Maxwell Taylor's Cold War

AMERICAN WARRIORS

Throughout the nation's history, numerous men and women of all ranks and branches of the US military have served their country with honor and distinction. During times of war and peace, there are individuals whose exemplary achievements embody the highest standards of the US armed forces. The aim of the American Warriors series is to examine the unique historical contributions of these individuals, whose legacies serve as enduring examples for soldiers and citizens alike. The series will promote a deeper and more comprehensive understanding of the US armed forces.

SERIES EDITOR: Joseph Craig

An AUSA Book

MAXWELL TAYLOR'S COLD WAR

From Berlin to Vietnam

Ingo Trauschweizer

UNIVERSITY PRESS OF KENTUCKY

Copyright © 2019 by The University Press of Kentucky

Scholarly publisher for the Commonwealth,
serving Bellarmine University, Berea College, Centre
College of Kentucky, Eastern Kentucky University,
The Filson Historical Society, Georgetown College,
Kentucky Historical Society, Kentucky State University,
Morehead State University, Murray State University,
Northern Kentucky University, Transylvania University,
University of Kentucky, University of Louisville,
and Western Kentucky University.
All rights reserved.

Editorial and Sales Offices: The University Press of Kentucky
663 South Limestone Street, Lexington, Kentucky 40508–4008
www.kentuckypress.com

Library of Congress Cataloging-in-Publication Data

Names: Trauschweizer, Ingo, author.
Title: Maxwell Taylor's Cold War : from Berlin to Vietnam / Ingo
  Trauschweizer.
Description: Lexington, Kentucky : University Press of Kentucky, [2019] |
  Series: American warriors | "An AUSA book"—Series title page. | Includes
  bibliographical references and index.
Identifiers: LCCN 2018042161| ISBN 9780813177007 (hardcover : alk. paper) |
  ISBN 9780813177021 (pdf) | ISBN 9780813177014 (epub)
Subjects: LCSH: Taylor, Maxwell D. (Maxwell Davenport), 1901-1987. | Taylor,
  Maxwell D. (Maxwell Davenport), 1901-1987—Political and social views. |
  United States. Army—Biography. | Generals—United States—Biography. |
  Cold War. | United States—Military policy. | United States—History,
  Military—20th century.
Classification: LCC E745.T317 T73 2019 | DDC 355.0092 [B] —dc23

This book is printed on acid-free paper meeting
the requirements of the American National Standard
for Permanence in Paper for Printed Library Materials.

Manufactured in the United States of America

 Member of the Association
of University Presses

Contents

    Chronology   vii
    Introduction   1
1. West Point   5
2. Cold War Frontiers   37
3. Reformer and Strategist?   68
4. Camelot's Strategist   101
5. Architect of the Vietnam War   137
6. Wise Man?   172
    Epilogue   207
    Acknowledgments   213
    Notes   215
    Bibliography   269
    Index   285

Photographs follow page 171

Chronology

August 26, 1901	Born in Keytesville, Missouri
1918–1922	US Military Academy (West Point)
1923–1926	3rd Engineers, Hawaii (Second Lieutenant)
1926–1927	10th Field Artillery (First Lieutenant in February 1927)
1927–1932	Language training in Paris and French and Spanish instructor, USMA
1935	Graduates from US Army Command and General Staff College, Fort Leavenworth, Kansas
1935–1939	US embassy, Tokyo (Japanese language training—promoted to Captain in 1937 and detached as military attaché to Beijing)
1940	Graduates from Army War College; promoted to Major; service in War Department and on a defense mission to Latin America
1940–1941	Commanding Officer, 12th Field Artillery Battalion
1941–1942	Office of the Secretary of the General Staff (temporary promotions to Lieutenant Colonel in December 1941 and Colonel in February 1942)
1942	Chief of Staff, 82nd Airborne Division (temporary promotion to Brigadier General in December 1942)
1942–1944	Artillery Commander, 82nd Airborne (temporary promotion to Major General in May 1944)
1944–1945	Commanding General, 101st Airborne Division
1945–1949	US Military Academy superintendent (promotion to Major General)

1949	Chief of Staff, US European Command
1949–1951	US Commander, Berlin
1951–1953	Assistant Chief of Staff for Operations (G-3) and Deputy Chief of Staff for Operations and Administration (promotion to Lieutenant General)
1953–1954	Commanding General, 8th Army, Korea (promotion to General in June 1953)
1954–1955	Commanding General, US Forces Far East and 8th Army (in 1955 also Commander-in-Chief, UN Command)
1955–1959	Chief of Staff, US Army (retired July 1959)
1959–1960	Director, Mexico City's Electric Company
1960	*The Uncertain Trumpet* published; moves to New York to direct the Rockefeller Center
1961–1962	Military Representative, White House
1962–1964	Chairman, Joint Chiefs of Staff (recalled to active service)
1964–1965	Ambassador, South Vietnam
1965–1969	President, Institute of Defense Analyses
1965–1970	President's Foreign Intelligence Advisor Board (chairman: 1968–1970)
1982	Congressional hearings on defense reform
April 19, 1987	Dies in Washington, D.C.

Introduction

In 1984 officials in Washington debated reforming the defense establishment and who should advise presidents on strategy in times of crisis. Maxwell Taylor, former chairman of the Joint Chiefs of Staff (JCS), John F. Kennedy White House insider, and one of the architects of America's war in Vietnam, told members of Congress that the JCS were divided by service interests and had never fulfilled their role as strategy advisors. He concluded the system should not be reformed—it should be torn down. The Goldwater-Nichols Act that resulted in October 1986 did not quite meet Taylor's radical proposal of a complete restructuring even though it enhanced the powers of the JCS chairman. This book considers what shaped Taylor's thinking. Through his career in the Cold War we can investigate critical questions from the vantage points of the military and the executive branch: What is the role of the armed services in national and international security strategies? Where do service interests and national interest intersect and what happens when there is less-than-complete overlap? What is the role of the JCS and their chairman? And how could the armed services prepare for vastly different challenges, ranging from nuclear war to conventional battle, counterinsurgency, and nation building?

Taylor was one of the most influential American soldiers, strategists, and diplomats in the twentieth century. He was also a controversial figure, both in his own time and in ours. Most of Taylor's contemporaries in the military admired his intellect and courage, but many felt he did not put it to good use. Army general James Gavin concluded he was a political operator who used his subordinates—men like Gavin—to score points or remove obstacles; President Dwight D. Eisenhower learned Taylor was a skilled bureaucratic infighter and one who tarnished Eisenhower's legacy; fellow JCS members Arleigh Burke (in the 1950s) and Wallace Greene and Curtis E. LeMay (in the 1960s) found him dishonest and untrustworthy; and two chairmen in the second half of the 1950s, Arthur Radford and Nathan Twining, clashed with Taylor over the role and mission of the army, nuclear strategy, and limited war. The most insightful historian of the 1950s army depicts Taylor as an aloof manager and flawed architect.[1] Within the army, led by Taylor from 1955 to 1959 in an incomplete transformation for atomic warfare, senior officers deflected Taylor's schemes, but he also inspired confidence and had career-long disciples.

In the policy realm, Taylor appealed to action intellectuals of the Kennedy era, including the president, his brother, Robert (who became a close friend and named his son born in 1965 Matthew Maxwell Taylor Kennedy), and Robert McNamara, who thought "Max was the wisest uniformed geopolitician and security adviser I ever met."[2] Was he the mastermind of an unlawful conversion of the JCS into a general staff for the defense secretary or the brilliant soldier-scholar tailor-made for the television age? Taylor himself coyly suggested he looked more thoughtful in conversations because he had to lean forward to hear, as an explosion during his early days in the field artillery had left him nearly deaf in one ear. As his son noted, this also made social interactions difficult for Taylor and contributed to the apparent coolness in most of his relationships.[3]

Among students of the Cold War era, Thomas Ricks describes Taylor as politicized and dishonest, and Robert Buzzanco considers him one of the "masters of war" in the 1950s and 1960s.[4] In H. R. McMaster's study of the origins of the Vietnam War, we encounter Taylor the manipulator, who contributed to the breakdown of trust between the joint chiefs and Presidents Kennedy and Lyndon B. Johnson.[5] We read about Taylor the architect of American escalation in Vietnam in army general Douglas Kinnard's history of the war.[6] We get carefully measured glimpses of Taylor in his autobiography and from a biography written by his son.[7] Yet we do not fully appreciate the depth of his opposition to Eisenhower's nuclear deterrence strategy and we do not know what made him both a hawk who pushed for the air war against North Vietnam and a more cautious strategist who argued against the massive deployment of ground forces to South Vietnam. We lack an assessment of how Taylor perceived the evolving challenges of war in an age that featured nuclear weapons and guerrilla fighters. Above all, we do not understand to what extent Taylor affected the national security establishment in the 1950s and 1960s and what lasting effects his actions had on the tensions in civil-military relations that have persisted since the mid-1940s.

The following chapters trace Taylor's varied career from West Point, where he served as superintendent of the US Military Academy from the summer of 1945 to the winter of 1949, to stints at the Pentagon—in the early 1950s as deputy chief of staff for operations and administration, then as the army's chief of staff, and as JCS chairman (1962–1964)—and to the White House, as an adviser to Kennedy (1961–1962) and Johnson (1965–1969). In between, Taylor served as US commandant in Berlin from the summer of 1949 to the winter of 1951, commander of the Eighth Army in Korea from February 1953 to the summer of 1955 (and in 1955 also commander of the US Far East Command), and, perhaps most fatefully, ambassador to South Vietnam in 1964 and 1965. Throughout the 1970s and early 1980s he weighed in on public debates over defense policy and global strategy.

Maxwell Taylor's Cold War traces the evolution of Taylor's thoughts on civil-military relations, military command and leadership, strategy and policy, and the evolving challenges of war. It is equal parts intellectual biography and a study of the national security state; it does not render Taylor's life. Taylor kept his public career and family life separate, and his wife, Lydia, did not seek the limelight. In his memoir, Taylor mentioned her and their two sons a mere fifteen times, mostly in the context of early meetings and births, and his son Jack did not dwell on Taylor's private life in his biography shortly after his father's death.[8] Addressing Taylor's role in the making of national strategy as well as his conclusions about nuclear and conventional war and deterrence, limited war, and counterinsurgency yields a more complete picture of the Cold War and the Vietnam War era that combines military, strategic, policy, institutional, intellectual, international, and diplomatic history. Taylor's career offers a fresh perspective because it bridged—and at times combined—military command, diplomatic postings, strategy advice, intelligence oversight, and policymaking in ways few others encountered. His experiences at different levels of army, Pentagon, and federal bureaucracy point out significant tensions, serious fault lines, the need for compromise, and the power of individuals in the American foreign and defense policy apparatus.

Taylor's chief lessons of the first two decades of the Cold War featured a firm belief in the nation's need to be prepared for limited war in the atomic age—first expressed in a 1948 lecture in London—and distrust in the dynamics of nuclear deterrence; recognition of the need to combine all military, political, economic, and other assets under one commander on the spot; awareness of the importance of alliances and a desire to arm local forces and let them fight their own battles, when necessay backed by American air- and firepower; and the overarching need for better integration of the process by which Washington conducted policy and strategy. In the latter realm, this is a history of failure and frustration, but it is also the story of unresolved issues in civil-military relations and American strategy that continue to reverberate in the twenty-first century. Even so, Taylor thought of himself as "a practicing optimist" in these trying times.[9] He was a micromanager who believed in building structures from the top down and might be best described as an incomplete humanist who veered toward hierarchies because they provided a framework beyond the frequent turnover of leading personalities in policy, strategy, or high command. In Taylor's world, even though he held a strong preference for the liberal arts and believed leadership rested on communication skills and sound judgment, people were dispensable as long as the proper system was in place. He himself was a master manipulator within the bureaucracy, but the system struggled in complex crises in the Third World, it may have led the United States into a war that could have been avoided, and it failed to yield a successful strategy for the Vietnam War.

1

West Point

At the end of the Second World War, Major General Maxwell Taylor, famed airborne commander and the first American general to land in France on D-day, moved from the Bavarian Alps to West Point. This was a homecoming. Taylor had been a West Point cadet and he had taught Spanish and French at the US Military Academy. It was where he had met his wife, Lydia ("Diddy") Happer, and where their older son, John Maxwell, was born. His brother, Thomas Happer, followed in 1934, while Taylor was at the Command and General Staff College at Fort Leavenworth, Kansas. George Marshall had selected him to run the academy, and Taylor would stay in the Hudson highlands until January 1949. Though young for the post at forty-four, he was a logical choice for superintendent, intellectually inclined and gifted with foreign languages, a general who understood the value of a liberal education. He aimed to balance the academy's emphasis on engineering with the humanities and social sciences. Taylor was never a team builder, and while he relished debate, he liked to make up his mind independently of majority views. He offended some faculty members and saw himself opposed by traditionalists, but the superintendent himself spent a good deal of time on public relations, touring universities from Stanford and UCLA to Virginia and Michigan, receiving a steady stream of visitors from Washington, businessmen, journalists, and foreign leaders, and speaking widely about his lessons of the war and his projections for the future. He also took advantage of the proximity to New York and became an active member of the Council on Foreign Relations, which afforded him a professional network he could put to use in his later career in policy and diplomacy.

Taylor's army was caught between demobilization and preparedness. Army leaders, with the support of President Harry S. Truman, proposed to meet manpower requirements with a fundamental shift in the

American military tradition: away from mobilization of untrained men and toward universal military training (UMT) to build up a reserve in peacetime. Dwight Eisenhower, for one, thought that the active army's land and air forces could then be reduced to 325,000 officers and men.[1] Generals like Marshall and Eisenhower also proposed that the armed services' high command and bureaucracy should be unified. Congress debated UMT throughout the second half of the 1940s, but the United States maintained the selective service conscription model of the world wars. Unification of the armed services was diluted, as the United States built the Defense Department while retaining three independent services (once the air force was split from the army in 1947). Instead of installing one general-in-chief, a preference held by Taylor throughout the Cold War, the wartime measure of the Joint Chiefs of Staff, providing advice by consensus, compromise, or disagreement, was made permanent in 1947.[2]

Maxwell Taylor

In his memoirs, Taylor painted himself as good shepherd of the academy. He faced four major tasks: careful study of what West Point was and what it should become; assessing the effects of World War II on the postwar army and the requirements for leadership in a draftee-heavy force; his role as spokesman for the academy to military and general audiences; and the maintenance of academic rigor, but also of accessibility for graduates from average high schools. Taylor mentioned his accomplishments only in passing: a curriculum shifting away from heavy emphasis on mathematics and engineering toward better balance between the sciences and humanities, and the concurrent ability to educate officers rather than churn out second lieutenants with tactical and technical expertise. The future army needed leaders who were loyal to the service, could think independently, and could communicate effectively with military professionals and citizen soldiers. Some aspects of Taylor's curricular reform, his expansion of the faculty, and his emphasis on physical as well as intellectual preparedness resembled the reshaping of the academy by Douglas MacArthur after World War I, which Taylor had experienced firsthand as a cadet.[3]

As he departed for West Point, Taylor solicited advice from senior generals in Europe.[4] The most candid response came from George Patton, who had tasked his deputy chief of staff, Brigadier General Paul Harkins, to form a study group. Harkins reported, "They all agree that the education at West Point should be liberalized. They thought that more English should be studied along with the languages. They agree with [Patton] that, upon graduation, graduates should take three or four years serving in more than one branch." Harkins surely caught Taylor's attention when he noted, "Many of the courses in higher mathematics, although they provide mental gymnastics, could be well provided in a more liberal education—languages, history and English." Harkins closed on a personal observation: "One of the primary efforts of the Academy is to make a man mentally and physically mobile and that he must retain this mobility whether at some social occasion dealing with foreigners in peace and more so while on the battlefield."[5] Taylor soon brought Harkins to West Point, and he succeeded Taylor's World War II deputy, Gerald Higgins, as commandant in 1948. Patton added his own touch: "Nothing I learned in electricity or hydraulics or in higher mathematics or in drawing in any way contributed to my military career." Instead, "much more emphasis should be placed on [military] history," English, and foreign languages, by requiring cadets to study two of four options: Russian, German, Japanese, or Spanish.[6]

Whereas Patton was characteristically blunt, the supreme commander in Europe responded more guardedly. General Eisenhower held that "the value of West Point has been amply demonstrated again in this war." He did not recommend specific changes to academics beyond insisting the academy should return from the wartime three-year curriculum designed to turn out young officers faster to a four-year program as soon as possible and noting that "efforts toward improvement should be centered more along the human than the technical side. Lessons of cooperation and coordination, in the spirit of friendliness and devotion to a common cause, should be stressed." Moreover, he approved of the trend toward placing greater demands on First Classmen, "treating them as quasi officers." Eisenhower concluded that the stress which joint and combined warfare had placed on those holding unified command positions suggested the need for structural change. He hoped to foster better understanding of the sister service by "frequent and intimate contacts between the Annapolis midshipman and the West Point cadet." Eisenhower thought a full-year student exchange program could facilitate it.[7]

Taylor was not among Eisenhower's top choices to lead the academy. He had recommended Taylor's friend Alfred Gruenther, also a West Point instructor during the Great Depression—when he and Taylor perfected a bathtub gin recipe—who had served on Eisenhower's staff during the war, and he thought Omar Bradley and Thomas Handy would be ideally suited.[8] Yet in his later assessment to Secretary of Defense James

Forrestal, when Eisenhower prepared to trade in his job at the Pentagon for the presidency of Columbia University in 1948, Taylor made the chief of staff's list of extraordinary army officers. He was in fine company: Bradley and Handy, fellow airborne commanders Matthew Ridgway, Anthony McAuliffe, and Gavin, Gruenther, and Lyman Lemnitzer, some thirty generals and rising staff officers in all.[9]

One year prior, in February 1947, Eisenhower, who served on the board of the Boy Scouts of America, had recommended Taylor to be the new leader of the youth group, a well-paying position Taylor declined on the grounds that he did not want to leave the army at a time of international crisis, especially not when he was trying to inculcate in his cadets a sense of commitment to a military career. He also noted that the army had given him "more rewards than I could ever have anticipated."[10] A visit to West Point from Amory Houghton, the president of the Boy Scouts, could not change Taylor's mind.[11] Perhaps a decade later, when Army Chief of Staff Taylor became a thorn in President Eisenhower's side, Eisenhower would come to regret Taylor's choice, but in 1947 he insisted he did not want Taylor to quit. Instead, Eisenhower reassured Taylor that he "would view your departure from the Army with something akin to dismay; your standing in my estimation is unexcelled."[12]

Eisenhower may have harbored doubts about Taylor at first, but with the exception of closer cooperation between the military and naval academies, the two men came to agree on most issues concerning West Point. Both thought the academy should educate leaders who held dear country and their own personal honor as well as West Point's honor system, which represented the cornerstone of the academy's values.[13] Taylor agreed with Eisenhower that the honor system should remain above being used as "a device for the detection of the violation of regulations." Instead, he hoped that the return to the four-year curriculum would "bring forth a more mature First Class capable of assuming authority in the management of the Corps beyond that possible during the war-time course," thus giving soon-to-be lieutenants more experience in leading men.[14]

Unlike Eisenhower, Marshall had watched Taylor's career closely since he had proved his competence on Marshall's staff at the outset of World War II. More importantly, Marshall knew that very few senior army officers could match the combination of scholarly mind, leadership, and courage that Taylor had displayed during the war. In a letter to Douglas MacArthur, Marshall rated Taylor as "among the half-dozen most conspicuously successful division commanders in the heavy fighting in Europe." The two men must have spoken about the future when Marshall, taking a break from the Potsdam Conference, visited Taylor's headquarters at Berchtesgaden on July 27 and 28. Perhaps Taylor reminded his chief of his experiences in Japan, where he served on the military attaché staff from 1935 to 1939 and, alongside Joseph Stilwell, trekked behind the Japanese army during its 1937 campaign in China. Marshall recommended Taylor for the planned invasion of the Japanese home islands. But he also wanted combat veterans to lead army schools and training programs, and when MacArthur did not respond, Marshall nominated Taylor as West Point's superintendent.[15] Taylor started in early September and knew that he owed his position to Marshall.[16]

The earliest seeds for his willingness to innovate as superintendent were planted when he experienced intellectual boredom in the inflexible curriculum as a cadet. Taylor, who grew up in the Missouri suburbs of Kansas City and attended technical college after graduating from high school at age fifteen, had entered West Point in the fall of 1918 as part of a class that was supposed to be ready for combat commands in France in time for the anticipated 1919 summer offensive. The end of World War I put a stop to such intentions, and Taylor's class got to take the full four years at the academy. Taylor had been drawn to all things military from a very young age, under the spell of stories told by his grandfather of daring raids as a Confederate cavalryman. Later in life Taylor came to suspect that at least some of these tales stretched the truth and he learned that his grandfather's missing arm was the result of a sawmill accident, not a war wound. But military operations and strategy remained Taylor's passion, though his perspective shifted over time from a romantic tinge to detached professionalism.[17]

At West Point, young Taylor, well read and quick to pick up languages and history, discovered he could rely heavily on prior knowledge for his coursework. Since there were no electives, he read philosophy and military history on his own. This extracurricular focus did not negatively affect his performance: Taylor graduated fourth in a class of 102 cadets. His career in the interwar army and his experiences in World War II deepened his sense that future army officers required the ability to think critically, communicate clearly, and learn about history and knowledge of world affairs. He also recalled how the superintendent for three of his cadet years, Douglas MacArthur, had applied his lessons of the First World War to the academy's methods, which resulted in the modernization of the plebe system, moderate liberalization of the curriculum, and the arrival of intramural sports for cadets who were not part of an intercollegiate athletic team.[18]

For Taylor, an avid tennis player, physical fitness, moral courage, and intellectual growth had to stand alongside technical expertise in the making of future army officers. He told the Class of 1946 that all great leaders "have been devoted to the welfare of their troops. Next, they have been richly endowed with human understanding. And finally, they have stood out by their professional competence and ability."[19] Taylor firmly held that leadership depended on the ability to think through an argument, state it compellingly to one's men, and communicate clearly in day-to-day interactions. Therefore, he placed equal stock in the humanities and in the sciences. Taylor noted in his later reflections that the army in World War II had faced few problems finding enough engineers and scientists, but it had found it harder to develop strong leaders. West Point was the ideal place for young men to be educated in the foundational skills that would enable them to become such leaders as their experience and technical expertise grew over time.[20]

West Point's primary focus had already shifted toward academics and away from military training when Taylor served as a foreign language instructor from 1927 to 1932. The curriculum, albeit less rooted in rote memorization than had been the case in the early twentieth century, still built toward a "general engineering education"—the assessment of the 1939 academic board review—and the department heads rejected new courses in the humanities and social sciences because they would displace subjects "of more practical and cultural value to the Army officers."[21] Just before Taylor returned to West Point in 1945, the War Department had asked for a course in Russian to be added to the foreign language options. The next year, 119 First Year students took Russian, though Spanish, French, and German remained more popular. Taylor, himself fluent in French, Spanish, and Japanese, later noted that "the dominant world position in which Russia was emerging from the war, militarily as well as politically, left no doubt as to [the course's] desirability."[22] In April 1947, Taylor received orders to move Russian into second place, below Spanish, among West Point's foreign language offerings.[23] Of the cadets who entered in 1948, 151 studied Russian, 199 studied Spanish, 111 French, 107 German, and 56 Portuguese.[24]

In between his stint as instructor and his return as superintendent, Taylor had seen more than enough combat and had served under some of America's most famous generals. After his return from Japan in 1939, Taylor commanded an artillery battalion of the 2nd Infantry Division at San Antonio. In July 1941, Marshall called him to Washington, which offered Taylor a pressure-filled education in policy and strategy. When the

United States entered into World War II, Taylor was among the staff officers who screened and summarized proposals for George Marshall. Two of his superiors in this task would lead the army in the early Cold War years: Omar Bradley and J. Lawton Collins.[25] Marshall was notoriously demanding. He requested succinct memoranda, persuasive argumentation, and independent conclusions. The task suited Taylor's disciplined mind and his tendency to view all issues as questions of logic and rational thought, and it reinforced his belief that communication, a sound knowledge base, and self-confidence were essential tools of command.

Once the United States joined the war after the Japanese attack on Pearl Harbor, an event that stunned Taylor as much as anyone else on Marshall's staff, it would have made sense to send Taylor across the Pacific. Yet Marshall balked at Stilwell's request that Taylor be allowed to join his headquarters in southern China. Instead, he sent him to Matthew Ridgway's newly activated 82nd Airborne Division to serve as chief of staff. Taylor found himself bored in a job that allowed for neither independent thought nor action, and he jumped at the opportunity to take over as the division's artillery commander in late 1942. In this position, he participated in the division's planning for the invasion of Sicily and he landed on the island as soon as the airborne infantry had established a foothold. Toward the end of his life, Taylor deemed it a "semi-joke" that he never saw a Japanese enemy in combat while his classmate at the Command and General Staff College, Albert Wedemeyer, who had spent two years at the German War Academy, served in Asia.[26]

By early September 1943, Taylor's linguistic and diplomatic skills and his readiness to make difficult decisions had caught Eisenhower's eye. Eisenhower sent him and Colonel William Gardiner, an intelligence officer with the army air force, on a mission to Rome, behind enemy lines. For a flimsy cover, in case they were picked up by German soldiers, Taylor and Gardiner were disguised as airmen shot down over the Tyrrhenian Sea. Once in Rome, they met with Marshal Pietro Badoglio, Italy's new prime minister, and General Giacomo Carboni, the corps commander in the capital city, in order to ascertain whether an Allied airborne landing at Rome could take German forces by surprise and accelerate the liberation of Italy. Plans for the operation had proceeded to the point where it seemed a foregone conclusion that it would take place, and Taylor had to race the clock. He bid his time in frustration as Badoglio's staff displayed more confusion than control. He found the Germans in a strong position to defend Rome and the Italian army unprepared to rise up against the ally-turned-occupier. Taylor called for a halt through a tenuous communications network, and the advance elements of Ridgway's division were already airborne when Taylor landed at headquarters in Tunisia and impressed on Ridgway that the planes had to be recalled.[27]

Some of the commanding officers, most notably General Walter Bedell "Beetle" Smith on Eisenhower's staff, and James Gavin, who would have led the first combat elements into Rome, thought Taylor had panicked. Robert Murphy, Eisenhower's political adviser, erroneously believed all of the airborne commanders had made up their mind out of distrust of the Italians before Taylor had reported in. Eminent naval historian Samuel Eliot Morrison, the sharpest critic, concluded with no apparent evidence that Taylor had fallen for Carboni's exaggeration of the Germans' strength.[28] But Ridgway, Eisenhower, and the army commander, Field Marshal Sir Harold Alexander, agreed with Taylor's assessment that the operation had a high likelihood of stranding an Allied force in an indefensible position, cut off from land forces far to the south.[29]

Following the Roman adventure, Taylor was appointed chief of staff of the Allied mission to the new Italian government in Brindisi, at the heel of the Italian boot, where Badoglio and King Victor Emmanuel II had relocated. The position challenged Taylor, but it left his desire for a field command unfulfilled.[30] An opportunity arose unexpectedly in February 1944 when the 101st Airborne Division needed a new commander after General William Lee suffered a heart attack. Eisenhower's plans called for the division to jump into Normandy ahead of the Allied landing. He turned to Taylor—a bold move, putting an outsider in charge of a critical asset of the D-day operation. Taylor knew that he had to win over his men quickly, but he also understood that a successful leader did not have to be loved. He impressed with his characteristic combination of effectiveness and eloquence, leading the Screaming Eagles into Normandy, then commanded the division in Operation Market Garden in Belgium and Holland, in some of the fighting in the Ardennes, and in the advance into Germany.

Yet Taylor missed the crucial first days of the Battle of the Bulge in December 1944. He was in Washington when his 101st Airborne was thrown into the battle for Bastogne against numerically superior German forces. In Taylor's absence, and because Gerald "Jerry" Higgins was in England to give briefings on the recent Market Garden operation, Brigadier General Anthony McAuliffe, the artillery commander, was in temporary command. Contrary to persistent rumors that Taylor was in Washington "to look for a more prestigious command," he had been sent by Ridgway to talk to army planners about the future of the airborne concept.³¹ This unpreparedness for the German offensive illustrated the extent of the surprise all the way from division commanders in Belgium to Bradley's First Army and Eisenhower's headquarters. Ridgway, the corps commander, was in England with Higgins and more than a dozen senior officers of the "Screaming Eagles" when the German offensive commenced, and Gavin had to step in to fill that gap. It helped matters that McAuliffe held fast at Bastogne while Taylor, who had learned of his division's plight from a pin on a War Department map, flew back to Europe and was approaching the battle zone on treacherous roads, at times even drawing fire from Americans who suspected he was a German saboteur. The 4th Armored Division, of George Patton's corps, beat Taylor to Bastogne by a day, opening the access road in the process.³²

In his Army Day address in New York in April 1946, Taylor reflected on the war and stressed the need for preparedness and the close connection of army and nation. He celebrated the victories of 1945 and painted a picture of American armies surging into Germany and joining the battle for Okinawa just twelve months prior. Yet he also reminded his audience that the months after Pearl Harbor had been dark and that the United States had been woefully unprepared to win its battles. Taylor noted that "the army had won the war" with the support of the navy, the mobilization of industries, and the backing of the nation. This army was "really America" and "democracy militant." Most of the millions who joined were not soldiers at heart, but civilians who understood their task, trained hard, and received the largesse of the nation, both in spiritual and material support. Some in the audience must have been taken aback when Taylor stressed the relatively low cost, measured in lives, of winning these decisive victories over Germany, Italy, and Japan, and veterans surely disagreed when he emphasized that discomfort had been kept at a minimum. Still, for a speech about glory on a day of celebration, Taylor struck a cautious tone and closed on the nation's need to remain vigilant and the army's need to be prepared for the global commitments the United States now faced. Educating officers to lead that army was at the heart of his mission.³³

Superintendent

In thinking about how to prepare officers for future wars, Taylor anticipated the reasoning of a more radical reformer in his wake, General Garrison Davidson, though he could not yet have known all the demands imposed by nuclear weapons. In 1957, Superintendent Davidson initiated a comprehensive review of the academy's curriculum. His description of the problem mirrored Taylor's thinking: "the Army must be prepared to undertake any of three types of war (general nuclear; limited nuclear; and limited non-nuclear) while maintaining a high state of readiness for all three. Each of these conditions poses special problems; all will demand highly competent, dedicated officers."[34] Part of what Davidson depicted was the need to maintain cohesion of widely dispersed small units as well as the general trend toward increasing technological sophistication. How could cadets be educated to perform well in a rapidly shifting tactical environment, with sufficient technological know-how to understand the options at their disposal, and with the mental agility to cope with unpredictable scenarios? Was there a sound balance between (1) leadership built on the humanities, (2) gauging the enemy, one's own men, and the environment, and (3) the mathematical and technological side of commanding armed forces in the atomic age?

Taylor made known his vision in March 1946. He gained cover by winning Karl Compton's agreement to write the foreword to his pamphlet "West Point Looks Ahead." The president of the Massachusetts Institute of Technology, whose son was then serving in the infantry detachment at the academy, was well placed to suggest that a four-year specialized degree in engineering presented an outdated model, as "all engineering educators agree that this situation calls for specialized training at the postgraduate levels or in the practical school of postgraduate experience," and that Taylor's emphasis on a well-rounded education met the demands of the times.[35] Taylor stressed both in his pamphlet and in a presentation to the war and navy secretaries the trend toward incorporating more of the social sciences and liberal arts in the curriculum at civilian technical colleges.[36] He built his case on two fundamental changes in context: atomic weapons and adjustments to mission and structure of the military that were hard to predict. Taylor outflanked traditionalists and engineers when he noted that War Department directives did not "make the Academy a mill for producing second lieutenants for any arm of the service. All the emphasis is placed on giving a broad foundation of culture, affording the graduate a base upon which to erect a rich and full life of service."[37] If the mission was clear, the way to attain it was contested.

Taylor identified four critical areas, the first of which, the return to a four-year curriculum, already had been determined by his predecessor, Major General Francis Wilby. It was to be implemented by dividing the current Third Class (sophomores) into the classes of 1948 and 1949.

Cadets were asked to choose their preference, though Taylor knew some arbitrary transfers were unavoidable.[38] His focus thus shifted to revising the curriculum, expanding and improving the quality of the faculty, and presenting a long-term plan for the academy's infrastructure. Taylor slyly credited Wilby with setting in motion the shift in the curriculum toward the humanities and social sciences, which would now take up a quarter to a third of a cadet's class time. He particularly stressed the importance of military history as "an instrument impressing the principles of leadership" on First Year (senior) cadets.[39] Of course, the sciences also needed to keep up with the times: electronics and communications were central features of the course in electricity, and the Physics Department educated cadets in atomic energy. Taylor sidestepped controversies and painted a rosy picture of a smooth transition from the abbreviated World War II course to a balanced four-year curriculum.

How much of his vision did Taylor implement? For one, he completed the return to the four-year curriculum. When the 630 cadets of the Third Class stated their preferences, a large majority opted to complete the wartime three-year course rather than the revised four-year program. Taylor and the academic board, made up of all department heads and the commandant, assigned the seventy youngest cadets who had opted for three years to the four-year track.[40] Taylor later reflected that the three-year course had been a tolerable compromise between the educational mission of the academy and the need to turn out officers for the war. But his observations of lieutenants returning from France as cadets after World War I always stuck with him and he feared that with a truncated academic curriculum West Point would be little more than an officer training school. Like Eisenhower, he thought four years were required to provide cadets with a modern liberal education.[41]

Taylor did not want to return to the prewar curriculum's heavy focus on engineering. To build his argument against internal opposition at the academy, he asked for a board of consultants to offer new directions. The group, headed by Compton and made up of two university presidents (Compton and Williams College's James Phinney Baxter) and seven army generals (most prominently Troy Middleton and Bruce C. Clarke), met in the fall of 1945.[42] Taylor addressed them at their first meeting on November 5, hosted luncheons at the Thayer Hotel and at cadet mess, and provided dinners and entertainment in his quarters.[43] The group spent three days visiting academic classes and instruction in military subjects. Colonel O. J. Gatchell, a member of the academic board and a professor of mechanics, had already briefed the group on prewar, wartime, and proposed postwar curriculums. Taylor had chosen six cadets that represented different educational and service backgrounds for interviews: one who had attended an engineering school, one who had attended a liberal arts college, one who had come straight from high school, one who had served in the Pacific Theater, and one each who was older or younger than the average. Compton's group also interviewed three temporary instructors who in civilian life had been experienced teachers of mechanical engineering, mathematics, and history.[44]

When Taylor reminded his guests of specific questions at hand, he emphasized the need to fulfill the War Department directive to provide a balanced and liberal education in the arts and sciences. "Your work," he told them, "will contribute to the shaping of a modern West Point capable of confronting the new problems posed by the military, political, and scientific developments of the late war." He directed their attention to "distribution of instruction time [which] is often a matter for study and debate. This distribution involves the balance between military and academic subjects and, within the latter, the balance between scientific and so-called liberal courses." He was keen on getting advice "as to the quality of the balance effected in the new four-year course." Taylor expressed concern about the demands on cadets, who would have to take four hundred additional hours of instruction over four years than had been the case before the war. He wondered "whether we are trying to teach the cadet too much. Is his time so full that he is unable to appreciate and evaluate what he receives here?" Yet, if he wanted to cut subjects or course material, Taylor needed ammunition: "If you feel that the course is over-loaded, what courses should be cut? I hope that you can give specific indications of where reductions of time should be sought."[45]

The Compton board was impressed with instruction and the curriculum, though Middleton, who had risen from the enlisted ranks and had once striven in vain to attend West Point, noted there was still too much weight on military instruction in the field and on the parade ground and that the balance should be shifted farther to academics.[46] All of the consultants agreed on the overriding value of a four-year undergraduate education, as broad as possible, with no need to focus on career specialization. The schools for infantry, artillery, and other branches would take care of that. Middleton conceded that a graduate from an ROTC program might have a short-term advantage in specialized knowledge, but argued that a sound education would allow a West Point graduate to catch up quickly. Compton's report proposed cutting back on military instruction to give cadets more free time; the group stressed that this could under no circumstances come from the academic curriculum. But the board members sidestepped the fraught subject of sciences and liberal arts.[47]

Middleton, who served as comptroller (and later president) of Louisiana State University, congratulated Taylor in a personal letter. The former commander of the VIII Corps in Europe thought "the idea of a Board of Consultants is an excellent one," because it introduced the academy to leaders of civilian universities: "I feel that more of my contemporaries, in our universities, should share the opportunity given me to visit the Academy." Middleton was particularly impressed by the cadets' "ability to express themselves" and by the "progressive attitude of your faculty. I found a keen desire on their part to improve their methods and to send forth into the military world an educated man of high ideals and character . . . [and] your faculty impressed me with a desire to keep abreast with changes in this rapidly changing world." Civilian schools could learn much from West Point, and the academy seemed on track to produce superior officers.[48]

Taylor used the report as justification for adding classes in history, sociology, and English. He also emphasized foreign languages, extracurricular speaking engagements, and formal debate as critical elements of officer education. In his June 1946 report, Taylor noted with satisfaction that the first account of World War II in the United States had been completed at West Point and that a subcourse (twenty-two lessons) in military government was in the making, with a textbook written by instructors who were World War II veterans.[49] The war made up almost half of the military history curriculum. Cadets in the First Class in 1947–48, for example, spent forty-four class periods (out of 105) studying the military history of the Second World War, including motion pictures and terrain models, and another seventeen on World War I.[50] The First Class course on the economics of war considered the conversion from a peacetime economy to a wartime one and investigated the economic performances of Great Britain, Germany, Japan, and the Soviet Union in World War II.[51] Stepping back, Taylor later recalled the growing importance of the social sciences and military history, his addition of a course on military psychology and leadership (following Army Chief of Staff Eisenhower's expressed desire for a course "in practical or applied psychology" taught by World War II commanders), and his efforts to strengthen the English Department and make literature a focal point of humanities education.[52]

Military psychology and leadership was first offered as a full course for First Classmen in 1947—forty-two hours between January and

May—and a fifteen-hour course module for those in the Second and Third Classes. It covered "the study of human nature, study of personnel management and placement at troop level, and the study of applied techniques."[53] Taylor had acted quickly upon receiving Eisenhower's letter. Within a year, he had built an Office of Military Psychology and Leadership in the Tactics Department, hired a professional psychologist, and appointed a director, an aptitude officer, and four instructors who were sent to Queens College in New York for a three-month training course.[54] The new course featured two elements: individual behavior of citizen soldiers and collective behavior (such as rumor, panic, and mobs), public opinion, and psychological warfare. It concluded with "practical and applied techniques arising from [those] psychological principles... which make for the effective leadership of American troops," with emphasis on training methods, information and education, practical handling of military personnel, relations with civilians, and public relations.[55]

Taylor had created this course against opposition from the academic board. When he raised the issue in a session in early 1946, only his handpicked commandant, Gerald Higgins, offered his consent. All academic department heads rejected the proposal, mainly because they did not see any room in the curriculum for a new course. But they also thought the subject overly abstract and impractical.[56] According to Higgins, it was a rancorous meeting and Taylor shut down the debate by calmly thanking the assembled faculty members for their advice. Then he informed them that the course would be launched in the next academic year. To preempt delay, he handed it to Higgins's Tactics Department rather than tasking an academic unit with assembling instructors and developing course content.[57] None of this sat well with the department heads, who were forced into unanimous consent on May 11—the day after Taylor had informed Eisenhower that "the Superintendent and the Academic Board, United States Military Academy, desire to introduce a course in practical applied psychology into the curriculum of the United States Military Academy during the academic year 1946–47."[58] It thus seems ironic that the academic board today meets in Taylor Hall, the building that houses the Office of the Superintendent and features a display of Maxwell Taylor's career accomplishments.

Because time for the psychology course would be taken from military instruction and because it would replace fragmented instruction on military leadership, small unit command, and a lecture series by distinguished officers, Taylor reasoned that it fell under "basic military training" rather than the "academic course" and should rest with Higgins's department. But it was transparent that he had outflanked the academic board.[59] This added to his difficult relationship with the faculty. Even reform-minded professors questioned Taylor's methods. Herman Beukema, who had been Eisenhower's classmate, was among them, as was Colonel George A. Lincoln, who had volunteered for a demotion so he could join Beukema's pioneering Social Sciences Department in September 1947.[60] Lincoln, too, was a West Point graduate (1929). A Rhodes Scholar who had studied politics and economics at Oxford, he was a close associate of George Marshall and a key contributor to the preparations for the Yalta and Potsdam conferences. Most poignantly, Lincoln believed in the foundational importance of a liberal arts education for future officers and public servants. Taylor recognized Lincoln's impact: "I would say that his influence upon many generations of cadets constitutes in the aggregate a greater contribution to national defense than that made by most general officers of the line."[61]

Beukema's disagreement with Taylor was not over the direction of reforms. His department, which Lincoln ran from 1954 to 1969, became an incubator of unconventional thinking in the decades after World War II.[62] Taylor, Beukema, and Lincoln shared a similar vision of the education of future officers. Style, however, was a different matter. Lincoln once noted Taylor's aide had the entire headquarters "in a lather" about the loss of two National War College lectures, which Taylor customarily received via back channels from Washington. Taylor, a micromanager, craved access to information that allowed him to make decisions on his own.[63] This desire for control may have set off Beukema, who reportedly asked Eisenhower "to tame" Taylor.[64]

Taylor had intervened in the social sciences curriculum. He requested that the international relations course for First Classmen in 1946–47 address "the implications of atomic fission" for 20 percent of the instruction time and he suggested Bernard Brodie's *The Absolute Weapon* as the core text. In addition, the department nearly tripled the sequence on international aid problems in the economics course.[65] More generally, Taylor hoped to broaden the academic experience of cadets and make them aware of global issues. To that end, and to foster both debate and exchange, he supported the creation of the Student Conference on United States Affairs, hosted annually since 1948, which included visiting students from leading civilian colleges and the Naval Academy, and he invited prominent guest speakers, including Dean Acheson, Averell Harriman, Dean Rusk, Allen Dulles, Nelson Rockefeller, and John J. McCloy.[66]

Beukema recognized the benefits for the social sciences in the revised postwar curriculum, but he insisted positive changes had been generated by the academic board and not by the superintendent's intervention.[67] The shift in allotted hours to his department meant that beginning in the 1947 fall semester upper-level courses allowed for in-depth instruction in economic geography, history of modern Europe and the Far East, US government, contemporary foreign government, military government (dropped in 1948), economics, applied military economics, and international relations. Specially qualified cadets in the Second Class could add instruction in Latin American or diplomatic history, and soon Russian and Middle Eastern themes were offered as well.[68] "That composite," Beukema noted, "provides the cadet with a background adequate for the objective examination of current world problems and trends, along with their motivating causes." This met Taylor's desire of producing officers who could adapt to a changing world and face a variety of challenges. Beukema thought, "At worst, the cadet has received a solid mental framework for post graduate study in international relations and eventually—staff duties and high command."[69]

Taylor knew that little lasting effect could be achieved without strengthening the teaching faculty. The question was how to replace the civilian instructors who had taken over during the war when army officers left to fight. Taylor and most faculty members disagreed on the way forward. The latter thought West Point was best served by regular army officers and USMA graduates. Taylor remained keen on retaining outstanding civilian instructors, and he asked for an additional professorship for each of the nine academic departments so as to free up the best instructors to teach. Taylor did not air the internal dissent over the composition of the faculty to the public. Instead, he pointed at the assessment of Compton's review board as evidence for the academy's success. Taylor noted they "commented most favorably upon the methods of instruction, the progressiveness of the teaching staff, and the modern equipment in the Academic Departments." To keep up with the demands of the mid-twentieth century, the Compton board had recommended nineteen additional permanent professorships, more than twice what Taylor thought he could get from Congress. To facilitate oversight, he embraced the academic board's request for a dean and nominated Colonel Roger Alexander, the head of the Military Topography and Graphics Department.[70]

Taylor hoped West Point graduates would prove to be broad-minded and deep thinkers as well as men of action. "Modern war," he noted, "pervades all phases of national life, so West Point must survey a field of equal breadth." This was not a school for second lieutenants. Indeed, "cadets should not live in a mental cloister; their interests must be catholic. As future officers in the Army, cadets should avoid the limited horizons which have often hemmed in military minds." Taylor, the soldier with an intellectual bent, feared the academy would return to placing too much emphasis on technique and technology: "In our concern to give the cadets the scientific tools needed in the new age, we must not forget that West Point is essentially a school for leaders."[71] He artfully made the argument for a balanced education and concluded that West Point should not be measured exclusively against other colleges, who could—and should—"always offer more advanced scientific and liberal courses to special students." West Point stood apart and "succeeds or fails in the future to the degree in which it continues to produce broad men of character, capable of leading other men to victory in battle."[72]

Unlike at civilian schools, West Point curriculum planners had to keep in mind that students needed to connect the mechanics of military training and specific points made in the classroom to the bigger picture, which included world affairs as well as future demands on army officers. Lincoln thought the academy had found the right method: "Throw elements of the big picture at the cadet and then follow up with nuts and bolts. If he starts with the nuts and bolts he may never realize toward what he should build." Lincoln as well as Taylor took pride in the success of their First Class in 1948. Only 11 percent fell below the median on the Graduate Record Examination, and the overall average of 590 for West Point students comfortably beat the 520 points average of seniors from civilian colleges.[73] Taylor concluded that "the average cadet is apparently getting a considerably better general education than the average male liberal arts student, the Military Academy seems to be graduating a much smaller percentage of really poor students than the average liberal arts college." His academy was "successfully performing its academic mission of providing 'a balanced and liberal education in the arts and sciences.'"[74] Still, except in the First Class, science and engineering subjects received significantly more classroom hours than social sciences and humanities: just over two-thirds of instruction time for the Fourth and Third Classes and three-fourths for the Second Class.[75]

Next to academics, physical activity provided opportunities for character development and team building. Taylor was an avid tennis player throughout his life and he pursued other single-player sports, but as a cadet he had admired MacArthur's push for intramural team sports and as a young language instructor he had played in the basketball league.[76]

Yet Taylor worried about too much emphasis on intercollegiate athletics. He know football allowed the academy to advertise the army to the American people, an opportunity enhanced by the first live national television broadcast of an Army home game on NBC in October 1946, against Columbia University.[77] But for Army football to retain its amateur lore, he needed to shift the program away from the emphasis on recruiting that had characterized the war years. Taylor also determined to end the showcase series with Notre Dame, which in the public's eye had taken on the characteristic of pitting the army against the Catholic Church. This proved controversial, but Eisenhower, himself an avid supporter of Army football, agreed. He concurred that Army's undefeated team should not play in the 1947 Sugar Bowl and should continue to forgo postseason football.[78] Yet Taylor never challenged the exalted position of coach Earl "Red" Blaik or the culture in a team that saw itself as above the academy's rules. The environment for the academic cheating scandal on Army's football team in the early 1950s was thus nurtured during Taylor's tenure and he turned a blind eye.[79]

Taylor was right in his assessment that the army (and West Point) needed positive advertisement. Americans later came to regard World War II as "the good war," but memory of the war was complex and contested in the late 1940s and few young men felt the call to service.[80] The academy felt the pinch. In June 1948, Taylor reported that the class which had entered in summer 1947 was small: congressional appointments had filled only 566 of 952 vacancies. Adjusted for separations, returning students who had been deferred in previous years, and the appointment of seven foreign students, the Class of 1951 stood at 606 cadets. Taylor hoped that a more efficient testing process and a decision by the Army Department to allow for more candidates to compete for a vacancy (four instead of three) would help address the shortfall, but at the end of June 1948 the Class of 1952 fell 169 short of filling the 824 vacancies.[81] Taylor's successor, General Bryant E. Moore, noted in June 1949 that the academy was on its way back to "normal peacetime attractiveness . . . to be expected after the usual postwar decline."[82] Yet, between 1947 and 1951, more than a quarter of all slots remained unfilled.[83]

Unsurprisingly for a man whose career in the war had progressed in two airborne divisions, Taylor personally saw to the foundation of West Point's airborne detachment in March 1947. It was not that he relished jumping out of airplanes. Taylor had only done so twice into combat (and no more than six times overall in his entire career), and he "viewed the parachute strictly as a vehicle to ride to the battlefield, to be used only when a better ride was not available."⁸⁴ In characteristically pragmatic fashion, Taylor was a proponent of a completely air transportable division that provided a blueprint for ready-made rapid response forces that could raise havoc with small, often scattered groups until reinforcements arrived on the scene.⁸⁵ But even if he was not a romantic, forever after 1944 Taylor remained proud of his 101st Airborne. The new program allowed cadets to partake in eighteen hours of airborne instruction, "stressing Airborne History, Airborne Equipment, Air Transportability, and the possible use of Airborne Troops in future wars."⁸⁶ And it permitted Taylor and Higgins to visit Fort Bragg for the cadets' July 1947 airborne training.⁸⁷

While Taylor was reforming the academy at home, he also had to defend it against critics across the country. The vast majority of World War II veterans did not share the army brass's faith in the effectiveness of the academy, an attitude typically derived from a nostalgic recollection of one's own cadet years and the sense of camaraderie and army culture thus instilled. Critics thought the military academy had harbored elites who did not want to fight and sheltered athletes from deployment into combat. They noted high numbers of cadets who never served after the war: 20 percent of the first two postwar graduating classes either quit or did not seek a commission. Even within the officer corps, West Pointers were seen as a protected group that got the best assignments and all-around favorite treatment. In the immediate postwar years, army officers called for steps to reduce tensions between USMA graduates and those of other institutions and complained about arrogant lieutenants who had sat out the war but claimed to know more than veterans who had won it.⁸⁸

In May 1946 Taylor appeared before a congressional committee that considered plans to convert the academy into a two-year postgraduate institution for graduates from civilian universities or from a unified service academy. The National Guard Association led the charge against West Point as an undergraduate school, drawing strength from President Truman's support for the proposal.⁸⁹ Later that year, in particularly forceful language that Taylor found "intemperate and shows a bitterness which all parties should attempt to eradicate," leaders of the National Guard called the reestablishment of the four-year curriculum at West Point a mistake because it could only mean the return of a caste system throughout the army.⁹⁰ In June 1947, the American Legion similarly asserted that the service academies were "undemocratic" and produced "narrow loyalty to one service." Better to educate young men closer to home in civilian schools.⁹¹ And in November 1949, after Taylor's tenure as superintendent had come to an end, John Bracken, president of the Reserve Officers Association, reiterated in an Associated Press interview that both West Point and Annapolis should serve as postgraduate schools.[92]

Taylor, who had surveyed the political landscape with the help of Major General Wilton B. Persons, the chief of the army's legislative liaison group, understood this was a serious threat.[93] In his testimony in May 1946 he rejected the proposal categorically and pointed out that he knew of no army officer with any ties to West Point who favored it. The value of the academy was that "we must have these young men in their formative years if we are to implant the principles in them which we try to implant."[94] After his testimony, Taylor jumped at the opportunity to invite prominent proponents of the postgraduate plan to visit the academy and see why it ought to remain an undergraduate institution.[95]

To persuade a wider audience, Taylor delineated the objectives and methods of the military academy in a November 1947 pamphlet. He worried that "perhaps only a few recognize West Point as the symbol of the democratic tradition of our armed forces, implanting the conceptions of devotion to duty and to country in the minds of the young men who wish to dedicate their lives to the career of arms."[96] Taylor appealed to history and the great leaders West Point had produced, and he stressed once again the Army Department's directive of a liberal education aimed "to give a broad foundation of culture, general both in academic and military fields." On the curriculum, he noted mathematics remained central, but now some 40 percent of instruction time was spent on social sciences and humanities. Taylor emphasized the importance of military history in the First Class as a critical tool to impart principles of leadership. He also made note of the greater complexity of science classes and the addition of the psychology course, and he pointed at the Compton board as evidence for a more general stamp of approval by leaving the impression that it was equally made up of civilian academics and soldiers.[97]

Taylor conceded problems with selecting the right cadets. Current attrition rates of about 25 percent were too high, and many more students struggled to keep up with the demanding curriculum.[98] This was an issue Taylor hoped to address in part by better testing methods, greater competition over available slots, and by the recent opening of a preparatory high school at Newburgh.[99] But his primary purpose was to knock down the argument that converting the academy to a postgraduate institution would enhance national defense. Only a four-year undergraduate school could prepare effective military leaders who "should have the finest training available for the practical reason that they may dispose of our lives and our fortunes." Taylor concluded that West Point was the "most democratic" of colleges and universities, since "cadets come from every walk of life and represent every class of society."[100] Here, too, Eisenhower agreed with Taylor, who had sought the chief's advice. Eisenhower thought it "a splendid exposition" and merely suggested two sentences on how duty, devotion, and honor flowed from West Point through the entire army.[101] Taylor made that the centerpiece of his concluding paragraph. The "West Point way" was "far from the only road to military success." But the entire army was "heir to West Point" and "as long as the nation has need of these attributes of character and leadership in and out of our armed forces," West Point played a central role in American life.[102]

Taylor knew that not everyone in uniform agreed. Air force general Curtis E. LeMay, then the commander of US air forces in Europe and never one to mince words, told two West Point professors who were visiting his headquarters at Wiesbaden in 1948 that "he saw no real need for West Point [and] stated that he had received more military training in the ROTC at Ohio State than a cadet at USMA receives." LeMay preferred a postgraduate school solution for students who had attained a civilian school bachelor's degree in engineering. As for character and honor, he said, "The Air Force and the Army, too, for that matter, needs technicians, not gentlemen." Where LeMay concluded officer training and education should be extended from four years to six, Taylor believed the four-year curriculum instilled a thirst for lifelong learning.[103] In a 2011 address at West Point, Defense Secretary Robert Gates quoted Taylor: "The goats of my acquaintance who have leapfrogged their classmates are men who continue their intellectual growth after graduation."[104]

Eisenhower, meanwhile, wanted to streamline the second- and third-year curricula at West Point and Annapolis and allow cadets and midshipmen to take one year each at either academy. This would serve greater cross-service cooperation and also allow for the air force to rely on the two existing schools rather than build its own. Taylor rejected this on the grounds that the two academies had vastly different philosophies. He concluded Eisenhower's plan required adding a fifth year to the curriculum and that "the resultant product would be neither a properly trained cadet nor a properly trained midshipman." Taylor also questioned whether young undergraduates who did not yet know their own service could teach its traditions to their peers. His "most serious objection to the exchange plan lies in the loss of identity of the two schools and the disruption of the unity of their educational pattern." For example, it would negatively affect what Taylor called "the spiritual features" of the West Point honor system.[105] Interservice contacts continued on a smaller scale, as when the cadets of West Point's Second Class and the midshipmen of the same year at Annapolis participated in two weeks of joint amphibious exercises in August 1947.[106] And a regular exchange program had started in the spring of 1946, wherein First Classmen visited Annapolis and senior midshipmen came to West Point for a weekend and immersed themselves in the lifestyle of the other academy.[107]

On curricular and structural change Eisenhower was in Taylor's corner. When Brigadier General Alexander retired at the end of August 1947 after nearly two years of service as the first dean of the academic board, Taylor hoped to establish that seniority was not the sole principle on which a successor would be chosen. He proposed Colonel Harris Jones, the head of the Mathematics Department, because the board should be run by officers who had significant managerial experience in their department, but also had five or even ten years of service left ahead of them. Once again Taylor created a *fait accompli* by securing Eisenhower's approval before presenting the notion to the board. Eisenhower "emphatically" agreed with Taylor's "logic and choice" and instructed him to send the formal recommendation to Washington. Jones was promoted to brigadier general and appointed dean on September 1, 1947.[108] Perhaps this contributed to Beukema's unease with Taylor's methods; he would have been next in line by seniority after Charles E. Morrison, the professor of modern languages, who reached mandatory retirement age in 1948.

Another point of contention was the composition of the faculty. In 1946, Congress approved Taylor's request for one additional permanent faculty member per department.[109] Traditionalists, who saw the academy's main mission in the realm of inculcating cadets with the proper West Point spirit and who believed in the continued applicability of the methods introduced by Superintendent Sylvanus Thayer nearly a century and a half earlier, balked at the idea of hiring a greater number of outsiders. Taylor, who believed the academy should educate future officers, not merely train them, preferred expertise over service record, but that did not mean West Point's departments or the superintendent could go about hiring scholars from the civilian academy. The instructional faculty consisted primarily of young, bright, and hard-working officers on short-term rotations. Taylor, who once had served in that role, did not object to the practice, though he would have liked to bring expertise and service needs into a better balance. At first, the automatic correction of wartime practices, when by necessity more civilian and reservist instructors had to be brought in, worked for the traditionalists. Taylor noted that by 1947 all but forty-two members of the West Point faculty were once again regular army officers and almost all had graduated from the academy. Taylor hoped that some postgraduate work in civilian schools would go a long way to improve his faculty. "40 of 60 new instructors in the Academic Departments," he noted in June 1947, "attended either one or two semesters at selected civilian educational institutions. This policy will undoubtedly increase the officers' value as instructors."[110] But as with so many issues he had hoped to address, the question of who made for the best faculty members remained unresolved when Taylor left West Point in early 1949.

One claim that advocates of ROTC, Officer Candidate Schools, and the National Guard could not make was cost. West Point was cheap in the late 1940s. Budget analysis from Lincoln for Taylor showed the academy, which typically produced less than 10 percent of newly commissioned second lieutenants, received $7 million from the federal government in 1948, with $7.5 million allocated for 1949. The other officer training programs totaled $421 million for 1949.[111] In light of those figures, Taylor's plan to improve infrastructure and building space was perhaps doomed to failure. The last significant overhaul had occurred in 1938, when the academy was built up for a corps of 1,960 cadets. Due to World War II, size had increased to an authorized strength of 2,500. Taylor proposed a $50 million building program for additional housing, mess, and training facilities and for the renovation of existing structures.[112] Here, too, Taylor left before changes could be effected.

Partly, this was the result of Taylor's own flaws: he always seemed more interested in putting reforms on the agenda than pursuing the detailed work of seeing them through. His micromanagement in other matters suggests that he allowed what he considered less than essential to slip through the cracks of the system.[113] Very little new physical plant was built or appropriated in the half-decade after the war, even though academic buildings, faculty quarters, and cadet barracks were bursting at the seams. Perhaps it was a blessing in disguise that the postwar entering classes did not exceed three-fourths of available appointments. Taylor did persuade Congress to fund 133 new family housing units in 1946 and 1947, about half of what was needed, but even then the high building costs in the rocky terrain on post rose to the point where these could only be made of the cheapest materials. It would take another decade until Taylor's successors had wrung enough money from Congress and the Army Department to renovate and expand academic buildings. The conversion between 1955 and 1958 of Thayer Hall from riding hall to the central academic building alleviated some of the pressure and also allowed for the conversion of an older academic building into a much needed additional barracks in 1959. The housing shortfall was addressed in the early 1960s.[114]

Strategy for the Atomic Age

In his years at West Point, Taylor reflected on his experiences in the Second World War. He recognized that his vantage point as a division commander had been that of a tactician, but he had also conducted missions in Italy that went beyond the operational realm and he had observed military and political leaders at work in the European Theater of Operations. What stood out to him was a changed meaning of strategy. It was no longer Carl von Clausewitz's concept of using battles to defeat the enemy's armed forces as Taylor had been taught, albeit with apparent reductionism, in 1934 and 1935 as a student at the Command and General Staff College. Strategy was now a task for the entire nation. Winning a total war required the mobilization of all resources and "employment of all sources of power with unified effect, in short, a total integrated strategy on the part of the Allied coalition bent on bringing Hitler down." Taylor thought Eisenhower had well understood the interplay of military force aimed at the will of the enemy, employment of industrial production as well as destruction of the enemy's industrial plant and infrastructure, diplomacy and coalition building, the importance of finance, and a host of other factors that now defined war. He had included representatives of all crucial departments, agencies, and interest groups on his staff and among his advisers. In World War II, Eisenhower was not a conventional strategist, but the leader of a total and integrated war effort, Taylor concluded, "like Caesar in Gaul." For Taylor, modern war required a unified commander who controlled all assets, military and otherwise, that the nation and its allies could put at his disposal.[115]

The emerging Cold War also started to come into focus for Taylor. In his thinking about leadership for the second half of the twentieth century, both Cold War concerns and wartime experiences intersected, as he stressed the likelihood of overseas deployment and the need to be prepared to command armies of citizen soldiers in moments of grave crisis. The realities of the Cold War at its front lines hit Taylor with stunning force in 1949, when he was sent to the army's European command at Heidelberg and then to Berlin. His subsequent experiences in the final months of the Korean War deepened his assumptions, but those had already begun to take shape between 1945 and 1949.

Nearly three years into his tenure at West Point, Taylor delivered the annual Kermit Roosevelt Lecture at the Imperial Defence College in London. By then he understood that the United States and Britain were once again in a cold war—he considered the decade from the Manchurian Incident to the attack on Pearl Harbor a first cold war—and that strategy was no longer a purely military concern. Taylor defined strategy as "the course of action taken by a nation to apply its national power to obtain its national objective." This meant determining the goals and then selecting the appropriate policies to attain them. Traditionally, he held, America's leaders could always agree on the objectives in the broadest sense, peace and welfare for the nation, but there had been considerable disagreement on the proper means and confusion as to what were means and ends. For example, Taylor noted, the Monroe Doctrine was understood by some policymakers as an end in itself while others thought of it as a means to a wider end. As a result of global and total war, American policymakers and soldiers now "took a broader view of strategy" and understood the need to plan for full-scale mobilization of all resources of the nation and its allies.[116]

Given the tremendous military victory in 1945, why were the United States and Britain now in a state that could not be called peace? Taylor noted that the Allies had been unable to translate military victory into full-blown success because their political leaders had failed to realize the need to maintain the "civil dimensions" of strategy: political will, economic mobilization, and psychological readiness. By the time they had awoken to the new realities of a global conflict, the Cold War had hardened. On the bright side, experience gained in both world wars helped to change course, albeit at the expense of building the unavoidable "machinery to establish a proper relationship between national resources, national objectives, and national policies." Taylor went on to describe the national security establishment of the early Cold War: he started with Congress and appropriations before turning to the president, national security council and other advisers, and intelligence gathering.[117]

The question now was not whether the United States had sufficient resources or the will to mobilize and prepare. The real issue, Taylor feared, was the congenital slowness of the democratic process, which remained enshrined even in the National Security Act of 1947, the law that codified the national security state. Moreover, though he believed the strengths of a democracy far outweighed its weaknesses, he expressed both concern and optimism about whether American policymakers could overcome the vagueness in defining policy objectives and specific ends. Perhaps the Second World War had alerted them to the need to be meticulous. Taylor detected three principles that had recently been put in place. The first was the broadest goal: "a secure world, based upon international cooperation." Here the emergence of the United Nations offered a hopeful sign. Second, the United States now intended to support likeminded people. Here Taylor pointed at the Marshall Plan, aid to Greece and Turkey, as well as monetary and material aid to China, Japan, South Korea, and occupied Germany as the key examples. Third, Taylor noted the US commitment to containment of Russia and of communism. These were clear objectives and there was a mechanism in place to offer advice to the president, regulate spending, and control the forces that mobilization unleashed.[118]

All of this meant very little if the armed forces could not enforce American goals and if military strategy and national strategy were not fully aligned. Taylor strongly supported the emergence of a unified military establishment and noted obliquely, "Regardless of the present difficulties, we feel that in the long run this new organization should give far greater unity of purpose and economy of military and financial effort than was possible under the old system." Taylor believed airpower played the dominant role in modern war and that absolute safety was no longer a feasible goal—something, he noted, his British audience understood very well. The US Navy could still keep enemies from American shores, but the air space could not be secured entirely. No matter how the enemy might attack, Americans no longer enjoyed the "protection of time." Hence, Taylor surmised, constant military preparedness was the order of the day. This, he thought, almost everyone in the United Stated could agree upon. The trouble started once different actors in the executive and legislative branches got to projecting the nature of a future war and distributing resources for the armed forces without making cutbacks to science, education, industries, and in the political sphere. At that point, parochial interests and diametrically opposed perspectives on war set in.[119]

What Britain and the United States needed, Taylor concluded, was a clear and shared vision of war. "The soundest of our prophets," he argued, "are inclined to visualize a war falling into three phases." These were initial defense and retaliation, counteroffensive and expansion of the network of bases, and all-out offensive. Unsurprisingly, given the tendency of military planners to refight the last war, Taylor's vision sounded much like a replay of the Second World War, albeit on a much shorter time line, at least in the first two phases. Taylor declined to address the relative merits of air force plans for intercontinental bombers and navy blueprints for super carriers. Instead, he outlined a way "to get at the fellow's vitals from many directions: from Japan, from India, through the Middle East, through Western Europe, through Scandinavia, over the North Pole." Given these options, "the choice of the direction of the principal effort will be the most important strategic decision of the war and will depend largely on what you and the other Western democracies will tell us in advance." Equally critical, wherever the United States drew the line based on assumptions of a defensible position ("on the Elbe, on the Rhine, along the Channel, behind the Pyrenees, in the Caucasus?"), it was vital to maintain "the morale of all of Western civilization" and stop the Soviet advance as far to the east as possible. This was the fundamental initial task for ground forces.[120]

Taylor turned in a radically different direction in the concluding section of his speech. What he had outlined was a broad emerging consensus, but it was not necessarily how a future war would unfold, and the farther from reality the consensus, the worse it was. Taylor disagreed with the widely held notion that airpower alone could defeat the enemy in the third phase of the war. But what troubled him more was the assumption that any such future war would be a total effort. Quite remarkably for 1948, merely three years after the end of the Second World War and with the United States holding a monopoly on atomic weapons, Taylor raised the possibility of limited war. He was concerned about the recurrence of conflicts like the Spanish Civil War or the Russo-Japanese conflict over Manchuria, and he held that "even more indirect forms of war must be considered. Just as strategy consists of elements other than military, so aggression can take forms to which conventional military means are no reply." The United States relied too heavily on air and sea power to respond to localized attacks or nonmilitary aggression. "In providing for United States security," Taylor warned, "our planners will have to make provisions for meeting an enemy who comes in strange and unconventional forms." This required a sound balance of air, sea, and land forces, continued education of military and political leaders, a fuller understanding of the enemy, and recognition of the need to maintain the morale of the home front at all costs. Taylor's argument about the defense of western civilization "for transmission to our children and not for looting by the Barbarians of the east" represented the mainstream of military and strategic planners. His thoughts on the possibility of less-than-total war did not.[121]

Of course, there were hardly enough American soldiers for such wars. Omar Bradley, who had succeeded Eisenhower as the army's chief of staff, had expressed his concerns about low manpower levels to the Senate Armed Services Committee in March 1948, two months before Taylor's London speech. The army had 542,000 officers and men under arms, and nearly half of them were deployed outside of the United States: 100,000 combat and 158,000 service personnel. There were 127,000 officers and men in the Far East, scattered throughout Japan, Korea, the Philippines, the Ryukyu Islands, and the Marshall and Bonin Islands. Another 101,000 officers and men were in Germany, Austria, and Trieste. Exacerbating the manpower shortage, the army still supported the air force with some 50,000 men in maintenance functions and nearly a third of its service and administrative personnel. Most of the 284,000 troops in the United States were thus either supporting overseas deployments or the air force, and Bradley "could muster no more than a handful of combat troops for the defense of the U.S. or for emergency employment overseas." Bradley and his staff estimated that unless all occupation forces came home, it would take an increase to 782,000 officers and men to meet all immediate tasks and build a 149,000-man mobile strike force in five combat divisions that could be deployed in a crisis.[122]

Taylor, who had hoped to complete his fourth year at West Point, was sent to Germany at the end of January 1949. What did he take away from his experiences? He liked the surroundings and returned to the Hudson in search of rest—for example, when he spent a weekend on the river on the superintendents' boat, at the height of the Berlin Crisis in August 1961.[123] And he resolved that one of his greatest regrets was not getting along with the academy board. He gave his protégé William Westmoreland, superintendent from 1960 to 1964, the "gratuitous advice" to cultivate the board, whose members had dedicated their careers to West Point. Doing that, and making sure the alumni were persuaded the superintendent had a positive vision and showed strong leadership, would go a long way to ensure a successful tenure.[124]

Others found that Taylor had moved the academy forward. Eisenhower, still at Columbia University but also de facto JCS chairman for parts of 1949, reported to his high school friend Everett "Swede" Hazlett, who himself had graduated from the Naval Academy, on the findings of a Defense Department study group on unification of the armed services.

The deliberations of generals (including Eisenhower), admirals, and civilian leaders bore no fruit in the main, but all agreed that the service academies were in good shape. Academic performance at West Point and Annapolis compared favorably to most of the nation's colleges. In comparing the two schools, board members found "the curriculum at West Point is somewhat more crowded and intensive and requires a greater number of hours of work than at Annapolis." Eisenhower expressed relief that such had not been the case when he had studied at the military academy, but he also noted concern with the remaining emphasis on rote memorization. "Frankly," he concluded, "I honestly believe it far easier if we do not place too much dependence in mere knowledge."[125] Taylor had moved the academy part of the way in Eisenhower's desired direction, but more reforms were to come in the later 1950s under Davidson.

Even though Taylor's relationship with members of the faculty had remained tenuous, Beukema thought Taylor had left the academy in fine shape. Referencing the findings of an external review board for the service academies, Beukema noted, "In all important respects West Point is 20 years ahead of all except a very small fraction of the universities and colleges. That comes from leading educators, not military brass."[126] Consciously or inadvertently underlining his unsentimental approach, Taylor did not hold an academic board meeting to formally introduce his successor, Major General Bryant Moore, in the same way Wilby had done for Taylor. Instead, he held a regular meeting on January 14, 1949, that approved the name change of the Department of Foreign Languages (from Modern Languages), discussed admissions and appointment rules, and considered the fundamental assumptions of a mobilization plan and its effects on the curriculum. Moore presided over the subsequent meeting on February 11 without inserting thanks to Taylor for his service in the proceedings.[127] In between, Taylor had bid the academic board and the staff of the academy a formal farewell on January 28.[128]

Some reform-minded faculty members were sad to see Taylor depart. George Lincoln, West Point's keenest observer of international affairs, credited Taylor with "enlightened evolutionary change" of the academy. He noted, "The Military Academy during the last three years has gone through a process of constructive change which would probably have been considered highly revolutionary if it had not been handled with great smoothness and vision." Moreover, this was not change for its own sake: "If West Point had not changed materially from pre-war, there is a question in my mind as to whether our existence would not have been seriously jeopardized." Lincoln, who had served in demanding positions on the War Department staff and retained an impressive network of friends in high places throughout the military establishment and the State Department, concluded, "The job of Superintendent of the Military Academy seems to be one of the most difficult personal jobs in world. He must be a commander, a man capable of instilling the foundational elements of military leadership, and the president of a college." In Lincoln's estimation, Taylor had made sure "West Point is equal to or better than the best in civilian colleges."[129]

After his tenure at West Point, Taylor remained engaged with questions of education and leadership. He recognized the intricate balance that needed to be struck between science, technology, and mathematics on the one hand and humanities and social sciences on the other, as new technology and worldwide deployments placed army officers in an increasingly demanding environment. In a speech at The Citadel in 1956, then Army Chief of Staff Taylor expounded on the demands of leaders in the global Cold War. He noted that military leadership rested on three attributes: human understanding, professional competence based on sound training, and strength of character. He concluded, "The requirements for character and human understanding have been with military leaders of every age and remain relatively constant. On the other hand, the requirements of professional competence become greater as our weapons systems become more complicated and as the possible combinations of military force become more greatly diversified." In this worldwide struggle in the nuclear age, future officers "must learn more of the language of science," but "they must speak also the language of politics and diplomacy—never forgetting that they are soldiers. Thus, the attainment of professional competence is an ever-widening requirement."[130] Soldiering and generalship had become more political, complex, and demanding, and it was at the military academies and in ROTC programs that cadets and faculty had to lay the foundations that allowed officers to cope with the Cold War.

Two decades later, Taylor returned to education and leadership in a lecture at the National Defense University. He claimed it was Eisenhower's request in 1945 for a course on the principles of military leadership that triggered Taylor's quest to understand what made strong leaders. By 1977, he had further delineated the category of human understanding, which he now defined as both intellectual capacity and inspirational qualities, with emphasis on the ability to craft and convey a clear argument, skills helped by the study of English and foreign languages as well as history and social and behavioral sciences. In addition, Taylor held that professional competence and strength of character had to accompany these more cerebral aspects of leadership. But could those be taught? Certainly clarity of expression could, and Taylor recalled that even as JCS chairman in the 1960s he spent too much time "acting as a high school English teacher, simplifying and purifying the language of important staff papers to make them readily comprehensible to civilian leaders." The message was clear: know your men, but also know your audience.

Taylor thought one of the essential steps for his own career had been his devotion to high school debate. He firmly believed that "professional competence and a trained intellect can be developed by standard educational methods." Teaching character was a more difficult proposition, but even there, much depended on "habits of virtuous conduct" and moral principles that could be learned from "precept, example, parable, and fable." Even inspirational qualities, though perhaps they could not be taught in a narrow sense, could be demonstrated to cadets and young officers "through studies of historical and contemporary examples" and officers could later draw on elements of their public speaking or their studies of sociology and mass psychology. Leading, then, was partly persuading, which could be done by example (physical) and language (intellectual). Taylor always aimed to combine both, and he thought a sound officer education should stress that from the outset.[131]

Taylor's record as West Point's superintendent was mixed. He had directed the return to the four-year curriculum and led a spirited defense of the academy's purpose. He had also implemented Eisenhower's wish for a course in military psychology and leadership and generally improved the education of future leaders (as opposed to the training of officers). Yet he had not pushed as far as he might have desired in balancing engineering and mathematics with social sciences, languages, and history. He had encountered significant resistance and some acrimony from the faculty that favored a conservative retrenchment. And he had not insisted that the honor code really apply to all cadets and allowed the football team to remain a group apart. As a reformer, Taylor was quick to make his own decisions and often too far ahead of his subordinates. He seemed to believe hearts and minds followed once new structures had been sketched.

Taylor was generally more inclined to think about structures than people. In terms of strategy, command, and defense establishment, several themes emerged in the late 1940s that defined Taylor's career for the next decades. One was his recognition that limited war and conventional warfare remained possible in the atomic age. Another was his sense that strategy was now a holistic national and even international endeavor. Finally, he believed that modern war required unified command that controlled all assets in the way Eisenhower had done in Europe. But Taylor was an incomplete humanist and his arguments rested more on logic, abstraction, and too linear and rigid readings of history than on intuition, empathy, and deeper thought on how men and machines would function in such conflicts. Now it remained to be seen whether he could be a successful theater commander, strategist, and administrator.

2

Cold War Frontiers

Berlin Commander

Major General Taylor arrived at the Cold War's front lines in January 1949, when the Berlin blockade and airlift were in full swing and the western alliance was taking form. He told Truman's adviser Bernard Baruch he regretted leaving West Point but he was thrilled to serve in Europe, where the United States had its primary military and political interests.[1] Taylor found the command arrangements in Germany confusing: "I went over to be the chief of staff—in effect, the chief of staff of the Army in Europe. They had a curious organization then. My actual title was deputy chief of staff." The reason for this ambiguity was General Lucius Clay, military governor and senior army commander, who spent his time at offices in Berlin and Frankfurt. Taylor recalled, "In effect, [General Clarence] Huebner commanded and I was his chief of staff. I was very happy in Heidelberg. By mid-summer . . . Clay came home and retired and John McCloy became the High Commissioner with headquarters in Frankfurt."[2]

Taylor spent just over half a year in Heidelberg. Life there was pleasant. The Taylors' quarters came with ample space to host delegations like the West Point cadets who visited in June. Relations between American soldiers and the German community were still tense, but showed signs of improvement.[3] The main task, defending Western Europe, seemed impossible. The army had fewer than 90,000 officers and men in Germany and could field two combat divisions, Germany was defeated and disarmed, and elements of the British and French armies were deployed in wars in Malaya and Indochina. Estimates at the time put the Soviets at 175 combat divisions, though there was less agreement on manpower levels and combat effectiveness.[4] Cold War icons like the Seventh Army (reactivated in November 1950) and the US European Command (established in August 1952) did not yet exist, and while the North Atlantic Treaty was signed in April 1949, there was no supreme commander for Allied forces until the end of 1950.[5] These odds notwithstanding, US forces spent much of 1949 in maneuvers to improve tactical mobility, communications, and interoperability of army, navy, and air force units, about 120,000 officers and men in all.[6]

In the summer of 1949, McCloy, who reported to the State Department, requested Taylor's move to Berlin. He had also submitted two other names—Gruenther and Wedemeyer—and Taylor believed he owed his assignment to propinquity. McCloy knew Taylor from War Department service in 1941 and missions in Italy in 1943 and thought he had the right combination of military, political, and diplomatic skills: "His present post is as exacting as anything that he was asked to do in the course of the war itself. Berlin has become almost an outpost and a symbol of American policy in Europe. The importance of having a man of high courage and quality there is self-evident."[7] In August the cool and calculating Taylor succeeded Brigadier General Frank Howley, whose relations with Soviet officials had been stormy.[8]

American officials assumed the biggest threat to their position in Berlin stemmed from another blockade, and military plans revolved around an airlift.[9] Since June 1948, America's Berlin policy had been one of crisis management and its response to the blockade a desperate play for time that extended for over half a year beyond when American diplomats had expected the airlift would falter.[10] Moreover, the airlift had not provided sufficient calories to feed 2 million people in West Berlin. Throughout the blockade Berliners bought food and other commodities on black markets stocked with goods smuggled into the city from the Soviet occupation zone in East Germany.[11] This success in improvisation, minus the unacknowledged reliance on East German foodstuffs, now had to be extended to day-to-day operations, just as the emergence of two German states deepened political divides and the Cold War expanded.

Taylor got to shape the new office of US Commander, Berlin (USCOB), and run parts of a devastated city.[12] He concluded Berlin could not be defended, but that it was worth staying since a successful West Berlin held tremendous propaganda value.[13] His first task was to restore confidence in the future of a free Berlin, and nothing was more critical than "timely financial and economic help."[14] Taylor liked to remind visiting dignitaries, "I'll ask you to consider the city as a beleaguered island in a hostile 'Red' sea more than a hundred miles from the nearest friendly coast. As such it is a constant hot spot in the cold war in which battle is joined in the political, economic and ideological fields."[15] He thought there should be a unified commander of the three western sectors, but at least his office controlled all American assets. Howley had commanded US armed forces, but other representatives of the military governor (or frequently Clay himself) had managed politics and economics. Acting as diplomat and general, Taylor reported to McCloy and Huebner's successor, General Thomas T. Handy. As visual reminder, Taylor displayed autographed pictures of his two bosses at his office.[16]

McCloy rated West Berlin's economy "in distress."[17] After the destruction in 1945 the Soviets had removed most remaining machine tools. In 1949 there was only 15 to 20 percent of the prewar industrial plant left.[18] Manufacturing output had collapsed accordingly: in July 1949 it was 19 percent of what it had been in 1936, and it only slowly increased to 28 percent by year's end. The city ran an 800 million Deutsche Mark (DM) budget deficit (roughly $160 million, nearly half of Berlin's annual expenditures), and no-interest credits and low-yield loans from the American, British, and French military governments—almost DM 800 million from American sources alone since June 1948—were not extended much beyond the end of the blockade in May.[19] Taylor estimated that 25 percent of the labor force was unemployed, and by January 1950 that number had risen to 30 percent. Berlin's economy suffered from lack of investment capital to modernize factories and infrastructure, the collapse of trade with the east, and a general sense of fear. Taylor knew why West Berliners remained steadfast: "A man without a job in West Berlin is still better off than a man with a job in East Berlin." The communist system provided no incentive for workers and "in 1949, thirty thousand workers in the iron and steel industry produced *one-half* the volume of production that thirteen thousand workers produced in 1936."[20]

Taylor and his chief economist, Howard Jones, worked closely with Berlin's elites. The new West Berlin Club offered a meeting space for social functions as well as political conversations with prominent citizens. Some of them served on an Economic Cooperation Administration (ECA) advisory committee Taylor had launched.[21] Taylor believed Marshall Plan aid was the decisive means to help West Berlin's economy produce at equal cost to that in West Germany.[22] "I attended endless christenings of new buildings and the dedication of housing areas," he noted, "getting very much interested in everything in Berlin. I've always said that when I left I knew more about West Berlin than I knew about Kansas City where I grew up in the United States."[23]

In mid-November 1949, Jones, McCloy, and Taylor persuaded Secretary of State Dean Acheson of "the necessity for substantial ECA assistance if further deterioration in the Berlin situation were to be prevented and Berlin started on the way to economic recovery."[24] Taylor welcomed the first installment in December as "a decided stimulant to Berlin's economy in its race to catch up with the production figures achieved in Western Germany."[25] With a steady supply of capital on the horizon, German manufacturers Telefunken, Daimler-Benz, and Siemens announced the reopening of factories in Berlin.[26] By mid-1950, DM 221 million had been allocated to provide loans to industry (DM 65 million), rebuild housing (DM 35 million), and help small firms, utilities, and agriculture.[27] In all, Berlin received over $350 million in Marshall Plan aid, primarily to improve infrastructure and boost manufacturing businesses and the construction sector.[28]

West Berlin remained poorer than West Germany on a per capita basis, and it depended on subsidies. Taylor noted that industrial production in 1950 still reached only 38 percent of what it had been in 1936, compared to 96 percent for West Germany. He ascribed it to "a creeping blockade, less dramatic but perhaps even more pernicious than the old all-out blockade" that the Soviets "turn on and off like a water faucet."[29] Still, he sounded optimistic in a talk to German economists in October. The western Allies had recognized the world was one economic entity and they were adjusting to free trade, fair valuation of currencies, and proper mechanisms to settle the international trade balance. "Here in Berlin," Taylor noted, "we have evidences of the effects of the [Marshall] plan on all sides. In spite of the losses arising from the dismantling by the Soviets as well as the direct effects of the war, the city has been able to start a far-reaching program of reconstruction." This required patience, but "the retooling of Berlin industry which is resulting will in the long run reduce production costs and improve the competitive position of Berlin vis-à-vis West German and world markets."[30] By 1954, manufacturing output had grown to 70 percent of prewar levels and exports had risen tenfold since the end of the blockade.[31]

Politically, Berlin remained suspended between east and west. Four-power coordination effectively ended in June 1948, but the three western sectors still operated jointly. Occasional meetings of all four commandants commenced in the summer of 1949, yet Soviet officers rarely partook in substantive policy discussions.[32] September offers an illustration: the meeting on the 13th progressed "in an atmosphere of unusual amiability," perhaps because the stakes were low and General Alexander

Kotikov, described by Howley as "a big, bulky man with flowing white hair, icy blue eyes, and a mouth like a petulant rosebud, his mind turned on and off automatically with switches operated in the Kremlin," had sent his deputy, Colonel A. I. Yelisarov.[33] The only concrete decision was to allow postal service delivery in each sector even if the mail bore different sector stamps. To the Americans' surprise, Yelisarov also permitted exploratory meetings of German officials from East and West Berlin on coordinating administration of the city.[34]

More typical was the Soviets' refusal to participate in meetings when the central issue, compensation for railroad workers, was thornier and Kotikov had no incentive to accept changes to western subsidies for East German (*Reichsbahn*) train operations. Taylor and his colleagues, the British commandant Geoffrey Bourne (since January) and French general Jean Ganeval (since 1946), resolved to put pressure on the Soviets to cease removing railroad equipment from the French and British sectors—the Americans had previously balked at the practice—and threatened the end of one-to-one conversion of railroad workers' wages for the two German currencies, which greatly overvalued the eastern mark.[35] This issue triggered a tense exchange of letters throughout the rest of the year.[36]

Soviet harassment along supply routes through East Germany continued for much of Taylor's one and a half years in Berlin, to the point of familiarity where the British high commissioner thought attempts to turn back vehicles at Soviet checkpoints were "minor vexations."[37] Still, increasing communist pressure in Europe and the Far East had Washington on edge. This could lead to poorly conceived actions. In mid-January 1950, Taylor's men seized the *Reichsbahn* building in Berlin to force the issue of transportation policy—a repetition of an earlier attempt by Howley—but they had to retreat when the Soviets responded by curtailing train traffic into the city. State Department officials feared Americans would not support another airlift as long as the Soviets let some trains and army convoys enter Berlin. Acheson asked Taylor and McCloy how the United States should respond to a full blockade and what the Allies and West Germans thought of an airlift.[38] By then, the stakes were raised: the Soviet Union had tested an atom bomb, China had fallen to communism, and State Department policy planners considered the enhanced conventional and nuclear armament policies proposed in NSC 68 later in the spring.

Taylor did not expect an outright military attack, but he concluded that economic and psychological pressure was part of Moscow's wider plan. He was convinced the Soviets intended to seize West Berlin as a step toward a Soviet-dominated unified Germany. Taylor feared a sequence of mounting attacks. First, the Soviets "might create political conditions favorable to some deal which would allow them to take over the city." If the Allies and Berliners held firm, the Soviets would likely accelerate "a campaign of economic attrition to hasten its economic collapse." After that, "the third and extreme line of action is that of winning Berlin by subversion and force." Taylor viewed West Berlin's economy as a neuralgic point, and fears of heightened political pressure and an impending attempt to overthrow West Berlin's government were running high in spring 1950.[39]

In late May, the communist Free German Youth (FDJ) staged a mass rally in Berlin of 400,000 members. East German accounts even claimed 700,000 participants, including 30,000 West Germans.[40] Henry Byroade, the State Department's principal desk officer for Germany, expressed concerns as early as February.[41] Allied officials feared this *Deutschlandtreffen* aimed at "possible mass invasion of the Western sectors of the city" and a coup that would place communists in charge of the magistrate.[42] Taylor was less alarmed. In March he assured Admiral Forrest Sherman, the chief of naval operations, that the rally would be "serious but not critical." In mid-April he told NBC's Ed Hasker the situation was "delicate, [but] far from critical," and he informed viewers of the German program *Welt im Film* of his World War II lesson that danger always looked greater from a distance.[43]

Taylor did not expect major disturbances, but he asked his entire command—some 1,800 officers and men in one infantry and one constabulary battalion, plus about 850 military police (supported by 1,300 British soldiers and MPs and over 800 French troops and gendarmes)—to display calm confidence and be ready to take up battle stations quickly. He gave orders for his men not to stand in place as a crowd control force, but to appear on the scene when needed, striking aggressively rather than letting tensions build and succumbing to acts of provocation. Above all, he reminded his officers, "use the minimum of force, a minimum of killing weapons." Should the crowd disperse, "let them run." Taylor recognized that "when we have to shoot on a Berlin street, we have accepted defeat to a certain degree. We have lost something we can never get back."[44]

The *Deutschlandtreffen* went by peacefully and it did not prove necessary to call on the five infantry battalions on alert in West Germany (two American, two French, and one British).[45] The May rally was an attempt at intimidation, but beyond propaganda bluster there was little evidence for a militant coup. Taylor's political affairs adviser concluded, "If the USSR were committed to take the city, it would have been taken."[46] General Handy commended Taylor for his "leadership in the planning, training, supervision, and execution . . . of a most difficult and complicated task."[47] Taylor himself mockingly apologized to the press for "a rather dull weekend . . . it came and went without conquest of the Western Sectors of Berlin which the Communists loudly proclaimed a few months ago." He ascribed this to the resolute response by the Allies and the people of West Berlin that had persuaded the Soviets the likely cost was not worth the risk.[48]

Taylor operated within a hardening political divide. By the fall of 1949, Acheson had concluded Berlin would remain divided as long as the two newly formed German states existed.[49] West Berlin's mayor, Ernst Reuter, following on public statements to the same effect by West German chancellor Konrad Adenauer, engaged in futile attempts throughout the spring of 1950 to arrange citywide elections.[50] Taylor saw propaganda value in Reuter's proposals, but he feared the Soviets could turn the tables and present plans for reunification that appealed to the people of West Berlin.[51] Taylor need not have worried. Soviet responses in May and June were, in Reuter's words, "so ridiculous there is no need even discuss it."[52] As West Berlin's ties to West Germany grew deeper, all major federal agencies opened offices, even though the city retained its autonomy (including its own postal service and exemption of its residents from military conscription).[53]

Those links notwithstanding, US officials wondered if they had developed deeper emotional ties to Berlin than the Rhineland Catholic Adenauer, who agreed with the position of the French: Berlin symbolized Prussian militarism and the ills of the old German nation-state.[54] Taylor vented his frustration in April 1950, after West Germany's finance minister told Berlin's treasurer he could provide only half of the DM 60 million earmarked for the month. This presented practical problems and depressed morale in the city, which had been declared a disaster area (*Notstandsgebiet*) by the federal government in mid-March so that more aid could be sent quickly.[55] Taylor told Economics Minister Ludwig Erhard and Vice Chancellor and Marshall Plan aid coordinator Franz Blücher that, while he had worked hard to get American orders for Berlin industries (DM 9.5 million from March to July 1950), he did not see the same commitment from German companies or the state. It was "high time that our friends in West Germany took really effective steps to assure that Berlin gets all the business that can be directed here under the terms of the Notstandsgebiet Law."[56] Taylor found working with local authorities, especially the resolute Reuter, congenial, but he knew he was operating at the "end of the trolley line."[57]

As for the German Democratic Republic, Taylor reported "unprecedented haste" in the constitution of the East German parliament on October 7—an unelected body that determined to postpone elections until late 1950 as one of its first measures—and he noted the de facto emergence of East Berlin as the GDR's capital. McCloy thought the postponement of elections presented "one of the most vulnerable points in the Soviet façade and we feel that it should be exploited to the full" by western media and information agencies.[58] But the formation of the East German state also provided the Soviets with a new tactic. They could now threaten to turn over control of access points to their East German clients and walk away from agreements on Allied rights in Berlin.

In cultural and ideological terms, Taylor considered Berlin a window for East Germans as well as a platform from which news media could project their message of freedom and prosperity. Taylor held that in the "daily propaganda struggle, on the West side we have the U.S. overt radio, RIAS [*Rundfunk im amerikanischen Sektor*]—it is our biggest gun and it reaches millions of East Germans. . . . There are also 10 daily West-licensed but not West-controlled overt newspapers."[59] Public relations work also entailed elaborate displays. In the spring of 1950, Taylor, Bourne, and Ganeval approved an international automobile show and the State Department called for a "Freedom Fair (*Freiheits Messe*)" to highlight the benefits derived from free institutions.[60] From geographic isolation, immersion in Berlin's daily life, and shared experience of what McCloy called "the fear and the pressure of this great force that is coming from the East" grew a sense of community that reminded Taylor of frontline comradeship.[61]

The Korean War put the defenders of West Berlin on high alert.[62] In the wake of North Korea's attack, with fears rising in Western Europe, McCloy, Handy, and Taylor presented the Truman administration with a call to arms in response to the question of what the United States should do in case of another blockade.[63] In its aggressive recommendations, it closely followed Taylor's draft of August 10.[64] They noted "the Soviet offensive against Berlin has never ceased since 1945; it merely waxes and wanes in intensity" and comprised "economic warfare, psychological warfare, subversive penetration, and increased pressure of political activity." One may now even expect "the *coup de grâce* by East German paramilitary forces," estimated at 55,000 officers and men and growing rapidly in strength. It was essential to persuade Soviet leaders "by encouraging dis-affection in the satellite nations" that their power base in Central Europe was tenuous and that an assault on Berlin would be premature and impossible to keep localized. This required building up Allied forces so the Soviets had to grow concerned about the cost of victory.[65]

The Allies' military position was weak. There were fewer than 10,000 American, British, and French troops in West Berlin and they could count on an 11,000-man police force. East German paramilitary forces alone had "the capability of possibly overwhelming this Allied garrison and certainly of bottling it up in a small area." Reserves would be hard to find since "Allied forces now immediately available to support the West Berlin garrison are committed by other operational plans in case of a general emergency." Consequently, "the position of the United States Commander, Berlin, is now militarily untenable." But the Allies could deter the communists and avoid war. For Taylor, it was essential that the Soviets understood that "an armed aggression from any source against Berlin means war." Berlin should build up its capacity to withstand a long blockade and the Soviets had to be told it would trigger responses designed to cripple East Germany's economy. Beyond that, "the Allies should maintain a tough, well-equipped garrison in Berlin, which will make any attack costly to aggressors and destructive to the city which they wish to use as a Communist capital." Finally, it was time to build a "West Berlin military organization capable of supporting and extending the effectiveness of the Allied garrison." As for a renewed airlift, the three strategists concluded it could "easily be disrupted and its effectiveness is questionable."[66]

Before the Korean War, no one had expected a direct military attack on Berlin, but now that sense of security was lost. The Allies, Taylor wrote, needed to maintain their foothold in Berlin "even at the risk of war." Doing so provided "numerous political and ideological advantages," but it was also a debt owed to the 2 million Berliners "who have linked their fate with the West" and it was an essential step to retain the support of West Germans while "Free Europe" was building up conventional armed forces to match those of "Soviet Europe." As a practical matter, this meant maintaining access rights to Berlin at all costs, building up "a sufficient balance of strength to discourage the *Bereitschaften* [East German paramilitary police] from ventures," and a "psychological campaign" to project greater strength than the western position presently held.[67]

Taylor thought the Soviets hoped to conquer Berlin without triggering a wider war through a blockade or an attack by East German paramilitary forces, which would likely grow to 140,000 men by May 1951. He doubted the feasibility of defending West Berlin's 103-mile perimeter. That would require some eighty battalions. Instead, he recommended a deterrent force that could make any attack very costly. For that purpose, the United States needed to augment forces to one full infantry regiment, supported by a military police battalion, administrative and support units, and German labor service units, and the French and British had to follow suit. Taylor was more optimistic about deterrence than about an airlift, which "would not be effective for any length of time," but while he could demonstrate strength, the Allies could not defend West Berlin.[68]

Taylor joined Handy and McCloy in an urgent call for West German rearmament. Until the outbreak of the Korean War, McCloy and his chief advisers had not seen an immediate need. Now Acheson made clear at the September 1950 New York NATO foreign ministers' meeting that German soldiers were needed for the Cold War. But would that not alienate the French, British, and other allies? McCloy also knew West Germans were not keen on taking up arms just half a decade after the end of the Second World War, and he feared rapid rearmament could endanger the nascent democratic experiment. Both he and his legal adviser, Robert Bowie, preferred a European army in which Germans could be integrated; the JCS thought it impractical to build a unified force from different military cultures and expressed concerns about logistics; and the French government first proposed a plan for a European defense community and later rejected it. By the time the first West German forces mustered, in 1955, the immediate crisis of the Korean War had passed and the Cold War had engulfed much of the world.[69]

To tap into all reservoirs, Taylor supported the October decision by the commandants of the western sectors and Reuter's magistrate to rearm the West Berlin police to prewar levels, add 3,000 officers, and build a volunteer reserve.[70] He would have found the 1955 observations of an English journalist and former intelligence agent agreeable: "The true garrison of the city is more than 2,000,000 strong, comprised of the Berliners themselves, without whom there could be no freedom in the city."[71] Above all, Taylor concluded, the western position in Berlin could be strengthened only if the British, French, and American governments agreed on a unified command and appointed a supreme commander and combined staff.[72]

Despite sounding the alarm, Taylor did not expect an imminent attack. In late September he reported "recent intensified Soviet . . . interference and antagonism." This included a shutdown of power deliveries, which West Berlin compensated for by faster depletion of coal stocks. Taylor backed Reuter's call for a West German embargo on steel shipments to the east as leverage to restart exchange negotiations. In addition, there had been provocative acts by both sides: West Berlin authorities had arrested six East German policemen, the communists responded by arresting twenty-six members of the West Berlin force who lived in the Soviet sector, and West Berlin retaliated by jailing another fifty-two East Berlin police officers. Moreover, two American soldiers had been detained, though they were released quickly and tensions lessened when all of the detained police officers were let go. Ominously, there had also been an eight-day standoff between British and Soviet troops after the latter had put up barricades at the sector boundary. Soviet authorities continued to interfere with traffic to West Berlin, most recently by detaining barges. Taylor concluded these were typical measures in the lead-up to mid-October elections and he recommended that "although Russian harassment should be met with firmness, feel this is no time for spectacular action."[73]

In the meantime, the earlier call to arms by McCloy, Handy, and Taylor had made its way to the White House for a strategy review. The JCS agreed with recommendations to reinforce the Berlin garrison but found other parts of the August 29 paper at odds with US policy.[74] Officials in Washington proved to be more optimistic than American commanders in Germany about the ability to withstand another Berlin blockade. National Security Council (NSC) members determined that stockpiles and airlift capacity meant western forces could hold out in Berlin for about half a year. Even more, "by increasing current personnel, primarily through recalls to active duty and security and maintaining aircraft from reserve stocks [airlift] capability can be increased" to where after seven months all of West Berlin's requirements could be met.[75] To Taylor this was wishful thinking. Food, coal, fuel oil, raw materials, medical supplies, and tobacco might last for four months. Building up stockpiles for a full year would cost DM 720 million, and limited transportation capacities meant it would take more than twelve months to bring in the required additional 445,000 tons of food and 1.45 million tons of coal.[76]

Late fall 1950 proved to be uncertain times for a strategy review. When George Marshall, who had returned as defense secretary, submitted the JCS recommendations to the NSC, the US Eighth Army and its South Korean and UN allies were driving north to the Yalu River. Soon thereafter, Chinese forces entered into the war and pushed the UN armies back southward, past Seoul. That did not change the situation in Berlin, but it altered perceptions in Washington and Western Europe. Already at their September meeting NATO foreign ministers had issued a stern warning: armed aggression in Berlin would trigger a wider war. In November the North Atlantic Council adopted an American resolution that extended Article Five protection to Berlin: any attack required the allies to take up arms. On the other hand, the NSC rejected Taylor's recommendation to deploy an armed convoy to open access routes in case of blockade.[77]

When Taylor was promoted in January 1951 to a post on the army staff, the western position in Berlin remained tenuous. His departure came just days after Eisenhower had arrived for an inspection tour of his new NATO command. NATO partners had agreed on the necessity of West German rearmament, and they had included West Berlin in their security guarantee, but practical steps were to be debated for another three and a half years and Berlin did not formally become part of the alliance. Taylor worked on the buildup of US forces in Germany from the Pentagon: "I was on the Washington end of the buildup, and of course very much in favor of it. I thought it was indispensable."[78] The West Berlin police force grew as well, but the goal of a 6,000-man volunteer reserve was abandoned because it was too expensive to pay for their service. Taylor also did not get his wish of a unified command for the western sectors of Berlin: the French blocked it and participated only nominally in a combined staff.[79]

Taylor's bosses found his work in Berlin stellar. McCloy thanked Taylor for his distinguished service "in a situation which required great tact and firmness and where strains were complex and heavy." Taylor had excelled at building personal relationships, and his projected image of professional resolve had impressed Berlin politicians, including Mayor Reuter. Writing to Taylor, McCloy passed on Reuter's "deep appreciation for the services you have rendered for the welfare of the city. He has particularly stressed your invariably considerate attitude toward the German authorities." At stake were "progress, stability and defense of the city and its people." McCloy knew he would be hard-pressed to find a successor equally adept in the military, political, and economic areas.[80] Handy had already noted in his 1950 performance report, "In the key spot of the cold war General Taylor has performed magnificently."[81] Clay, a close observer of events in Berlin, concluded that Taylor was the most influential of all US commanders and no one after him was given the same "almost plenary powers."[82]

Taylor remembered his time in Berlin fondly and remained interested in the city and its people. In February 1958 he told West Berlin mayor Willy Brandt that he still read his copy of the Berlin daily *Der Tagesspiegel*.[83] Berlin had served as Taylor's initiation to Cold War realities. In such an exposed position it was necessary to think broadly in military, diplomatic, economic, psychological, and political terms and to combine all assets under "a single authority for a common purpose."[84] He had also observed firsthand that it was essential to control the narrative of events, and he singled out his almost daily meetings with the British and French commandants and Reuter. The chief lessons Taylor took from his time in Berlin included the need to rely on local populations for self-defense and the value of a deterrent force. More ominously, Taylor also learned that American credibility was a core measure for allies. In Berlin, this was a positive lesson, as Taylor could observe the favorable reaction of politicians—even those on the left—to American intervention in the Korean War.[85] Elsewhere this linkage of credibility to the commitment of armed forces would prove to be less apt.

Pentagon Planner

Paul Harkins, later a commander of Military Assistance Command, Vietnam (MACV), and previously commandant at West Point, remembers arriving at the Pentagon with Taylor, "who had sort of adopted me after General Patton."[86] Taylor embraced his new job as head of the army's operations branch and, from mid-1951, as deputy chief of staff for operations and administration, a position that put the newly promoted lieutenant general in charge of the day-to-day running of the army. His friend Charles Bolté served as the other deputy chief of staff, tasked with planning and JCS work. Both were given much leeway by their chief, J. Lawton Collins, who could thus focus on his role as JCS designated officer for the Korean War.[87] Taylor knew that many army officers saw service at the Pentagon as trite, but he held it was necessary if an officer wanted to "reach his whole capacity" and understand the strategic rationale: "Until you've lived in this city and worked in it in some relatively high, moderately high at least, position to see how it works, you can't believe it in the first place and hence you're not guided by that experience when you are in the field with heavy responsibility related to what takes place in Washington."[88]

Back at work in Washington for the first time in a decade, Taylor found the army reeling from postwar demobilization, the Korean War, and the still shifting form of the national security establishment.[89] Army leaders had lost the unification debate. There was no general-in-chief as the president's military adviser and the army now was one of three autonomous services overseen by a defense secretary and a corporate body of service chiefs.[90] Universal military training once more appeared for discussion in 1951. Yet again Truman and the army could not muster enough support and the proposal was dropped quietly in 1953 by one of its former champions, President Eisenhower.[91] Atomic weapons and large standing forces were new in the American experience, as were massive deployments like the buildup from one to six divisions in Germany. Keeping those forces balanced between armor and infantry and enabling them to hold the west bank of the Rhine River proved difficult. In June 1951, Collins explained to Eisenhower and Handy why he could not send them the 1st Armored Division for at least another year. A decision by Congress meant the army could not activate a National Guard armored division to round out its twenty-one-division force. Consequently, the US VII Corps, tasked with meeting the enemy in Hessen and the Palatinate, remained made up of infantry divisions and poorly suited to mobile defense.[92]

When the United States intervened in the Korean War, the army had fewer than 700,000 officers and men under arms and its four divisions in Japan lacked heavy weapons and tanks. The Eighth Army's preparedness in June 1950 remains subject to debate, but the army's combat effectiveness on the whole had declined sharply since the end of the Second World War.[93] In 1950 and 1951, the army more than doubled in size to 1.5 million officers and men, but the Korean War also brought new frustrations once it became clear this was not an unrestrained fight to the finish. Few in the defense establishment had followed Taylor's 1948 argument about limited war, fought by conventional armies. Instead, US war planners counted on the use of the atom bomb to make up for manpower deficiencies.[94] The confluence of war in Korea and State Department policy planner Paul Nitze's April 1950 (NSC 68) proposal of conventional and nuclear rearmament, calling for the annual defense budget for the next five years to grow from under $13 billion to $35 or even $40 billion (plus $10 to 12 billion for allies), may have boosted the army, but it was unclear what role land forces were to play in future wars.[95]

The domestic climate was increasingly defined by Cold War histrionics. Senator Joseph McCarthy (R, Wisconsin), who suspected communists and fellow travelers were in every office of the government, would soon attack the army. Not even World War II heroes were safe: Senator

William Jenner (R, Indiana) asked George Marshall a series of hostile questions in his September 1950 confirmation hearing for the post as defense secretary about the loss of China to communism before denouncing him as "a front man for traitors."[96] In the short term, the Korean War helped the army rebuild its personnel strength, defense budgets went up, demobilization changed to rearmament, and the nation seemed to pull closer together. But even in 1951 there were signs of declining public support for the war effort, many Americans doubted the wisdom of President Truman's decision to relieve General MacArthur, and the global and militarized nature of the Cold War required new strategic thinking.[97]

One episode that shed light on how Taylor reacted to the political climate was the 1952 court-martial of General Robert Grow, military attaché in Moscow, whose diary had been copied for publication in an East German propaganda piece by a British defector.[98] It revealed that Grow was privately calling for war and assumed World War III would erupt in 1952. Taylor and General Alexander R. Bolling, head of Army Intelligence, pushed for a court-martial to address the security breach even though CIA and State Department officials advised against it. Did Taylor aim to retaliate for charges by Grow that the 101st Airborne Division had inadequately supported his 6th Armored Division in the breakout from Bastogne?[99] It seems more likely that Taylor deemed Grow's laxness in keeping the diary away from public eyes too egregious, while Grow, who had been offered the option to retire, saw the court-martial as the only way to clear his name. Ultimately, he was reprimanded for dereliction of duty and security infractions and retired in 1953 after a six-month suspension from command.

Taylor's job was complex. He told students at the Army War College that "many of these problems far transcend the area of competence or experience to be expected of soldiers." In the fall of 1952 this included advising Collins and Army Secretary Frank Pace on "the rate of exchange for the won [currency] in Korea, the desirability of exploitation of Saudi Arabian oil or for the effect and influence of the Voice of America in the cold war."[100] Earlier, Taylor had weighed in on desegregation, psychological warfare, and force structure for South Korea's army. On the latter, he informed Pace that while "the long-range strength requirement of the ROK force cannot be estimated at this time," US generals in the Far East assumed that with American aid the Koreans could sustain up to ten combat divisions.[101] Taylor could draw on his recent experiences in Berlin when he advised Truman's Psychological Strategy Board, headed by former army secretary Gordon Gray, on "caring for refugees from Iron

Curtain countries" who could provide information and perhaps serve as agents for operations in Eastern Europe.[102]

On race relations, Taylor supported General Matthew Ridgway's initiative to integrate combat units in Korea. Ridgway, who was deeply religious, acted from "human and military" motivation. Taylor simply noted everyone he talked to in Korea and Japan in the spring of 1951 supported integrated combat units. He also thought positive experiences in Korea would lead to desegregation of the rest of the army.[103] Not everyone agreed. Taylor's staff had to fend off a request to expand segregated units from Army Field Forces commander Mark Clark and Assistant Chief of Staff for Personnel Anthony McAuliffe, who had filled in for Taylor at Bastogne. McAuliffe, trying to address an influx of African American recruits that could not be absorbed by existing segregated outfits, suggested that Taylor should activate new units. He expressed concern that from May to August African Americans made up as much as one-fifth of the replacements scheduled for deployment to Korea. Taylor and his aides, citing budgetary constraints and policy directives, rejected the request.[104] After he had commanded the Eighth Army, a "strange mixture of nationalities and races with their Caucasians, Negroes, Puerto Ricans, and Koreans," Taylor, reflecting the implicit racism of the early 1950s, noted in his impressions on the Korean War that small unit commanders "obtained much better results from their polyglot units than we had a right to expect."[105]

In thinking about reorganizing combat units, Taylor kept informed about what West German planners—many with firsthand experience fighting the Soviets—thought about division size, armor, maneuverability, and firepower. Following discussions in February 1951, he applauded their rearmament plans, even though he may have been disappointed that they called for 250,000 officers and men, only half of what the JCS had expected.[106] Taylor approved of much smaller armor-heavy divisions than the American model for NATO's central front. Major General George Hays, McCloy's military deputy, told Taylor that World War II generals and rearmament planners Adolf Heusinger and Hans Speidel believed the abundant availability of motorized vehicles gave smaller divisions an equal punch and the threat of enemy airpower required nimbler units. They deemed 10,000 officers and men to be ideal and recommended an upper limit of 12,500 (with one tank for every twenty infantrymen), far fewer than the over 15,000 that made up an American infantry division (with one tank for every forty infantrymen). Hays thought adopting the German model would increase US divisions in Europe from six—in itself an expansion by five divisions due to fears caused by the Korean War—to ten without going above 110,000 officers and men in combat units and "without impairing their combat efficiency."[107] For now, the war in Korea delayed action about future army divisions, but Taylor would return to the issue in the mid-1950s.

The army's budget soared during Taylor's two years at the Pentagon, though army planners understood these gains were temporary. Based on the premise of NSC 68, the JCS recommended that the army should add one combat division—for a total of twenty-one—by 1955.[108] The army's share of the defense budget for 1951 had been set at $4.27 billion, but after June 1950 this was raised to $19 billion (of a total of $48 billion). For 1952, Marshall's Defense Department asked for over $60 billion, including $21 billion for the army. The Truman administration lowered the 1953 defense budget to $47 billion, of which the army received $13 billion even as the war in Korea continued. The air force received more than $20 billion in the same year and the navy had almost caught up to the army.[109] Money seemed likely to dry up again, especially once Dwight Eisenhower, who campaigned on a platform of fiscal responsibility, was elected president in November 1952.

What did Taylor make of the war in Korea? The most controversial decisions had already been made when he settled into the Pentagon job: MacArthur had landed at Inchon and moved north across the 38th parallel, China had entered the war, Ridgway had rallied the Eighth Army, and MacArthur was about to be relieved from command. Taylor later reflected that MacArthur had proper authority to advance into North Korea because of his mandate from the United Nations and, therefore, also from the US government. That reading of the past may be open to interpretation, yet Taylor, informed by his own command experience in Korea, also thought the campaign was poorly conceived. He criticized the split into two commands—Eighth Army and X Corps—with next to no direct communications between them, and he thought the amphibious landing on North Korea's east coast left the X Corps in an exposed position. Taylor questioned the push to the Yalu, where MacArthur's forces would have to guard a front line of over 400 miles, perhaps facing over a million Chinese troops operating from home bases. Why not hold in a defensible position near the 38th parallel, where the waist of Korea was about 125 miles wide? Taylor approved of President Truman's decision to fire MacArthur, which, he claims, took him by surprise.[110]

As Taylor prepared to leave for Korea, the army was operating at the outer limits of what could be sustained. Briefing Defense Secretary Robert Lovett, who had taken over from an ailing Marshall in September 1951, Frank Pace noted "the capability of deploying units of acceptable combat readiness overseas in accordance with the requirements of the Emergency War Plan, approved by the Joint Chiefs of Staff, despite logistic deficiencies close to the limits of acceptable risk."[111] Even that was a leap of faith. Taylor's operations division concluded in July 1952 that at the approved strength of 1.5 million, the ready reserve was dangerously low. Over 700,000 officers and men were deployed overseas and only the 82nd Airborne Division could be sent to deal with an emergency on top of the war in Korea and the buildup in Europe.[112]

Pace conceded that if another war broke out in the first months of 1953 the army would have to rely on "inadequately trained units or to delay deployment.... Lack of reinforcement in the quality or at the time required would jeopardize the combat effectiveness of our forces already committed overseas."[113] The army staff had already concluded preparedness for a global war could not be attained until 1955–56, instead of 1952–53 as the plans drawn up in 1950 required.[114] Support of Korean forces had cost $2 billion for 1951 and 1952, and the estimate for 1953 was another $1.3 billion. ROK ground forces had increased from 282,000 officers and men in ten divisions in mid-1951 to 463,000 in twelve one year later. This had forced the army to restrict training in the United States to conserve equipment. Together with the war itself, training demands had also depleted mobilization reserve stocks and had required diverting equipment slated for other allied countries. If the Korean army were increased to twenty divisions, as some commanders in Tokyo and Seoul urged, the US army would have to contribute an additional $2 billion in 1953.[115]

Korean War

When Taylor arrived in Korea in February 1953, the war had long settled into a bloody stalemate. Frustration abounded. MacArthur had proclaimed there was no substitute for victory, implicitly rejecting geographic limits in a war where President Truman did not authorize attacks in China or the use of atomic weapons.[116] Armistice talks had been under way since the summer of 1951, but progress was slow and the end not in sight. Acheson summed up the mood in the United States: "If the best minds in the world had set out to find the worst possible location in the world to fight this damnable war, politically and militarily, the unanimous choice would have been Korea."[117] Taylor, who reported to US Far East and UN commander Mark Clark in Tokyo, was now in charge of running the war on the ground in Korea.

Taylor took command from General James Van Fleet. He had observed the war from the Pentagon and was familiar with the strengths and weaknesses of the Eighth Army, one of the reasons why Collins had recommended him for the job.[118] Taylor rated Van Fleet a "superb trainer of troops, especially of foreign troops." This had been apparent in Greece in the late 1940s, and it showed again in Korea. But the two generals disagreed on how to protect the front line. Taylor thought there were too many men deployed forward of the main line of resistance: "I found so many outposts and I thought they needed to be thinned out. We were wasting troops on outposts and in retaking outposts."[119] The Eighth Army's mission was defensive. Taylor's corps, divisions, and regiments patrolled a 155-mile battlefront "to maintain contact with the enemy and insure against the enemy encroaching upon friendly positions. . . . Pressure against the enemy was maintained across the Army front, consistent with the requirements for low ammunition expenditures and friendly casualties." Fighting consisted primarily of raids, chance encounters of patrols, and "light enemy harassing attacks against UN outpost positions." Such attacks were aimed mainly at South Korean divisions, which defended more than ninety miles of the front.[120]

Chinese and North Korean forces outnumbered the men in Taylor's command, but the difference was not dramatic: the April estimate of a force just over 1 million officers and men in seven Chinese armies (rated from fair to excellent by US intelligence) and two North Korean army corps (rated poor and good) was typical for 1953. Against this stood some 735,000 South Korean, American, and other UN forces. Even though enemy forces had more supplies stockpiled near the battle lines than at any previous point, these numbers made a general offensive unlikely, though they allowed for limited-objective attacks.[121] The problem, Taylor noted in his postwar report to Army Chief of Staff Ridgway, was that the mountainous terrain negated much of the American advantage in firepower. Chinese and North Korean infantry had "covered routes of approach and sheltered assembly areas, difficult to reach with our shells and bombs. The hills restricted the use of armor to the narrow valleys which were often blocked by mines, obstacles, or flooded rice paddies. Tanks were reduced to the role of stationary pillboxes supplementing the fire of our ground weapons on the MLR [main line of resistance]."[122] Taylor rushed his report ahead of a more detailed Eighth

Army study because he felt "some, indeed much of the experience gained in Korea may serve to guide the formulation of future military policy."[123]

Most of the burden of combat rested on the infantry. Taylor concluded American infantry "was called upon to fight extremely bloody local engagements which, while restricted in scope, attained an intensity rarely known in our previous wars."[124] On February 13, his second day in command, the Eighth Army suffered 213 casualties, including eleven Americans killed and fifty-four wounded.[125] Enemy forces were assembled in twenty-eight infantry divisions, supported by the equivalent of one armored division, five artillery divisions, eight independent artillery regiments, and two anti-tank divisions as well as elements of one rocket launcher division. Most of these units remained quiet that day. Taylor reported that "three enemy attacks, from two platoons to company strength against outposts of the 3d ROK Division marked the noticeable ground action. . . . Elsewhere across the Army front, only widely scattered patrol contacts and enemy engagements were reported." UN forces inflicted an estimated four hundred casualties on Chinese and North Korean troops, including three hundred killed. Taylor noted, "the enemy will probably initiate limited-objective attack" within the next two days.[126]

In the meantime, Van Fleet had complained bitterly about an artillery ammunition shortage. Taylor had been tracking the issue for Collins since the fall of 1951.[127] He did not find a critical shortage and thought "Van was ill advised in allowing his criticisms of the ammunition situation to get mixed up in politics. . . . Getting it into the press . . . was most embarrassing to the hard working people in the Pentagon who were doing everything under the sun to be sure that the Eighth Army lacked nothing in the battlefield."[128] While there may have been an insufficient number of 155-mm shells by early 1953, there were more than enough of the 105-mm type. Perhaps the problem rested with Van Fleet's approach: "Van prided himself on the size of the consumption of ammunition. The rumor was that Artillery officers got, if not decorated and promoted, at least commended for the number of rounds they fired."[129] Van Fleet aired his grievances about limited war, political shackles, and digging in on the defensive in a candid article in *Life* magazine.[130]

When Van Fleet was still in command, he and Clark had acknowledged that the Eighth Army was firing vastly more ordnance than the enemy (at a ratio of forty to one in January 1952, four to one that September, and ten to one in December), but they felt this was justified in defensive and offensive operations as well as to deny the enemy freedom of movement. Clark noted that division and corps commanders by the end of 1952 were rationing 155-mm howitzer and 60-mm and 81-mm mortar shells. For him it was a simple calculus: "The relatively high ratio of our artillery and mortar fire to the enemy's is fully justified by the reduced casualties and our success in repelling the recent attacks with heavy Communist casualties."[131] Taylor, a field artillery officer for much of the interwar period, believed in more judicious application of firepower, though he himself was forced to blast away liberally when Chinese forces attacked in the spring and summer. He did not feel the pinch as much as Van Fleet had done: in May 1953 he could tell the commander of the 25th Infantry Division, General Samuel T. Williams, there were enough artillery shells to "allow any reasonable expenditure of ammunition" even when the division was training away from the front lines.[132]

While he was critical of Van Fleet, Taylor mostly concurred with the findings of Major General Ray Porter, the commander of Taylor's former 101st Airborne Division, who visited Korea in February and March. Porter decried the effects of troop rotation and replacement policies that had left the Eighth Army with a severe shortage of experienced junior and noncommissioned officers. He also noted that while morale may be deemed satisfactory, it was based on "comforts and conveniences rather than courage and confidence" and led to "general timidity and inefficiency in patrolling."[133] Taylor, who did not fully agree with Porter's assessment of insufficient aggressiveness, recognized that his headquarters did not have a good grasp on small-unit actions by patrols and at outposts. His solution showed his penchant for micromanagement: he asked patrol leaders and company commanders to brief him and his staff. From Taylor's perspective this provided "first hand information on the techniques and tactics peculiar to ground action in Korea," though as a practical matter it was unevenly applied, since those who suffered heavy casualties or had performed exceedingly well were given priority.[134]

In late March the Chinese attacked. The hard-hit 1st Marine Division suffered 540 casualties between March 26 and 28.[135] This was some of the heaviest fighting that American forces in Korea had seen in half a year, but while giving up prominent terrain features like Old Baldy on March 23–24 meant the loss of defense in depth for the 7th Infantry Division, it did not alter the strategic situation. Taylor could point at enemy casualties (an estimated 1,800 killed, 1,630 wounded, and 14 prisoners taken from March 26 to March 31), and he deemed it unwarranted to spend more of his men and materiel in attempts to recover lost ground.[136] Total enemy casualties for March ran up to 12,500, including an estimated 6,800 killed.[137] Taylor's assessment was unchanged: expect further limited-objective attacks but no general offensive in the near future.[138]

Fighting slowed down significantly in April, though there were four-day battles for outposts Vegas (1st Marine Division) and Pork Chop Hill (7th Infantry Division). American casualties for the month declined from nearly 5,000 in March (including 366 killed in action) to just over 2,000 (299 killed in action).[139] There was good news elsewhere: cease-fire talks at Panmunjom resumed on April 26 after breakthroughs in the prisoner of war question, following an Indian proposal that a neutral commission could assess individual cases and once Clark had approved an exchange of over 6,500 sick and wounded prisoners in return for 684 captured UN forces. Taylor welcomed released prisoners at "Freedom Village" at Munsan-ni on April 20 and 21.[140] The time was right for an armistice agreement. Stalin's death in March and uncertainty over future Soviet support had unsettled Mao and Kim Il-Sung, who worried, too, about President Eisenhower's warning of significant escalation, including the use of atomic weapons. Mao and Marshal Peng Dehuai, the commanding general in Korea, concluded that China had successfully confronted the western empires, restored its status, and emerged as the leading communist power in Asia.[141] The main holdout was South Korea's President Syngman Rhee, who staged mass demonstrations that called for "Unification or Death" and "Drive to the Yalu."[142]

Taylor and Clark had inherited the POW issue that had long dogged the cease-fire talks. Screening in early 1953 revealed that some 70,000 of the 132,000 Chinese and North Korean prisoners in UN camps had no desire to be repatriated. Rhee threatened to derail the Panmunjom talks by releasing prisoners. US ambassador Ellis Briggs colorfully rendered Rhee's attitude that spring: "Rhee then immediately went into his 'Victory or Death' act which remained theme song of meeting lasting nearly two hours."[143] Rhee's recalcitrance invited punishment. The final Chinese offensives in June and July focused on sectors held by South Koreans both because of the perceived weakness of the ROK army and to help Rhee overcome his opposition to the cease-fire agreement.[144] Clark assumed that Rhee was worried the Americans might leave and thought he needed "a security pact signed, sealed, and delivered before the armistice becomes effective."[145] If he feared the United States would withdraw from Korea, Rhee badly misread the mood in Washington. The Korean War had hardened mind-sets, and the response—by Eisenhower as much as by Truman—was to strengthen the policy of containment and apply it around the world.[146]

On May 11, Chinese and North Korean forces attacked at several points. What followed was heavier fighting than in March. Taylor and his new chief of staff, Paul Harkins, concluded that the enemy intended to seize key terrain features so as to allow their negotiators to put pressure on the UN side. In the course of May, two ROK divisions were forced to abandon a half-dozen outposts, but the Eighth Army held forward of the main line in most places. Taylor shuttled between the front and activation ceremonies for new ROK army units, and he maintained his regular schedule of visiting corps and division commanders. He also witnessed demonstrations against the cease-fire talks and attended training exercises. In the days after May 11, Taylor and Rhee stepped up the pace of joint visits to frontline units to assess the tactical situation and bolster the morale of the defenders. Among those who distinguished themselves in the May battles was the Turkish Brigade, which fought as part of the US 25th Infantry Division. In heavy fighting from May 28 to 31, the 25th Division inflicted some 3,200 enemy casualties and absorbed over 64,000 rounds of incoming artillery and mortar fire, an unusually high number that indicated a change in enemy tactics. The Turkish Brigade lost 104 killed, 324 wounded, and 47 missing.[147] Oddly enough, amid the battles Taylor also received—and denied—a request from South Korean army leaders to deploy ROK units to Indochina to assist the French and the Vietnamese National Army in their war against the Viet Minh.[148]

Taylor admired the tenacity of the Chinese soldiers, who fought against the odds and held their positions despite heavy shelling and American air superiority. He was impressed by how "the Chinese would simply, slowly and patiently work their way across no man's land, often without being detected and take sometimes days in doing it, then form in spite of our patrolling, and launch an attack on an outpost with very little warning." They usually did so under the cover of darkness "so as to limit the effectiveness of our automatic weapons and of our artillery." This was countered by close-in fire support: "We eventually fortified our outposts so that our men could stay right in their positions and call down our artillery to fire upon them. The Chinese were extremely good at locking themselves with you so closely that you used these weapons with great difficulty and only in selected areas where you could protect your own troops." It was an uneven fight against a determined foe: "I gave the Chinese very high marks as a rugged determined infantry, but didn't even know they had any artillery until the very end."[149]

Taylor's prime objective was to facilitate the conclusion of an armistice and hold the line that sat astride the 38th parallel. Taylor well understood President Eisenhower's desire to see the war come to an end without much additional loss of American lives. As one of his first orders, Taylor required troopers to wear their new flak jackets at all times, and he made it clear commanding officers would be held accountable for operations that invited casualties. Unsurprisingly, this contributed to risk aversion by corps, division, regiment, and battalion commanders, who now aimed to avoid contact with the enemy whenever possible.[150] It could also mean ceding ground, as in July when Taylor and I Corps commander Bruce Clarke rejected pleas from General Arthur Trudeau (7th Infantry Division) to commit reserves to reclaim Pork Chop Hill. Clarke later noted, "Our history is too full of holding useless real estate at a great cost in casualties." Taylor and Clarke met with Trudeau early on July 10 before Clarke made the decision to evacuate the outpost altogether.[151] Taylor reported dryly: "Two enemy battalion attacked outpost PORKCHOP in the 7th US Division sector. Friendly withdrew on order."[152] As long as the enemy suffered heavy casualties (1,860 killed and 920 wounded on July 11) and the main line could be held, it did not matter who sat on what hilltop even though it opened Taylor up to criticism of squandering a hard-fought tactical victory.[153]

Enemy attacks had intensified in June and July. This was the worst fighting the Eighth Army had seen since the Chinese spring offensive in 1951. Once again, Taylor and his staff ascribed it to the interplay of fighting and negotiating. Chinese forces deployed entire divisions and the main thrust hit the ROK II Corps in the central sector, south of Kumsong, but fighting picked up elsewhere, too. This time the defenders could not hold the main line in all places: the ROK II Corps sector was breached at a length of thirteen kilometers. Taylor shifted three of his reserve divisions to that hot spot and they helped establish a new defensive line just south of the old one. These were bloody battles: over 52,000 UN troops (the vast majority Koreans) were killed, wounded, or missing, and the enemy lost more than twice as many men.[154]

Taylor and Mark Clark were dismayed by the performance of the ROK II Corps: "Three of its four divisions in line behaved rather badly, withdrawing to a depth considerably beyond the line they were ordered to form upon." Moreover, "some units withdrew without much pressure from the enemy. Some came back by regiment; others in smaller units; and some as stragglers." The problem, they noted, was poor leadership. Their verdict: most ROK generals were in over their heads once they got promoted beyond battalion and regimental command.[155] Instead of focusing his full attention on the front, however, Taylor also had to deal with the fallout from Rhee's decision to allow 25,000 North Koreans to escape from POW camps on June 18 in an effort to sabotage an imminent truce. For the next week, this meant conference after conference with Rhee, Briggs, Clark, and others. Only when Assistant Secretary of State Walter Robinson arrived in Seoul, on June 25, could Taylor once again devote most of his time to the ongoing battles.[156]

Instead of trading casualties, Taylor, promoted to four-star general in June, checked the enemy with his field artillery and relied on air support from the Far Eastern Air Forces (FEAF). American casualties, frustratingly high at 63,000 (including 12,300 killed in action) in the two years since armistice talks had begun, now grew more slowly. The vast majority of the 64,000 UN casualties in battles from April through July were South Koreans. Taylor's field artillery fired close to 8 million rounds in those four months, over 60,000 shells a day on average; in July, when Chinese forces expended their highest monthly total of artillery rounds (375,000), Taylor's artillery launched over 2 million—and that was still 700,000 fewer rounds than in June.[157] The FEAF, commanded by General Otto Weyland, meanwhile hoped to force communist leaders to sign the armistice agreement by targeting the civilian population. Weyland, from the air force's increasingly marginalized Tactical Air Command, had voiced reservations about the feasibility of striking North Korea's dams so as to destroy the rice crop. He worried about the world media's response to a starvation campaign. But Weyland's planners persuaded him after a series of successful attacks on railroad dams in May. And Mark Clark seemed prepared to take even more drastic steps.[158]

In the spring of 1953, Clark requested upward of three hundred atomic bombs for targets in North Korea. Eisenhower had publicly flirted with the idea in February, when frustrations over the stalled armistice talks mounted. Now the NSC authorized preparations for an atomic war plan. Clark, CINCPAC Admiral Arthur Radford, who had proposed the use of atomic weapons to President-elect Eisenhower during a visit to Korea in December 1952, and SAC commander Curtis LeMay, who wanted to strike China, were to meet in Honolulu in July for an "Atomic Annex Coordination Conference." There is no clear evidence that Taylor knew about potential escalation to atomic war, but he did ask a visiting General Collins in late June how atomic weapons could be acquired for the Eighth Army and how they might be delivered or replaced in case of general war with the Soviet Union.[159] In the end, a two-week air campaign against North Korea's rice crop in late May yielded terrifying results, but planning for atomic war stopped when the armistice, signed on July 27, appeared imminent.[160] Taylor was later convinced that a combination of attrition in the field and airpower had ended the war on favorable terms.[161]

The change from war to peace was jarring. The battles in July had topped anything Taylor had seen in Korea in scope and intensity. And then, Taylor's staff noted, "at the end of the month, in a rapid transition from the violence of the battle which had been raging in central Korea, the entire Eighth Army front was quiet as friendly and enemy troops withdrew from their respective MLR's to new positions two kilometers to the rear of the former front lines."[162] Battle casualties for the final month of the war had been heavy: 5,325 killed in action (638 Americans), 18,667 wounded (3,636 Americans), and 5,637 missing in action (422 Americans). With close to 30,000 total casualties, July provided a grim illustration that a war of posts cost thousands of lives for no strategic gain.[163] The enemy suffered much worse. The Eighth Army estimated 18,540 Chinese and North Korean soldiers killed and 9,400 wounded on July 15 alone, 790 killed and 390 wounded on the war's last day, and a total of 71,800 enemy casualties (25,100 killed) for all of July.[164]

On July 19, Taylor had the dubious distinction of presenting Rhee with the news that an agreement at Panmunjom was near. Taylor reported that "the president had received his message without reaction." One week later he was back in Rhee's office with confirmation that the armistice would be signed the next morning.[165] Taylor had attempted to prepare his unit commanders for the implications of a truce in a mid-June radio broadcast. He stressed that it did not mean peace and they had to remain on high alert, ready to resume fighting if the enemy broke the agreement. It was also necessary to educate the troops so that there would be no casual acts in violation of the armistice. Taylor made clear he would hold commanding officers responsible for dereliction of duty on the part of their men.[166] Manning the battle stations south of the demarcation line was a familiar mix of South Korean, American, and UN forces. Taylor's command had relied heavily on South Korean troops, which reinforced his lesson from Berlin: arming local people for self-defense was a critical feature of preparedness. At the time of the armistice, Taylor could draw on just over 780,000 officers and men. More than half a million were Koreans and almost 35,000 came from Britain and the Commonwealth (19,840), Turkey (6,340), and nine other countries fighting under UN command. There were 234,000 American soldiers and marines in Korea when the guns fell silent.[167]

Once the armistice went into effect, Taylor's army had to prepare defensive positions at least two kilometers south of the DMZ. In August, "the situation in Korea [was] unique. Two armies face each other, organized for battle, separated by a narrow strip of demilitarized territory." Taylor reminded his soldiers to be prepared for sudden resumption of hostilities. To maintain the Eighth Army's effectiveness and morale he stressed military training and information and education programs. In the first days of August, Taylor participated in discussions with Rhee, Briggs, Secretary of State John Foster Dulles, and Army Secretary Robert Stevens on the defense treaty between the United States and South Korea that was concluded on August 7. And he was faced with reports that the communists held back POWs. In fact, the last American POW to return was an air force captain, Theodore R. Harris, on September 6. Army Major General William Dean, the most prominent POW, who had fallen into North Korean hands in the early battles of summer 1950, had come home two days earlier.[168] On the other hand, as late as October, there were still some 23,000 North Korean and Chinese prisoners who had refused repatriation. About a third of them returned to the PRC, while over 14,000 went to Taiwan.[169] Taylor also got to turn to more immediate postwar questions and met with a delegation led by Van Fleet, now the director of a pro-Korea lobby group in New York, and former (and future) State Department official Dean Rusk, who hoped to improve public health, education, and living conditions in South Korea.[170]

In the months after the cease-fire agreement, Taylor found more time to do what he had done in Berlin: work closely with the senior US economic adviser, C. Tyler Woods, and help local government and businesses rebuild the economy. Initially, this meant "bettering the overall economic situation in Korea through construction, allocation of supplies and material and by direct troop aid to the Korean people." Spontaneous aid included unprompted actions by American soldiers and marines, who by the end of September had built, rebuilt, or supported ninety-seven orphanages, seventeen schools (with nineteen more under construction or planned), sixteen churches (six more under construction or planned), and five hospitals. In all, American soldiers had provided free labor and material worth $1.4 million in August and September.[171] Taylor offered some $15 million worth of construction material his army no longer needed to help Korean building trades and industries. This soon developed into a wider program: Armed Forces Assistance to Korea (AFAK).[172]

By early 1954, reconstruction and rehabilitation of Korea had become one of the five main missions of Taylor's command. The Eighth Army still needed to guard against attack from the north and monitor compliance with the armistice, maintain training, educational, and recreational programs, and dispose of "non-repatriated prisoners of war." However, it had become "not only a combat organization, but was also an effective instrument for peace and reconstruction. Its influence upon the government and people of Korea cannot be measured."[173] Eisenhower approved Taylor's rehabilitation program for Korea after Taylor pitched it as a "community type welfare program" to Assistant Secretary of Defense John Hannah in August 1953. Just as Taylor had begun to centralize the local efforts by American soldiers in the final days of the war, Eisenhower was putting him in charge of coordinating economic rehabilitation efforts in Korea more generally.[174] But at $15 million, this seemed like small change. By the end of August 1953, the United States had provided the Republic of Korea with over $4.5 billion in aid and assistance ($3 billion of that in logistical support for ROK forces).[175]

The AFAK made the most of its small purse, and Taylor provided labor, knowhow, and equipment free of charge. Soldiers built schools, churches, libraries, cultural centers, communications facilities, and highways, improved public health, reconstructed transportation facilities, provided vocational training and flood control, and supported land reclamation. Taylor served as program director and diverted Eighth Army resources as long as it did not interfere with combat readiness. He also added $9 million from his own budget, asked for $3 million each from the logistics and air force commands, and set aside another $1.75 million to help rebuild Pusan after a devastating fire.[176] Not everyone in the Eighth Army embraced performing free labor to rebuild South Korea. An inspector general investigation into an anonymous letter to the *Chicago Tribune* discovered "many men do not understand the meaning and significance of the AFAK program." Some felt pressed into voluntary service. Taylor concluded this was the result of a lack of awareness and instructed IX Corps commander "Hanging Sam" Williams to ensure troop information sessions better explained the program.[177]

With the shooting war receding into the past, the Eighth Army needed to build new defensive positions. Maintaining readiness required novel ideas. In early December Taylor ran "the first army-wide command post exercise ever conducted in the face of an armed and hostile enemy." It involved all command echelons and staff sections of the Eighth Army. Everyday business included explaining to American soldiers why they were still in Korea as well as constructing new recreational facilities and offering educational programs, which Taylor considered to be a critical morale boost. Soldiers could receive instruction equivalent to an eighth-grade education or take more advanced vocational or technical classes during duty hours. Taylor encouraged those with a more academic bent, and prewar education, to enroll in correspondence courses with the University of California. Still, most American soldiers yearned to return home, and the staff needed to consider how to draw down without harming the defensive capability of the Eighth Army and the growing ROK army.[178]

Thinking about the war's lessons, Taylor drew on a study by X Corps commander Major General Reuben Jenkins. Jenkins concluded, "The highly centralized control necessitated by this theater has tended to reduce the aggressiveness and initiative of commanders producing a potentially dangerous weakness." He noted the failure of corps and division staffs to check and assist at the next two lower echelons. Turning to replacements, Jenkins praised on-the-spot instruction in Korea, but he also revealed that training in the United States had never fully adjusted to the tactical requirements of fighting in the mountains. Replacement units often arrived in rough shape, insufficiently trained and weakened by the long journey across the Pacific. Results had improved once the army shifted from shipping entire combat units to sending four-man replacement teams. On the controversial question of artillery support, Jenkins concluded it had been more than adequate, though he recommended increasing 105-mm howitzer batteries to eight guns, furnishing more 240-mm howitzers to cover the entire front of a division, and improving fire control of corps artillery.[179]

Taylor returned to thinking about the design of future army divisions. Jenkins had focused on infantry divisions and concluded regimental commanders were overburdened with administrative tasks that reduced their ability to lead in combat. Infantry regiments, Jenkins held, had become too reliant on tanks and vehicles in general. It would be better to pool those at division level and increase the regiments' firepower by adding BARs, 81-mm mortars, and 105-mm recoilless rifles to all battalions.[180] Taylor, doubting that these adjustments would yield more effective infantry divisions, proposed a modular battle group for the ROK army that could be adapted to conventional and nuclear battlefields and facility dispersion, built on a division of five major combat elements instead of three. His hope that the South Koreans would serve as guinea pigs was disappointed when ROK army generals opted to retain the triangular division structure.[181]

James Gavin, also a decorated World War II airborne general, had come to similar conclusions as Taylor.[182] While in command of the VII

Corps in Germany in 1953, Gavin observed that only armored divisions, with their combat commands that had worked well in the Second World War, were sufficiently adaptable.[183] Infantry had to become quicker to disperse and reassemble, and cavalry units needed to be made airmobile by helicopters. As the depth of the battlefield increased due to new missile technology, communications would become ever more important. Gavin suggested that battalions needed the kind of equipment regiments had in World War II, and regiments that of divisions. The atomic battlefield would be deeper, wider, and less defined by fixed front lines. Gavin, like Taylor, proposed battle groups that were smaller than the existing regimental combat teams and could be dispersed widely in order to present less of a target to atomic attacks.[184]

Army Chief of Staff Ridgway endorsed the battle group concept. He, too, recognized that atomic weapons made essential the ability to disperse rapidly. Firepower would be decisive in future battles, but maneuver remained crucial in order to concentrate all available forces at the point of decision. Alfred Gruenther, Ridgway's successor as NATO commander, and his deputy, Field Marshall Bernard Law Montgomery, were also concerned about tactics designed for set-piece attacks of artillery and infantry supported by tanks that reminded Montgomery of the First World War.[185] Gruenther ordered his division commanders to think about defensive operations that forced the enemy to concentrate multiple divisions that could be struck with atomic weapons. He and Montgomery came to a similar conclusion as Taylor, Gavin, and Ridgway: smaller formations, quick decisions and improved communications, and the ability to disperse and assemble rapidly.[186] But where Taylor (as well as Heusinger and Speidel) favored smaller divisions, Gruenther envisioned brigade actions, with divisions assembling only in desperate situations, and Ridgway and Gavin concluded divisions would have to be increased in size.

In Tokyo, the new Far East commander, John E. Hull, believed Taylor was just as deserving of the command when Clark retired: "The only competitor I had was Max Taylor who had command of the Eighth Army in Korea, had done a very outstanding job. He really deserved promotion and I thought maybe serious consideration was given to him for the job." Hull, formerly Collins's vice chief, was delighted to work once again with Taylor, who had impressed him by his efficiency and polish as deputy chief of staff. Hull "greatly admired his ability and was delighted to have him there in Korea in command of the Eighth Army and later on before I had finished my tour, I gave him the Army Command in the

Far East." That decision was the result of Hull's determination that the Eighth Army's commander should have full control over his logistics and communications rather than having to go through Tokyo to deal with officers in Honolulu and elsewhere in the Pacific.[187]

As for Taylor himself, by the spring of 1954 he wondered what was next. Ridgway met with Lydia Taylor to explain the uncertainties about personnel decisions. The Taylors seemed particularly concerned about whether they should maintain their household in Washington. Maxwell Taylor told Ridgway "I am certainly not restless in my present assignment. Apart from the inevitable separation from the family which I like no better than any other soldier in Korea, the command of the Eighth Army has been and is a most satisfying professional experience for which I am most grateful." He looked forward to a trip home for a few weeks' leave. Tongue in cheek, Taylor added, "Ed [Hull] concurs in these dates although we understand that any absence from Korea depends upon the situation at the time. You remember I missed the first week of the Bulge and don't want to be missing again if the shooting starts a second time."[188] In the meantime, pet projects like the AFAK and day-to-day administration kept him busy. In the second half of 1954 Taylor was asked to take part in discussions with Hull, Rhee, and Briggs about regional security concerns, such as the effects on Korea of the Geneva Accords for Indochina and the implications of Chinese artillery attacks on islands in the Taiwan Strait.[189]

Taylor succeeded Hull as Far East commander on April 1, 1955. Three months earlier he had moved to Camp Zama, southwest of Tokyo, where the Eighth Army headquarters and the Army Forces Far East headquarters had been combined. Rhee had seen him off with a ceremony that included elements from every ROK army division, South Korea's political elite, some 10,000 spectators, and the award of the country's highest honor.[190] John Foster Dulles considered Taylor to be the successor to his former boss, J. Lawton Collins, as ambassador to South Vietnam.[191] But Ridgway's retirement left a vacancy at army chief of staff in the summer of 1955. Taylor, though critical of Eisenhower's defense policy and the strategic doctrine of absolute nuclear deterrence, was chosen to fill the spot. Three decades later, Taylor reflected that this meant the end of his "exclusively military activities." What followed was a career in strategy and policy.[192]

3

Reformer and Strategist?

The President and the General

President Eisenhower and Defense Secretary Charles Wilson interviewed Taylor on February 24, 1955. Since Taylor harbored doubts about the administration's strategy and budget priorities, the central question concerned his "willingness to accept and carry out the orders of civilian superiors."[1] Taylor had just fought in a conventional war and believed limited war could erupt in Europe; he did not think nuclear weapons by themselves were a credible deterrent. He put it bluntly in an interview: "The atomic weapon has existed since 1945, and during this period several wars have been fought, but no atomic weapons have been used at all, anywhere."[2] In other areas Taylor's thinking resembled Eisenhower's: both preferred alliances over unilateral actions, recognized the importance of NATO to American security, favored arming local forces, and desired a more centralized Defense Department. Over time they also came to agree that the JCS were close to dysfunctional. Yet to Taylor neither Admiral Radford nor General Nathan Twining of the air force presented an attractive option for an empowered chairman. As a first step of asserting his independence, Taylor fended off Wilson's request to pick his deputy. Taylor selected Williston B. Palmer.[3]

Taylor had not been Army Secretary Robert Stevens's first choice. When Ridgway announced he would not seek a second term, Stevens looked to Al Gruenther to guide the army through troubled times. Taylor became chief of staff because Eisenhower felt Gruenther, who had taken on the NATO command in 1953 after serving as Eisenhower's and Ridgway's chief of staff, could not be spared in the midst of German rearmament and political, strategic, and diplomatic concerns facing the alliance.[4] Taylor faced stiff headwinds: Eisenhower thought service traditions and separate identities stood in the way of unified war planning and procurement. He stated it forcefully to Congress in 1958: "Separate ground, sea and air warfare is gone forever. If ever again we should be involved in war, we will fight it in all elements, with all services, as one single concentrated effort."[5]

Following the Korean War, Eisenhower had adjusted American strategy. The president feared excessive emphasis on military mobilization in a perpetual Cold War could undermine the robust economy and limit the nation's political freedoms. He saw nuclear deterrence as a cost-effective alternative to conventional arms. Consequently, the army's share in defense appropriations declined sharply.[6] "Hanging Sam" Williams, who had moved from Tokyo to commanding the Fourth Army at Fort Bliss, darkly warned, "There may be increasing pressure to deactivate the Active Army, based on the thought that Guard units or Reserve units can be sent to an active theater almost immediately."[7] Taylor had to address that the army did not have a major role in the wars pondered by JCS chairman Arthur Radford or SAC commander Curtis LeMay.

Despite personal admiration for Eisenhower, Taylor's day-to-day job pitted service interests against national interest and the president's desires. He thought massive retaliation, the strategy built on the assumption atomic weapons served as an absolute deterrent, almost immediately "reached a dead end . . . many world events have occurred which cast doubt on its validity and exposed its fallacious character." The Korean War had revealed that possession of atomic weapons did not deter all wars.[8] He once thought differently. Taylor described how he first learned about the atomic bomb from George Marshall in late July 1945. This seemed to be a weapon that could have saved tens of thousands of American soldiers' lives if it had arrived sooner and "now we have a weapon which can keep the peace and never again will a Hitler or a Mussolini dare to use war to impose his will upon the Free World." But in the subsequent decade, Taylor had come to realize atomic weapons were not "sufficient to assure the security of the United States and its friends."[9] His 1948 London speech suggested the conversion happened soon after World War II.

By the time Taylor arrived in Washington, nuclear saber rattling shaped the strategic discourse. Eisenhower recognized the arms race would continue unabated unless someone changed its trajectory. His proposals for peaceful use of atomic energy and a mutually agreed upon inspection regime of both superpowers' nuclear programs fell on deaf ears. Still, the president hoped his administration could limit federal spending and maintain steady economic growth without causing much inflation. In his last year in office, federal spending had indeed been reduced to 10.4 percent of the gross national product (from 16 percent at the height of the Korean War), and in 1956, 1957, and 1960 the United States maintained a balanced budget. To accomplish this, Eisenhower and his defense secretaries, Wilson (1953–57), Neil McElroy (1957–59), and Thomas Gates (1959–61), held the defense budget at about $40 billion and American strategy rested on the threat of nuclear weapons, greater efforts to build up allied conventional forces, and more active use of psychological and covert operations. The catchphrases of the day were the "New Look" and "massive retaliation."[10]

When administration and Congress reduced the 1955 defense budget by $5.5 billion, the army sustained the entire cut. Its budget dropped to $7.6 billion, about one quarter of defense appropriations. Senate Republicans were told that in 1956 "about two-thirds of projected Defense Department expenditures will be for air power and related programs—more than was spent for these programs in any previous peacetime year."[11] Within three years, the army's share of the budget had declined from 38 percent to under 22 percent.[12] Even so, defense consumed much of the federal budget. Truman's $13 billion defense budget for 1950 had amounted to one-third of all federal expenditures. By the time Eisenhower was elected, the defense share stood at over two-thirds.[13] The military seemed to have trouble spending it all: the Defense Department had available more unspent money from previous years' appropriations ($38.5 billion) than Congress had allocated for 1957 ($36.8 billion).[14]

Fiscal concerns and the need to offer a stronger force for the defense of Western Europe shaped army reform. Ridgway had argued against the New Look and massive retaliation and hoped to delay force reductions until West German and Japanese troops had been raised to fill the gaps in Europe and the Far East. But German rearmament proceeded slowly and Japan's new constitution barred anything other than a small defense force for the home islands.[15] Ridgway did not believe tactical atomic weapons would reduce the need for manpower. They greatly enhanced firepower, of course, but there was no evidence to suggest that a combat unit so equipped would need fewer men. Instead, Ridgway held, ample conventional forces remained necessary to prevent war. Poorly defined plans to rely on an atomic army and conventional reserves did not meet his approval. He feared it would take too long to prepare reserve units for combat and ship them to Germany or Korea.[16]

Eisenhower expected Taylor to unmoor the army from its post–World War II notions of the nature of warfare and make combat divisions leaner and more mobile. He issued instructions on the eve of Taylor's swearing in ceremony echoing the advice he had given European generals four years prior: US army divisions were too large and did not present a blueprint for NATO forces.[17] Now he told Taylor to move the army into the atomic age and to replace manpower with technology, as the Korean War surge to 1.5 million officers and men was coming to an end. Eisenhower and Taylor expected the army brass to oppose these steps. Taylor noted that once the requisite studies were completed, he might have to make an arbitrary decision; this foretold his controversial decision to implement the pentomic division. But what seemed like accord between Taylor and his president was built on different understandings of military strategy for the Cold War.[18]

Taylor predicted firepower would win future wars. Like Ridgway, he acknowledged the need to be prepared for conventional war, but his emphasis was on tactical atomic weapons. Taylor explained that strong ground forces in Germany ensured that atomic weapons could be used against Soviet divisions before they had closed with the bulk of NATO's army. He believed "one of the primary purposes of ground combat will be to discover, or to develop, targets for our weapons, so that . . . we can virtually destroy any target on our front, so that our movements thereafter will largely be in the nature of exploitation."[19] He insisted on the defense of Western Europe, for if the Soviets overran it, the United States would be faced with deciding whether to use nuclear weapons on friendly nations.[20] Despite contrary evidence in army staff studies, Taylor proclaimed increased firepower with atomic weapons would lead to smaller combat units, but he cautioned that the need for supporting units would not allow for significant overall manpower reductions.[21]

By the summer of 1955 Taylor had spent ten years in positions that made him think deeply about education and leadership, defense and diplomacy, and the army's mission and strategy. His chief lessons from Berlin and Korea centered on credible deterrence, which required a sufficiently strong American presence on the ground in allied nations; recognition that war could be general and limited and that the latter need not remain conventional; the overconfident assessment that firepower and attrition had led to the Korean armistice agreement and one could count on a similar dynamic in other conflicts; and the need to arm local forces in Europe and Asia. In February 1956 Taylor noted that close to 7,000 officers and men were training over two hundred army divisions in some sixty countries around the periphery of the communist bloc and in South America. He rejected the argument that the United States and its allies could not match the enemy's manpower as "largely a slogan that doesn't have much validity."[22]

Taylor's lessons and experiences also moved him to consider deeper questions of strategy and alliance politics. What he had observed from Korea in the transition from Truman to Eisenhower filled him with concern. In the spring of 1955 Taylor wrote his "National Military Program," a plea for deterrence based on a flexible strategy. Less than a year later he submitted it to Wilber Brucker, the new army secretary. The JCS rejected Taylor's strategy paper during their March 1956 retreat in Puerto Rico. When Hamilton Fish Armstrong, the editor of *Foreign Affairs* and a friend of Taylor's since they had met at the Council on Foreign Relations, invited Taylor to publish the core argument, Wilson's Defense Department denied the necessary clearance.[23] Armstrong thought this violated Taylor's freedom of expression and remained bitter about the experience for another decade.[24]

Taylor's thinking had returned to themes in his 1948 lecture at the Imperial Defence College. Since then he had experienced multifaceted conflict in Berlin and limited war in Korea. Neither suggested nuclear deterrence was the appropriate strategy for all Cold War theaters. Taylor noted that in order to "preserve the security of the U.S. and its fundamental values and institutions," national assets and resources had to be bundled to maintain "military strength which is capable of dealing with both general war and aggression under conditions short of general war." He built on the argument of his recommendations for Berlin: "Military strength of the U.S. and her allies must be so constituted as to prevent war if possible, limit war as it occurs, and successfully defeat any aggression that may threaten the national interest." This required deterring the Soviets from launching atomic war, but "in the approaching era of atomic plenty, with resulting mutual deterrence, the Communists will probably be inclined to expand their tactics of subversion and limited aggression." Taylor anticipated a spectrum of threats. Unless the United States projected strength at all levels, any aggression could escalate to nuclear war or lead to the loss of "a large part of the Free World."[25]

At a minimum, Taylor argued, the United States had to be "capable of deterring war, both general and local, and winning local war quickly. In relying on deterrence we must bear in mind that Communist advances in technology and preparedness may render today's deterrents inadequate to restrain the Soviet Bloc tomorrow." He cautioned that there was no reliable way of predicting singular threats that could be met "by any single weapon system, strategic concept, or combination of allies." Instead, "the National Military Program must be suitable for flexible application to unforeseen situations." Preparing for the unknown required maintaining a technological lead over the Soviets, developing "a deterrent, atomic delivery system capable of effective retaliation against an enemy" and "a continental defense system . . . strong enough to prevent an enemy from delivering a crippling blow to the Continental United States." It also required "ready forces of the Army, Navy, and Air Force capable of intervening rapidly in any areas where local aggression may occur." Taylor noted this might include the use of atomic weapons and required adequate logistics. Finally, he advocated strengthening the reserve at home and providing "military and economic aid programs capable of developing indigenous strength and confidence among our allies and of assisting in the deterrence and defeat of Communist aggression."[26] This was Taylor's version of flexible response in the mid-1950s, still calibrated for big wars and the Soviet Union.

In early 1956 Taylor tried to rouse Congress to pay for local deterrence and the ability to fight limited wars with proportionate means. He emphasized deterrence through balanced forces, the need for a versatile army, the deterrence mission of overseas-deployed forces and the need to provide a sufficient strategic reserve to back them up as well as the army's role in training and assisting two hundred foreign divisions. Taylor planned for the atomic battlefield because there was neither money nor manpower to build an army that could operate on the entire spectrum of war.[27] When asked explicitly about the 1957 defense budget, Taylor replied that he considered "the funds allocated marginally sufficient to maintain the Army I have described." But for a force that could fight with nuclear and conventional weapons in any environment he preferred 1.5 million men in twenty-eight divisions instead of the projected 850,000 in fourteen.[28]

When Taylor sent Radford his statement for the Senate Armed Services Committee, the JCS chairman annotated it liberally. One passage that caught Radford's eye and yielded a question mark and an exclamation point (in red ink, the only usage of that color in the fifteen-page document) summarized Taylor's strategic priorities: "Only after allocating the national resources necessary for those 3 purposes—of deterring general and local war and of winning local war—should we proceed to satisfy the residual requirements for fighting a general war."[29] Taylor pointed out to staff officers that the NSC assessed a Soviet attack on the United States to be the least likely scenario. Thus, the armed forces should be prepared to deal with the more realistic threat of local and proxy attacks. Too much emphasis on airpower left the free world vulnerable to limited and local aggression. Taylor concluded it was unwise to pursue policies that would alienate potential allies.[30]

Eisenhower vented his anger about the parochialism of the armed services in a candid letter to "Swede" Hazlett: "My most frustrating domestic problem is that of attempting to achieve a real coordination among the Services." There had been many meetings and sometimes it seemed consensus was within reach, "yet when each service puts down its minimum requirements for its own military budget for the coming year, I find that they mount at a fantastic rate." He mused, "The kindest interpretation that can be put on some of these developments is that each service is so utterly confident that it alone can assure the nation's security, that it feels justified in going before Congress or the public and urging fantastic programs." He knew, of course, that this was a case of institutional interests clashing with the greater good. Eisenhower told Hazlett that he had tried to make the chiefs understand they had to act as a corporate advisory body, not as an assembly of interests of their particular services. He concluded, "I simply must find men who have the breadth of understanding and devotion to their country rather than a single Service that will bring about better solutions than I get now." The exception was Radford, no longer the aggressive champion of sea power of the late 1940s.[31]

For Taylor, JCS debates and presidential policies cut to the heart of his army, which was down to 1 million officers and men in eighteen divisions in June 1956. In subsequent years, he fought off proposals from Radford, Twining, and CNO Arleigh Burke to cut it to 800,000 or less. Radford's 700,000-man proposal struck Taylor as particularly counterproductive to reliable deterrence. Eisenhower's guidance pointed at 850,000 officers and men by 1959; there might then be further cuts. In the end Taylor and his successor, Lyman Lemnitzer, a brilliant staff officer with limited command experience, could claim partial victory: 873,000 army officers and men in fourteen divisions in June 1960.[32] Still, this seemed insufficient to address major crises. In February 1959, facing Soviet threats over Berlin, Burke and Taylor released statements that the United States could handle any crisis (Burke) and deal with the Russians in Berlin (Taylor). When pressed by columnist Drew Pearson, Taylor "amended his statement to say that we were ready in Berlin if the American nation mobilized."[33]

Pressure on the army abated in the aftermath of the *Sputnik* shock. Soviet advances in missile technology alerted congressional leaders that the US military did not have the projected technological edge and that the size of the active armed forces was thus a bigger problem than had been assumed.[34] After the *Sputnik* satellite launches in October and November 1957, the NSC reviewed defense policy and the JCS were directed to give greater consideration to a force structure adaptable to limited war. Many high-ranking military and civilian officials assumed a force capable of fighting general war could cope with limited conflict. Taylor disagreed. He argued that armed forces built for limited war might adapt to general war, but while "there's nothing of use in the little war not applicable to the big war . . . the reverse is not true."[35] In 1959, Taylor's position was reinforced by a study conducted for the Senate Foreign Relations Committee, which found strategic nuclear deterrence had to be supplemented by tactical nuclear and conventional ground forces that could halt any Soviet attack without automatically triggering escalation to general war.[36]

Privately, Eisenhower was less sanguine about nuclear weapons than he projected in public. He told John Foster Dulles in September 1953, "I am doubtful whether we can, as a practical matter, greatly increase the emphasis we are now placing upon assuring our lead in non-conventional weapons." Eisenhower also knew the United States could not pull back from worldwide force deployments: "While it is true that the semi-permanent presence of United States Forces (of any kind) in foreign lands is an irritant, any withdrawal that seemed to imply a change in *basic* intent would cause real turmoil abroad."[37] In thinking about strategy and policy, he considered finance and economics as well as military strength and favored a unified military command and strong defense secretary. His experience had shown that warfare required fully integrated application of air, land, and sea power.[38] Yet throughout his presidency Eisenhower faced challenges to fiscal restraint and centralized decision making from the armed services. Even the air force, the winner in the 1950s defense budgets, fought a running battle with the White House over a supersonic bomber (B-70) and a versatile plane that could operate from orbit (Dyna-Soar). Eisenhower opposed both but did not cut them because he held that the president should not become involved in research and development projects. It was left to Robert McNamara to cancel both during John F. Kennedy's presidency.[39]

Reflecting on his relationship with the president, Taylor admitted they did not see eye to eye on the premise that underwrote American strategy. Taylor agreed on the importance of economics. He had learned as much in Berlin and Korea. But for all his belief in a synthesis of political, economic, and psychological assets, he still held that military strength had to form the core of strategy or peace might be lost. Where Eisenhower worked from economics toward military strength and banked on nuclear weapons as cost savers and credible deterrents, Taylor saw the need to be prepared for limited land wars that did not have to escalate to intercontinental nuclear war. To project credible deterrence required a flexible strategy and more money than Eisenhower was willing to spend. Yet Taylor later concluded Eisenhower had been better than his successors at thinking in terms of organizations as well as people. He had made better use of the committee structure of the NSC, whereas John F. Kennedy relied on a smaller inner circle and intuition.[40] Moreover, Taylor knew the army was not shut out from the White House. Colonel Andrew Goodpaster joined Eisenhower's team in 1954 as de facto staff secretary and confidant, and in the president's second term Major John S. D. Eisenhower, self-proclaimed "young Turk, pro-Army," moved from the army staff to work for his father.[41]

The fundamental disagreement between Eisenhower and Taylor was about how much the nation should spend on military means and whether deterrence had to be multifaceted. Contrary to the stereotypical image, much of it painted by Taylor himself, Eisenhower did not assume the United States could rely solely on nuclear weapons delivery systems, with intermediate-range and intercontinental missiles at the top end of the arms race in the second half of the 1950s. The president knew well that the United States needed armed forces that could confront aggression of all types, from local crises short of war to Soviet threats over Berlin. He did, however, calculate on the psychological effect of nuclear saber rattling and, like the leading European allies, feared flexible response could lower inhibitions in the Kremlin to test American resolve with small-scale military moves. Taylor, as well as many congressional Democrats and fewer Western European strategists, feared the opposite was true: Soviet leaders would not believe the US threat of retaliation over seemingly minor attacks. Would the United States risk destruction of New York or Washington to protect or avenge Hamburg or Paris?

John Foster Dulles did not think so. By 1958 the once formidable proponent of massive retaliation told Eisenhower he no longer had faith in American strategy and concurred in the nuclear deterrence policy only because of the sensitive nature of the subject. Dulles had concluded US strategic doctrine "is rapidly outliving its usefulness and that we need to apply ourselves urgently to finding an alternative strategic concept." Defense Secretary McElroy agreed that the State and Defense Departments should form a study group to consider the outlines of a new strategy for the Cold War.⁴² The time for absolute nuclear deterrence had passed with Soviet breakthroughs in the field of missile propulsion. The fundamental difference between the early years of the Eisenhower era and the late 1950s was that the homeland no longer seemed safe.

But if strategy consensus could be shifted, what kind of army was best suited for the Cold War? Taylor inherited politically infeasible proposals from Ridgway's staff on the future combat division. Despite his rejection of massive retaliation as "repugnant to the ideals of a Christian nation [and] incompatible with the basic aim of the free world in war, which is to win a just and enduring peace," Ridgway had set about reforming the army within the confines of nuclear strategy.⁴³ Yet maneuvers in 1955 revealed the proposed Atomic Field Army (ATFA), with a much leaner infantry division of 13,500 officers and men and three combat commands with maneuver battalions that could be added as the situation required, could not last in protracted combat. Closer inspection suggested that the amorphous nature of the atomic battlefield required more troops to defend both wider fronts and deeper battle spaces and to maintain communications, control, and reconnaissance functions. Army planners concluded that infantry divisions could not be reduced to less than 17,000 officers and men and that armored divisions needed 14,000.⁴⁴ Taylor knew this violated the basic principles of economy of the Eisenhower administration. It also ran counter to Taylor's vision of atomic warfare.

Reforms were complicated further by the poor relationship between army leaders and Defense Secretary "Engine Charlie" Wilson, the former president of General Motors. Ridgway detested Wilson for his unwillingness to listen to positions he disliked and his criticism that the army had done little right even in the Second World War.⁴⁵ He was not the only one on the JCS who disliked Wilson—James Gavin related another service chief's assessment of Wilson as "the most uninformed man, and the most determined to remain so, that has ever been Secretary." Wilson and the army staff were approaching the point of open hostility.⁴⁶ Policy advisers at the White House and Pentagon even suggested the army should serve as a post-conflict force that could be charged with reestablishing order after a nuclear exchange and occupying conquered territory.⁴⁷ Ridgway found his time was "spent in the unhappy task of defending the US Army from actions by my superiors which, to my mind, would weaken it, physically and spiritually."⁴⁸ While he still held fast to the principle of civilian control of the army, Taylor now had to ponder how far he could push the boundaries.⁴⁹

Once he had decided to retire, Ridgway took a parting shot in a letter to Wilson, which appeared in the *New York Times* against Wilson's orders. Ridgway pointed at Soviet superiority in numbers that would force the United States to strike first with atomic weapons. He found this morally reprehensible, but he also believed the United States needed the option of meeting conventional attack with conventional forces. Ridgway judged US forces to be "inadequate in strength and improperly proportioned to meet [alliance] commitments." He cautioned that atomic superiority of the United States was temporary. Furthermore, the United States was lacking the "mobile-ready" force called for by defense officials in public statements, and America's allies would be defeated in detail if the Soviets waged a global war.[50] Taylor had to redress these shortcomings. He recalled, perhaps mellowed by the passage of time, that he got along with Wilson, who he described as "likeable personally but very unsure of himself as the ultimate arbiter short of the president."[51] That inability to force the will of the administration on a divided group of service chiefs was the main reason why Eisenhower eased Wilson out of office in 1957.

Ridgway endorsed Taylor's selection and "turned over [his] duties as Chief of Staff to that brave and brilliant officer, General Maxwell D. Taylor."[52] He added in a private letter: "I want you to know, as I think I told you some weeks ago, of my complete confidence that the Army and the Nation will be admirably served thru your conspicuously superior, high-principled, forward-thinking, and virile leadership."[53] Ridgway's assessment of Taylor's character stemmed from their shared experiences in World War II: Taylor's performance when the 82nd Airborne Division landed in Sicily with Ridgway in command and Taylor as artillery commander, and Taylor's leadership of the 101st Airborne Division when Ridgway served as corps commander.[54]

Limited War

The army's force structure depended on its mission, which Taylor thought should be the deterrence of limited as well as general war in Europe. His definition of limited war included the use of tactical nuclear weapons.[55] He intended "to improve the combat readiness of the Army in support of a strategy of Flexible Response and to improve its morale depressed as it was by the precedence given to the needs of the Navy and Air Force by the ex-Army man in the White House."[56] In spirited debates with his fellow service chiefs, Taylor defended the assessment that limited nuclear war was indeed possible.[57] He did not think this would lead to a reduction in the need for overall manpower even though combat divisions could be reduced in size. Instead, in 1961 he told General Speidel, by then NATO's land forces commander for the central region, that tactical atomic weapons "impose many casualties and cause substantial physical damage; they also carry with them a risk of escalation."[58] Moreover, it was not enough to deploy six nuclear-armed combat divisions to Germany. The army needed reserves, transportation capacity, and an operational concept that reflected the changing nature of warfare.[59]

Ridgway held off on voicing his opposition to national policy until the *New York Times* letter and his 1956 memoir. Taylor was more politically astute and searched for creative ways to address the problems facing his army. He walked a fine line, voicing public support for Eisenhower's defense policy and strategy while simultaneously offering behind-the-scenes opposition to it. For example, despite his agreement with their position, he distanced himself in May 1956 from a group of colonels on the army staff who had leaked information to the *New York Times* about air force and army antiaircraft missiles. In July, another leak to the press revealed Admiral Radford's proposal that the army should be cut further and that up to a third of American soldiers could be withdrawn from Europe.[60]

William Westmoreland, then serving as Taylor's staff secretary, recalled that this was "a group of very bright, young officers. Many . . . had their MS degrees, but also officers that had a reputation of being innovators, so to speak—activists," and that they resembled similar cells in the navy and marines in the 1940s unification battle. One of them, George Forsythe, later recalled that Taylor had let him know this was "a dangerous assignment and that if we were ever 'uncovered' he 'wouldn't know us.'"[61] Under pressure from the White House and Wilson, as Westmoreland recalled, Taylor determined these men had to be moved from the Pentagon. Vice Chief of Staff Palmer noted that one of the colonels was promoted to brigadier general as commander of an antiaircraft unit in the capital region, another went to the Army War College, and the lone general whose career supposedly was destroyed by the incident had already filed for retirement. Palmer thought there had been no punishment.[62] Westmoreland, who did think the officers had been "scattered to the winds," nevertheless concluded that "it gave visibility to efforts that all of us felt were contrary to the best interest to national defense. The result was that Radford was overwhelmed and in the final analysis General Taylor's efforts were reinforced."[63]

It was a rare victory. At the end of the Eisenhower administration, only eleven of fourteen army divisions were combat-ready.[64] Any defense of Germany seemed impossible. The chiefs agreed that nuclear weapons had to be used early on and that even then the main line at the Rhine and Ijssel Rivers might fall. Radford argued that immediate use of tactical atomic weapons was necessary if American forces came under attack by the Soviets. Nathan Twining questioned the assumption there could be major military operations after a prolonged nuclear exchange. Taylor agreed that there was no option to defend Europe or the Middle East without nuclear weapons at that point, but he held that land warfare remained possible.[65]

These discussions about the nature of warfare afforded Taylor another opportunity to impress on the other chiefs the need for a more flexible strategy. He felt nothing had prepared him better for this task than his passion for debate in high school.[66] When Radford attempted to codify the immediate use of nuclear weapons in all war plans, Taylor objected. He argued that the threat of massive retaliation would deter Soviet aggression only as long as the United States had a significant advantage in the number of warheads and long-range delivery vehicles. He feared the Soviets would catch up by the end of the decade. At that point, rapid automatic escalation no longer made sense. Instead, the US military needed to develop capabilities to respond to limited aggression with measured force. Taylor believed possession of tactical nuclear weapons served as deterrent, prevented the enemy from massing forces, and limited aggression. Their use could offset the Soviet numerical advantage and bring about the stalemate that would force the enemy to decide whether to escalate. Taylor rejected the idea that US ground forces in Germany served only as a trip wire to trigger a nuclear war.[67]

In the public's eye, he received help from the serialized publication of Ridgway's memoirs in the *Saturday Evening Post,* beginning in January 1956. Ridgway blamed a sinister conspiracy within the administration for deciding on cuts to the army prior to listening to advice. The public reaction showed that the army had friends among the media, including the *New York Times* and *Washington Post,* and among congressional Democrats.[68] Taylor publicly defended the administration against the charge of political meddling. Privately, he urged retired generals to help maintain the momentum created by Ridgway's memoirs and let Americans know about "the proper composition and strength of our defense forces. In the discussions of new weapons there is the danger that the continued indispensability of land forces may be obscured in visions of more attractive solutions to national security."⁶⁹ When one of the recipients, retired National Guard brigadier general John Ross Delafield, inquired if he could give a paraphrased account to the press, Taylor's chief of information responded that the chief of staff saw this as an excellent opportunity to educate the public.⁷⁰ This illustrated why Radford considered Taylor an untrustworthy double-dealer who seemingly accepted JCS decisions and then continued to resist without risking direct exposure himself.⁷¹

Taylor pressed for greater flexibility with Eisenhower and Radford in May 1956. The NSC, he suggested, had begun to work notions of responding to enemy threats and actions into recent policy papers, but the other chiefs believed all war was going to be nuclear. Taylor worried about the commitment of resources to nuclear war at the expense of preparedness for limited war. Eisenhower bluntly stated the army was less essential to the fighting in the first year of a war against the Soviets than other services and more "vital to the establishment and maintenance of order in the United States." He added a warning that foreshadowed a central issue of the Vietnam War: the Korean War had shown inflicting damage and casualties might not get US forces closer to victory. In local wars, US armed forces were to provide "mobile support, with the Air, Navy, and Army supporting weapons, and perhaps put in several battalions at critical points . . . we would not, however, deploy and tie down our forces around the Soviet periphery in small wars." Chillingly, Eisenhower noted the feasibility of using tactical atomic weapons against military targets in such wars.⁷² Taylor agreed with the sentiment not to get bogged down in small wars, but the conversation deepened his sense of alarm. Eisenhower foreshadowed the attitude summarized by Wilson at an NSC meeting in July 1957: "maximize air power and minimize the foot soldier."⁷³

In a talk at the Council on Foreign Relations in May 1956, Taylor outlined his vision for balanced conventional and nuclear forces. He left no doubt that he intended to alter national military strategy from Eisenhower's massive retaliation to a more proportional response.⁷⁴ To facilitate this shift and adapt the army for atomic war, Taylor proposed a transformation. The pentomic division, comprised of five battle groups, armed with atomic weapons and tasked with defending wider frontages and a much deeper battle space than its predecessor, was to be the first step. Since the army's views about future war did not fit the mainstream of the defense establishment, reform had to be presented in compliance with current policy and strategy. Specifically, since limited war was not a fashionable concept, Taylor needed to find a structure that appeared well suited for general war while allowing improvement of the capacity to fight limited wars. The pentomic division was intended to enhance the army's position with respect to the other armed services, help redefine its role in the Cold War, and contribute to a change in national military strategy.[75]

If Taylor succeeded partially at reforming the divisions, he failed to implement the wider transformation.[76] He believed a dual-capable force for conventional and atomic warfare could be achieved only if the army's budget were significantly increased.[77] In the meantime, he focused on the atomic battlefield. Taylor assumed converting combat divisions to the pentomic structure would force a rethinking of tactics, doctrine, and technology. General Clyde Eddleman, then on the army staff, related he had proposed the battle group as an ad hoc outfit and wanted to retain the regiments. His idea was to build combat teams as needed by adding infantry or mechanized components and artillery strength.[78] Taylor preferred more drastic changes and drafted plans for the new division himself. As Westmoreland recalled, "Taylor personally worked that out, and he would come in with diagrams that he would draft at home and I would send them to the staff and they would review them." Staff officers expressed doubts about the new division, "but General Taylor felt that he had to do something—something new, to give the Army a modern look."[79] Taylor had thus made his arbitrary decision and, as with some of his reform proposals at West Point, he rushed it into action.[80]

In the summer of 1956 Taylor called for a pentomic airborne division of 10,000 to 12,000 officers and men, and soon thereafter he expanded the concept to infantry. His idea derived partly from his experience with airborne operations.[81] Each battle group was to have the capability to fight in all directions, forcing the enemy to mass forces and present targets for atomic weapons. Taylor did not explain how they could avoid annihilation themselves or whether the commander of a division could effectively control five battle groups and the battle group commander five companies.[82] Taylor pressed on because he felt making tactical atomic weapons organic to the division would lead to thorough consideration of their proper employment. Contemporary critics charged that this was nothing but a public-relations stunt in which Taylor responded to Wilson's challenge to "sex up the army."[83]

In the pentomic division, proper combination of firepower, movement, and skilled personnel would determine the success of ground forces. Rockets and guided missiles were to provide most of the heavy firepower. Mobility was also significant because rapid dispersion and concentration of force were the most important tactical principles on the atomic battlefield. Taylor stated that lightweight equipment, thin-skinned troop carriers, and army aviation were essential. Even though he pleaded the army needed capable soldiers, hoping to reverse a trend in which most young men went to the more glamorous options in the air force and navy, his argument was built on structures and machines more than men.[84] The basic idea, succinctly put by an army captain, seemed sound: "concentrate to fight—disperse to live."[85] Taylor explained to senators that the wider, deeper, and less linear atomic battlefield required supreme mobility and firepower for small, self-contained units. Leaving aside dispersion and the defensive, Taylor noted that "the problem of the ground commander will be to find the enemy, to determine his configuration, and then to destroy him by directing atomic fire upon him, using his own organic weapons or calling down the fire of distant missiles deployed to the rear. Thereafter the commander will need instant mobility to exploit the effects of this destructive fire."[86] But the pentomic division was not suitable to all formations. Converting the 101st Airborne Division in 1957 without prior field tests of the design revealed serious flaws. It lost 5,600 officers and men, gained rocket launchers, but had to give up all 155-mm howitzers to become fully air transportable. The pentomic airborne division had neither enough manpower to fight for protracted periods of time nor sufficient artillery support to confront Soviet forces in Germany.[87]

If the airborne division seemed flawed as a result of making it lighter, infantry divisions revealed deeper problems of the pentomic scheme. They were pared down to 13,700 officers and men, still larger than Eisenhower and Taylor would have liked. Conversion was slow, especially in the Seventh Army, where some of the battle groups did not receive their fifth rifle company until 1960. Shortages of armored personnel carriers that also affected armored divisions meant only one battle group at a time could be mechanized and only one additional battle group could be motorized even if the division stripped all light trucks from its transportation battalion. This made timely dispersal, rapid concentration of force, and orderly retreat to defensible positions impossible and it left three battle groups inutile.[88] Worse, communication systems to coordinate all five groups were lacking and the elimination of regiments as combat units threatened the army's esprit de corps and left lieutenant colonels without a command.[89]

For public consumption, emphasis was put on tactical atomic weapons. Nuclear weapons "were the going thing and, by including some in the division armament, the Army staked out its claim to a share in the nuclear arsenal." Taylor claimed Defense Secretary Wilson had directed him to "request . . . 'newfangled' items with public appeal instead of the prosaic accoutrements of the foot soldier."[90] Wilson followed Eisenhower's guidance: "Because scientific progress exerts a constantly increasing influence upon the character and conduct of war, and because America's most precious possession is the lives of her citizens, we should base our security upon military formations which make maximum use of science and technology to minimize numbers in men."[91] For new conventional equipment, Taylor approved a program intended to replace light, medium, and heavy tanks with a main battle tank and an airborne assault vehicle, and he expected the M113 armored personnel carrier to come online as an air-transportable vehicle.[92] The pentomic division proved useful for procurement, but most new conventional weapons did not reach US forces in Europe until after the pentomic experiment itself had been abandoned in 1961.[93]

The Seventh Army faced difficult odds even though the gap with Eastern bloc armies had grown smaller since 1950. Army studies called for the employment of 151,000 theater and tactical nuclear weapons in the defense of Western Europe.[94] American generals in Europe concluded that the headquarters of the Seventh Army and US Army, Europe, should be consolidated to improve command and control. Taylor disapproved: "We have in the Seventh Army a highly successful going concern—probably the best trained, best equipped, most combat ready field army in the Free World." He knew NATO commander Lauris Norstad could not maintain full control over the land battle from his headquarters at Fontainebleau, but found it was better to maintain strategic, operational, and tactical command at different headquarters and improve communications. The Seventh Army's units already had "frontages greater than any which we have ever anticipated before. In order to assure the control of a front of some three hundred miles and to effect a close tie-in with the Northern Army Group, I would consider that an army group headquarters would be needed in spite of the small number of divisions and corps."[95]

At a time when NATO forces were tasked to defend positions well to the east of the Rhine River, Seventh Army leaders found the pentomic army wanting in some of the most critical aspects of modern warfare: fire support, mobility, and communications. Donald Bennett, the Seventh Army's chief of operations, concluded that infantry divisions lacked trucks and armored personnel carriers.[96] Most damaging for an army that relied on the application of heavy firepower, the Seventh Army's artillery commander concluded that infantry divisions lacked sufficient conventional and atomic weaponry. He feared the reorganization had taken away the strength of American artillery: centralized command, flexibility, and massing capability.⁹⁷ Logistics looked little better. Williston Palmer, now deputy commander of US forces in Europe, noted that support units had been "cut below the safety point. If we were involved in a shooting war, it is doubtful that our combat forces could be supported by the current logistical support forces."⁹⁸

Many officers derided the pentomic division. Westmoreland, who had moved on to command the 101st Airborne Division, readjusted it to the point where the pentomic structure remained only as facade. Leaders at the Command and General Staff College, tasked with developing new operational doctrine, fought the concept so vigorously that Taylor decided to replace the commandant. He brought in Lionel McGarr for Garrison Davidson, who was made superintendent at West Point. McGarr, too, found the concept unworkable and by 1958 focused more on unconventional than atomic warfare.⁹⁹ Harold K. Johnson, just prior to becoming army chief of staff in 1964, opined that the pentomic division "would have had a difficult time fighting its way out of a wet paper bag."¹⁰⁰ Other soldiers, like Anthony Herbert, a platoon leader of an infantry battle group in Germany in 1959, thought the reorganization made no sense from an operational perspective. It had to be a publicity ploy. He feared greater dispersion was of little help on an atomic battlefield, as radiation would destroy all life in a wide area. He also recognized a problem that had been largely ignored in the planning stages: the gap between senior commanders and junior officers once the regimental and battalion command levels were combined at battle group. Perhaps this could have been made to work with an improved communications system, but not with existing technology.¹⁰¹ Taylor, anticipating new equipment, expected such problems to be solved in the near future.

By 1959 army planners were considering fundamental changes, and in 1961 Eddleman, now vice chief of staff and previously commander of the Seventh Army, introduced the Reorganization Objectives Army Division (ROAD).¹⁰² He found inspiration in the West German division-and-brigade structure that NATO leaders had endorsed as an ideal formation.¹⁰³ Eddleman proposed three brigades in a division, based on the building block principle of assembling task forces as the tactical or strategic situation required by adding combat battalions, just as he had intended for the mid-1950s reforms.¹⁰⁴ Taylor's transformation had proved too ambitious, as he attempted to alter the army's mission, the structure of its combat divisions, future weapons technology, and tactical and operational doctrine in short order. But it had served a different purpose. Taylor hoped to transform the army; he needed to prove its utility in the nuclear age. The reorganization had given the army room to redefine its mission from war fighting to deterrence. ROAD had greater staying power and more firepower and mobility, but one should not assume it could have been approved in 1956. It also benefited from the arrival of weapons and equipment ordered for the pentomic division. Both types were built primarily for atomic war and seemed less well prepared to engage enemies in insurgencies and conventional wars outside of Europe.[105]

Taylor stated as early as 1955 that the ideal army should "include forces that would be readily available to carry out separately any of our various missions." This entailed a ready force to meet the commitment to NATO as well as one for contingencies outside of Europe. He concluded the ideal solution would be "exceedingly difficult to attain" and that the army would have to do its best within available means.[106] Still, Taylor maintained publically that "the American Army must achieve greater combat readiness to deter not only the big war, but also the small war which may occur any place about the world." To meet all eventualities, "we are stressing so much the air transportability and strategic mobility which are indispensable for a prompt reaction to unexpected aggression. We feel that the small war must be deterred, or won quickly; otherwise, it may extend to the big war which would be a disaster to all participants."[107]

JCS chairman Arthur Radford was sufficiently concerned about Taylor's moves to ask staff officers to investigate his public statements. What did he think constituted proper balance between armed forces for nuclear deterrence, conventional or tactical nuclear war, and brushfire wars, which represented the near future in a global Cold War? The report, presenting excerpts from seventeen speeches and statements between July 1955 and May 1956, was on Radford's desk in October 1956. Taylor had stressed several common themes to army staff, the press, and public audiences across the country: the army needed strong reserves to be prepared for all eventualities, a rigid strategic doctrine and force structure built on just one form of deterrence was insufficient, the nation needed to regain strategic flexibility, and future wars could come in all shapes and sizes.[108]

Taylor did not ignore guerrilla warfare, but he did not make it a central feature of his public pitch on the army's mission. In his 1957 year-end reflections to the press, Taylor stressed deterrence and limited war in Europe, the development of tactical atomic weapons, the army's progress in the space race, the tensions between the armed services, and how much overseas commitments and the budget stressed the army. He did not mention Vietnam, even though he was aware it was a more likely future battlefield than Germany. He also knew there was no winning political argument in preparedness for such a war, but there was much to gain from appearing to modernize the army for nuclear war. When pressed by reporters on tactical nuclear weapons in a war in Southeast Asia, Taylor noted that "our Army forces should arrive prepared to use these weapons," but how such a war was fought depended on the desires of the local government. Any war carried great risk of escalation, but by "our visible readiness to deal with the situation [we] then have reasonable hope that the challenge will not present itself." Put differently, the same logic applied to deterrence and war fighting in Germany and Vietnam.[109]

Similarly, Taylor had told the Association of the United States Army convention in October that the army's greatest advances in a year filled with crises in Hungary and at the Suez Canal had come in the pentomic conversion and the missile program. Plainly, the atomic army took precedence in a world of *Sputnik* and likely increases in Soviet aggressiveness.[110] Still, the army was building strength to meet challenges at the periphery of the Cold War: "The prompt suppression of small war situations," Taylor told senators in June 1958, was one of the tasks of "a mobile combat ready strategic force at home."[111] He had just designated a four-division Strategic Army Command. On paper this gave the army the rapid reaction force Taylor advertised, yet in case of a wider war reinforcements for Europe alone would have consumed all four divisions, and three more that were slated for Korea. If the Cold War remained calm in those theaters, Taylor could send two divisions each to simultaneous conflicts in Indonesia and the Middle East.[112] But as the intervention in Lebanon from July to October 1958 showed, the JCS were too concerned about Soviet moves to deploy the strategic reserve, which would have tied up most of US airlift capabilities. Instead, they sent a marine task force and a reinforced airborne battle group from the 24th Infantry Division in Germany.[113]

Early in his tenure as chief of staff, Taylor had found little support for his arguments on flexible response from senior officers. One exception was CINCPAC Admiral Felix Stump, who implored Wilson in June

1957 to help the military prepare for limited wars. Otherwise, the United States would fall "into a position of complete inferiority to Russia by losing cold wars in succession if we do not have the power to win them. Without such power, Russia can conquer all Asia piecemeal and in small increments too insignificant to be the cause of risking an intercontinental war." Stump read recent statements by Air Force Chief of Staff Thomas White and the new JCS chairman, Nathan Twining, as evidence that "this danger is not fully understood by them."[114] By 1958, CNO Burke and Marine Corps Commandant Randolph M. Pate had come to support the call for limited-war capability and John Foster Dulles had made known his new thinking.[115] By then, only White and Twining insisted that armed forces built for general war would also suffice in a limited war environment and that any war against the Soviets would be general and nuclear.[116]

Twining resented limitations imposed by political leaders upon military commanders. He and White feared US nuclear strategy was insufficiently aggressive and could fatally delay escalation to all-out attack on the Soviet Union.[117] As an example, Twining cited the Korean War, where President Truman's refusal to authorize the use of airpower north of the Yalu River had kept US forces from winning the war. Unlike Taylor, Twining thought war in Europe could not remain limited and argued more generally that limited war was a "philosophy of weakness."[118] This was in line with NATO strategic guidance, which held that alliance forces had to employ nuclear weapons at the outset of general war with the Soviets, even if the enemy did not do so first, or else Europe would be overrun.[119] Yet even though Twining and White were in the minority on the JCS, Eisenhower steadfastly supported their position.[120]

Taylor embraced political science scholarship on limited war. He may have nourished the seed for the most provocative book in his May 1956 talk at the Council on Foreign Relations. Avoiding direct critique of the administration, Taylor assured his audience, "we are doing quite well with our military preparations for the present." Much of the rest of the talk suggested otherwise.[121] Taylor had appeared at the invitation of John J. McCloy, now the council's chairman. In the audience was a young Henry Kissinger, who directed the council's study group on nuclear weapons and foreign policy. Kissinger agreed with McCloy's realist worldview and Taylor's argument about land forces and the possibility of tactical nuclear war in Europe.[122] He, too, concluded massive retaliation ceded the initiative in foreign policy and did not provide means to address lesser threats than nuclear war.[123] Kissinger's book, along with his critique of the administration's foreign policy on television programs such as *The Mike Wallace Interview*, moved him into the spotlight and added to a public debate of limited war.[124] Surprisingly, *Nuclear Weapons and Foreign Policy* was well received by Eisenhower's friend Senator Henry Cabot Lodge Jr. and by Goodpaster, who presented some twenty-five pages of notes to the president.[125]

Administration officials, including Eisenhower and Defense Secretary McElroy, showed greater receptiveness to consider limited war in the policy reviews of 1958 and 1959, but it became obvious that strategic nuclear deterrence and sufficient military capability for limited war could only be achieved if the defense budget was increased significantly. Eisenhower prioritized fiscal policy for medium-term economic growth and security over short-term improvements in the defense posture. At least the Defense Department seemed in steadier hands with McElroy Still, he told "Swede" Hazlett, "this whole business of inter-service rivalries has been greatly distressing to me, and to all of us. I am sure you are as sick as I am of public debates among Generals and Secretaries of the various services."[126]

As Eisenhower's presidency was nearing its end, limited war remained a point of discussion at the White House. Eisenhower's science advisers noted in August 1960 that the defense establishment lacked an integrated plan or structures for limited warfare and airlift remained insufficient. Moreover, guidance from the defense secretary had not been updated substantially since 1956. Among pressing concerns, "the Army is now prohibited from performing in a manner adequate to its needs, while the Air Force is not providing for development and procurement appropriate to the task," specifically, tactical aerial reconnaissance and air support. Eisenhower agreed: "The more the services depend on nuclear weapons the dimmer the President's hope gets to contain any limited war or to keep it from spreading into general war." However, he "did not intend to say that the possibilities for tactical weapons should be neglected." After seven and a half years in office, Eisenhower concluded, "notwithstanding the inevitably increased reliance on nuclear weapons . . . we should not neglect the task to contain limited or local aggression."[127]

Army Missiles and Falling Out

In leading the army, Taylor fell into the same patterns as at West Point. He thought more about structures than people and believed the way to affect change was to build it from the top down. He also micromanaged in some areas (such as the pentomic division) but remained aloof in others (such as the growing crisis in command). From 1954 to 1956 the army lost 132,000 officers, and Taylor's friend Higgins, who retired as a major general, summed up the frustrations of many of his peers: "If present trends continue the Army will soon become a service support agency for the other armed services."[128] Senator Richard Russell (D, Georgia), the new Armed Services Committee chairman, expressed his concerns to Taylor in October 1955, noting that he had discussed reasons for leaving the army with a number of officers. He was surprised that "very few of the young men [gave] inadequate compensation as a reason for leaving." Instead, slow promotions, separation from dependents resulting from overseas service, shortage of housing near army bases in the United States, and lack of access to postgraduate schools or civilian universities ranked high on their list of grievances.[129]

Taylor told Russell that Congress should also improve access to medical care for dependents—about 40 percent did not receive it—and provide proper benefits for dependents of service members who died. But he dismissed concerns about promotions (which were already improving) and he did not think the cost of sending more officers to postgraduate schools was warranted.[130] Taylor assumed tweaking the system would resolve the crisis. Instead of cutting down on bureaucracy, as proposed by the other army leaders, Taylor hoped giving major generals division commands at a younger age and relying on statistical analysis from the army's career management division would provide better opportunities for rising officers. He believed scientific management should be added to money, men, and materiel as one of the four essentials.[131] It did not lead to the desired outcome. World War II and the Korean War had swept large numbers of reserve officers into active service. By 1960 over two-thirds of active duty army officers were still reservists or short-termers even though the officer corps had shrunk by a third since 1953. The number of experienced regular army officers had declined precipitously and the army's crisis in command had deepened.[132]

Taylor grasped the need for the army to be active in missile development. The space race had gripped the public's imagination, and Taylor feared the army would fall irreparably behind its sister services if it did not make breakthroughs in the field. This fed into his public relations strategy, anchored by television (*The Big Picture*) and radio programs (*The Army Hour*).[133] Taylor hoped senior officers, in presenting the army to the public, could stress the progressive, forward-looking, and versatile nature of an institution that "attaches the greatest importance to human values." Doing so might attract more qualified young men.[134] Missile technology offered ways to show that the army was just as advanced as the air force and navy. This clashed with Eisenhower's notion that from a technical and fiscal perspective the air force (and, once Polaris had emerged as a submarine launch system, also the navy) should develop medium- and long-range missiles. While Taylor made the argument for the army missile program, in public and private he often seemed aloof and let his subordinates, above all James Gavin, carry the brunt of the fight against Wilson, Radford, and the air force.

In 1955 Eisenhower allowed the army missile program to proceed only because Defense Secretary Wilson warned that transferring it to the air force could delay long-range missile development by a full year. Even so, the president was concerned about redundancy and infighting between the services.[135] Taylor noted in a January 1956 press conference: "The Army . . . is developing a medium range missile, a 1500-mile missile. The Army expects to spend more and more of its money in continuing efforts to expand its missile system." He concluded ground-to-air and ground-to-ground missiles "will give our forces tremendous destructive firepower ranging far ahead of and above our front lines, that is, high into the enemy air space, and deep into the vital sources of strength of our enemy ground forces."[136] The army held a strong position: rocket and missile development was well under way, propelled by German scientists led by Hitler's former rocket engineer Dr. Wernher von Braun. Taylor did not dwell on the odious connection. In his idealized vision, "the Army is the versatile and flexible member of the defense team. It does not depend for success on the blind destruction of the big bang . . . [and] retains the ability to vary the application of military force to the needs of the moment, to make 'measured' rather than 'mass' retaliation."[137]

Eisenhower remained doubtful. In April 1956 he reiterated his opposition to redundancy in missile development and air transport, another area where the army and air force could not find common ground. Eisenhower stressed that it was not good enough for any one of the armed services to argue it needed weapons, vehicles, or equipment because it lacked faith in the other services. He asked how the army planned to use long-range missiles. Taylor seemed taken aback: the army was developing long-range missiles because it had the experts and facilities, but there were no concrete plans for their use. Taylor then moved on to seemingly safer ground, speculating they could be placed in North Africa to provide fire support for the defense of Western Europe. Goodpaster summarized

Eisenhower's response: "The President referred to this as flanking fire, indicating that he thought front-line people might be rather worried as to its accuracy when it was firing from such a distance. He also referred to the communications problem of bringing fire down when and where needed, from distant launching pads."[138]

Such doubts notwithstanding, Eisenhower hedged his bets. In August 1957 Wilson reported that the army's Jupiter intermediate-range ballistic missile had made good progress. "The difficulty," he noted, "was that the group of German scientists located at Huntsville desired to get into longer range missiles. The Army's viewpoint was that these missiles were really large mortars." Wilson thought cutting the program would deepen "a large service morale problem." He also stated the long-range Redstone missile system was already outdated. According to notes taken by his son, Eisenhower responded to such uncertain advice by stressing that "the technical angles, which include cost and procurement, are not matters for the President. However, he reemphasized his desire that the Army not feel that it is forbidden to develop a good missile which has the capability of firing 500 miles."[139]

The army's missile program produced tactical delivery systems that could be useful on the atomic battlefield. Taylor showcased that family of missiles in the summer of 1958 at Fort Bliss, outside El Paso, Texas, and the nearby White Sands Missile Range in New Mexico. The goal of the two-day exercise was "to acquaint key members of the executive branch of the Government, Joint Staff agencies, and certain prominent members of the public with the characteristics and capabilities of the Army's family of missiles." These included the Dart, Little John, Honest John, Corporal, Lacrosse, Nike Ajax, Nike Hercules, Hawk, and Talos systems. Taylor thought this would "give our guests an appreciation of the Army's current capability in the surface-to-air and surface-to-surface missile fields."[140] As missile development had morphed into the space race, Taylor was attracted by the publicity without worrying about costs. Eisenhower's science adviser, MIT president James Killian, thought this was unsustainable: "The Army will have an increasing budget problem to maintain [Army Ballistic Missile Agency] at the level to which it has become accustomed."[141] When Eisenhower announced the impending transfer of the army's missile program to NASA, he stressed that the army's missile team had "shown its high technical proficiency through splendid accomplishments.... The contemplated transfer provides new opportunity for them to contribute their special capabilities directly to the expanding civilian space program."[142] Taylor, by then retired, called it "unhappy news" but also recognized "it was probably inevitable" and concluded it "may in the long run best serve the interests of our country."[143]

The fights about missile development contributed to a falling out with General Gavin, who considered Taylor "absolutely cold and impersonal."[144] Gavin, notoriously cantankerous, also deemed Eisenhower "an enigmatic and devious person. He was also a rather complex man and could be charming when the occasion called for it."[145] Gavin's career derailed following controversial Senate testimony in December 1957, in the wake of the *Sputnik* launches, when he accused the armed services of having bungled missile development and offered a condemnation of the White House, the Defense Department, and the JCS. Senator Lyndon Johnson (D, Texas), whose staffers pointed out that army leaders were angry about delays in missile development and "the doctrine of air supremacy," had prompted Gavin's statements.[146] Within days, Staff Secretary Westmoreland told Gavin he would have to serve a fifth year at the Pentagon. Gavin, who thought he had a firm commitment from Taylor for a field command, considered this a betrayal and submitted his request to retire. When it took Army Secretary Brucker until early January to grant his wish, Gavin blamed Taylor for stalling.[147] Westmoreland had a different view: Gavin retired because he had crossed the line in his criticism of Eisenhower and Wilson and the two-week delay that upset Gavin had simply been caused by the timing of his request on December 23. Taylor, Westmoreland claimed, had not been involved at all.[148]

In his memoir that appeared soon thereafter, Gavin did not spare the army. But he reserved most of his criticism for the administration and the defense establishment. They were missing the fundamental shifts in warfare in the nuclear age.[149] Privately, Gavin told a friend that Taylor, Wilson, and Radford had been the main reasons for his retirement. The latter two were wrong on army missiles and stuck in past conceptions of warfare. Taylor simply could not be trusted: "All personalities and friendships aside, he made our role a very difficult one. . . . The problem was that Gen. Taylor would agree with us, or with me when I saw him personally, on issues, then he would go to the Joint Chiefs and agree with Radford."[150] Gavin concluded Taylor, "a very troublesome man," had used him to "tell half-truths on the Hill so he could tell the big ones later."[151]

Gavin's retirement coincided with fears that *Sputnik* validated Soviet premier Nikita Khrushchev's boasts of breakthroughs in ICBM development. On November 7, Eisenhower received an alarming report from his committee on science and defense (known as the Gaither Committee though its chairman, H. Rowan Gaither, had been forced to resign by progressing lung cancer). Their report, which had morphed from an investigation of how to protect the American people from nuclear attacks and fallout to a broader assessment of deterrence, urged Eisenhower to spend $44 billion over five years on top of the current defense budget. This included $19 billion for accelerated ICBM development, a more potent and less vulnerable Strategic Air Command, and greater limited war capabilities for American and allied forces as well as $25 billion for missile defenses and fallout shelters.[152] Taylor had made his pitch for conventional and tactical nuclear forces to the committee and argued that "development of the anti-ICBM system should be accelerated to the extent of a national priority equal to the national priority accorded the development of the ICBM."[153]

Eisenhower presented the report to the NSC but otherwise kept its findings secret. Leaks to the press contributed to charges of a missile gap by Senator Stuart Symington, former air force secretary and member of the Armed Services Committee, columnist Joseph Alsop, and Senator John F. Kennedy, who later emerged as the Democrats' choice for the 1960 election.[154] The NSC discussed the Gaither Report for much of the first half of 1958. Privately, Eisenhower agreed with most of the committee's findings, but he was not prepared to invest in greater limited war capabilities or an extended program to build fallout shelters and he did not admit publicly that he had doubts about nuclear deterrence. Instead of adding $8–10 billion per year, Congress raised the defense budget by $4 billion. The bulk went to air force and navy ICBM development and Intermediate-Range Ballistic Missile (IRBM) deployment.[155]

One area where Eisenhower and Taylor still found common ground was defense reform. When the president pushed for reorganization in 1958, Taylor joined the effort and made the argument that the JCS needed an empowered chairman who could overrule the service chiefs and present his own views to the president as those of the committee. The service chiefs also should lose their direct access to the White House. The Defense Department could thus remove "all unnecessary obstacles . . . between the source of responsible decision and the agency for its execution." In February Taylor advised to Eisenhower's committee on government reorganization, which included McElroy, the recently retired Gruenther, and Twining and his predecessors Radford and Omar Bradley, to propose installing "a Director of Joint Military Plans and Operations, who reports to SecDef through the JCS chairman." He thought this would prevent the JCS from meddling in planning and day-to-day operations. Instead, the chiefs could focus on strategic concepts and force structure, determine broad military policy, give advice to the defense secretary and president through the chain of command, designate unified, joint, and specified commands, and develop joint doctrine.[156]

Both Taylor and Eisenhower were satisfied with the Defense Reorganization Act passed in July, even though Eisenhower had been dismayed about language in earlier drafts that provided service secretaries and chiefs with access to senators and congressmen in a way that "suggests that Congress hopes for disobedience and interservice rivalries."[157] Taylor stressed that the House bill under review in the Senate "will, in fact, provide for the unity in strategic planning and in military command which I consider essential to our national security." He liked that it strengthened the chain of command from the president to the defense secretary and regional commanders. Taylor did not dwell on its failure to remove the JCS from the chain of command when he noted, somewhat legalistically, "This legislation is so written that each Service chief, in the exercise of supervision over the members and organizations of his Service assigned to unified and specified commands, shall do so in such a way as to be consistent with the full operational command of the commanders of unified or specified combatant commands." At least the commander on the ground now had "full operational command, over all forces assigned" and no one but the president could approve a transfer of forces from one command to another.[158]

Taylor was alarmed about the vulnerability of the United States and its allies. In January 1959 he had presented new members of Congress with "a qualified no" to the question of whether the army was prepared to meet its missions. He simply lacked the funds to buy newly designed weapons systems necessary to stand up to the superior numbers of the Soviet military.[159] In February 1960, half a year after he had retired from active service, Taylor lobbied senators aggressively for the capability to wage limited war. Soviet advances in nuclear weapons and delivery vehicles meant there was no justification for nuclear deterrence alone. Moreover, even when the United States had held the monopoly "it did not keep the peace." Now, "our manned bomber force is a dwindling military asset. Our long-range missile force is limited in size, uncertain in reliability, and immobile upon exposed bases." Worse, the United States had no anti-missile defenses and inadequately protected the population from fallout. The alternatives were strategy change and greater defense spending or "military inferiority, and there is no living long with communism as an inferior."[160]

Taylor and SAC commander Thomas Power, who testified in joint hearings of Johnson's Aeronautical and Space Committee and Symington's Preparedness Investigation Subcommittee, agreed on one point: the US military needed more money. Taylor put the bill at $50 to 55 billion per year. He wanted more men and hardware for ground forces and implementation of Gaither Report proposals for fallout shelters as well as renewed emphasis on Jupiter missiles to "partially offset the missile gap." Power requested bombers and ICBMs. And whereas Power made the case for massive retaliation, Taylor pitched flexible response.[161] This entailed a thorough review of "how much is enough for all categories of operational functions" and required "a small mobile and secure missile force and a fully modernized Army and supporting services; a revised structure for the military budget to show clearly what it buys in terms of operational forces; and a new statement of roles and missions to show what we really mean by Army, Navy, and Air Force."[162] In his crescendo, Taylor anticipated the reforms Robert McNamara would soon bring to the Pentagon's budgeting process.

Taylor explained his critique in more detail at the US Army War College the next day. He stressed that the United States had spent too much on nuclear weapons and not enough on limited war capabilities. Coupled with the loss of an edge in technology and with parity in nuclear capability on the horizon, this put the nation at risk and it was past time to abandon all pretense of massive retaliation. Taylor did not blame Eisenhower and instead noted that the system had become unwieldy. The NSC, Defense Department, and JCS had all failed at providing a "strategy which we can all understand and which we can all execute." The NSC had not crafted the synthesis of political, economic, psychological, and military strength; the JCS were split on too many issues; and the defense secretary was too reluctant to settle them. Quick fixes could be made if the United States returned its focus to the army's Jupiter IRBM project and built up limited war capabilities, at first simply "by better organization, by improved joint planning and training, by developing a feeling of true cooperation between the three services." But since he also insisted the army should be given control of all assets for the land battle, including air support, Taylor's plea for unity sounded like a call to lift the army to the top.[163]

Taylor made similar points to a range of audiences throughout 1960.[164] In mid-June he reminded senators that the budgeting system led each service to buy its own weapons systems without full consideration how these would contribute to functions shared by all armed services. It would be better if the bureaucracy thought in terms of missions such as deterrence, atomic retaliation, overseas deployments, and limited war.[165] In November, Taylor told students and faculty of the National War College that they had to guard against assumptions that limited war was simply "a particular brand of war like guerrilla, mountain, or desert warfare" instead of covering the whole spectrum short of general war. He reminded his audience, too, of the "Great Fallacy"—indeed, he spelled it with capital letters—of thinking that preparedness for general war "includes and replaces the need for limited war readiness."[166] Limited war was the only rational option since nuclear war, "international suicide," violated Clausewitz's definition of war as "the continuation of politics by other means." Unfortunately, Taylor noted, the Defense Department and various armed services had been so intently focused on general war that no one knew whether the United States could wage a limited war.[167] Taylor's critique was unfair because the NSC had considered the very studies of limited war in different theaters that he called for. Yet it rang true because the Defense Department and JCS did not act upon the conclusions. Taylor hoped President-elect Kennedy would change the dynamic, based on his publicly stated opposition to massive retaliation and his use of missile-gap rhetoric in the campaign.

Taylor followed Ridgway's example and published an account of his frustration with national security policy. But where Ridgway had placed his criticism in the later chapters of a memoir, Taylor took a more direct approach. *The Uncertain Trumpet* was a scathing indictment of the national security system and the shortcomings of massive retaliation. It offered a passionate plea for a greater role for ground forces and for flexible response. In his last months in office Taylor had leaned heavily on his staff, especially on William E. DePuy and John Cushman, to help him sharpen the argument. His vice chief, Lyman Lemnitzer, later recalled that he acted as de facto chief of staff while Taylor spent most of his time drafting his book.[168] Taylor recognized that American strategy resembled "a hybrid which, by the time of my departure from the Pentagon bore some resemblance to the strategy of Flexible Response soon to be adopted by the Kennedy administration."[169] But this did not go far enough.

Independent of what he felt for Eisenhower, or the president for him, Taylor could not be reappointed for a third term as chief of staff, and JCS chairman Nathan Twining was expected to serve until 1961. In March 1959 McElroy had offered Taylor the NATO command in Europe, but Taylor opted for retirement.[170] Once he had accepted the lucrative position as director of Mexico City's main electrical utility company, Taylor also turned down Eisenhower's request to lead a study group on disarmament that the president hoped to get under way in the fall of 1959.[171] Eisenhower was not dissatisfied with Taylor's service and he was impressed by the army's weapons development. After viewing a 1960 demonstration at Fort Benning, Eisenhower described almost lyrically the perfect integration of soldier, scientist, and nation: "I felt this oneness, this unity, of America producing these tremendous and wonderful weapons, with a great organization taking them from the producers and the scientists and learning to use them so expertly."[172] By then Taylor had walked away, but Eisenhower had not pushed him out. Any hard feelings stemmed from Taylor's book.

Taylor did not pull his punches about the defense establishment and strategy in *The Uncertain Trumpet*, but he protected Eisenhower, whom he mentioned merely half a dozen times (and just twice in the chapter on "The Failure of Decision-Making," once laudatory and once mildly critical).[173] Radford and Wilson, both in office for just over half of Taylor's tenure as army chief of staff, each appeared twice as often and in less flattering light. Even before his book appeared in print, Taylor had appealed to the public in a series of articles in *Look* magazine.[174] He took aim at political supervision, the role of the chairman of the JCS, and the JCS altogether. He thought the joint chiefs received insufficient guidance from the National Security Council, since the Basic National Security Policy papers, themselves often the result of compromise on the NSC, remained too vague, especially at times when the service chiefs were fighting over their roles and budget shares.

The New Look, Taylor wrote with some justification, "was little more than the old air power dogma set forth in Madison Avenue trappings and now buttressed upon Massive Retaliation as the central strategic concept."[175] Taylor acknowledged how far Dulles and others in the administration had moved from their original concepts and he decried the lack of decision-making that kept massive retaliation in place nonetheless.[176] The culprit was the tedious bureaucracy. The JCS were not designed for collective action and their divisions or any disagreements with the president and defense secretary were exploited by Congress. To remedy the latter, Taylor suggested that the JCS should serve as military advisers to the legislative branch as well as to the executive.[177] Or, better yet, he "would dissolve the JCS as it now exists and replace it by a single Defense Chief of Staff for the one-man functions and by a new advisory body called provisionally the Supreme Military Council." The sinister name choice notwithstanding, Taylor proposed a rather innocuous group of three four-star generals and admirals who had recently retired or were in their final tour of duty and would no longer be listed on the active roster of any particular service.[178]

Had Taylor crossed the line that divides professional advice from open challenge to civilian control of the military? In the judgment of Morris Janowitz, an astute observer of civil-military relations at the time, Taylor had "resisted urging by members of congressional subcommittees to continue [his] opposition in public debate" while still in office.[179] Taylor had waited to condemn the JCS system until he had retired. In December 1957 he had been given an opportunity to do otherwise. Gavin's controversial Senate testimony had just become public and Taylor was asked at the National Press Club what he thought of Gavin's argument to replace the JCS. Taylor responded blandly that he hoped Gavin's ideas would get a fair hearing, especially since he, Taylor, had also believed in the need for a stronger chairman before he became chief of staff. Yet, "whether it's growing conservatism or whether perhaps experience leads one to be slow in reaching final conclusions, I am not nearly as sure now as I was then." The evasion was not truthful, but it allowed Taylor to register faint critique without sounding prepared to challenge the president or defense secretary.[180]

Lucius Clay, who had helped Eisenhower build his political campaign and select his first cabinet, concluded that Gavin had done what any retired military officer was allowed to do: he had vented his frustration and moved on to build a career as a businessman. Taylor on the other hand was political. He had consciously boosted the opposition party in an election year and returned to serve the new administration.[181] Arleigh Burke criticized Taylor for abusing his access to the White House to gather evidence: "Some of the material in his book, was derived from a very informal conversation, where the President wasn't thinking of how that could be used. . . . The President never intended what Max thought he implied or intended."[182] Nathan Twining also recalled that an offhand remark Eisenhower made at a White House cocktail party became a centerpiece of Taylor's evidence.[183] Burke and Twining seemed to refer to a December 1958 dinner with all stakeholders in the budgeting process. Yet if Taylor suggested Eisenhower chided the chiefs for a lack of "team play," he also praised Treasury Secretary Robert B. Anderson and ascribed criticism of the chiefs as insufficiently aware of economic factors to "several officials."[184]

The president himself felt betrayed by the public nature of Taylor's critique. Eisenhower responded tersely to a reporter's question about *The Uncertain Trumpet*: "I should think he has the right to his own opinion."[185] In conversation with Gordon Gray and Goodpaster, Eisenhower revealed that he wished he could take disciplinary action. Gray reported the Pentagon's legal assessment that retired officers could be disciplined just as if they were still on active duty, but he suggested Eisenhower did not want to make Taylor a martyr by pursuing the matter. The president mused about the case of General Johnson Hagood, who had been forced to retire in 1936 after criticizing the spending of the Franklin D. Roosevelt administration on New Deal measures, but then he dropped the issue.[186]

Taylor's long career in the army had ended on a sour note, and it also looked as if he had lost his fight to make the army equal again to the air force and navy in budget share and relevance. In Europe, NATO partners viewed a retreat from the threat of massive retaliation as an invitation for local aggression. In the United States, ICBMs, SAC, and the nuclear navy held sway in public imagination. War plans still proceeded in the tracks set in the mid-1950s. When newly elected president John F. Kennedy reviewed the integrated war plan, he found it was little more than an enhanced target list for air and missile strikes on Eastern Europe and the Soviet Union.[187] There still seemed no major role for the army in the main theater of the Cold War. That the new president and his defense intellectuals were talking about waging limited war in Third World countries only heightened the anxiety. Taylor himself soon became a central actor in the definition of policy and strategy. In the spring of 1961, Kennedy called on Taylor to run the investigation of the botched attempt by CIA-trained Cuban exiles to overthrow Fidel Castro, and from that sprung a permanent presence of the general in the inner circle of another president.

4

Camelot's Strategist

At the end of 1960 the Taylors moved to New York, where Maxwell had agreed to run the new Lincoln Center for the Performing Arts. Fate and politics intervened. *The Uncertain Trumpet* had caught the attention of John F. Kennedy and Taylor placed an article in *Foreign Affairs* as a timely reminder. Armstrong opted to publish it because it "put his case up to the new administration."[1] As Taylor settled in New York, Kennedy was confronted with a host of crises, from Cuba and Congo to Berlin, Laos, and Vietnam. The disastrous failure of the Bay of Pigs invasion in April proved a breaking point for Kennedy (and Defense Secretary Robert McNamara) with the military establishment. Kennedy turned to Taylor for a troubleshooter, then appointed him to his Foreign Intelligence Advisory Board, and finally installed him in a new post at the White House: military representative of the president.[2] What exactly this entailed remained unclear. When asked to draft his own job description, Taylor opted for an ambiguous letter that did not paint him in any corner of the bureaucracy.[3] Taylor's job appeared to many observers, including General Lemnitzer himself, to be set up as counterweight to the JCS chairman.[4]

Contrary to common understanding, Taylor's position was not entirely unprecedented. Eisenhower had leaned on Andrew Goodpaster as de facto chief of staff and liaison to the military. Goodpaster was deemed so essential to White House communications that Kennedy asked him to stay on for the first two months of the new administration.[5] Eisenhower himself had returned to Washington as Truman adviser and informal chairman of the JCS for the first half of 1949.[6] Taylor left an impact on civil-military relations to match that of Eisenhower (pre-presidency), and he was involved in translating the vaguely defined strategy of flexible response into practical reality in crises in Europe, the Caribbean, and

Southeast Asia. Intellectually, despite his advanced age (Taylor would turn sixty in August 1961), he fit the mold of the best and the brightest, those academics and business executives Kennedy brought to Washington. Taylor and Robert F. Kennedy, the president's brother and attorney general with an outsized role in unconventional aspects of foreign policy, developed a close friendship.[7]

The General at the White House

Kennedy's White House was in need of better organization. In May 1961, National Security Adviser McGeorge Bundy complained that the president rarely had more than six to eight minutes for a briefing on national security matters and spent most of it asking about what he had just read in the newspapers and worrying about leaks. He needed to set aside a regular time and designate a coordinator for input from various agencies and departments.[8] Taylor, Bundy, and JFK's military aide, General Chester Clifton, took up that task jointly from early July, but briefings were scheduled at irregular times and often skipped over several days. They became more and more infrequent in 1962. Kennedy also did not follow Bundy's advice to call for NSC meetings at a fixed time and in regular intervals.[9] In this structure, individuals with access to the president, like Bundy and Taylor, had a great deal of influence in policy decisions.[10]

While Taylor found his way into the president's inner circle, his relationship with the joint chiefs was less friendly, even though his ties to Lemnitzer helped cover up some of the friction and he often reinforced JCS advice.[11] The chiefs resented the notion of a watchdog at the White House, and Burke and LeMay pegged Taylor for a master manipulator. The arrangement confused foreign visitors: West Berlin's Mayor Willy Brandt thought Taylor was the JCS chairman during the Berlin crisis in the summer of 1961, and the German news magazine *Der Spiegel* saw him as the architect of plans to rearm conventional forces in Europe.[12] JFK and McNamara determined to retire or reassign gradually the service chiefs after the Bay of Pigs fiasco. In the meantime, Kennedy conveyed his expectations to the chiefs in a letter drafted by Taylor. Beyond restating what was already well understood—the JCS served as "my principal military advisor . . . I expect their advice to come to me direct and unfiltered"—Kennedy was looking for broad-mindedness: "I regard [the chiefs] to be more than military men and expect their help in fitting military requirements into the overall context of any situation, recognizing that the most difficult problem in Government is to combine all assets in a unified, effective pattern." Taylor held that it was critical that military advisers weigh political, economic, and ideological factors.[13]

Even prior to his election, Kennedy had concluded that the United States needed a strategy that afforded appropriate means to address different kinds of challenges. Flexible response was a deliberately vague concept. There was no signature document akin to NSC 68, and Kennedy did not approve the drafts of annual policy reviews.[14] In 1960, Taylor had written that flexible response "would restore to warfare its historic justification as a means to create a better world upon the successful conclusion of hostilities."[15] Senator Kennedy told him in an April 1960 letter that *The Uncertain Trumpet* had greatly influenced his thinking on defense policy.[16] One air force planner, Brigadier General Noel Parrish, claimed Taylor and Gavin spent weekends at Hyannis Port and wrote Kennedy's campaign speeches on conventional forces and less immediate reliance on nuclear weapons.[17] But while Gavin had ties to the campaign, Taylor did not meet John F. Kennedy between a 1948 speaking engagement in Boston and the spring of 1961, outside of Senate committee hearings, yet he observed from Mexico City that Kennedy's thinking on strategy resembled his own.[18] Taylor did not mention that while flexible response may have elevated the credibility of deterrence at levels below nuclear war, it did so at the cost of higher likelihood of getting drawn into shooting wars.

Robert S. McNamara, the new defense secretary, concluded that the current force structure left the United States without the capability to respond proportionately in local conflicts. In February 1961 he lamented that American forces overseas were "strongly oriented in their war plans, current capabilities, materiel procurement, and research and development, towards general nuclear war." Consequently, the contribution of ground forces to deterrence was modest. McNamara recommended that "the primary mission of our overseas forces should be made non-nuclear warfare."[19] At a cost of $740 million, he proposed to increase the budget for army Special Forces (in line with JFK's interest in irregular warfare), increase army personnel, conduct more training exercises, enhance air and sea transport, build greater stockpiles of ammunition and equipment, and improve research and development.[20] He also wanted to increase the army from eleven to sixteen combat-ready divisions. And McNamara and his deputy, Roswell Gilpatric, changed the defense budget from a service-defined to a functions-based model: money was allocated for nuclear deterrence and limited war capabilities. Taylor, too, had stressed this point and on one occasion, a January 1960 talk at the Council on Foreign Relations, Gilpatric had been in the audience.[21] Now Taylor was a reviewer of the proposed 1963 budget at the White House.[22]

The Sino-Soviet rift and a multipolar world required greater awareness of the global Cold War. Taylor surveyed the shift in the first half of the 1960s in a March 1966 lecture at Lehigh University: "Whereas in the past we have had a single principal enemy, the Sino-Soviet bloc, which absorbed all or virtually all of our attention, now we have not only two major adversaries, the Soviet Union and Red China, but additionally other troublemaking powers which must be taken into account." This meant the United States had to keep constant watch "in all directions in anticipation of the emergence of forces inimical to our national purpose."[23] In the early 1960s these included Cuba's Fidel Castro, Egypt's Gamal Abdel Nasser, Indonesia's Sukarno, and North Vietnam's Ho Chi Minh. The United States needed to be prepared to deter the Soviets, confront Chinese aggression, and face the spread of wars of national liberation.

Like Kennedy, who expressed similar sentiments in his inaugural address, Taylor believed the United States needed to win the hearts and minds of people in Asia, Africa, and Latin America. Subversive revolutionary war had erupted before, but South Vietnam offered the opportunity to expose the myth of invincibility of wars of national liberation. Taylor left unexplained why the outcomes of the Greek Civil War, Huk Rebellion in the Philippines, and Malayan Emergency—all defeats of the insurgent movements—had not already done so. He also projected too much of his Korean War experience into the 1960s. He observed that it was possible to employ military force as a means to affect a negotiated settlement if the enemy was persuaded the war "can be made costly, dangerous, and doomed to failure."[24] This was an ominous conclusion, for what might have worked in Korea was not equally applicable to Vietnam.

Taylor, who also noted the need to remain on guard in Europe and to keep up nuclear and conventional armaments, emphasized the threat of communism spreading to some ninety emerging nations with conditions of poverty and social injustice. The magnitude of the task required a selective response. The countries most in danger were those closest to the Soviet Union, China, North Vietnam, or Cuba. It was possible to discern a predictable sequence of events and intervene early, perhaps before military action had become necessary. In most cases aggression centered on an underground political structure aimed at rural areas, later bolstered by guerrilla forces. The goal of the insurgents was to win cooperation or silence of the people and destroy their faith in the government's ability to provide security. For governments facing an insurgency, it was essential to convince the people they were better off under their rule than that of the insurgents. This required first and foremost making the people "feel secure for both the short and long term, although the latter is the more important."[25]

Taylor explained "our new military policy" at an awards dinner in early 1962. Just two decades earlier the United States had awoken to the reality of no longer being protected by ocean waters and allied armies. Any remaining sense of complacency was shaken between 1947, when President Truman determined a pro-western Greece was worth American investment, and 1949, when the Soviet Union acquired the atom bomb. Yet nuclear deterrence strategy in the 1950s neither met the complexity of the world situation nor delivered lower defense budgets. Taylor quoted from Kennedy's January 1962 State of the Union address to highlight the change: "We have rejected any all-or-nothing posture which would leave no choice but inglorious retreat or unlimited retaliation." Flexible response did not mean the United States had given up on the strategic deterrent. It remained crucial to impress upon the Soviets the certainty of destruction from an American nuclear counterstrike. But this had to be supplemented "by an ability to deter those limited aggressions which might appear tempting to a potential enemy if we appeared muscle-bound with our nuclear strength." Taylor also emphasized the threat of insurgencies and pointed at the "undeclared para-war" in Vietnam as the most prominent example. He noted this was not new; Americans themselves had practiced it against the British. Counterinsurgency required "particularly skillful blending of all our resources—political and economic as well as military, and constitutes a challenge to the ingenuity of our national leaders." Flexible response could meet such threats, as in Vietnam, while also preparing the US military for conventional and nuclear war.[26]

For all their seeming agreement, Kennedy, McNamara, and Taylor had different understandings of flexible response and the relative importance of deterrence in Europe and conflicts in the developing world. Countering McNamara, Taylor voiced doubts about placing too much emphasis on conventional warfare. NATO ground forces were too small for conventional defense and did not compose an ideal deterrent. He conceded he had "advocated larger conventional forces which would give us some choice other than all-out retaliation or retreat," but Taylor feared McNamara had gone too far when the defense secretary extolled the conventional forces underpinning flexible response in speeches at the University of Michigan and the NATO Council meeting in Athens in the spring of 1962. Taylor told Walt Rostow, "It has always seemed to me that the aim of our military policy should be to increase the available alternatives in the possible uses of military force and thereby achieve a graduated series of possible responses." But this had to include nonconventional means: "The development and use of very low yield atomic weapons for battlefield use has always seemed to me to offer the possibility of a very valuable intermediate stage in any escalating series of responses." He feared McNamara's course might eliminate this option.[27]

It did not help that McNamara's speeches came just as France, disgruntled with American unwillingness to help build its nuclear arsenal, was turning away from Washington and West German leaders were questioning the resolve of the new administration. Taylor thought the way to address this was to assist the French in return for guarantees that Charles de Gaulle's *force de frappe* would become an integral part of a NATO tactical and theater nuclear arm. Washington could then keep Bonn from exploring its own nuclear weapons program or moving closer to Paris in a second power center within the western alliance. This included pushing NATO's forward-defense line as far to the east as possible to project security for the West German population. Doing so required reliance on tactical nuclear weapons, but McNamara, Secretary of State Dean Rusk, and Kennedy did not agree entirely.[28] Taylor was thus not exactly the architect, but he played a significant role in defining the framework of flexible response. He owed his position to an early misstep of the administration.

Kennedy had turned to Taylor in April 1961 when the failed attempt by CIA-trained and American-supported Cuban exiles to land in the Bay of Pigs had embarrassed the White House. Together with Attorney General Robert Kennedy, CIA director Allen Dulles, and CNO Burke, Taylor was to consider what had gone wrong and what lessons it held for the future. Kennedy made clear Taylor was in charge and that the other three board members were to comment. The president may have been thinking about a wider review, for he told Taylor, "It is apparent that we need to take a close look at all practices and programs in the areas of military and paramilitary, guerrilla and anti-guerrilla activity which fall short of outright war. I believe that we need to strengthen our work in this area." This suggests he hoped Taylor could provide advice to the administration beyond the study of Operation Zapata.[29] Taylor insisted in the Senate's Church Committee hearings on intelligence operations in 1975 that he understood his task in the narrow sense of investigating the Bay of Pigs fiasco and that it took several more months before he started managing the counterinsurgency program.[30]

Taylor and his colleagues began their hearings with CIA officers on April 24 and presented their first cut, an oral briefing, to Kennedy on May 16.[31] Taylor's written report followed on June 13. He concluded that it had made little sense to allow the CIA to run a large paramilitary operation that required substantial military support. The JCS should have taken the lead in planning and coordination from November 1960, when the magnitude of the operation had become apparent. Taylor also felt too many officials had given the green light to their parts of the operation because they were anxious to move ahead as long as the Cuban Brigade was well prepared and motivated. The biggest problem did not rest with either the Cuban exiles or the CIA plan, but with miscommunication within a new administration where military commanders and civilian leaders had not gotten to know one another. The chiefs, Taylor made clear, should have spoken out forcefully. In April 1964 he recalled his amazement that military officers had deemed feasible the plan for an amphibious landing and 1,200 men holding a thirty-six-mile beachhead long enough for an uprising to galvanize. He concluded the that JCS had hesitated to intervene because it was not their plan and, therefore, their place.[32] That attitude, Taylor noted, was antiquated. He would have preferred US military intervention to the fiasco that ensued and was critical of the unwillingness of CIA and military officers to confront Kennedy when the president decided on the morning of D-day to cancel planned air strikes.[33]

To insiders, Taylor's findings appeared duplicitous. Two CIA officers claimed they told him the president and attorney general had approved an assassination plot against Castro, which Taylor did not include in his report. There is no conclusive evidence on why he remained silent, or whether Richard Bissell, who had coordinated the operation, and Grayston Lynch, who had served with the Cubans, really told him about it. In a phone call to Burke, Lemnitzer voiced frustration about Taylor's interpretation that the JCS had approved the invasion plan.[34] But the chiefs had not made an unequivocal statement against it, nor did they reveal an internal assessment of a 30 percent likelihood of success. Instead they presented McNamara with a rosier prognosis: the operation could succeed without direct intervention of US armed forces. In his testimony, Burke, who concluded the chiefs had morally (if not technically) approved the plan, expressed regret that he did not make his concerns known.[35] Lemnitzer's distinction that the chiefs had been asked to appraise but not approve the plan sounded like splitting hairs.[36] Still, while nobody involved with the Bay of Pigs operation looked good in hindsight, Taylor placed less blame on the White House than on the agencies that advised the president. The CIA's history of the investigation concluded that while Taylor blunted some of Robert Kennedy's attempts to shape the findings, he actively deflected criticism from the White House.[37]

Taylor's report advanced six recommendations. First and foremost, the US government had to acquire the capability to run large-scale paramilitary operations. This required an oversight body to coordinate political, economic, ideological, and intelligence assets, modeled on the Special Group, established in 1954, that had as its constituent members the CIA director, JCS chairman (since 1957), and undersecretaries of state and defense. Second, if it was a large operation with military-trained personnel, it should be run by the Defense Department. Third, the Kennedy administration needed an inventory of paramilitary assets to determine what had to be added. Fourth, President Kennedy had to define his expectations of the JCS. In particular, he needed to make clear that the chiefs should weigh in on any military issues no matter what agency had crafted the plans. Fifth, the lessons of the Bay of Pigs operation had to be absorbed by all principal department and agency heads, and Taylor asked for a line-by-line review with the president, vice president, secretaries of state and defense, attorney general, CIA director, and national security adviser. Finally, he implored Kennedy to revisit policy objectives for Cuba and weigh possible courses of action against Fidel Castro's regime.[38]

Subsequently, Taylor helped plan for staging an uprising to overthrow Castro. Operation Mongoose, directed by air force brigadier general Edward Lansdale with support from the CIA and Defense Department, was to combine infiltration, sabotage, and propaganda operations in Cuba.[39] In March 1962, Taylor proposed a shift from the White House's hopeful assumptions about effects of a local uprising to formulating concrete plans for an invasion. While events in Cuba could serve as a pretext for decisive military action, they could not bring about regime change. The chiefs agreed and noted that the United States had sufficient military forces ready to strike. Yet President Kennedy was not prepared to go along, and in April McNamara and Rusk also conveyed their opposition to Taylor's scheme. Operation Mongoose also seemed to run in parallel with rumored plans to assassinate Castro. Taylor testified in July 1975 before the Church Committee that he was unaware of such plans, and both he and Lansdale confirmed that Robert Kennedy had never approached them about it.[40] President Kennedy suspended Operation Mongoose in October 1962 to reduce risk factors during the Cuban Missile Crisis.

Taylor also provided briefings on his report outside of the inner circle. On June 23 he went to Gettysburg, with mixed feelings. Not quite three years later he quipped that he brought along Allen Dulles "as a bodyguard." Taylor had not seen President Eisenhower since his retirement and knew full well that his memoir had made him unpopular with his former boss. But his trepidations were unfounded: "General Eisenhower was his usual friendly and sunny self and expressed happiness that I had been willing to return to the government." With the uncomfortable visit behind him, Taylor met Senator Russell and Representative Carl Vinson to help ward off a congressional investigation.[41] He found the Bay of Pigs operation had been a heavy blow to the administration. Three years later, Taylor concluded that "it took weeks and, indeed, months for proper relationships to be restored among the officials who were responsible for the Bay of Pigs. The Administration never entirely recovered until October 1962 when its members turned in a magnificent performance in handling the threat of missiles in Cuba."[42]

Beyond the immediate conclusions he put before the president, Taylor also gained a deeper sense of the departments, agencies, and services involved in discrete operations in the Cold War. Action abroad, in the military, political, and economic realm, required careful coordination. That was difficult to attain in a system defined by personalities and parochial interests. Taylor's new committee added another layer to an already cumbersome bureaucracy, but in his thinking a high-powered oversight group for counterinsurgency would give all invested agencies and departments a seat at the table. It could observe the landscape and discuss policy recommendations for the president that could not easily be taken on by any particular interest group.[43] The result should have been better integration of American assets for foreign policy, economic aid, military assistance, intelligence operations, and information campaigns. In reality, Taylor's Special Group (CI) struggled to translate theory into practice. The new body grew from the Special Group (Augmented) that John F. Kennedy created after the Bay of Pigs operation to coordinate US actions against Fidel Castro's regime. Facing the rising threat of insurgencies and revolutionary war, Taylor's new group could propose counterinsurgency doctrine, put in motion training programs for military and civilian officers, and monitor events in over half a dozen countries deemed in critical condition. Yet on-the-ground coordination beyond Washington boardrooms was hard to effect. When he arrived as ambassador in Saigon in the summer of 1964, Taylor found the country team operating in parallel tracks to the Military Assistance Command and the South Vietnamese government.

Cuba remained part of Taylor's portfolio, but he also began to work more directly on other crises. The vehicle to oversee Operation Mongoose and look at wider counterinsurgency planning was the Special Group (Augmented), led by the attorney general, Taylor, and Lansdale, who had gained experience as adviser to Philippine defense minister (later president) Ramon Magsaysay at the height of the campaign against the Huk and as a confidant of South Vietnam's President Ngo Dinh Diem. President Kennedy increased funding for the military's Special Forces community, but he, too, understood that counterinsurgency required a holistic effort. By mid-1962, that included a new five-week interagency training seminar on "Problems of Development and Internal Defense" for senior officials deploying to developing countries. Taylor and his colleagues estimated that 360 people would take the course in 1963—125 from State, 75 from Defense, 70 from the Agency for International Development (just launched in March 1961), and 45 each from the CIA and the US Information Agency.[44] Junior- and mid-level officials attended training for company and field grade officers at armed forces schools, while senior Defense and CIA officials reported to staff or war colleges and USIA, AID, and State Department officials took a course at the Foreign Service Institute. The Special Group (CI), an offshoot of the augmented group, developed guidance on coordinating the actions of several agencies, assessing the politics and culture of different countries, and linking American and local efforts.[45]

The Special Group (CI) convened in January 1962. Taylor was at the helm and regular members included the JCS chairman, CIA director, national security adviser, deputy secretary of defense, deputy secretary of state for political affairs, attorney general, and AID administrator.[46] Their immediate focus was on Southeast Asia. South Vietnam was the "counterinsurgency laboratory," and by June 1962 thirty-eight officers had been sent there and another thirty were assigned as observers in Thailand (seven), Laos (ten), Latin America (five), and Europe and the Middle East (eight). Thirteen more were "on rotation" in Laos, Thailand, and Latin America.[47] By the summer of 1962, these efforts also led to a framework for counterinsurgency strategy.[48] Nevertheless, this fell short of actionable doctrine, and neither the Special Group nor other interagency groups ever solved the basic problem of coordinating one unified strategy across the armed services, State and Defense Department offices, the intelligence community, and other governmental agencies invested in counterinsurgency efforts.

Taylor outlined his preferred strategy in a talk at the National War College in May 1962 about "the growing birth pains of this program" to combat communist insurgencies. He explained that the Kennedy administration had been forced to widen its focus from inherited crises in Congo, Laos, and Cuba to subversive insurgencies more generally, a threat that had not been considered for US force structure policies and nuclear strategy in the 1950s. And yet, guerrilla war was nothing new in military history and guerrilla operations had by the mid-twentieth century become a primary tool of undeclared warfare. It was time for American officers to shed their assumptions about guerrillas as a supporting means in conventional wars. Instead, the nation and its armed forces had to prepare to combat wars of liberation, which Taylor suspected were part of a worldwide strategy promoted by Soviet leader Nikita Khrushchev.[49]

History, Taylor asserted, played a crucial part in identifying the traits of futures foes. The Special Group (CI) had identified half a dozen common features in twentieth-century insurgencies. First, they were communist-inspired even if, as in Cuba, the initial motivation may have been nationalist. Second, they arose in "backward areas" where the societies of "young nations were struggling for modernization." These were usually people recently freed from colonialism who could be riled up against the West as an extension of the old colonial order. Poor economic conditions and low standards of living added to political instability and uncertain social hierarchies. Third, insurgent movements shared the goal of claiming political power and controlling the nation's resources; these were political movements with the aim of taking over the state. Fourth, insurgencies unfolded in predictable stages, beginning with infiltration of political parties, the armed forces, or labor unions. Fifth, with a political base, public support, and logistics in place, insurgents shifted from clandestine political to low-grade military tactics. Finally, once ambushes and sabotage had worn out government forces and the insurgent movement had gained sufficient strength, the insurgency would evolve into a costly war of attrition, usually employing guerrilla tactics but sometimes culminating in conventional battles.[50] Taylor assumed all insurgencies applied Maoist tactics. This assessment clouded his ability to draw distinctions about local movements, meaning countermeasures were calibrated to defeat an ideal-type insurgency.

Since the Cuban revolution and the crisis in South Vietnam were likely to fuel new insurgencies, the United States urgently needed to find ways to defeat subversive revolutionary movements. The deepening crisis in Laos and Vietnam already had forced the administration to adopt ad hoc measures, but now the Special Group (CI) had completed taking stock of the United States' worldwide paramilitary capabilities—American advisers, equipment, and Special Forces, plus local armed forces—and it was time to craft an integrated strategy to draw on the strengths of all departments, agencies, and services invested in the fight. Taylor, quoting extensively from the group's charter and touting its early success in establishing training courses, envisioned his group as an advisory body akin to the JCS and NSC. The most immediate steps were (1) to ensure all actors in the armed services and the bureaucracy (including State, Defense, Labor, CIA, AID, USIA, and FBI) were on the same page and (2) to build a school where Americans and allies could learn the trade of discovering clandestine subversive movements and improving the social, political, and economic conditions that fueled them. This long-term goal of early recognition and relatively inexpensive policies to help young nations "break through the modernization barrier" had to be matched by military means to combat insurgencies already in the field or close to moving from political to military tactics.[51]

Taylor sketched the conditions of victory, a hard-to-define concept in these irregular conflicts. Prevention was the surest route to success, and governments needed an early warning system to alert them to deteriorating conditions, allowing them to intervene early. Active counterinsurgency required three fundamental structures: a stable and friendly local government, a well-versed country team at the American embassy to bring to bear all assets in one concerted effort, and an "adequate monitoring organization" in Washington to "direct the necessary resources rapidly and effectively to the area under attack." Taylor stressed that the country team had to determine what was needed; Washington could not gauge the best combination of resources and armed forces. He noted ominously, "I recommend a study of Vietnam which is a laboratory for the study of insurgency," but thought the United States was turning a corner: until recently no one knew "how the war was going" but now "we have reasonable hope of getting hard intelligence in the future." With better knowledge of enemy and context it should be possible to connect the government in Saigon and the people across the country.[52] Counterinsurgency also required drastic changes to the US armed forces. John F. Kennedy told West Point cadets and Superintendent William Westmoreland, at their June 1962 commencement, if "freedom is to be saved" the army needed to become "a wholly different kind of force and, therefore, [devise] a new and wholly different kind of military training."[53]

Even though the Kennedy administration invested more heavily in Special Forces, the only tangible change in the high command seemed to be the addition of a counterinsurgency adviser to the JCS, marine general Victor "Brute" Krulak, whose conception did not always mesh with Taylor's. But counterinsurgency was a wider field. Taylor himself was particularly proud of the courses at various schools in the Defense and State Departments and at other critical agencies that were to provide counterinsurgency instruction to some 57,000 military and government officers in 1962–63. Traditional boundaries of military and civilian functions no longer applied: "Diplomats find themselves arguing the merits of competing weapons systems to convince reluctant allies of the need for conventional forces. US military men find themselves engaged in civil activities in underdeveloped countries which have nation-building and social progress as their objectives."[54] It was telling that Taylor's June 1962 University of Pittsburgh commencement address on "our evolving national strategy" did not mention Europe and focused on insurgencies and the counterinsurgency effort.

Taylor and Kennedy's Wars

Among Kennedy's inherited crises was one over Berlin that had erupted in 1958, when Khrushchev threatened to sign a peace treaty that would leave East Germany in a position to control access to West Berlin. The western response, as well as Khrushchev's apparent unpreparedness to act on his threat, tamped down the initial phase, but when the seemingly untested John F. Kennedy entered the White House, Khrushchev, under pressure from East German leaders facing a massive stream of refugees escaping to the West through Berlin, saw another opportunity.[55] Khrushchev's June meeting with Kennedy in Vienna deteriorated to the point where a shaken JFK told *New York Times* reporter James Reston and British prime minister Harold Macmillan that Khrushchev had been ruthless in testing his resolve.[56] After Vienna, Kennedy prepared for the possibility of armed conflict. Emergency measures included an increase in the defense budget, the buildup of conventional armed forces, augmentation of US troops in Europe, the call-up of reserves, and larger numbers to be drafted. Kennedy left the impression that Americans should brace for war in his July 25 television address, even though the speech did not contain a declaration of national emergency as hardline adviser Dean Acheson had proposed.[57]

It thus came as a relief when the Soviets and their East German clients did what Walter Ulbricht, the GDR's Stalinist leader, had proclaimed would not happen: they built a wall to retain their own people. This was "a hell of lot better than war," Kennedy exhaled when he learned of the developments on August 13. But tensions in Berlin continued to build until American and Soviet tanks confronted one another at Checkpoint Charlie in late October.[58] That summer and fall, Kennedy frequently called on Taylor's advice. Taylor counseled a mixture of firmness and caution, to ensure that the United States was not seen as weak and to avoid inadvertently triggering a nuclear war. The main questions on his mind were the feasibility of an airlift, the risks involved in sending military columns to Berlin, and questions of command in the city. He also weighed in on mobilization and expansion of American capabilities in Europe.

Prior to the building of the Berlin Wall, Taylor had sought creative solutions to the mounting diplomatic crisis. At the end of July, following on Kennedy's prime time television broadcast, Taylor proposed that the administration might step back from attempts at active negotiations and review the defense of American rights in Berlin. He concluded reflexive retrenchment to insist on rights that "are of no real value" and that "we would like to get rid of . . . if an honorable way could be found" made little sense. To Taylor, the point of the American presence in Berlin was about the safety of the people and honoring an American commitment. These were reasons to be prepared for war, but he also concluded that "our position on Germany and West Berlin should be no tougher than that of the West Germans" and "we can probably accept any settlement which they indorse." Taylor thus drew a distinction between defending concrete positions and tying American credibility to abstract principles.[59]

Taylor also distinguished between military and commercial airlift, and while he deemed resorting to the former an admission of defeat, he advised Kennedy to plan for the latter. On July 21 Taylor noted that the daily target of flying 4,000 tons of food and fuel into Berlin was attainable even if the Soviets jammed electronic devices and forced pilots to navigate by sight. Current stockpiles of fuel (with the exception of liquid fuel for transports) and food for US forces were sufficient to hold out for six months, though Taylor asked for an increase in medical supplies above the four months' worth that were in stock.[60] Six days later he advised the president to "forget about a military airlift and drop it from discussion." If push came to shove, such an operation could be assembled quickly. In that, Taylor knew the president could draw on the experience of Curtis LeMay, a veteran of the 1948 airlift and now the chief of staff of the air force. In the meantime, the United States should update plans and ready anti-jamming electronic equipment for a civil airlift, "but make no visible preparations."[61]

After the wall went up, Taylor joined McGeorge Bundy in recommending a military air transport to Berlin in case the Soviets or East Germans closed road and rail access, even unescorted if there was ground fire that would make fighter jets just another target. This would make plain for the whole world to see that US intentions were peaceful while exposing the callous aggression of the communists. Here was an as yet hypothetical game of chicken that followed plans drawn up in the 1950s; judging from past experiences, it presented a low-risk option to show resolve without inviting escalation.[62] When Kennedy instead followed the advice of Generals Norstad and Lemnitzer on automatic tit-for-tat escalation, Taylor urged clarification.[63] He deemed it necessary to fight for Berlin, but warned against creating a policy of automatic escalation that left Kennedy no choice but to forge ahead into nuclear war. Perhaps, as Taylor claimed later, he took air corridor interferences less seriously than other advisers because he had seen so much of it during his days in Berlin.[64]

Escalation from a ground forces probe appeared more likely. At the mid-August White House meeting when Kennedy decided to send reinforcements to Berlin, Taylor joined Lemnitzer in objecting to stranding another army unit in an indefensible position. They conceded that political considerations, presented by Rusk, were significant and that deploying a battle group would bolster the morale of the people in Berlin and signal resolve to the Soviets, but all it did from a military point of view was subtract from meager NATO forces in West Germany.[65] Taylor did not comment further on JCS plans for the movement of a six hundred-man battle group to West Berlin. Some safeguards were built in: the commander should await further orders if his troops were blocked at the border and he should not initiate aggressive actions even when harassed along the way. Should the Soviets or East Germans block the route, however, he was to attempt to remove the obstacle unless he deemed the opposing forces too large for any chance of success. Should the battle group come under attack, they were to return fire and proceed or retreat, again depending on the size of the enemy force. This put great responsibility in the hands of an army colonel, who had to determine whether to launch what might escalate into a wider war, yet Taylor did not register any qualms and the move on August 20 proceeded relatively smoothly.[66]

Taylor's aide Laurence Legere, his jumpmaster into Normandy on D-day, vented his frustration with the policies of Kennedy's team in a remarkably candid memorandum. "The Soviets," Legere noted, "have made us look like monkeys, weak monkeys and we can't wait to demonstrate our masochism by crawling back and begging them please to negotiate, so that we can give up something else to them." He hoped to move his boss to a hardline position and suggested Washington should only negotiate once the Soviets had torn down the wall and ended the illegal split of Berlin. In the meantime, the United States should build up its armed forces and "inform [Moscow] that we will go to war before we can forego our rights in and access to Berlin." Legere was convinced the French and West Germans would back this policy.[67]

Amid the crisis, the relationship of Kennedy and Norstad grew more tense. Norstad and Bruce Clarke, the commander of American forces in Germany, resented the arrival of retired general Lucius Clay in Berlin as the president's emissary, a move Taylor had brokered. Clay's desire to provoke a crisis so as to expose the hollowness of Soviet threats of letting East Germany control access to Berlin, led to the tank standoff on October 27–28. The Soviets backed off, but American commanders in Europe were concerned about adventurism by the Kennedy administration.[68] Just prior to the tank standoff, Kennedy had decreed that interference with access to Berlin short of a full blockade was to be countered by a platoon-sized probe. After that the United States would resort to economic embargo, maritime harassment, and U.N. action while mobilizing the armed forces. Next, a force larger than a single division was to advance to Berlin. If all else failed, Norstad was to launch nuclear weapons in "limited tactical employment . . . to achieve . . . significant tactical advantage such as preservation of the integrity of Allied forces committed, or to extend pressure toward the objective."[69] Norstad opposed the emphasis on conventional military operations and favored greater reliance on the nuclear deterrent than the Kennedy administration was willing to concede. Rusk, for example, had argued as early as that summer that the United States should build up forces to fight the Soviets in a conventional campaign of several weeks by the end of 1961.[70] When his pleas fell on deaf ears, Norstad refused to alter NATO planning.[71]

Norstad had already warned the joint chiefs that escalation from local to general war would not follow Washington's model. He argued it was essential to maintain the nuclear capability of his command and that "the Concept of Operations pertaining to aggression Less than General War establishes the proper courses of action for ACE [Allied Command Europe]. Specifically, it would be necessary, if possible, to force a pause in the continuity of military action."[72] This referred to operational plans that contained the option to fight with conventional weapons for a short period of time during which general nuclear war might still be avoided. But despite his need for more ground forces, Norstad preferred that six army divisions in the strategic reserve not be deployed to Europe, since "NATO would not agree to a 12 division assault up the *Autobahn* in an attempt to reach Berlin . . . [and] the divisions could not make the difference between success and failure in general war." Half of the divisions could be deployed within two weeks if the crisis worsened, and the remainder, as well as two marine divisions, could follow within one month.[73] Taylor disapproved. Sending up to eight divisions in one month seemed implausible and "would result in delivering units pell-mell into a strange environment which might soon become one of combat." He concluded, "It is hard for me to view this as a serious proposal."[74] In late November, Washington dropped plans to deploy additional combat divisions, as the Berlin crisis seemed to be abating, but Norstad and Kennedy no longer found common ground and in the fall of 1962 Lemnitzer took over the NATO command.[75]

The crisis in Indochina also caught up quickly with the new administration. Eisenhower alerted Kennedy in their transition conversations to the immediate problem in Laos. Throughout early 1961, the Pentagon, State Department, and White House watched forces of the recently overthrown neutralist government seize the Plaine des Jarres and the communist Pathet Lao surge in the north and east. Taylor, though not yet officially at the White House, was invited to a May 1 NSC discussion on whether the United States should intervene. Dean Rusk feared inaction in Laos would mean the beginning of the end of American alliances. Undersecretary of State Chester Bowles was convinced the United States and China would be at war by the mid-1960s, but for now it was critical to win over neutrals like India and Burma, and it was unwise to start that war over Laos. Lemnitzer reported that the chiefs were split: LeMay and Burke recommended to fight, George Decker and David Shoup were opposed. Taylor, otherwise silent, agreed with the army's chief of staff and the marine corps commandant, and President Kennedy preferred seeking a diplomatic solution.[76]

A few weeks later, Walt Rostow, then a leading advocate for greater commitment in Southeast Asia on the NSC staff, suggested that Kennedy send Taylor on a fact-finding mission. The particular issue at hand was a request from South Vietnam's President Ngo Dinh Diem to expand his army from 170,000 to 270,000 officers and men. Rostow sensed the civil war in Vietnam was reaching a new phase (and feared that its climax would coincide with the escalating crisis in Berlin), but the American commitment was not yet firm or irreversible. He assumed large-scale intervention could only occur with United Nations backing. But in the short term, Taylor, Lansdale, with his relationship to Diem and his brother Ngo Dinh Nhu, and guerrilla warfare expert Lucian Pye could investigate whether Diem's proposal was militarily sound, his operational plan fully integrated, the rural population engaged by government policies, and the proper balance of political and military measures developed.[77]

Taylor saw no need for a rushed decision. Diem had just recently been given the means to build up his forces from 150,000 to 170,000 officers and men. Taylor and the joint chiefs believed there could be some benefit to adding another 30,000 troops, but that would take over half a year and it was better to await assessments of the effectiveness of Diem's growing army. Taylor noted that the administration needed a clearer sense from the Saigon embassy, the Military Assistance and Advisory Group (MAAG) in South Vietnam, CINCPAC, and the Defense Department of what the end goal for South Vietnam's army should be. This was partly an economic calculation, but it also had become apparent that building up armed forces could not serve as an end in itself.[78] Kennedy decided not to dispatch Taylor to Vietnam, and wondered, too, whether Diem expected the United States to pay for the buildup of his army. He noted there had been agreement on jointly paying for the 20,000 men that were now being trained.[79] The Kennedy administration's caution toward Diem was soon challenged by events in Vietnam.[80]

Taylor recognized that intervention in Southeast Asia might become unavoidable. On July 26 he told Kennedy there needed to be "a rational analysis of the need for military forces in Laos and Thailand, as well as in Vietnam." There were no plans in place to halt infiltration through Laos from North to South Vietnam. The Southeast Asia Treaty Organization's Plan 5, the best military option for Laos, focused on population centers, but it did not address the border regions in the east. The Royal Laotian Army, even if supported by Hmong fighters in these remote areas, was incapable of securing Pathet Lao strongholds. Taylor concluded that the United States needed to establish "a secure base in the south of Laos, capable of covering the flank of South Vietnam and capable of providing a point of support for operations in the North [of Laos]." Doing so required support from South Vietnam and Thailand. Taylor did not say whether American forces should become directly involved, but he had concluded the security of South Vietnam was a regional issue: "To answer the question of the future size of the Vietnamese Army, we need a strategic plan for the entire Southeast Asia area." Following his penchant for structures, Taylor suggested an interdepartmental Southeast Asia task force.[81]

Two weeks later, Taylor advised Kennedy to lay the groundwork for a public relations campaign on why the United States had to step up its military efforts, either as advisers or by more direct intervention. Kennedy sensed the difficulty of crafting a compelling narrative of North Vietnamese aggression in Laos and South Vietnam. Failing that, the president noted, any "military action against Northern Vietnam will seem like aggression on our part."[82] Taylor had joined Rostow in making the argument that Hanoi was "the regional source of aggression" that destabilized Laos, South Vietnam, Cambodia, and Thailand. It was better to attack North Vietnam than to try to secure the population centers in the Mekong River valley in Laos, which offered little hope of wresting control of the border with Vietnam from the communists.[83] For Rostow, who had already advocated air strikes against North Vietnam, this may have been an extension of his World War II experience, when he served as an Office of Strategic Services analyst, identifying lucrative targets in Germany and occupied Europe for Allied airpower.[84] For Taylor, it grew from his experience in Korea.

Neither Kennedy nor Taylor stated why it was so difficult to counter Ho Chi Minh's image as a freedom fighter and champion of national unity and independence from western oppression, but it seems both men understood the short-term advantages of a closed-off dictatorship in projecting a coherent message for the world to consume. When Kennedy dispatched Averell Harriman to Paris and Geneva to work on an international framework for the neutralization of Laos and a coalition government that linked centrist and leftist factions in an uneasy partnership with the pro-American right, Taylor sensed a darker future. He sided with those in the administration who saw the Ho Chi Minh trail as essential to the National Liberation Front (NLF) and rejected State Department counterinsurgency planner Roger Hilsman's position that the South Vietnamese insurgency, though boosted by cadre from the North, was homegrown and capable of functioning entirely on local resources.[85]

That fall Washington approached a fork in the road in Vietnam, and Taylor advocated for firmer commitment to Diem after an October visit alongside Walt Rostow. Kennedy instructed Taylor to look at internal security and external defense and consider wider regional implications of the current crisis. He hoped Taylor could find ways of "urgently improving the effectiveness of South Viet-Namese forces, including the rapid provision of additional equipment, manned if necessary by U.S. personnel," and accelerated training and expansion of South Vietnam's armed forces. Kennedy added: "I should like you to evaluate what could be accomplished by the introduction of various levels of SEATO or United States forces into South Viet-Nam, including the role, composition and probable disposition of such alternative force levels." What he was looking for was not "orthodox measures," but rather "unconventional forms of assistance which we might bring to this situation if we apply all our initiative and ingenuity."[86] Taylor divided his task into seven parts: assessment of the socio-political environment, military conditions (subdivided into operations and training, logistics, and intelligence), political warfare (Rostow's domain), unconventional warfare (Lansdale's), covert activities, military assistance, and economics.[87] Taylor and Rostow met with Diem, Vice President Nguyen Ngoc Tho (who the Americans thought had a better understanding of the situation), Ambassador Frederick Nolting, MAAG commander General Lionel McGarr, CINCPAC Admiral Harry Felt, and other American and Vietnamese officials.

Their findings proved to be a step toward US military intervention. In late 1961 hawks were advocating deployment of American soldiers to Vietnam, Laos, or both. Rostow proposed airborne and seaborne infiltration missions to destroy military installations in North Vietnam, and called for 25,000 SEATO troops along South Vietnam's border with Laos. This would free American naval and air power to be deployed against North Vietnam's capital and the main port, Haiphong, and might keep the United States from getting drawn into a guerrilla war.[88] The JCS feared Rostow's plan invited defeat in detail and instead favored on-the-ground intervention in Laos, bolstered by some 20,000 American soldiers at Pleiku, in South Vietnam's Central Highlands.[89] Admiral Felt suggested a more comprehensive set of attacks that included downing North Vietnamese planes, harassing troop and supply movements from the air, attacking military installations, mining the approaches to Haiphong, launching small amphibious raids, and landing sabotage teams either by air or sea.[90]

While these proposals were not adopted, Washington braced for rough seas. State Department officials anticipated a military coup in Saigon and updated contingency plans to reflect the hope that Tho, backed by General Duong Van ("Big") Minh and other Army of the Republic of Vietnam (ARVN) leaders, might seize the presidency if Diem fell.[91] Part of the frustration stemmed from ARVN's perennially low level of aggressiveness. Its commanders seemed more interested in graft and political power than in combating enemy forces and eliminating political cadre. In Saigon, Taylor and Diem argued about the best military strategy against guerrillas: Diem asked for more troops to provide security for cities and villages, Taylor held that offensive operations were cheaper and more promising than defensive ones. He wanted South Vietnam's army to strike at guerrilla bases and infiltration trails, and he feared the deployment of US troops would make the ARVN even more passive. Diem insisted there would be no negative psychological effect from the introduction of US armed forces and that the Vietnamese people would welcome greater commitment. He asked for tactical aviation, helicopter companies, coastal patrol forces, and logistics support units to be deployed now and for combat forces at a later point. But when Taylor inquired about an integrated political, economic, psychological, and military plan, Diem only offered vague promises.[92]

Taylor concluded there was "a critical political-military situation in SVN brought on by western policy in Laos and by the continued buildup of the VC and their recent successful attacks." Add in severe floods in the Mekong delta and one could understand how low the public's confidence in Diem's government had sunk. On the military side, the ARVN lacked reliable intelligence and seemed paralyzed by "an unclear and unresponsive channel of command" and by immobile mind-sets of ground forces commanders. What resulted was a "passive, fragmented defense conceding the initiative to the enemy and leaving him free to pick the targets of attack." The political situation, too, was volatile, but there was no viable replacement for Diem. Taylor had learned from Tho and "Big" Minh that the government had little reach into the provinces and lacked qualified administrators who could connect hamlets and municipalities to the capital. Military success could alleviate the crisis in confidence, but South Vietnam's politics would remain frayed.[93] Tho implied Diem's autocratic methods were partly to blame for the lack of loyalty across the country. He also noted most people in rural areas did not favor the communists, but they were inadequately protected by government forces and lived in fear.[94]

To meet the military crisis, Taylor concluded the United States needed to help South Vietnam block infiltration from Laos into the Central Highlands, gain better intelligence, and provide helicopters and light aircraft, which would allow ARVN units to take the offensive. He also raised the possibility of inserting a "flood relief task force" of medical, engineer, signal, and transportation elements and combat troops as a "military reserve in case of heightened military crisis," a point he reiterated to Kennedy, Rusk, McNamara, and Lemnitzer in an "eyes only" cable. Taylor explained that combat forces were needed to protect logistics operations and US bases. He also warned, "Any troops coming to VN may expect to take casualties."[95] Taylor added that it was not his intent to use the flood emergency for more than a much needed assistance program. But it would be all for the better if such a force could meet the psychological need for greater American commitment without the White House having to send three divisions earmarked in the current SEATO plan.[96] Kennedy deemed these cables explosive enough to ask Taylor to keep them in strict confidence.[97]

The size of the force to be recommended was contested. Military officers on Taylor's mission peddled numbers well above 8,000, and some also wondered about Laos. Lansdale, after meeting with Nhu, reported that Vietnam's leaders were stunned by the neutralization agreement that emboldened the communists and left them in control of the border area. Like Rostow, Lansdale thought the United States needed to attack the root of the problem and launch sabotage missions against North Vietnam.[98] Taylor hoped ARVN Ranger units, up to 5,000 officers and men made airmobile by two US Army helicopter companies (412 officers and men, and forty H-21 as well as four H-13 helicopters) under MAAG command, could shore up the border if American forces acted as reserves to free up the men.[99] MAAG chief Lionel McGarr questioned whether the US Army battle group Taylor had in mind for the Mekong delta was enough. Taylor snapped back it was McGarr's job to make sure American forces were adequately protected. In February 1962 McGarr was relieved and the command upgraded: Taylor's protégé Paul Harkins arrived to lead the Military Assistance Command, Vietnam (MACV), a new operational headquarters to match the growing American presence.[100]

The Taylor-Rostow report was complete by early November. Their main conclusion inspired hope that prompt and energetic action could lead to victory without "a U.S. takeover of the war." Recommendations included more military advisers, more hardware (the planes and helicopters Diem had asked for, but also artillery pieces and ammunition), logistic support, and, on Taylor's insistence, a US military task force of some 8,000 officers and men as well as an enhanced military assistance command for the nearly 5,000 advisers after the augmentation. Taylor anticipated concerns in a November 1 cable from Saigon. He recognized the risk of an escalatory dynamic that would require even more US troops and the possibility of a wider war in Asia. However, he suggested, a small force could make a significant contribution and signal commitment to Saigon and other allies. Unless he acted now, Kennedy might be faced with the need for a much greater effort later.[101] An 8,000-man force seemed moderate. The new interdepartmental task force for Vietnam proposed setting the ceiling at 100,000 officers and men.[102] Taylor had concluded the situation could be rectified by a tolerable effort that would keep the onus of fighting enemy guerrillas to the South Vietnamese.

The main sticking points for Kennedy and his principal advisers were whether Diem was the right man to back and the proposal to send combat forces. Rusk, most State Department officials, and those in CIA, AID, and USIA invested in civic action programs deemed it too soon. Few went so far as Harriman, Bowles, and economist John Kenneth Galbraith, the ambassador to India, who argued the United States should seek a neutralization accord for Vietnam alongside that for Laos.[103] Galbraith even suggested Harriman should serve as US ambassador in Saigon.[104] Senate majority leader Mike Mansfield, a student of Southeast Asian history, noted that troop deployment smacked of colonialism and would, at best, provide a slim margin for the regime while costing the United States untold billions of dollars for many years to come. More likely, it would trigger a wider conflict that could spiral out of control and become a global and total war. Mansfield counseled shaking up the US leadership in Saigon and appointing a new ambassador who would be in charge of the entire American effort. But unless the South Vietnamese government could rouse its people, this was not a war that could be won.[105] The majority of Kennedy's advisers, on the other hand, saw Vietnam as the critical battleground for Southeast Asia. If anything, more vocal opposition came from hardliners in the Defense Department and the JCS who feared the policy to neutralize Laos in cooperation with the Soviet Union was bound to fail and that pressure on South Vietnam would increase.[106]

Taylor could gauge support and opposition at a Saturday morning meeting with senior officials the day after he submitted the report. According to notes taken by Lemnitzer's naval aide, the president, who was not present, was "instinctively against the introduction of US forces." McNamara argued that an 8,000-man force was too small to make a significant impression but that it would undoubtedly commit the United States for the long run. Why not insert a much larger force now? He assumed six to eight divisions were needed to "meet Communist escalation in SEA," but perhaps it was best to set aside that discussion and focus on the importance of the region to the United States.[107] McNamara alerted the president to his views, supported by the JCS, before the NSC met to discuss Taylor's report. He offered reassurance and revelation: the armed forces were sufficiently large to send "the ultimate possible extent," 220,000 officers and men, to Vietnam.[108]

U. Alexis Johnson, undersecretary of state for political affairs and Taylor's acquaintance since they had served in Tokyo before World War II, favored sending troops but thought they should go to the Central Highlands rather than the Mekong delta. George Ball, undersecretary of state for economic affairs, contrary to claims in his memoirs that he "strongly opposed the recommendations of the Rostow mission," argued for a larger force commitment and rejected the limitations built into Taylor's plan.[109] Rostow agreed that Hanoi had to be the ultimate target, but suggested following Taylor's "limited actions" for now while preparing the public for what was to come. Lemnitzer backed McNamara in pushing against the 8,000-man recommendation because it would result in "combat forces being thinned out in an area in which it is hard to operate. We must commit the number of troops required for success." But what exactly was success? Richard Bissell, representing the CIA, agreed with Taylor, whose recommendations "represent action, not talk" and shifted US policy away from the wrong track pursued in Laos. Taylor noted that Kennedy had asked for a plan that allowed South Vietnam "to win their own war." For him the report was a step toward carefully calibrated escalation. It represented an early example of what would later be called the strategy of graduated pressure.[110]

Kennedy accepted all recommendations except for the troop deployment. Both he and Robert Kennedy noted that, for domestic political reasons, statements on future deployments should stress that there was no firm US commitment and that any such force should be made up of SEATO contingents.[111] In practical terms, the new policy meant increasing the ARVN's airlift capacity with US army helicopters, light aircraft, transport planes, and US personnel under MAAG command. Kennedy authorized deployment of additional American officers who could engage in reconnaissance flights, photography, and "instruction in and execution of air-ground support techniques, and for special intelligence." The United States also provided small craft and personnel to help the South Vietnamese patrol their coastal and inland waters. In order to free up ARVN units for combat, the US-led training program and material support for the civil guard and local self-defense forces was greatly increased. Kennedy also adopted Taylor's recommendation of a countrywide survey of the political, social, economic, and military conditions that helped fuel the insurgency and he promised greater economic assistance and flood relief as well as top priority for counterinsurgency projects.[112]

Kennedy's decision was codified in NSAM-111 in late November. On the morning of the NSC meeting intended to confirm it, Bundy still hoped for the commitment of "about a division when needed for military action inside South Vietnam," which he deemed necessary to stave off defeat.[113] Despite his reticence to commit American combat forces, Kennedy had determined to double down on the success of Diem and the Republic of Vietnam. In return, Diem was to put South Vietnam on a wartime footing. Yet Diem remained tentative and the ARVN on edge. In late February renegade air force officers strafed the presidential palace and Diem still had not fully committed his army to the counterinsurgency effort. By then, Taylor sensed, JFK was in a fighting mood. In preparing Lemnitzer for a meeting with the president, Taylor noted that Kennedy wanted to talk about military means to secure the border between South Vietnam and Laos and to discuss US and SEATO plans to resist North Vietnamese or Chinese intervention in the wars in South Vietnam and Laos. Taylor alerted Lemnitzer that this was a good time to ask for any additional military measures he deemed necessary.[114]

In the meantime, Kennedy had moved to step up the air war. Just days after his decisions on the Taylor-Rostow report, he approved an escalation in South Vietnam's air campaign against enemy strongholds and allowed American forces to use defoliants and herbicides for route clearing and crop destruction operations. This included use of napalm and the beginnings of less discrimination between friend, foe, and those in between.[115] Rusk recommended a program controlled from Washington, cited British practice in Malaya as precedent, and thought this did not violate "any rule of international law concerning the conduct of chemical warfare."[116] Operation Ranch Hand, the air force campaign that spread chemicals over South Vietnam, started in January 1962.[117] Whether it was a conscious decision or inadvertent alignment of tactical steps, late 1961 was a moment of commitment and escalation.

JCS Chairman

In the summer of 1962, Kennedy decided to send JCS chairman Lyman Lemnitzer to Europe as NATO commander. Instead of promoting any one of the service chiefs, a group of men Kennedy distrusted, he selected Taylor, who was called back to active service, to become the next chairman. Taylor's confirmation hearings in August 1962 proceeded amicably, even though senators wondered whether the critic-as-chairman would subvert the system. The first question, framed in friendly terms by Leverett Saltonstall (R, Massachusetts), prompted Taylor to clarify his views. After all, in *The Uncertain Trumpet* he had argued that the JCS was in dire need of reform, if not revolutionary change. Taylor reassured the senators that he was not "returning, if you gentlemen confirm me, as a crusader for change, but rather to make the present system as effective as possible." He noted that a new team and changed climate at the Pentagon would allow the chiefs to thrive.[118] When Margaret Chase Smith (R, Maine) raised concerns that his close association with the president could tempt Taylor to convert the JCS chairmanship into that of a general-in-chief, he responded that he aimed to take up the same position Lemnitzer had held and that his role at the White House had not, as Smith inferred from press reports, placed him above the JCS in the chain of command. He was right about the latter, but seemed less than truthful in projecting his role as chairman and principal military adviser.[119] For now, Taylor tabled his concerns about the dysfunction of the system and worried instead about building a better relationship with McNamara, who had been "a very hard taskmaster for the Joint Chiefs of Staff." Taylor sensed that leaving the White House could reduce his influence.[120]

Taylor took up the chairmanship just in time for the Cuban Missile Crisis. John F. Kennedy presided over the swearing-in ceremony at the White House on October 1, and his brother administered the oath.[121] Soon thereafter the detection of Soviet missiles in Cuba offered a serious challenge to national security. Taylor learned of the crisis from Defense Intelligence Agency director Joseph Carroll at an October 15 dinner at Fort McNair.[122] Fortunately, Taylor recalled, the administration had found its footing since its rough start in 1961. This had been a slow process, and perhaps Taylor thought it was incomplete until he had moved to the Pentagon. Taylor concluded that the way in which Kennedy and his advisers responded in October 1962 should be the model for sound crisis management.[123] In contentious discussions of the NSC and its ad hoc Executive Committee, Taylor conveyed the JCS's call for air strikes against the missile sites and for preparations to invade Cuba. As late as October 22, the day of Kennedy's television address that made the crisis public, Taylor advocated for air strikes and a 90,000-man invasion force.[124] Yet his personal opinion was subtly different: Taylor knew military actions entailed great risk, and even though he favored air strikes and an invasion, he signaled support for Kennedy's course, a naval quarantine and pressure on Khrushchev as necessary.[125]

Taylor's primary fear was not nuclear war over Cuba, which he deemed unlikely, but Soviet actions against Berlin.[126] Perhaps Taylor's position as a cautious hawk was a reflection of his doubts about the feasibility of nuclear war. In April 1963, for example, he voiced grave concerns about the air force's preferred counterforce strategy. Taylor did not believe the Soviet missile force could be destroyed, and even if the United States had the capability to do so, it would not deter limited aggression.[127] Taylor noted that during the Cuban Missile Crisis he was simultaneously considered a hawk (on the NSC) and a dove (by the other chiefs). Taylor's colleagues objected to what they considered timidity, and they felt hamstrung by a micromanaging president who would not allow naval commanders to make on-the-spot decisions and a defense secretary who nearly came to blows with CNO Admiral George Anderson.[128] They did not accept Taylor's argument that "this was not really a military situation, but a political situation; it just happened that the pawn being used by the Government were military toys."[129] Taylor recalled his feeling of "relief and joy" at the news that the Soviets had turned their first ships around, and he credited Kennedy for the peaceful deflection of the immediate crisis.[130] Like the other principals, Taylor did not know about Soviet nuclear-armed submarines closing in on US Navy ships and how close the world had come to nuclear war.[131]

The JCS did not trust that the Cuban crisis had ended with the private deal between Kennedy and Khrushchev.[132] In mid-November, Taylor presented Kennedy with a readiness report: the armed forces were "in an optimum posture to execute CINCLANT OPLANs 312-62 (Air Attack in Cuba), and 316-62 (Invasion of Cuba)." The Strategic Air Command had put one-eighth of its planes on airborne alert and the Continental Air Defense Command had shored up readiness in the southeastern United States. Amphibious and assault forces were ready to land in Cuba at any point within seven days of the commencement of air strikes. In case Kennedy opted for war, Taylor had ordered the 5th Marine Expeditionary Brigade, some 9,000 officers and men, into the Caribbean to join the assault forces, and he proposed placing the 5th Infantry Division and one combat command of the 2nd Armored Division in ready reserve for the operation, adding over 25,000 officers and men to the follow-on forces. This posture could be maintained for seven days. If the United States lowered readiness to Defense Condition Five, which the chiefs did not recommend, that time span would increase to ten to twelve days.[133] That same day Kennedy ordered the return to regular readiness posture, closer to peace than to war. To celebrate the outcome and mark an ending to the crisis, Kennedy visited military and naval installations in Florida on November 26.[134]

Vietnam remained central to Chairman Taylor's attention. The RAND Corporation conducted one of the first substantive war games for the JCS in the summer of 1962. Taylor, still at the White House, led the enemy (Red), assisted by State Department Southeast Asia expert William H. Sullivan, who had recently served as Harriman's deputy for the Laos talks. Over the course of a week, representing ten years on the calendar, Taylor's team entangled Blue (led by CIA director John McCone) in a protracted war. Sullivan recalls that Red forces "were everywhere on the map of Indochina. We had overrun most of Laos, and we controlled the countryside of South Vietnam and the cordillera into Cambodia."[135] Taylor built his strategy on Maoist guerrilla warfare, accepting heavy casualties and waging a propaganda battle as well as a military effort. Sullivan ascribed the success of Taylor's forces to tenacity and support from the Soviet Union and China. Blue deployed half a million American troops, which led to an active protest movement at home and near isolation in world opinion. Air force generals protested: the rules of the game did not account for the effects of strategic bombing and interdiction of enemy supply lines. McCone concluded that the United States should avoid getting into a major war in Vietnam.[136] War games in April and September 1964 (Sigma I and II) seemed to confirm the outcome of the 1962 exercise: graduated pressure was bound to fail. Taylor's conclusion was different: war was unavoidable and it should be fought with a combination of airpower and South Vietnamese ground troops backed by American forces near the population centers.[137]

The battle of Ap Bac in January 1963 should have offered cause for concern, but American officials fell back into their familiar patterns of crisis management. The engagement, fought some thirty-five miles southwest of Saigon, pitted a People's Liberation Armed Forces battalion against ARVN units that were roughly four times larger and who had the overwhelming advantage in firepower, including US air support from helicopters. But ARVN forces remained poorly prepared for close combat and many officers were unwilling to accept casualties. As a consequence, ARVN troops never moved behind enemy lines to close the ring and the PLAF battalion inflicted heavy casualties and escaped intact. Many South Vietnamese soldiers remained in their armored personnel carriers and did not dismount to join the fight. Perhaps worst of all for American observers, the guerrillas shot down five of the helicopters that were deployed and damaged another nine. Only one escaped unscathed. The result was a propaganda victory for the NLF even though the South Vietnamese army held the battlefield. Lieutenant Colonel John Paul Vann, an adviser to ARVN forces, accused their officers of cowardice and called the effort a "damn miserable" performance, though there was considerable blame on flawed intelligence and decisions made by American advisers. It was unclear whether MACV fell for falsified reports. Harkins seemed unconcerned, and Army Chief of Staff Wheeler and Krulak returned to Washington with an optimistic report. Taylor and McNamara agreed that Diem and his army still offered the best path forward. Vann complained that Taylor was unwilling to meet with him when he returned to the Pentagon to raise the alarm.[138]

If Taylor and McNamara came to agree on Vietnam policy, their positions on conventional and nuclear strategy in Europe were far apart. This underscored the malleability of flexible response. Its chief architect on military issues, McNamara, could suggest as early as 1962 that NATO might not have to resort to nuclear weapons if the Soviets attacked in a limited war. Taylor reminded the defense secretary that his own assumptions on war in Europe included tactical nuclear operations. He also deemed impractical the multilateral nuclear force proposal that had arisen late in the Eisenhower administration and was kept alive under Kennedy, even though Taylor supported the idea in principle and hoped something like it could draw France into a fuller partnership. The differences were pronounced: McNamara anticipated a shift to conventional defense; Norstad and Lemnitzer did not believe Europe could be defended without resorting to nuclear war; NATO partners resisted the shift from nuclear deterrence strategy to flexible response until the mid-1960s; and Taylor thought deterrence depended on projecting strength at all levels of war.[139]

In November 1963 Taylor objected to telling Kennedy a conventional defense of Western Europe could be possible: "There is insufficient recognition of some of the critical aspects of the defense of NATO such as the shallowness of the combat theater and the decisive advantage accruing to an aggressor in concentrating his forces swiftly for the attack of a critical sector." He found it "difficult to conclude that for the present a successful defense can be effected by NATO forces without the early use of tactical nuclear weapons. I believe this to be the unanimous judgment of the military leaders of NATO, US and European, and I would be loath to have the President receive a different impression." Taylor also took issue with attempts to quantify combat effectiveness in mathematical formulae, and so did the other chiefs, except for LeMay. Taylor's main objection was that no higher math could take all variables into account. He noted "weather, terrain, proximity of the enemy, time of day, status of supply and equipment, physical condition of troops, their courage, morale, leadership" and concluded, "The most important factors, courage, morale and leadership, are not subject to physical measurement." For Taylor this meant that at best about a quarter of factors that determined victory or defeat could be quantified.[140]

Unsurprisingly, then, Taylor did not wholeheartedly embrace the quantitative analysis of the whiz kids, the group of Defense Department officials who McNamara had called to Washington from businesses and think tanks with the goal of remaking Pentagon culture. Taylor thought the goal, greater efficiency in the bureaucracy of the armed forces, was laudable, but preparing for war required a significant human element. Yet he approved of the changes to the budgeting process and, as long as the whiz kids recognized their own limitations, he knew they could be of great help in controlling what outgoing President Eisenhower had called the military-industrial complex. Taylor added scientists to that realm, noting it was very difficult for political leaders and the service chiefs to keep track of the specialized developments in science and technology.[141]

The Joint Strategic Objective Plans for 1968 and 1969 were the main strategy planning exercise for Taylor's JCS. The process started at a late December 1962 meeting at Palm Beach, where the chiefs resolved to align JSOP-68 planning with McNamara's new budgeting model. In the spring they presented their five-year force planning goals and cost estimates. Revised projections followed on October 1. The nearly year-long planning exercise yielded, in Taylor's assessment, "the most thorough [analysis] of any JSOP within my experience." The chiefs were split on army size, tactical fighter aircraft, and ICBMs. Taylor ascribed the latter to "major uncertainties" in the reliability estimate of American and Soviet missiles and the potential for new ICBM systems.[142] Taylor and Wheeler wanted to retain the current twenty-one tactical air wings, whereas LeMay and Anderson argued for twenty-five. McNamara endorsed a twenty-four-wing tactical air force by mid-1968, some 1,740 aircraft in all. On army size, McNamara sided with the majority: sixteen combat divisions were enough if reserves could be mobilized to address a secondary crisis. Wheeler had argued for eighteen, so as to be able to deploy nine additional divisions overseas in case of two simultaneous wars. The question remained how to fight in Europe. McNamara thought conventional defense of the Rhine River was possible; Taylor, considering the eastward advance of the main line of resistance to the Weser and Lech Rivers, concluded tactical nuclear forces were needed, too.[143]

The analysis for JSOP-69, in the spring of 1964, pitted LeMay's faith in interceptor planes over surface-to-air missiles against the rest of the chiefs, who concluded the proper mix of air-defense forces could lower destruction caused by a Soviet nuclear attack from a worst-case scenario of losing 48 percent of the industrial plant and up to 73 percent of the American people to a best-case one of losing less than 23 percent of the industrial plant and a third to half of the population. McNamara had little faith in missile defense and instead relied on the offensive deterrent, expressed in his notion of mutual assured destruction.[144] He again committed to twenty-four tactical air wings and sixteen active army divisions, with six of them to be added to the five American combat divisions already in Europe in case of a prolonged defense of the Weser–Lech line. There were, however, two problems with JSOP-69 on the defense of Western Europe: the base assumption, rejected by Wheeler, Marine Commandant Greene, and new CNO David McDonald, that the invasion of Europe would follow a month after a communist assault on Southeast Asia and the lack of NATO reserve divisions to reinforce the defenders. Instead of fifty-one divisions, only forty-two were projected to be available thirty days after the beginning of hostilities, including eleven US army divisions.[145]

The national security establishment saw fundamental changes in the early 1960s. The State Department's influence over foreign policy waned in the Kennedy years. Bundy and his staff as well as McNamara played a more central role.[146] The chiefs faced their own problems: they never regained Kennedy's and McNamara's trust after the Bay of Pigs. One solution was to change the leadership, and indeed, Lemnitzer found himself moved to NATO while others retired: Air Force Chief of Staff Thomas White was replaced by LeMay in June 1961 after having served his full two terms, and Shoup retired in December 1963 after four years as marine commandant, but CNO Anderson, himself only in brought to replace Burke in the summer of 1961, and Army Chief of Staff Decker did not receive reappointments. Taylor built a close relationship with McNamara throughout his tenure as chairman. He also did not have to contend with a military representative at the White House. Yet the service chiefs did not feel their positions were honestly reported and they thought Taylor represented the president.[147] He himself concluded working closely with the president had prepared him to "anticipate better than otherwise your requirements in terms of military advice."[148]

Taylor wanted to act as the primary adviser to the president and defense secretary. Reforms of the National Security Act in 1953 and 1958 had opened the door for a stronger chairman, albeit not one who could silence the service chiefs, who retained access to the president. Therefore, Taylor needed to lean more heavily on McNamara and on his rapport with Kennedy. This did not increase the functionality of the JCS and left the group in a weakened position to shape strategy where it was most needed, especially in the escalating crisis in Vietnam. Taylor violated the spirit of the law, and his actions deepened the problems in what he would later depict as a JCS system that had never worked properly. He also stepped on his colleagues' toes when he asked his assistant (a position authorized by the 1958 reorganization), Andrew Goodpaster, to preside over meetings whenever Taylor was away.[149] This went against common procedure that the most senior of the service chiefs stepped in as acting chairman—though that remained the practice when the JCS had to be represented at NSC meetings in Taylor's absence. Yet if Taylor had desired to build a new kind of JCS that ran entirely through the chairman, he surely would have picked a different assistant. Goodpaster was respected for transparency, honesty, bureaucratic and diplomatic skills, and self-reliance.[150]

Despite Taylor's influential contacts, he found himself suspended between JCS consensus against a nuclear test ban agreement and White House wishes for the limited test ban treaty in the summer of 1963. Taylor insisted he would not have supported a comprehensive test ban. Unlike his colleagues, however, he backed the limited treaty. Taylor knew the treaty was stillborn if the JCS came out against it in Senate hearings, and he applied considerable pressure on the service chiefs to present unanimous support. They compromised: the limited ban still allowed for underground testing and for research and development of detection capabilities, and support could be qualified on conditions that allowed Western observers access to testing sites in the Soviet Union. Still, this was, as the official history of the JCS noted, "an abrupt about-face" in which the chiefs endorsed Taylor's draft paper and "abandoned a position they had consistently advocated over the past two years."[151] Taylor concluded in the spring of 1964 that the treaty "had even greater importance in the psychological-political area than I thought at the time." It had "opened a door" in managing the Cold War confrontation with the Soviet Union.[152]

Taylor's tendency not to mention disagreement among the JCS at NSC meetings—some called it outright fabrication of consensus—was on display in February 1964. The discussion was on whether the president or secretary of defense should make a public statement about Oxcart, a supersonic reconnaissance plane. Proponents feared a leak would eventually reveal the existence of some thirteen planes (and planned procurement of more) and they argued it was best to explain the necessity for supersonic air lift—their cover story for the A-12 Oxcart—to the American people, especially since, as McNamara noted, the cost of development of the plane and its engine, including the acquisition of the first thirteen planes, had been cheap at about $1.5 billion. Taylor favored revealing the program and, as CIA Director McCone noted, did not point out that LeMay had dissented from the JCS majority. Consequently, the NSC decided to make public the existence of an earlier version (A-11), but keep secret the CIA model (A-12) for reconnaissance missions.[153]

Stepping away from the crises for a day, Taylor returned to West Point in June 1963 to address the graduating class. He chose to preach the creed of American ingenuity while also alerting these future army officers that they could expect to be welcomed in exotic locales but viewed as harbingers of militarism at home. "Uncle Sam has become a world-renowned soldier in spite of himself," Taylor intoned, taking his cues from Ralph Waldo Emerson's 1857 observation that the American scholar was no longer dependent on European thought. In Taylor's view, the American soldier, too, had broken away from European models. Somehow the largely isolated officers of the interwar army had managed to develop American conceptions of civil-military relations, strategy, and technology and American soldiers had found American solutions to military problems since at least the Civil War. Taylor pointed out that lieutenants could now expect to serve as advisers in Iran or as defenders of Western Europe. But at the same time "clichés about men on horseback . . . [and] trouble distinguishing what is military and what is militaristic" meant many in the nation looked askance at professional soldiers. The army already knew what some Americans had yet to learn: there was not "wholehearted acceptance at home of the continuing need for a large and respected military profession."[154]

Taylor was back in Vietnam in September 1963. In the meantime, a new ambassador, Henry Cabot Lodge Jr., and a cabal of Washington officials had offered support for a military coup. Their cable signaling US backing to plotters, sent by Harriman and Hilsman, had not been cleared by Rusk or McNamara. Taylor considered it a betrayal of the president, who was spending the weekend at Hyannis Port.[155] There appears no evidence Taylor had signed off on—or even seen—the August 24 telegram, though Hilsman later claimed Taylor, Gilpatric, and CIA Deputy Director Richard Helms had approved it.[156] The plotters did not proceed at that point, but since Kennedy—despite expressing outrage—did not rescind the telegram to Lodge, it appeared the administration was now hedging its bets. In an interview with Walter Cronkite, JFK hinted at the need for a more popular government in Saigon, and Lodge kept open channels to disaffected generals within the ARVN. Rusk, McNamara, and Taylor argued that the administration should continue to back Diem. A fact-finding mission of General Krulak and State Department official Joseph Mendenhall returned with incompatible findings: Krulak suggested the war was going well and Buddhist protests would pass; Mendenhall reported a religious civil war. Kennedy, wondering whether the two men had visited the same country, dispatched McNamara and Taylor, who suggested victory was possible by 1965 and that the 16,000 American military advisers could then be withdrawn.

Taylor remained convinced Diem was the best available leader in Saigon. He and McNamara also agreed it was necessary for Washington to force Diem on a course toward political and economic reforms. For that purpose, perhaps misreading the military and political crisis and the personality traits of Diem and Nhu, Taylor and McNamara proposed that Kennedy should make a public statement about the withdrawal of 1,000 military advisers by early 1964. This has led to significant debate among historians and White House aides, some of whom believe it was meant to be the first step of a general withdrawal and that it clearly signaled Kennedy would not have escalated the war.[157] Others are not persuaded; Taylor called the move "subtlety that backfired," aimed entirely at Diem as a firm message. When journalist Stanley Karnow asked in 1979 if Taylor thought Kennedy would have withdrawn short of victory, Taylor chuckled: "Can you imagine Jack Kennedy as a voluntary loser?"[158]

When the plotters assassinated Diem and his brother on November 1, 1963, America's involvement in Vietnam deepened. At least, that was Taylor's conclusion in hindsight: it was now much harder for anyone in Washington to say the cause was lost.[159] Taylor argued that the US government had the moral obligation to help Diem's successors, a position codified in NSAM-288 in March 1964.[160] It assumed the staying power of the United States in Vietnam, based on the assessment of Taylor and McNamara, who had visited the country shortly after the January coup that brought General Nguyen Khanh to power, much like NSAM-273 had done in early December when General Minh was in charge. Taylor believed airpower could stem the tide and called for attacks on North Vietnam. But he disagreed with the service chiefs on the scale of operations in debates that continued into the summer. At a Honolulu conference in early June, Taylor argued that the US military should commence less than all-out attacks and allow for future escalation. Air Force Chief of Staff John P. McConnell recommended "a sharp, sudden blow . . . to paralyze the enemy's capability to move his equipment around and supply people in the South." Taylor preferred what he assumed to be Lyndon Johnson's preference: "demonstrative strikes" that could be increased in intensity if initial raids did not yield the desired results.[161]

Taylor showed greater optimism than the intelligence community after Khanh's ascent to power. The latter feared that a changing cast of generals in control in Saigon made effective pacification nearly impossible and would force the United States to withdraw or go to war. Taylor thought it was possible to get back to the relative stability and counterinsurgency success of the fall of 1963 when, he believed, "we were winning in the countryside." The United States now had to do its utmost to stabilize the new regime and allow it to pursue the national pacification plan. It was also necessary to open a new front and "place pressure on Ho Chi Minh" that went beyond sabotage operations. For Taylor, it was time to turn to airpower and begin hitting select targets in North Vietnam. President Johnson seemed receptive: he noted that it was "essential to carry the fight to the enemy" and asked for the planning of operations against North Vietnam to be accelerated.[162]

There were limits to how far Taylor was willing to go. Upon returning from a trip to Vietnam with McNamara in March, Taylor rejected McCone's proposal to deploy nationalist Chinese armed forces from Taiwan in the Mekong delta, asserting that the JCS would unanimously oppose this if it were put before them. On the other hand, Taylor concurred in McNamara's recommendation to ready capabilities for retaliatory strikes against North Vietnam and cross-border operations into Laos if the intensity of attacks in the South increased.[163] As discussions on airpower deepened, it also became more apparent that Taylor underestimated the enemy's air defense capabilities and discounted the likelihood of Chinese or Soviet intervention with fighter jets as long as the strikes were small and in isolated areas, a category that he felt included Haiphong harbor. This, too, pitted him against McCone in NSC meetings.[164] In mid-1964, Lyndon Johnson favored McCone's cautious line on airpower and did not want to approve overt attacks on North Vietnam until the regime in Saigon had gained control over South Vietnam's politics.[165]

Taylor had been a problematic JCS chairman. He was too close to Kennedy, and the general's budding relationship with McNamara (as well as Kennedy's and McNamara's distrust of their generals and admirals) meant that Taylor acted more as a presidential aide than as an independent adviser. His colleagues, who felt they were being treated more like subordinates, could never rely on Taylor to convey dissenting positions or trust that they were fully informed about critical issues. Instead, Taylor reinforced Kennedy's and later Johnson's base instincts rather than challenging them when necessary. Nowhere was this more apparent than in the lead-up to full-blown American engagement in the Vietnam War. Taylor's sharpest critics, most notably Greene and LeMay, were right about the structural problems Taylor's chairmanship had introduced, or at least deepened. Their own advice, to bomb North Vietnam and take the war to the real enemy (in LeMay's case including inevitable war with China), sounded no more apt.[166] Taylor favored airpower, too, albeit within the boundaries of limited war. These tensions remained on display after the JCS chairman became ambassador to South Vietnam. Earle Wheeler, Taylor's successor as JCS chairman, could not restore the JCS to a more independent and trusted position in the Pentagon or the administration.

5

Architect of the Vietnam War

Ambassador

Taylor returned to Vietnam in July 1964 to take charge of the embassy and the military assistance effort. Contrary to his fears when he was offered an ambassadorship to France, in 1961, this did not "cost me my wife who had always said she would not be an ambassador's wife any place."[1] Taylor believed the most important goals were to buy time for the regime in Saigon to stabilize and to enact a joint South Vietnamese-American counterinsurgency program. He later claimed he had reached these conclusions in the fall of 1961 and that presidents Kennedy and Johnson held the same views.[2] Throughout the Vietnam War, Taylor stuck to the observation that devising a strategy was not hard, yet it was impossible to execute it in a time span tolerable to the American people. If the United States failed in Vietnam, Taylor feared, China would act more aggressively in the Far East and fresh insurgencies would erupt across Asia and Africa.[3]

President Johnson made a public show of confidence in Taylor at the swearing in ceremony at the White House. Johnson, in a letter prepared by Taylor, also stressed that the ambassador's "responsibility includes the whole military effort in South Vietnam and authorizes the degree of command and control that you deem appropriate."[4] Taylor thus ranked above William Westmoreland, the newly installed commander of MACV, and he bore heavy responsibility for how the United States responded to the communists' 1964–65 offensive. That Lyndon Johnson had selected a general as ambassador worried editors of the *New Republic*, who considered the president's Vietnam policy deeply flawed and saw Taylor as the architect of plans to bomb North Vietnam, though they chose not to reveal their position until after LBJ had been elected that November.[5]

On paper Taylor was a sound choice. He knew the actors and the context of the war in Vietnam and he could assert his authority over MACV. He also had experience in handling a prickly ally, Syngman Rhee, and he had led efforts to help Germans and Koreans recover from war. By sending Taylor, Lyndon Johnson projected the desire for a tough stance and increased the likelihood of escalation. U. Alexis Johnson went as Taylor's right-hand man, even though Rusk, over customary scotch and soda, had offered him an ambassadorship in his own right.[6] William Sullivan, who worked briefly as Taylor's chief of staff before moving as ambassador to Laos, thought the president picked Taylor because he understood the civilian and military integration required in a limited war. Sending an executive agent of Taylor's stature, Sullivan concluded, allowed LBJ to focus on his Great Society project.[7] Sending the JCS chairman and an undersecretary of state to an embassy underscored the seriousness of the crisis.[8] The task, as Rostow noted, was infinitely complex: Taylor had to "try, simultaneously, to manage a war and to bring along the beginnings of democracy in South Vietnam. D-day was sure easier."[9]

Few ambassadors get to shape strategy. But Taylor not only had been put in charge of all military and civilian efforts, he also had a back channel to the White House due to the president's request to receive a weekly personal report. This was Taylor's vehicle to advocate for a better balance between pacification and war fighting.[10] Soon he would return to advocating air strikes in Laos and North Vietnam. Yet Taylor was also cautious. He provided a prophetic statement in April 1964 on why he had opposed sending American forces to Laos in 1961: "It was quite clear that we should not get in the position of fighting for a country that wouldn't fight for itself."[11] Even if the ARVN fought well, Taylor and those at the embassy considering pacification knew that unless Saigon was "able to establish civil government behind the clearing troops, nothing is accomplished by sweeps except ARVN casualties and losses of weapons, and some inconvenience to the VC." Americans could not win the war for the South Vietnamese, and there was no military path to victory.[12]

The weakness of Khanh's regime was on display in the summer of 1964. This forced Taylor to amend his initial assessment: instead of building from political stability toward pacification, securing population centers and hamlets came to the foreground; and instead of focusing on political and military operations in South Vietnam, Taylor increasingly pondered the right time for an air campaign against the North and cross-border actions in Laos. Both could bolster morale in the South and slow

North Vietnamese infiltration along the Ho Chi Minh trail, but Taylor's real target was the political will of the leadership in Hanoi, of which Taylor knew very little. Just then North Vietnam's leaders exploited the political weakness in Saigon, initiating a substantial military offensive—still applying guerrilla tactics—in the fall and winter of 1964. They assumed a vast uprising would topple the regime in Saigon as peasants and some urbanites rallied behind the NLF, which could then establish a new government before the arrival of US ground forces. The events that led to the cataclysmic Vietnam War were thus the result of misreadings in Washington and Hanoi.[13]

Khanh tried to butter up Taylor: South Vietnam's people liked recent American appointments and morale was improving. Taylor reassured Khanh of US support and told him of a new body at the embassy, a mission council composed of the heads of civilian agencies, the MACV commander, and the ambassador himself, where Taylor intended to coordinate all American assistance projects and the military advisory effort. Taylor had alluded to this at the swearing in ceremony: U. Alexis Johnson was his right hand and Westmoreland his left.[14] Khanh wanted more active American participation in the military and pacification campaigns. Taylor suggested Saigon deploy more troops to hold areas that the ARVN had cleared. The manpower requirements could be met by relying more heavily on paramilitary forces. He then inquired about tensions between religious group, recruitment for government and military service, and desertion rates. Khanh sounded upbeat but acknowledged that Buddhist leader Thich Tri Quang was hard to control when he was among his followers in Hue. The conversation closed on an ominous note: Khanh pointed at the difficult balance between independence and partnership, and Taylor "reminded him of the saying about necessity to hang together or hang separately."[15]

Diplomatic niceties aside, Khanh distrusted Taylor. He feared the ambassador favored "Big" Minh, the lead plotter against Diem, whom Khanh had moved into the largely symbolic position of chief of state. Moreover, Khanh disliked the ambassador's authoritarian style that also chafed CIA operatives in Saigon and Langley, albeit for different reasons. Taylor, in turn, saw Khanh as a weak leader, overly invested in political intrigue and too eager to project the message of attacking North Vietnam.[16] By the end of the summer, tensions ran so high that the South Vietnamese leader presented a list of grievances to his CIA confidant Luc Conein, who was then promptly sent home by Ambassador Taylor.[17]

American assessments of the situation in South Vietnam in the summer of 1964 varied. Based primarily on public opinion in Binh Hoa province, the USIA concluded that the rural population preferred Khanh's government to the NLF. Their most common aspirations were government credit, material aid, hospitals, schools, irrigation projects, and assistance for agricultural development. Even the much-maligned strategic hamlet program remained viable if security was provided, government officials were not corrupt, resettlement costs were paid, and free elections were held. Overall, "the overwhelming need is for reassurances of physical security."[18] Yet the PLAF posed a mounting threat, with over nine hundred military attacks, ambushes, bombings, sabotages, and terror attacks in one week in July, the highest number since the fall of 1963, and the government failing to extend control outside of the major cities.[19] The best the United States could hope for, thought Taylor, Rusk, McNamara, and Wheeler, was for Khanh to "maintain order, keep the pacification program ticking (but not progressing markedly), and give the appearance of a valid government." US options were defined by holding up the regime and boosting morale in the South, which topped military considerations of how best to combat the enemy.[20]

Taylor reported that the PLAF was growing in strength and getting bolder. US officials estimated their strength at 23,000 to 34,000 full-time fighters. Attacks in the northern part of the country occurred more frequently. Taylor and Westmoreland concluded that MACV needed more men: 21,000 by the end of the year, with another 1,000 to be added by the spring of 1965.[21] Taylor also described recent surprise attacks against ARVN Special Forces camps in I Corps, which defended the northernmost military region, that showed the enemy had reliable intelligence while government forces lacked support from the local people. In an assault on one ARVN outpost by two PLAF battalions on July 11 and 12 and in the subsequent ambush of relief forces (five poorly trained militia companies of the Hoa Hao sect), PLAF forces displayed foresight, skill, and tenacity. Taylor speculated that these attacks aimed to prevent road-building projects from reaching into the interior and to spoil the success of pacification in coastal areas south of the demilitarized zone.[22]

With the quality of the PLAF rising, the ARVN needed to adjust their tactics. But more than just responding to enemy actions, South Vietnam required a stronger effort in the implementation of its pacification program. Taylor recommended adding advisors to ARVN battalions, increasing American presence in critical districts, and beefing up Special Forces in the Central Highlands that could "carry on an effective offensive counterguerrilla program—something we have done only to a limited degree in the past."²³ Taylor estimated the minimum required augmentation at some 2,100 support personnel, an additional 700 to 900 officers and men assigned to South Vietnamese battalions or district headquarters, and nearly 600 more to serve with the Special Forces. This nearly doubled the number of American advisers to lower-echelon units likely to see combat. Michael Forrestal, the NSC staff officer for Southeast Asia, suggested a White House announcement about the anticipated increase in American casualties so as to preempt a backlash in public opinion.²⁴

The JCS recommended more severe measures. They proposed missions by unmarked American aircraft—not to be flown by US crews—against military targets in North Vietnam, including the mining of rivers and ports to punish Hanoi. The chiefs also raised the possibility of air and cross-border ground operations into Laos up to battalion strength—including American advisers—to interdict traffic on the Ho Chi Minh trail.²⁵ CIA director John McCone was concerned about Hanoi's response to such an escalation and reiterated that it could lead to the introduction of Soviet- or Chinese-made fighter jets. Moving into Laos was less likely to trigger additional escalation.²⁶ Ambassador Leonard Unger rejected air strikes in Laos, arguing they would not do much good in slowing down resupplies for the PLAF, but would unsettle the country's unsteady politics. Taylor, too, advised caution. He needed time to develop a coordinated Vietnamese-American air offensive, particularly since Khanh had embarked on a "March North" propaganda campaign and seemed intent on all-out war.²⁷

Taylor came to question "the rationality and good sense of a dangerous opponent" when North Vietnamese patrol boats attacked the American destroyer USS *Maddox* in the Tonkin Gulf on August 2. But while he thought Hanoi had gravely miscalculated, he also lamented the lack of an American response to the attack. Taylor pointedly rejected as inadequate the White House statement that the attack had been repelled and operations off North Vietnam's shores were to continue; he believed leaders in Saigon—as well as in Hanoi—would see this as a sign of weakness. At minimum, Washington should announce that North Vietnamese patrol boats found in international waters would henceforth be attacked, the United States would conduct regular surveillance flights in North Vietnam's air space, and harbors used by patrol boats would be mined.²⁸

The ambassador applauded retaliatory air strikes after the phantom August 4 attacks on *Maddox* and *C. Turner Joy*. Taylor saw American credibility at stake in Vietnam and the entire region. He also felt that the air strikes boosted morale in Saigon. He did not seem to ponder the implications of Hanoi's "impudent actions" that reminded him of "Khrushchev's rashness in introducing missiles into Cuba" for a rational-actor limited-war strategy.[29] Taylor pushed for quick resumption of infiltration and sabotage operations under Operation Plan 34-A. He hoped small teams of South Vietnamese, who arrived by air or sea, could destabilize the local economy and politics in the DRV.[30] Later Taylor claimed he did not think 34-A operations amounted to much: "These were little patrol boats going up and firing a few mortar shells . . . I had such a low regard for the quality of 34-A."[31] Taylor recognized the concept: as chairman of the Special Group and later the JCS he had approved comparable operations against Cuba so as to keep the armed forces on alert and convey to the people there were groups that resisted the regime.[32]

Taylor, supported by McCone, thought a sustained air war against North Vietnam should follow once the South Vietnamese government could defend its homeland. As long as politics in Saigon were volatile, air attacks on North Vietnam seemed too dangerous. For now, the United States should maintain destroyer patrols and conduct aerial sweeps over international waters in the Tonkin Gulf. But Taylor did push for aircraft to begin "US armed reconnaissance missions in Laos panhandle, progressively attacking most clearly identified infiltration installations . . . to strike specified fixed targets, to attack road traffic in specified areas and to conduct fire-suppressive attacks with appropriate ordnance against antiaircraft defenses as needed." Once conditions suggested improved pacification around Saigon and joint planning with South Vietnam's armed forces was complete, probably by early 1965, the United States should begin attacking North Vietnam.[33]

Laos held a key to success in South Vietnam, and Taylor opposed a renewed effort at negotiations that could allow the communist Pathet Lao greater control along the border.[34] Yet in his August 10 report to the president, Taylor indicated grounds for optimism. Military advisers saw hopeful signs across South Vietnam. The communists knew they could not win on the battlefield and thus conducted a terror campaign with the goals of neutralization akin to the Laos agreement and coalition government. Saigon, however, remained weak, and while Khanh had defused some of the tensions between Buddhists and Catholics, most South Vietnamese did not trust in his leadership. Security was the critical issue: if Saigon projected strength, the people of South Vietnam would follow. Taylor lauded the buildup of regular and paramilitary forces to close to half a million officers and men, and noted the declining desertion rate—half of what it had been in the spring—and improving morale in the army. He estimated that the share of the population under government control could be increased by year's end to 47 percent, with 39 percent contested and 14 percent under NLF control.[35]

The embassy now had four main objectives. Politically, it was necessary to bolster Khanh's government; in pacification, the main efforts should focus on strategically important areas around Saigon following the Hop Tac Plan devised by the regime, MACV, and the embassy, but the campaign also needed to be improved nation-wide and "show-window" social and economic projects in secure urban and rural areas should attract the population. Militarily, the United States likely needed to strike North Vietnam in the coming year. In public relations, it was crucial to keep the American people informed of policies and progress in Vietnam.[36] In the coming months the US effort should focus on denying North Vietnamese infiltration and developing strength for "deliberate escalation of pressure against North Vietnam" come January. To meet a North Vietnamese offensive, three ARVN divisions could be deployed to I Corps once the Saigon area was secure. In the short term, American and Vietnamese armed forces should recommence 34-A operations and naval patrols in the Tonkin Gulf, launch U-2 reconnaissance flights over North Vietnam, and prepare operations in Laos.[37]

Khanh wanted to expand the war more aggressively. The communists were experts at guerrilla warfare, held the people and armed forces of South Vietnam hostage, and could not be beat at their own game. He concluded, "We must turn to the kind of conventional military operations which we understand and not continue to try to fight their kind of war which is new to us." In a conversation with General Alden Sibley, who had been MAAG logistics chief in Vietnam in 1960–61, Khanh suggested there was no cause for concern about Chinese intervention and that the people of North Vietnam were ready for change. Khanh could unify the country. In an aside, he noted that Ho Chi Minh was "too old to come to the office and that the real power is held by several of his principal lieutenants, two of whom are Moscow oriented communists rather than Peking sympathizers." Though Sibley reported this to Westmoreland and Taylor, there were no signs Khanh's insight was taken seriously.[38]

Where Taylor feared the US response to the Tonkin Gulf attack was perceived as weak, the JCS believed reprisal air strikes (Operation Pierce Arrow) showed resolve and that the United States had recovered the initiative.[39] Admiral Sharp, on the other hand, told Westmoreland of his "concern over the vulnerability to possible VC attack of heavy concentrations of recently deployed US aircraft on airfields such as Bien Hoa,

Tan Son Nhut, and Danang." He worried that PLAF fighters would destroy planes and cause significant psychological damage. Sharp wondered whether ARVN forces could secure US airfields and bases and keep insurgents from launching mortar attacks.[40] McGeorge Bundy, meanwhile, suspected the US military was not giving priority to Vietnam. He also worried about China, which was getting close to testing its first atomic bomb and might act more aggressively thereafter.[41]

Taylor was optimistic about joint American and Vietnamese planning and endorsed plans for operations in Laos. Soon, he reported US air force pilots had been flying missions—not disclosed even to MAAG and MACV commanders—against NLF positions at the border since late 1961 instead of merely monitoring the performance of their Vietnamese trainees.[42] In time, two or three ARVN battalions might conduct reconnaissance and raids in Laos and it seemed prudent to allow advisers to cross the border with those units, partly to relieve "some of the steam building up in local military." Taylor noted that no more than two battalions should be deployed at a time and that MACV should have full control over air and ground operations. Westmoreland expected any further US escalation to be met by joint PLAF and PAVN attacks in I Corps. This required rapid reaction capacity, ideally by keeping a US marine battalion offshore at Danang, with additional forces on alert in Okinawa. Taylor made clear he did not think the United States should deploy combat units—only marines to secure American bases. Finally, on air strikes in North Vietnam, the arrival of MiG fighters made use of South Vietnamese propeller planes risky, but Taylor thought it was still possible to find relatively safe targets for them while American fighters and bombers could operate more freely.[43]

The JCS deemed Taylor's time line for enhanced American operations overly cautious. They concluded that by the end of the year the South Vietnamese government would be on the brink of collapse. Quick and resolute action was needed. The chiefs, noting that the United States was "already deeply involved," held that "only significantly stronger military pressures on the DRV are likely to provide the relief and psychological boost necessary for attainment of the requisite governmental stability and viability." They also advised "direct and forceful actions," notably Lao, South Vietnamese, and Thai operations in the Laotian panhandle, pursuit of PLAF forces into Cambodia, and air strikes in North Vietnam.[44] The latter was pressing since "accelerated and forceful action . . . is essential to prevent a complete collapse of the US position in Southeast Asia."[45]

McGeorge Bundy had not yet joined the ranks of the air-war hawks.

Instead he reflected on the possibility of stepping up the land war, where "a couple of brigade-size units put in to do specific jobs about six weeks from now might be good medicine everywhere." He told Lyndon Johnson that McNamara was "very strongly against" sending marines to guard US installations "for reasons that are not clear to me." Bundy was prepared to go further: "A still more drastic possibility which no one is discussing is the use of substantial US armed forces in operations against the Viet Cong. I myself believe that before we let this country go we should have a hard look at this grim alternative, and I do not at all think that it is a repetition of Korea."[46] Neither Bundy nor Johnson raised the upcoming presidential election, but it is an indication of the crisis in Vietnam that the national security adviser pondered a greater effort on the ground for the fall of 1964.

By early September, Taylor conceded there was little hope for stability in Saigon. In just over two weeks in August, Khanh had been forced out and Minh had ceded the office of chief of state to a military council, only for both antagonists to return to their old positions in the first days of September. Conflicts between Buddhists and Catholics, southern nationalists and neutralists, and other political groups and military factions had deepened to the point that some in Washington wondered whether the ambassador could leave Saigon to participate in strategy review meetings at the White House. Taylor did participate. In the embassy report for September he called for attacks on North Vietnam, beginning on December 1. "Before initiating these pressures," he advised, "US and allied military forces would be positioned to meet possible Chicom/DRV reaction. Escalating actions would then begin, taking the form of any desired combination of attacks on Lao infiltration routes and/or on targets of appropriate categories in DRV." Until then, South Vietnamese forces should step up sabotage operations in the North and conduct "modest crossborder operations into Laos." Americans in South Vietnam should help "get going some kind of government worthy of the name while shoring up morale and holding enemy activities in check." Taylor concluded, "We see no quick and sure way to discharge our obligations honorably in this part of the world. This forecast is fairly grim but the alternatives are more repugnant. We feel that we should take the offensive generally along the lines recommended herein and play for the international breaks."[47]

Westmoreland added an equally concerning assessment. He feared the armed forces of South Vietnam were beginning to come apart. The most important countermeasure was to protect officers from political interference and retributions that had rocked the army in late August and early September. If civil-military relations could be repaired, Westmoreland hoped, the military picture was bound to improve. The army had a steady influx of recruits, lower desertion rates, better training and equipment, and greater tactical proficiency, partly due to the influx of American advisers at the battalion level. On the other hand, junior officers and NCOs needed more training, the government and the military lacked capacity to find and process sufficient numbers of recruits for more ambitious operations in the future, the size and role of paramilitary forces needed further definition, it was unclear how Special Forces could best be utilized, the agencies involved in the pacification process lacked close coordination, and South Vietnamese and American armed forces still had no authority to attack infiltration routes in Laos.[48]

Bundy summed up the consensus of the meetings in Washington on September 7 and 8. In the coming weeks American diplomats and generals needed to focus on "thickening the thin fabric of the Khanh government" and think more carefully about how to increase pressure on Hanoi. Specific points followed Taylor's recommendation: resumption of naval patrols and 34-A operations in North Vietnam, and authorization of South Vietnamese attacks and Royal Lao air force strikes in the panhandle of Laos. Finally, the US military should be prepared to retaliate in case of attacks on American installations. Bundy noted that it made little sense to engage in provocative actions, such as running naval patrols closer to the coastline, "but by early October, however, we may recommend such actions." Drawing North Vietnam more openly into the war seemed only a matter of time, but timing hinged on political progress in Saigon.[49]

The critical question was whether the situation in Vietnam had deteriorated so far that air strikes against the North were necessary right away. The air force chief of staff and marine corps commandant thought so, but others on the JCS and McCone agreed with Taylor, who wanted to wait until South Vietnam's government had attained a modicum of stability and asked for yet more advisers. Rusk added that playing for time might afford breaks from deepening divisions in the Sino-Soviet bloc, which could limit military options for Hanoi and Beijing. McCone cautioned that he saw signs of a tiring population in the South that was beginning to display anti-American traits. Perhaps, Taylor and Rusk mused, Khanh had been chastened by the political crisis and might develop a keener sense of responsibility to his people in the coming weeks. The conversation did not turn to a substantial assessment of North Vietnamese motivations.[50]

The result of the strategy review was codified in National Security Action Memorandum 314. It green-lighted the resumption of 34-A operations and naval patrols by up to three destroyers in the Tonkin Gulf, albeit far outside of the twelve-mile zone. The United States opted to begin serious talks with the Laotian government on how to coordinate air strikes, American aerial reconnaissance, and future ARVN ground operations in Laos. American forces were put on alert to respond to communist attacks on US bases in South Vietnam. Lyndon Johnson stressed the importance of pacification and included the reminder that military actions should not come at the expense of socio-economic projects. "Larger decisions" loomed in the background, but for now the critical issue was strengthening the GVN.[51] As it was, US and North Vietnamese escalation was progressing on parallel lines in the fall of 1964.

Taylor wasted no time in trying to turn what he had learned in Washington in his favor. At a meeting in Saigon on September 11 with the ambassadors to Thailand and Laos, the Saigon embassy pushed for cross-border operations. U. Alexis Johnson, with Taylor waiting out bad weather in Honolulu, argued for hard-hitting strikes by both US and Vietnamese forces. He advocated a twelve-day air campaign that could significantly reduce the communists' ability to move troops into South Vietnam. ARVN units should be permitted to pursue insurgent forces into Laos, capture enemy stocks, and dismantle supply points. Laos and Thailand should offer the veneer of participation by allowing American planes to depart from Thai air bases and by cooperation of the Royal Lao army and air force in the border areas of northern and western Laos. The ambassadors compromised: the US air force could destroy five bridges in Laos, but the Lao air force should take on the remaining important targets. Johnson hoped South Vietnamese ground forces could operate along Route 9 in Laos. Penetration raids of less than twenty kilometers conducted by ARVN companies did not require prior authorization from the Lao government.[52] For now, such plans did not proceed, but they indicated the degree of concern of American commanders and diplomats in Indochina.

Chronic instability in Saigon became acute with a failed September 13 coup attempt. Since Taylor assumed military operations had to be rooted in a stable government, he spent most of his time trying to shore up Khanh's tenuous hold on power and began to ponder how the United States could carry more of the burden without taking over the war. Taylor's depiction of events in mid-October highlighted the confused state of Saigon politics: "formation of a new government and impasse between

High National Council and Khanh. Difficulties of HNC in draft plan for new government. Issue of Minh as Chief of State with Gaullist-like powers. Fear of Khanh and his unwillingness to step down as Prime Minister. Khanh's desire for Armed Forces to report directly to Chief of State (not Minh). U.S. efforts to modify role of Chief of State." The immediate crisis was defused on October 26 when Khanh resigned (but remained commander-in-chief of the armed forces), seventy-one year-old Phan Khac Suu was appointed chief of state, and former mayor of Saigon Tran Van Huong was named prime minister. This was not a long-term solution, as factionalism and divides between civilian leadership and the armed forces remained.[53] Taylor later told Robert Komer, when Huong was again under consideration to serve as prime minister, that while he was "brave and determined, he moved slowly at best about the government's business."[54]

The Hawk: Calling in Airpower

Throughout the fall Westmoreland and Taylor grew increasingly concerned and recommended a more muscular military effort. Yet neither called for American combat ground forces and MACV doubted the utility of airpower beyond operations against staging areas in Laos and South Vietnam. Taylor, on the other hand, had long believed the United States had to strike North Vietnam at some point. At a meeting of the joint chiefs with Lyndon Johnson ahead of a Taylor-McNamara trip to Vietnam in March 1964, Chairman Taylor had argued for an expanded air campaign. Wallace Greene registered disagreement with Taylor's preference for gradually increased pressure. He believed the communists would respond with an escalation of their own once US planes started bombing North Vietnam, and he favored unrestrained air strikes from the outset. Yet he also warned "this would result in a major campaign, smaller perhaps, but similar to that which had taken place in Korea, and that there was risk of a possible escalation into another world war." Greene may have been right and Johnson was telling Taylor not to return with recommendations to escalate.[55] But just four months later, Johnson put Taylor in charge of US operations in Vietnam.

When a mortar attack on the American base at Bien Hoa on November 1 killed four US servicemen and hit twenty-seven aircraft, Taylor called for retaliatory air strikes against North Vietnam. President Johnson instead asked about sending ground forces, a step neither Taylor nor

Westmoreland were prepared to recommend.[56] In a phone conversation with the president on November 25, Taylor again lobbied for air strikes against targets in North Vietnam and Laos. The call had been prompted by Taylor's desire to disavow newspaper reports that he was considering resigning his post if Johnson did not act on his recommendations at an upcoming meeting. For his part, Johnson expressed frustration with a *New York Times* story that featured Taylor's recommended strategy. Taylor admitted to background conversations with reporters but reassured the president he had not given interviews on the record.[57]

Taylor had concluded it was time to change the dynamic in Vietnam. He thought the United States might have to settle for a government that "can speak for and to its people, can maintain law and order in the principal cities, can provide local protection for the vital military bases and installations, can raise and support Armed Forces, and can gear its efforts to those of the United States." Once the political context was more stable, Saigon and the United States would launch a counterinsurgency offensive. At that point the US military should "persuade or force the DRV to stop its aid to the Viet-Cong and to use its directive powers to make the Viet-Cong desist from their efforts to overthrow the government of South Viet-Nam." Meanwhile, the Johnson administration should permit increased clandestine operations in Laos and North Vietnam, including reprisal bombings and continued infiltration by South Vietnamese commandos. But while this might boost morale in the South, only an expanded American war effort could uproot communist strength and erode the resolve of North Vietnam's leaders.[58]

Publicly, Taylor still insisted that a stable government in Saigon was a precondition for an expanded war, but privately he suggested otherwise. He told Rusk, "We do not expect such a government for three to four months. Do we withhold all action against the DRV (except those of the morale-sustaining type) until we get this minimum government? What if we never get it?" He favored "going against the North anyway."[59] Yet Taylor rejected JCS recommendations to take on a greater share of the war in South Vietnam, as well as to pursue PLAF fighters into Cambodia. This violated "the principle that the Vietnamese fight their own war in SVN" and there was no reason to expect greater success in finding and fixing enemy units in Cambodia. For Taylor, the only path to ending the war was to get Hanoi "to wind up the VC insurgency on terms satisfactory to us and our SVN allies."[60] Doing so required carefully calibrated pressure, but Lyndon Johnson should not overreact to the attack at Bien Hoa and send combat battalions.[61]

Westmoreland read Taylor's recommendations with growing anxiety. In late November he alerted JCS chairman Earle Wheeler to a vital area of disagreement: "We must assure ourselves that GVN is established on reasonably firm political, military and psychological base before we risk the great strains that may be incurred by vigorous external operations." He was more optimistic than Taylor and Alexis Johnson, who "tend to think that we can't wait for these conditions to develop and that present government requires morale boost by way of immediate dramatic action well beyond pattern of present policy. I feel that there is good prospect of things holding together until March or April." By then ARVN should be in much better shape to deal with enemy attacks that would result from a US air campaign. Neither Taylor nor Westmoreland had any desire to take over the ground war, but Taylor seemed prepared to take greater risks because he assessed the political situation as more desperate.[62]

Saigon was again in the throes of a crisis brought on by public demonstrations and increasing doubt about the military's—or at least Khanh's—loyalty to Tran Van Huong. The opening line of Taylor's report to Lyndon Johnson did not inspire confidence: "Huong's government has survived its second week."[63] Upheaval in Saigon notwithstanding, Taylor traveled to Washington for the crucial meetings about the air war with a plan in hand. Despite a precipitous decline in PLAF attacks in October and November, putting those months below the average for 1964, Taylor's assessment was bleak: the counterinsurgency program was under serious assault across the country, and in the northern provinces the communist offensive posed an immediate threat.[64] The north could soon be cut off from the capital region, as the PLAF was gaining control of Quang Ngai and Binh Dinh provinces from the highlands to the coast. Taylor, who was in the dark about the extent and intent of North Vietnam's effort, feared that while the ARVN had made great strides, the continued weakness of the regime in Saigon made successful pacification ever more unlikely.[65]

Embassy officials also considered other structural problems. Taylor had learned in mid-October that the fundamental flaw in South Vietnam's pacification program was the government's neglect of the national police, which stood at well below 30,000 men instead of the 71,000 that were deemed necessary. The problem, as the US Operations Mission chief noted, was that without sufficient police forces, the link between holding and building in the "clear, hold, and build" approach to counterinsurgency was severed. If South Vietnam needed to counter even small-scale acts of terrorism by diverting the ARVN from the fight against enemy main units, there was "little point in pressing other components of pacification."⁶⁶ In Washington, Taylor did not dwell on that weakness and instead focused on North Vietnam's role in the war and on the need to attack infiltration routes in Laos.

In South Vietnam's northern provinces that were now under assault, the PLAF had hardly been a noticeable presence just a year prior. Some of their recent success, Taylor noted, could be ascribed to South Vietnamese weakness, but most of it rested on DRV support for the insurgency and the ability of the NLF to replace even heavy losses. Taylor admitted that intelligence data and military reports provided no compelling explanation of how the communists consistently found large numbers of recruits—he concluded coercion alone did not suffice—and why their morale remained high. "If, as the evidence shows, we are playing a losing game in South Viet-Nam," Taylor warned, "it is high time we change and find a better way." That required the Americans and their Vietnamese allies to "establish an adequate government in SVN; second, improve the conduct of the counterinsurgency campaign; and, finally, persuade or force the DRV to stop its aid to the Viet-Cong and to use its directive powers to make the Viet-Cong desist from their efforts to overthrow the government." Lyndon Johnson had to decide to widen the war or accept the loss of South Vietnam. One thing was clear, however: pacification ultimately depended on the strength of the Saigon government.⁶⁷

The December 1 White House meeting led to an expanded war effort. The goals remained unchanged: to get Hanoi out of the South and return to the 1962 agreement for Laos. To meet these objectives, Lyndon Johnson and his advisers resolved to embark on a thirty-day air campaign that could be extended as initial results warranted. In addition to seeking closer coordination with the South Vietnamese and Laotian governments and diplomatic efforts to gain support from Great Britain, Australia, New Zealand, Thailand, and the Philippines, the White House authorized intensified military actions. This was the beginning of the US air war in Laos. Johnson also authorized joint American and South Vietnamese reprisal air strikes for PLAF attacks, with targets, including troop concentrations, supply depots, airfields, ports, and naval facilities, restricted to areas south of the 19th parallel in North Vietnam. Washington held off on deploying more air assets or moving destroyers to patrol stations in the Tonkin Gulf. These and other steps could be taken after the first thirty days.⁶⁸

The president instructed Taylor to press Saigon for more aggressive counterinsurgency operations. At least, the government should be able to bring ARVN and militia forces to authorized manpower levels, conduct successful military operations and civic action programs in the capital region, strengthen the police, grant more authority to provincial governors, and show a stronger presence in the countryside.[69] Johnson also wanted his ambassador, who he suspected of pushing for a more aggressive strategy via the press, kept on a shorter leash. McGeorge Bundy told his brother William, then the assistant secretary of state for Far Eastern affairs, that he had to supervise Taylor more closely. McGeorge, who did not think Taylor fully understood the nature of the war and remained lukewarm about his appointment as ambassador, noted the president wanted regular updates of "what is being said to other countries" and "what Max is saying in Saigon." Lest William Bundy should feel uncomfortable, his brother suggested he could route reports through Rusk.[70]

Taylor's frustrations found more private expression. The Taylors foreshadowed the difficulties with waging the kind of war that was coming in their holiday letter: "I try to attend the funeral services here of our lads who have been killed on duty, and these occasions are both frequent and sad. So frustrating not to be able to distinguish friend from foe, even in the streets, and the ragged workman pushing a load of charcoal next to you can easily have a grenade in his pants pocket. The commies infiltrate easily, too, and unfortunately do not look any different from the rest of the natives. The job they did preparing the way for the treacherous raid on the Bien Hoa airfield a short time ago was murderous. We cross fingers and hope and pray that the new government will prove to be a strong one."[71] This featured the main elements of what equally haunted Westmoreland and, later, Creighton Abrams: the inability to know who was an enemy, communist infiltration at all levels of government and facets of life, the expertise in guerrilla operations that the enemy already exhibited, and the general weakness of South Vietnam's government.

Taylor counted on a strategy of "controlled escalation." At first, he argued, American pilots might use airpower to limit infiltration by attacking "staging areas, training facilities, communications centers and the like." But Taylor did not assume an anti-infiltration campaign would sufficiently weaken the NLF's or North Vietnam's resolve. He concluded "this kind of attack could extend to the destruction of all important fixed targets in North Viet-Nam and to the interdiction of movement on all lines of communication." He foresaw a division of labor: US forces were to defend South Vietnamese air and sea space, while the ARVN and the South Vietnamese militias were responsible for security on land, including the protection of American bases. Unlike Westmoreland, Taylor did not expect that an air campaign all but committed the United States to deploy combat ground forces. He believed it was possible to fight a war for limited political objectives with airpower.[72]

The objective was a negotiated settlement, not military victory. Taylor thought it was essential to open channels to Hanoi and Beijing, to make sure communist leaders understood the price they would pay for continued operations against Laos and South Vietnam, but also to communicate that the United States did not seek to threaten the independence of North Vietnam. This could be attained if the United States followed three principles: "Do not enter into negotiations until the DRV is hurting . . . never let the DRV gain a victory in South Viet-Nam without having paid a disproportionate price . . . keep the GVN in the forefront of the combat and the negotiations." This was an optimistic proposal that assumed leaders in Hanoi equally perceived the war as limited rather than absolute, and it ignored JCS war games that predicted stalemate resulting from measures such as those Taylor now proposed. Taylor himself had guided the communists to political victory in the 1962 iteration. Did he hope that real-life bombing would trigger a different response? Taylor later suggested his optimism stemmed from misreading why China and North Korea had agreed to a settlement in 1953 and from a false sense that American airpower could again force Asian communists into a compromise peace.[73]

Whereas Taylor had moved away from insisting on stable government in the South before strikes against the North could commence, the president and his key advisers had not yet done so. Lyndon Johnson posed a series of probing questions in the December 1 meeting. After all, Taylor's situation report on November 24 had noted serious political strife but "a good military week with Viet-Cong activity low and government activity both high and effective."[74] LBJ wondered, too, how Diem had managed to keep all factions in South Vietnam in check. Taylor believed he had involved them all in the political process and played off some against others, and he had held the army's support. Above all, Diem had been courageous, a trait Taylor now claimed to see in Huong. Johnson reminded Taylor he had said the same about Khanh a few months earlier. Next he asked whether the United States could do more to win over the people. McCone indicated he had spoken with the Pope to assert his influence over the Catholic minority. Johnson wondered if the communists had a foothold among the Buddhist bonzes. Taylor thought so, yet assumed it was impossible to remove their influence and necessary to get to know them better. Above all, would North Vietnam not send its army south if the United States started bombing? When Taylor replied he did not think so, Johnson likened it to MacArthur's judgment in the fall of 1950 that China would not intervene in the Korean War.[75]

Johnson, Taylor, and McNamara expressed concern that the South Vietnamese government took US willingness to raise the stakes for granted. According to McGeorge Bundy's notes, Taylor insisted, "We can improve in-country problem; we can't win without."[76] Johnson seemed to understand jet planes could not intercept guerrilla fighters and the South Vietnamese army needed to wage a more effective campaign. Specifically, he asked why a 200,000-man regular army was losing to 34,000 guerrillas. Johnson omitted the 60,000–80,000 PLAF militia fighters Taylor included in his estimate, but he also did not count government paramilitary forces. Taylor pointed out that in successful counterinsurgencies government forces had held ten-to-one or even twenty-to-one superiority. When the conversation turned to combat forces, Taylor responded he did not recommend deploying them unless Johnson decided to "go North." Taylor reiterated his preference for controlled escalation wherein the United States helped strengthen the regime, stepped up reprisal bombings to reduce infiltration and boost morale in the South, and began attacking North Vietnam to erode the war effort.[77] He returned to Saigon with orders to plan joint Vietnamese and American air strikes against the North in Phase II of an American air campaign, but he had not attained a commitment that the United States would move against the DRV.[78]

Taylor spent most of the following weeks trying to keep Khanh, still the army's commander, from reclaiming political power. He hoped a conditional commitment by the Johnson administration to start attacks on North Vietnam once the Saigon government had reached certain performance benchmarks would incentivize other generals to help Huong right the ship. Without that, escalation was pointless; without escalation South Vietnam would fall and the United States would lose Southeast Asia.[79] On January 11, 1965, Johnson agreed to the lowest common denominator as the precondition for escalation: "a government in whose name we can act and to whose request for assistance we can respond." Taylor recommended strikes against North Vietnam from mid-February.[80] It was thus a major blow when Huong resigned in late January after the military council withdrew its support. That finally forced Lyndon Johnson to decide on escalation without political stability.

Taylor got his wish when Johnson authorized reprisal strikes against military targets north of the DMZ after PLAF attacks on American facilities at Pleiku (February 7) and Qui Nhon (February 10).[81] Much like the president, Taylor did not think planes could defeat guerrillas, and he dismissed "Douhet theory," which predicted airpower to be decisive. The point was to use "the most flexible weapon in our arsenal of military superiority to bring pressure on the will of the chiefs of the DRV."[82] This argument on war as a communications exercise resonated with LBJ.[83] For now the president was not willing to act on rumblings by McGeorge Bundy that Taylor was a politically spent force who did not have the diplomatic tact to shape events in Saigon. Rusk, who thought it would be a "mistake to return him," nevertheless suggested the compromise of making Taylor CIA director.[84]

Early in 1965 Robert Kennedy told Taylor he was being made a scapegoat and lacked defenders in Washington.[85] By early March, McGeorge Bundy reminded President Johnson it soon would be time to bring Taylor back from Saigon. Bundy, summarizing a conversation with McNamara and Rusk, pointed out that Taylor lacked the light touch in dealing with people: "Max has been gallant, determined and honorable to a fault, but he has also been rigid, remote and sometimes abrupt." Perhaps age was a factor, as Bundy pointed at the need for a "younger man" to serve as chief of staff if U. Alexis Johnson was promoted to ambassador.[86] Two weeks later Bundy expressed the hope that Lyndon Johnson had settled on a new ambassador, with Alexis Johnson as deputy and "an operational Chief of Staff like John McNaughton."[87] McNaughton, then the assistant secretary of defense for international security affairs and McNamara's closest aide, seemed to be a hawk on Vietnam, but privately he opposed escalation.[88] US policies, Bundy thought, could still succeed if there were "a fully coordinated U. S. effort under the leadership of an Ambassador who understood the essentially political nature of the problem and applied himself to decentralized action with U. S. advice, assistance, and support at every level." The president, however, disagreed. His annotation on the memorandum read: "See me. This doesn't look like it's very workable to me."[89]

For now, Taylor stayed in Saigon and remained influential. The response to the February 7 strike by the PLAF's 409th Battalion against Camp Holloway and the adjacent American helicopter base at Pleiku that caused the death of eight American soldiers and left 126 wounded enhanced Taylor's importance for the president. Taylor, Westmoreland, and Bundy, in Saigon for consultations, quickly agreed on a decisive response.[90] Taylor then ordered immediate reprisal air strikes by US and South Vietnamese forces against staging areas in North Vietnam. He also advised President Johnson it was time to order all dependents of American officials out of South Vietnam. Lydia Taylor left on February 18. Taylor knew this was a crucial step, since LBJ had refused reprisal strikes for the December 24, 1964, bombing of US officer quarters at the Brinks Hotel in Saigon at least in part because he feared for the safety of American women and children in Vietnam. The issue had been batted back and forth between Saigon and Washington throughout January.[91] Johnson's public statement closely resembled a draft written by Taylor that blamed escalation of the war on Hanoi and made the case for continued American resolve in the defense of South Vietnam's freedom, though he opted to relegate word on the air strikes to a White House press release.[92]

Just as soon as Bundy had returned to Washington, Lyndon Johnson decided to move to Phase II of the December 1 program. The president authorized Taylor to share his decision with political leaders in Saigon, a move Taylor hoped would help calm the waters. Yet LBJ hesitated to set a date for Operation Rolling Thunder as long as Soviet premier Alexei Kosygin was in Hanoi and the Soviet response to an American air war against North Vietnam remained uncertain.[93] Taylor advocated for a rapid start of the sustained air campaign, then euphemistically called "graduated reprisals." Taylor did not believe that inflicting damage on men and materiel on the Ho Chi Minh trail would appreciably lower the rate of infiltration, though he conceded hitting them would help impress on Hanoi the cost of continued support for NLF operations. And that was the point: "Our effectiveness in influencing Hanoi leadership will, in the long run, determine the success or failure of our efforts in both North and South Vietnam."[94]

To make that point, Taylor proposed stepping up "frequency, size, number and/or geographic location of the reprisal strikes and of related activities such as Barrel Roll [in Laos] and 34-A. An upward trend in any or all of these forms of intensity will convey signals which, in combination, should present to the DRV leaders a vision of inevitable, ultimate destruction if they do not change their ways."[95] But as the United States moved from reprisal strikes to strategic bombing, priorities were muddled. Bundy hoped to boost morale in the South and show US commitment, Rusk thought it could provide diplomatic leverage, the JCS hoped to cut the umbilical cord that kept the insurgents alive, and McNamara joined Taylor in assuming airpower could break the will of leaders in Hanoi to keep up their war effort.[96] Westmoreland warned against an air war before the ARVN and US military were ready to defend South Vietnam. Taylor did not see escalation of the land war as an inevitable result of Rolling Thunder.[97]

Political stability in South Vietnam remained a troublesome issue. Since the summer of 1964, Taylor had worked with three different heads of state and three prime ministers (two of whom, Khanh and the incumbent in early February, Nguyen Xuan Oanh, had held the office twice). One week after the Pleiku attack, Oanh was ousted and replaced by Phan Huy Quat, a physician and veteran politician. Westmoreland's and Taylor's frustration with the infighting showed when they recommended a delay in launching Rolling Thunder because "the South Vietnamese Air Force is too exhausted from recent internal military goings on to participate."[98] In his February 23 report to the president, Taylor called it "the most topsy-turvy week since I came to this post. A new government installed, a coup attempted against the commander-in-chief [Khanh], the coup suppressed, the commander-in-chief deposed by those who had put down the coup."[99]

This even topped the blowup in December when Taylor had confronted yet another group of plotters. "Do all you speak English?" he asked some of South Vietnam's most senior generals, including air force commander Nguyen Cao Ky and IV Corps commander Nguyen Van Thieu. "I told you all clearly at General Westmoreland's dinner that we Americans are tired of coups. . . . I made it clear that all our military plans which I know you would like to carry out depend on governmental stability. Now you have made a real mess."[100] Taylor soon sent General John Throckmorton, Westmoreland's deputy, to apologize, but his relationship with those in the military who worked against Khanh in 1965 was fraught with tension.[101] Rumors in the Saigon press corps that Taylor had asked Khanh to step aside as commander of the armed forces required an official denial from the embassy.[102] At least the February events had now removed Khanh, "the troublemaker," as Taylor noted. Perhaps Quat's government could get on with the war.[103]

It soon appeared that it could not. Like his predecessors, Quat struggled with local and religious factionalism, had little control over the military, and felt the weight of war fighting and pacification at once. In his March 31 report, Taylor stressed relative calm on the military front and improvements in the public presentation of the new government, but he still doubted that South Vietnam's leaders had built up enough strength to implement an ambitious nation-building program. On the other hand, the bombing campaign against the North had lifted spirits and Taylor thought, "We must seize this moment of relative government stability . . . to make a determined effort to increase our effectiveness and that of the GVN." His embassy would guide pacification programs, but it was all a question of finding the proper balance between military and other means and making sure not to extend the grasp of Saigon's forces beyond their reach.[104] Taylor was overly positive in his assessment of progress in pacification, noting the effectiveness of airpower in impeding PLAF operations and stressing fewer incidents in II Corps and improvements in refugee resettlement in Binh Dinh province. Perhaps this was because he was set to return to Washington for discussions on the air war and deployment of combat forces.[105]

Backing into the Land War

By the spring of 1965, Taylor and Westmoreland had parted ways on the need for American soldiers. Whereas Taylor favored airpower and a small footprint, Westmoreland built his plans on securing US air bases and combating the PLAF with American ground forces. In January 1965, Westmoreland had made it known that MACV required 75,000 American combat personnel, the equivalent of thirty-four battalions. Taylor found these figures "startling." That, he held, "would bring us into greater conflict with the Vietnamese people and government." He advised President Johnson to stay the course, "increase the size of the armed forces of Vietnam, to improve their combat effectiveness, and, in conjunction with an expanded police force, to maximize their contribution to pacification." Taylor proposed adding 80,000 officers and men to the ARVN and militia forces and 10,000 to the national police. This was "preferable to the commitment of a large number of US security forces to static guard missions in South Vietnam."[106]

Taylor considered Rolling Thunder the most important of three "blue chips" the United States could play in negotiations toward a political settlement. Preparing for the Washington meetings in early April, he provided a statement on the desired end game: "We would like to be assured that the DRV has ceased its support of the VC insurgency, that the main force VC units and all VC personnel so desiring, move back into North Viet-Nam, that the former VC remaining in South Viet-Nam are prepared to become law-abiding citizens, that the Communist communications network between North and South Viet-Nam is dismantled and that some form of international inspection exists to verify the consumption of these actions. Likewise, there should be some arrangement subject to verification that Laotian territory will no longer be used as a channel of infiltration into South Viet-Nam."[107] This was not particularly likely at the moment, but Taylor drew his optimism from the Korean armistice and thought history could repeat itself.

That did not mean the North Vietnamese would simply trade their military position in the South for an end to strategic bombing. Taylor thought a bombing halt could be linked to a cease-fire in place whereby PLAF main units surfaced into the open while awaiting evacuation to the North. This required the reinstatement of an international control commission, much like the one that had been put in place in the 1954 Geneva Accords. "Also," Taylor warned, "we must be prepared to resume bombing if negotiations break down or if the DRV does not live up to its agreements." This first phase entailed an end to "VC incidents" and the right of government forces to move freely. Next, all American and communist forces would withdraw, possibly in incremental steps, but Saigon would have to accept that PLAF and PAVN units would keep their arms. In the final phase, "there would be the pay-off whereby the United States would engage itself to provide political and economic support for both North and South Viet-Nam to assure the viability of both countries as independent, recognized states."[108]

The turn to strategic bombing did not signal the end of pacification. When Taylor returned to Saigon from the Washington talks, he carried with him fifty-four new nonmilitary programs. He vented his frustration after receiving word of additional projects: "This mission is charged with securing implementation by the two month old Quat govt. of a 21-point military program, a 41-point non-military program, a 16-point [Carl] Rowan USIS program and a 12-point CIA program. Now this new cable opens up new vistas of further points as if we can win here somehow on a point scale."[109] Taylor worried Congress and government officials introduced too many new programs and the American public did not know how heavily the United States was invested in trying to solve political, economic, and social problems in South Vietnam.[110] At the same time—indeed, in the same cable to Bundy—Taylor objected to the rush into a land war that he gleaned from JCS recommendations. "Mac, can't we be better protected from our friends?" Taylor wondered. He knew "everyone wants to help, but there's such a thing as killing with kindness. In particular, we want to stay alive here because we think we're winning—and will continue to win unless helped to death."[111]

Despite his outward show of resolve, Taylor did not hold out much hope for pacification. In a meeting of the mission council with Army Chief of Staff Harold K. Johnson on March 5 he had outlined the problems facing the American effort. At the root, Taylor noted, was "the provision of adequate security for the population; that without security most of our other programs are rendered either impossible or of marginal effectiveness." The three primary obstacles to providing security were "lack of satisfactory progress in destroying the VC insurgents in the countryside, the continuing capability of the VC to replace losses and increase in strength and our inability to establish and maintain an effective government." Of course, Taylor stressed, the NLF depended on DRV support and perhaps the strategic air campaign would affect some change. But it was next to impossible to control 2,500 miles of land and sea frontiers, and Taylor conceded that while it would be best if South Vietnamese forces could operate in Laos, Cambodia, and North Vietnam, he recognized the validity of "political arguments which impose restraints on such operations." He also recognized South Vietnam's land and air forces were too small to conduct such operations on a sufficient scale.[112]

The question that exercised American military and civilian officers was how to help bring about a more stable South Vietnamese government, build stronger armed forces that can gain control in the countryside, and improve the integration of different threads of the pacification effort across the country, but particularly in those rural areas where the NLF had its most fertile recruiting grounds. Even before his ambassadorship, Taylor had recommended a shift from broad sweeps to clear and hold operations, notably in his advice to Diem in early October 1963.[113] Yet Taylor was never one to succumb to fatalism and now he presented General Johnson with a specific plan in "areas where, if progress can be made, we will be striking at the sources of our fundamental difficulties." His proposal built on improving the ARVN's mobility, expanding training capacity, making military service more attractive to young South Vietnamese, delineating how existing forces should be used, introducing "U.S. manpower to offset present shortage in Armed Forces of GVN," using "U.S. Navy resources to strengthen surveillance of coast and waterways," accelerating bombing campaigns in Laos and North Vietnam, "expanded use of Peoples Action (Quang Ngai) Teams," addressing the economic blockade and the mounting refugee problem in central Vietnam, improving "procedures and equipment for resources control," and strengthening South Vietnam's public information programs. Those may have been realistic goals, but as long as the political situation in Saigon remained volatile and North Vietnam found fairly easy access into the country to support NLF operations, Hanoi held the stronger hand in the war.[114]

Once Lyndon Johnson had launched the air campaign, he moved rapidly toward the deployment of combat forces, urged on by his national security adviser.[115] When the president approved the initial deployment of two marine battalions to Danang in early March 1965, Taylor, who had talked him down from the four battalions requested by Westmoreland, still hoped combat units would serve as a deterrent to North Vietnamese operations and not as a force combating the southern insurgents.[116] He also warned that more direct use of US airpower in South Vietnam against NLF targets was an ill-advised step toward taking over the war.[117] Once the marines had landed, Taylor channeled his own hopes in an assessment of improving morale across South Vietnam. The Vietnamese saw it, he reported, as the "strongest, most concrete evidence to date of US determination to honor its commitment to SVN." He surmised, "growing body of Vietnamese opinion senses hope less in terms of possibility of victory of Viet Cong than of placing GVN and US in strong negotiating position vis-à-vis Hanoi." The key was to not get drawn deeper into the morass until South Vietnam's government could begin to "exploit the improved atmosphere."[118]

Taylor maintained his reservations about bringing in additional combat units. On April 14 he expressed astonishment at the "eagerness in some quarters to deploy forces in SVN." He hoped plans to accommodate some 50,000 US troops were just one of several contingencies and would "not interfere with essential work in preparation for less ambitious but more probable developments."[119] Taylor followed up in a separate cable with a more general point. He feared JCS arguments for further reinforcements "could be adduced to justify almost unlimited additional deployments of US forces." Taylor acknowledged that US combat units were far superior to those of the ARVN, but he warned of equating operations and strategy: "The mounting number of foreign troops may sap the GVN initiative and turn a defense of the GVN homeland into what appears a foreign war. The increasing presence of more Americans will give Peking grounds to press military reinforcements on Hanoi. Frictions will grow between the Vietnamese and their white allies; it will become increasingly difficult to steer US and GVN policy on parallel lines."[120] He concluded, "For both military and political reasons we should all be most reluctant to tie down Army/Marine units in this country and would do so only after the presentation of the most convincing evidence of the necessity."[121] Bundy forwarded the second cable to Lyndon Johnson, noting, "Direct orders of this sort to Taylor would be very explosive right now because he will not agree with many of them and he will feel that he has not been consulted."[122]

For now, Taylor held fast to the argument that the ground war was

South Vietnam's to fight and that pacification could not be achieved by foreign troops. He had regarded the deployment of marines as part of an experiment in counterinsurgency, not the beginning of a more aggressive American part in the ground war. Taylor had assumed the White House and Defense Department were resigned to hold off on making final decisions on ground forces until the Americans in Saigon and Washington could assess what difference the marines made in the northern provinces. He saw no need to take rash steps and asked Rusk to stop the planned deployment of the 173rd Airborne Brigade.[123] Matters came to a head at an April 20 conference in Honolulu, a meeting ordered for the principal military and strategy advisers by Lyndon Johnson. McNamara passed it off to the press as a routine event to review the effort to provide "logistical support and training and advisory personnel" for the South Vietnamese government. The questions he faced before departing from Andrews Air Force Base and as he was leaving Honolulu suggested some reporters saw through the ruse, but no one seemed to sense that the United States was about to take over the ground war. That allowed McNamara to insist publicly that only small numbers of additional advisers were going to be sent. He evaded the sole direct question on additional combat forces.[124]

Taylor was in the minority, holding that continuous air strikes, even without expanding the list of targets, would cause consternation in Hanoi. McNamara, McNaughton, William Bundy, Wheeler, Sharp, and Westmoreland all favored either an expansion of the list of targets or periodic bombing pauses, and no one seemed to believe the war could be won in the North unless Lyndon Johnson removed all restraints. Therefore, it was necessary to demonstrate that communist forces could not win in the South. Taylor warned of the effects of taking over South Vietnam's war, but he accepted the compromise of nine additional battalions between Westmoreland and Wheeler, who had wanted more, and McNamara, who had proposed fewer. Taylor fell in line because he had read a recent cable from McGeorge Bundy as evidence that LBJ had decided on Americanization of the land war.[125] Some officials in Washington even suggested integrating ARVN and American forces under MACV's command, but Westmoreland demurred: it would cause disillusionment in Saigon. Earlier, Taylor had likened it to an attempt "to hook up a fire hydrant to a garden hose."[126] The alternative, however, was to wage parallel wars while also trying to maintain a delicate balance of war fighting and pacification against an enemy who could act as an insurgent or conventional force.[127]

There remained disagreement on how to employ US ground forces. Westmoreland believed he needed to throw US battalions directly into the fight across all of South Vietnam. Taylor argued that US troops should instead support the ARVN and secure enclaves around the major cities and ports. Unlike James Gavin, who championed a defensive enclave strategy, Taylor recognized that US forces eventually would be needed in inland areas where the enemy was strongest. Westmoreland, too, saw securing enclaves as "an essential interim step," but argued his forces needed to go on the offensive immediately, before the enemy drove from Laos across the highlands to the coast south of Hue and cut the country in half.[128] Once he had accepted the ground force deployment, Taylor displayed surprising optimism. Where McNamara estimated a war of one or two years, Taylor hoped "a favorable settlement should be possible from a combination of continued air attacks and by introduction of sufficient US and third country forces to demonstrate to Hanoi that the Viet Cong have no ultimate chance of success. This process will probably take months; how many months is impossible to estimate."[129] As long as the strategy focused on breaking Hanoi's will, escalation on the ground could accelerate the process.

McNamara, himself a recent convert to the ground war option, had moved rapidly after the Honolulu conference.[130] Two days after the meeting, Taylor received timetables and areas of operations for additional army and marine units. There were already over 33,000 American soldiers and marines in South Vietnam, as well as 2,000 South Koreans; between May 1 and June 15, another 14,200 Americans, 4,000 Koreans, and 1,250 Australians were set to follow. Adding in approved augmentations of units already in Vietnam (11,000 men) and logistics troops (23,000), McNamara projected US strength by mid-June at thirteen combat battalions and 82,000 officers and men.[131] Just then MACV confirmed the first battalion of the 325th PAVN Division operating in Kontum province, though Taylor thought elements of that division had been in South Vietnam since at least February.[132] Taylor secured Quat's agreement to the increased American presence on April 27.[133] These were portentous times for US foreign policy: on April 30, a brigade of the 82nd Airborne Division landed in Santo Domingo to keep purportedly pro-Cuban forces who had seized the capital from establishing control over the Dominican Republic.

In the air war, ambiguity reigned well into the Rolling Thunder campaign. On June 1, Undersecretary of State George Ball asked for Taylor's assessment of the best path forward. Ball, the lone dissenter in the inner circle of advisers and now on a mission to find reasons to de-escalate, noted, "We have now reached a point in planning for successive Rolling Thunder operations where we must be clear as to precisely what we are trying to do." The need to determine basic objectives three months into a war effort suggested that American strategy was adrift. The fundamental problem was continued disagreement in Washington and Saigon on whether the war had to be won in the South or by air strikes against the North. If it was the former, the air campaign had to remain limited and, as Ball noted, it was essential to avoid targeting the Hanoi-Haiphong area for fear of drawing China and the Soviet Union into the war. At least with respect to China, this was a legitimate fear. In that scenario, bombing had to be calibrated to raise morale in the South, lower it in the North, cut down on infiltration, and isolate the battlefield. If airpower was supposed to win the war, Ball wondered how much risk the United States should take in hitting military installations at Hanoi and Haiphong.[134]

Taylor remained convinced of Rolling Thunder's viability and held that a negotiated settlement could only result from pressuring North Vietnam's leaders. At Honolulu he had agreed with McNamara that Hanoi should remain off limits: the point was to instill fear, not to "kill the hostage."[135] But Taylor and Alexis Johnson thought separating the air and ground war was a false premise: "The air campaign in the North and the anti–Viet Cong campaign in the South . . . are two parts of a single coherent program. The air attacks have as their primary objectives the termination of Hanoi's support for the VC whereas the campaign in South Vietnam has as its primary objective the destruction of the Viet Cong military apparatus within the country." There was no need for defeatism but also no quick road to victory: "A change in DRV attitudes can probably be brought about only when, along with a sense of mounting pain from the bombing, there is also a conviction on their part that the tide has turned or will soon turn against them in the South."[136] Taylor did not think of victory in terms of military operations leading to the enemy's surrender. He thought of it in shades of gray: at some point Hanoi would accept that South Vietnam would remain independent.

After the Honolulu conference, Taylor had lost influence in the remaining debates on troop deployments. On May 17 he signaled his approval of the June arrival of the 173rd Airborne Brigade, a move he had found premature just a month earlier. Partly, this shift stemmed from an instinct to follow orders once the president had determined a strategy, but Taylor also had come to agree with Westmoreland's reading of the crisis.[137] His biggest fear was no longer that the United States would take over the war, but rather that doves in Washington would extend peace feelers to North Vietnam as morale in South Vietnam deteriorated.[138] Even so, Taylor still resisted some of Westmoreland's requests. In early June, when MACV called for 140,000 American troops, McNamara, on Taylor's urging, agreed to only four additional battalions, for a total of 70,000 US forces in Vietnam. In this context, Taylor noted, he provided details of the military buildup to senators for the first time. He also alerted them, perhaps unwittingly, to a fundamental concern: the State Department was just then pushing Saigon "to promulgate a statement of war aims."[139]

By late spring, Taylor and Westmoreland were deeply concerned about the political and military situation. Quat had proven to be indecisive and was under attack from southern nationalists, militant Catholics, the Cao Dai and Hoa Hao sects, and the head of state, president Phan Khac Suu. Taylor advised the State Department that this meant the generals, who had withdrawn from active politics in recent months, were likely going to reassert their power in hopes of forming a stronger government. The military situation was even worse. After two months of relative quiet, PLAF units up to the size of regiments had stepped up ambushes throughout May. Guerrilla operations, harassment, sabotage, and terrorist attacks paralyzed the country, and the ARVN struggled to contain even just one major enemy thrust at a time. Taylor expected regiment-size attacks in all four corps areas by the summer and battalion-size attacks in all provinces. In addition, there were now two PAVN divisions in the northern sectors (I and II Corps). Far from dissuading Hanoi, the air strikes had led to a faster pace of infiltration and military operations. It would soon be necessary for US ground forces to prevent a collapse of South Vietnam.[140]

Westmoreland, who saw his assumptions about the air war validated, was more pessimistic than Taylor. A MACV study that compared who controlled the countryside in January and April found that the bombing campaign had no measurable effect and the crisis had deepened to an alarming degree in I and II Corps.[141] By the end of June, the enemy had forced all major roads into II Corps to be closed, military and civilian supplies had to be airlifted, and a new prime minister, Nguyen Cao Ky, had pleaded for more American ground troops.[142] The more aggressive military effort against South Vietnam that Westmoreland had foreseen had materialized, and now he needed a massive influx of soldiers just to return to the fragile state of late 1964. Westmoreland warned the

JCS that even the forty-four battalions he requested could not win the war. Instead, he hoped they would restore the military balance in favor of South Vietnam by the end of 1965. Forty-four battalions were the outer limit of what American and Vietnamese infrastructure and logistics could presently support. In 1966, Westmoreland predicted, he would require another influx of combat forces to wrest the initiative from the enemy.[143]

By the time Lyndon Johnson gathered his advisers just before his July 28 announcement that the army was going to Vietnam, Taylor had begun to spin US intervention as another Cold War battle like the one in Korea. In a July 12 telegram to Rusk, he argued that an American war in Vietnam would not be like that of the French. Unlike the colonial power, which fought for greed and grandeur, the United States would fight to help a free people resist communist encroachment. He believed this did not go unnoticed: "Many Vietnamese draw analogy between SVN situation and Korean police action in which United States came to aid of victims of foreign communist aggression."[144] U. Alexis Johnson explained in late July that he and Taylor now agreed on the need to deploy combat forces in Vietnam even though they did not foresee victory. Defeat was intolerable because it would strengthen the Chinese position across developing nations.[145] The result was mission creep: Hawk missiles were brought in to protect the airfield at Danang, and this required marines to guard the missiles. Similarly, the 173rd Airborne Brigade that was deployed at Bien Hoa proved to be not enough. "Looking back on it," Johnson concluded, "I think where we fell down was not making clear at any point along the line to the President the decisions that he might eventually face. The whole thing just sort of crept up on us, and it crept up on him, with each decision following the other decision."[146] Bundy thought along the same lines. In his "history of recommendations for increased US forces in Vietnam" in late July 1965, he reminded Lyndon Johnson how quickly the mission had expanded within three months from 33,000 to 180,000 authorized troops and from base defense to offensive combat.[147]

Taylor returned the keys to the embassy to his predecessor, Lodge, in late July. Bundy had pressed Lyndon Johnson to speed up the transition after the emergence of the new administration of Generals Ky and Thieu in June. In Bundy's view, Taylor no longer had the necessary energy, and Bundy also raised concerns about the quality of Taylor's team. Above all, Bundy asserted, Taylor was too heavily involved in military planning, and embassy officials had not established close links to Ky's cabinet.[148] U. Alexis Johnson, who liked working for Taylor, conceded that the general lacked the "sympathetic disposition to influence the Vietnamese," even though he found him much superior to the "flamboyant" Lodge, who seemed equally ill-informed about military matters and the South Vietnamese people.[149] In mid-July, Lodge arrived in Saigon alongside McNamara and Generals Wheeler and Goodpaster. Taylor presented his assessment of the American buildup in Vietnam and his concerns about the military's request for 175,000 men by the end of the year. He identified two variables that made projections difficult. The performance of South Vietnam's government remained unsteady and the enemy was gaining strength. It was also uncertain how the NLF and North Vietnam would respond to American escalation.

The new strongmen in Saigon, then three weeks in power, provided a briefing on July 16. Economics Minister Truong Tai Ton, who impressed the Americans as the most competent cabinet minister they had ever met in Saigon, made clear that "we are in a total war." Winning the war without losing the peace required balancing military and economic needs. For example, "galloping inflation could be as catastrophic as a military disaster." US economic aid had to be carefully calibrated to allow Saigon to build strength and maintain independence. Defense Minister General Nguyen Huu Co and Nguyen Duc Thang of the general staff noted that South Vietnam's military needed to add three Ranger battalions and seven task force headquarters, four marine battalions, and one squadron each of jet aircraft and attack helicopters. The main immediate concern was to build up the general reserve, which was depleted by the need to combat the PLAF and PAVN offensive. Thang noted that while the situation in I Corps had greatly improved, the same could not be said for the Central Highlands, where the 325th PAVN Division was wreaking havoc, or the Mekong delta, where PLAF forces were making inroads. He asked that a "U.S. Assault Division" be sent to the highlands and an infantry division to the delta. Inverting Taylor's preference, Thang suggested the Americans should conduct "search and destroy" operations in thinly populated areas, while the ARVN would focus primarily on pacification and population centers.[150]

Taylor was hopeful when he left Saigon. The embassy and MACV were performing well, improvements in logistics that would soon allow for hundreds of thousands of American soldiers to operate in South Vietnam were impressive, and the new regime of Ky and Thieu promised greater stability. His initial assessment in mid-June had been less flattering. While Ky was "a well-motivated, courageous, and patriotic officer," he was also "completely without the background and experience necessary for an assignment as difficult as this one," and his air force adviser thought him "a naïve, inexperienced politician and civil affairs administrator."[151] Typical of the American experience in South Vietnam, however, he was also the latest best hope despite his infamous interview with a British newspaper in which he noted that Vietnam needed several Hitlers.[152] Taylor hoped the decisions of the spring and summer of 1965 had reversed the dynamic and that the defeat of the Republic of Vietnam no longer appeared imminent. On a personal note, he took pride in the arrival of the 101st Airborne Division and of his son, Captain Thomas Taylor, whom he and Westmoreland welcomed at Cam Ranh Bay in a scene depicted in the army's television program *The Big Picture*.[153]

The introduction of US ground combat forces in 1965 may strike us as a sharper departure today than it appeared at the time. Even in *In Retrospect* McNamara refers to the United States as being at war in Vietnam as early as April 1964, and Rusk noted at an August 1965 press conference that "our combat troops did not arrive until late 1961, and during 1962, and subsequently."[154] As he left Saigon, Taylor thought the United States had a feasible strategy for the Vietnam War and he told journalists that was the greatest accomplishment of the past year.[155] In his lectures at Lehigh University in the spring of 1966 he outlined the strategy's four tenets. First, US and South Vietnamese forces were building up strength to attack enemy units. This would reveal weaknesses in the insurgency and destroy the myth of invincibility that had arisen around the communist movement. Second, Rolling Thunder aimed at eroding military capability and political will in North Vietnam while boosting morale in the South. Third, a comprehensive pacification program consisting of political, social, and economic projects promised to build stronger ties between the regime in Saigon and the people of South Vietnam. Finally, in the international arena American diplomats hoped to increase pressure on Hanoi and initiate negotiations that could end the war.[156]

To Taylor this made for a comprehensive package. "We have to be successful in breaking the back of the Vietcong main guerrilla force in the South," he noted, and "we have to use our air arm constantly to remind the Hanoi leadership that it is going to get tougher all the time." He admonished soldiers and political leaders to remain patient with Saigon: "We can never relax our efforts in raising the efficiency of government in the South and in shoring up the fragile economy." But there could be no victory without diplomacy and "we must be constantly prepared for negotiations."[157] He failed to remark on the variables: Saigon's performance, Hanoi's strength (as well as that of the NLF), and American public opinion. Hanoi's diplomats and publicists gained ground in the battle for global public opinion, and in the US uneasiness about the war effort and opposition to the war mounted after 1965. The goal was not to win but instead to give South Vietnam a fighting chance. This was hardly an argument to win over the American public.[158]

Taylor justified escalation as a response to North Vietnam's offensive in the wake of the coup against Diem. But if it was necessary to prop up anti-communist forces in South Vietnam, it remained unclear how to link the four parts of the American strategy. The body count and other metrics seemed to offer measures of success for operations against PLAF and PAVN forces, but without better knowledge of enemy strength, determination, and ability to recruit locally as well as infiltrate new troops from the North, the data proved meaningless.[159] For the air campaign against North Vietnam, there were no applicable metrics: how does one gauge the state of mind of an unknown enemy? Taylor pointed at "broken bridges, the interrupted highways, the inoperable rail lines, the airfields out of action, the ports which cannot be used," but while such destruction would have greatly depleted the efforts of a western military, the same could not be said about communist forces in Vietnam. And Taylor's coda, that one could observe desperation in the feverish pace of repairs and of daytime movement of supplies during the thirty-seven-day bombing pause in late 1965 and early 1966, seemed implausible.[160] It does not appear American observers knew enough about the leadership in Hanoi—or the Vietnamese people—in order for the second, third, and fourth tenets to be practical.

Taylor recognized there were different layers to the Vietnam War: the big war, local wars, and the "criminal war"—in Lodge's words—that included assassinations and terror attacks. Taylor reminded Americans in the fall of 1965 that the killings of over 3,000 local officials in the past two years, put in proportion to population size, translated into "66,000 [American] mayors, city managers, heads of school boards, and similar officials" dead at the hands of brutal assassins.[161] Taylor knew victory could not be defined in conventional terms. He also followed his own interpretation of the domino theory. The issue was less whether neighboring countries would fall in the wake of a communist triumph in Vietnam, but rather how America's allies would react to a withdrawal and whether insurgencies would erupt elsewhere. Taylor was "deeply convinced that such a disaster would propel a shock wave of dismay which would spread rapidly from the epicenter in South Vietnam, extending around the globe, which would affect every international relation we have and every alliance, including NATO."[162]

If Taylor's reading of free-world opinion was questionable, his sense of the enemy was less well developed. With few exceptions, like the State Department's China expert James Thomson, who grasped the degree of determination of the leadership in Hanoi, LBJ's advisers simply did not know what they were up against.[163] Taylor's performance in July 1965 offered a telling example. In his last days at the embassy he presented a detailed analysis of a recent article by the North Vietnamese defense minister, Vo Nguyen Giap, the architect of victory over the French in the 1950s. Taylor construed Giap's call for resolve that culminated in reassuring his readers of eventual victory in a long struggle as an admission that the "special war" in the South could no longer be fought under the pretense of being a "local war."[164]

By the fall, working once again as presidential adviser, Taylor had convinced himself that the deployment of ground forces and the buildup to 125,000 officers and men in Vietnam was necessary to help South Vietnam address manpower shortages and prop up the regime in Saigon. He pointed out that in the past year the NLF had added some 60,000 men by way of infiltration from the North and "ruthless impressment of South Vietnamese recruits." South Vietnam had added 140,000 men to its armed forces, government militias, and national and local police, but the counterinsurgency effort required close to a ten-to-one numerical superiority. Taylor insisted counterinsurgency was a sequential matter in three stages. The foundation was military action "to free the people from Viet Cong terrorism and intimidation." Next came the task to preserve security and "re-establish governmental services, this is the work of the local administrators and the police." Building on security, the government could win the loyalty of the people if it provided the desired education, health care, and standard of living. And, in parallel, Saigon had to ensure the people knew what their government was doing for them.[165] But he forgot his Korean War lessons on skill and determination of the enemy: "We have learned to respect the Oriental soldier as brave, hardy, disciplined, and eminently teachable." In 1954 Taylor had concluded that the war "showed the complete subjugation of the individual communist soldier to his leaders, and their utter disregard for human life in pursuing their ends."[166] What if the enemy in Vietnam was just as determined?

Despite such inconsistencies, Taylor was one of the few officials who considered the war as a layered structure of air war, ground war, counterinsurgency, and pacification. All four needed to be pursued vigorously, but only the United States was in a position to hit Hanoi. This was an exercise in communicating that victory for the communists was impossible. The result should be a settlement much like the one in Korea, with two independent states and a long-term American presence in the South. It was perhaps sound strategic theory in the abstract, but it suffered from fatal flaws in its specifics: Taylor misread communist leaders in Hanoi, or rather, he did not read them at all and assumed they were much like the ones he had dealt with in Korea. He overestimated the ability of South Vietnamese forces to hold off the PLAF and PAVN, and politics in Saigon remained volatile. Finally, he never reckoned with the dynamic of escalation: once airpower failed to deliver results, the deployment of ground forces was a near certainty. His advice in the spring of 1965 had been self-defeating.

1. Brigadier General Taylor looks on as Italy's Prime Minister Marshal Pietro Badoglio reads the declaration of war on Germany in Brindisi, October 1943. (National Archives, Army Signal Corps)

2. General Taylor, ready to jump in Operation Market Garden, September 1944. (National Archives, Army Signal Corps)

3. Taylor shakes hands with a worker who helped complete a Marshall Plan-funded housing project in Berlin, May 1950. (National Archives, Army Signal Corps)

4. The three commandants of the western sectors (from left: Taylor, Ganeval, and Bourne) join Lord Mayor Ernst Reuter at a reception in Berlin, November 1950. (National Archives, Army Signal Corps)

5. Lieutenant General Taylor ponders his new command in Korea on a Pentagon map, January 1953. (National Archives, Army Signal Corps)

6. Taylor inspects the front lines in South Korea, February 1953. (National Archives, Army Signal Corps)

7. Taylor salutes the colors at the ceremony where Syngman Rhee awarded the Eighth Army with the presidential unit designation, July 1953. (National Archives, Army Signal Corps)

8. Taylor and his fellow chiefs of staff in March 1956 (from left: Admiral Arleigh Burke, General Nathan Twining, Admiral Arthur Radford, Taylor, and General Randolph McC. Pate). (Kenneth W. Condit, *History of the Joint Chiefs of Staff*, vol. 6, *The Joint Chiefs of Staff in National Policy, 1955–1956*)

(*Above*) 9. Taylor inspects US Army, Europe, forces at Baumholder, Germany, 1957 (Carter, *Forging the Shield*) (*Below*) 10. President John F. Kennedy with Taylor and JCS chairman Lyman Lemnitzer at the White House, July 1962. (John F. Kennedy Presidential Library)

11. Just prior to the Cuban Missile Crisis: Kennedy confers with Taylor and Robert McNamara in the Oval Office, October 1962. (John F. Kennedy Presidential Library)

12. During the Cuban Missile Crisis: Kennedy confers with ExComm members McGeorge Bundy, Paul Nitze, Taylor, and McNamara, October 1962. (John F. Kennedy Presidential Library)

13. Kennedy poses with Taylor and his fellow chiefs of staff (from left: David Shoup, Earle Wheeler, Curtis LeMay, Kennedy, Taylor, and George Anderson) outside the White House, January 1963. (John F. Kennedy Presidential Library)

(*Above*) 14. John F. Kennedy's funeral procession from White House to St. Matthews Church, November 1963. (John F. Kennedy Presidential Library)
(*Below*) 15. Taylor and Nguyen Khanh at the commemoration of the tenth anniversary of the partition of Vietnam, July 1964. (National Archives, Army Signal Corps)

16. General Westmoreland and Taylor meet the press in South Vietnam, 1965. (Stewart, ed., *American Military History*, vol. 2)

(*Above*) 17. Ambassador Taylor greets his son, Captain Thomas Taylor, in South Vietnam in July 1965. (National Archives, Army Signal Corps) (*Below*) 18. Secretary of the Treasury Henry Fowler, Taylor, William Bundy, Robert McNamara, and Lyndon Johnson en route to the February 1966 Honolulu Conference. (Lyndon B. Johnson Presidential Library)

19. Taylor, partially obscured by McNamara, at the November 1967 Wise Men meeting with Lyndon Johnson. (Lyndon B. Johnson Presidential Library)

20. Taylor pondering Vietnam at a White House meeting on January 30, 1968. (Lyndon B. Johnson Presidential Library)

6

Wise Man?

Following his retirement ceremony at the State Department in September 1965, Taylor returned as consultant to the president. He was uneasy about his uncertain role, but accepted the call to assess US foreign policy and Vietnam War strategy. He noticed mounting opposition to the war effort in Washington and across the country and he expressed concern over the lack of control over the war's narrative exhibited by the Johnson administration. Above all, Taylor lamented the lack of centralized oversight of various efforts in Vietnam and in counterinsurgency more generally; he felt this should be done in a committee of senior advisers from all critical departments and agencies. His new creation, the Senior Interdepartmental Group (SIG), languished with no clear guidance from the State Department, which served as coordinator. Ironically, given his own tendencies, Taylor feared the White House was more interested in getting new ideas off the ground than in seeing through lasting and well-coordinated efforts.[1]

Counterinsurgency and the War in Vietnam

In addition to joining the President's Foreign Intelligence Advisory Board, Taylor took over as president of the Institute for Defense Analyses (IDA), a think tank that worked for the Defense Department and JCS. When Clark Clifford succeeded McNamara at the Pentagon in early 1968, Taylor took Clifford's spot as chairman. The PFIAB did much of its work in panels of two or three members. Taylor was a hands-on participant with a seat on the most important oversight groups. Together with Clifford, he assessed the overall effort of the intelligence community and evaluated the role of the CIA director. With his one-time critic over the Rome mission, Ambassador Robert Murphy, Taylor oversaw overt intelligence and the CIA budget. With Murphy and former Truman and Eisenhower adviser Gordon Gray, Taylor worked on covert intelligence and covert operations and Taylor and Gray kept track of the Defense Intelligence Agency.[2] Taylor's area expertise was East Asia and the Pacific, and by 1968 he also served on the Near Eastern and South Asian affairs panel.[3]

His roles in the PFIAB and IDA kept Taylor connected to the Pentagon and the intelligence community, and his relationship with Lyndon Johnson allowed him to retain influence at the White House. Three themes stand out from Taylor's assessment of the picture in Vietnam: his unwavering support of strategic bombing in hopes of forcing North Vietnam to negotiate on American terms, his lack of understanding of the leadership in Hanoi, and his growing uneasiness with the inability of the Johnson administration to sell the necessity of the war to the American people. Taylor also ran up against an old problem: agencies and departments in Washington struggled to coordinate foreign policy, particularly in complex and overlapping fields like war and counterinsurgency.

To strengthen the counterinsurgency policy process, Taylor again worked with U. Alexis Johnson, who had returned from Saigon in September 1965 and spent a year at Foggy Bottom before moving to his own ambassadorship in Tokyo. Johnson recalled in August 1967: "Both of us were deeply impressed, particularly during our period in Saigon, with the fact that our government really wasn't organized to deal efficiently and effectively with things that cut across many departments and agencies, particularly something such as the war out in Vietnam."[4] Taylor felt that too many departments, agencies, and committees made for ponderous deliberations. The Special Group (CI) had languished since 1962 as policy demands shifted from planning to implementation.[5] Now Taylor proposed a group made up of senior representatives from State, Defense, the CIA, the White House and NSC, USAID, and USIA as well as invited representatives of departments and agencies affected by a specific issue. This group was to be led by the undersecretary of state as an executive chairman, a leader who had the right and responsibility to make decisions and was not merely a facilitator of discussions. As a practical matter, this group—and the interdepartmental regional groups of lower-level advisers—did not serve as a faster route to decisive action. But Taylor's thought process in setting it up revealed his desire to have one presidential adviser in charge of military, political, social, and economic assets. He envisioned SIG as an alternative to the JCS.

Averell Harriman, ambassador-at-large and the second-most influential official at the State Department, feared that Taylor risked diluting the effectiveness of counterinsurgency assets by putting them on too wide a field. Using the example of Latin America, Harriman argued that Soviet tactics had "undergone a change of emphasis, probably due to the success of Latin American governments in defeating attempts to organize terrorist and guerrilla action. The trend now is to encourage the development of popular or united fronts in which the Communist Parties would try to play eventually a decisive role." This was not militant insurgency, yet Taylor did not seem to draw the distinction. "Of course," Harriman noted, "support of terrorist activity has not been abandoned, particularly by the Chicom factions. In addition, the training and organizing for possible guerrilla insurgency is in some cases being maintained for use if the opportunity develops." The more immediate danger was political: the loss of elections in Chile had been avoided in 1964, but it could happen elsewhere, and that would weaken the US position in the western hemisphere. Harriman feared that by conflating political and militant threats, Taylor shifted the US response entirely into the military realm.[6]

Harriman misread Taylor, who rejected the term counterinsurgency precisely because it implied a strong military bent; his preferred terminology was "subversive aggression" to be met by "counter-subversion." He agreed it was best to keep the framework broad and inclusive.[7] In January 1966, Taylor offered his findings to Lyndon Johnson. He emphasized that interdepartmental operations were still poorly coordinated, though less so on the ground where an embassy's country team offered a sound mechanism that could relatively easily be adjusted to give the ambassador greater executive control. In Washington, parochialism and insularity impeded early recognition of a subversive movement and effective countermeasures before an insurgency had taken root. Only a high-ranking cabinet official, ideally the secretary of state, could get so many independent or autonomous agencies to act in unison. It was necessary to recover "the missionary zeal" of the early 1960s.[8]

SIG started meeting in March 1966, but Taylor's plans faced resistance.[9] He hoped the new committee would not add another layer to an already stifling bureaucracy but rather act as a "coordination filtration mechanism" that allowed assistant secretaries of state to monitor regional developments more thoroughly and move information of troubling signs through the hierarchy more rapidly.[10] While everyone agreed on the need to recognize potential subversive aggression at the earliest point so that the United States and the local government could destroy the base for an insurgency and address the root causes that might fuel militant resistance, few department heads liked having to work with the newly formed

SIG, which they regarded as merely an additional watchdog. Still, in July 1966 SIG formally accepted the tasks that had previously rested with the Special Group.¹¹ The most immediate need was to build top-quality local police forces, but for long-term success, US military forces and civilian agencies needed to be more closely linked in assisting vulnerable countries. Doing so required pressure from the president.¹²

In Vietnam policy, Taylor supported the efforts of NSC staff officer Robert Komer, an ally since 1961, to ensure coordination across civilian and military realms. Lyndon Johnson had tasked Lodge with running "the other war," and the ambassador installed his deputy, William Porter, as pacification director. In April 1966, the blunt Komer, known in Washington for his incendiary memoranda as "Blowtorch Bob," took on the effort from the White House. Taylor weighed in on the finer points of the pacification effort, for example, when he proposed that one way to motivate South Vietnamese officials might be to promote the most active province chiefs on the spot.¹³ Komer relayed Westmoreland's concerns that this would just be another means for favoritism in a corrupt regime, but he embraced Westmoreland's plan that half of all ARVN units in I, II, and III Corps, and a quarter in IV Corps could take up counterinsurgency as their primary task. Komer concluded, "We've got to get the civil side thinking as boldly."¹⁴ In September 1966 Westmoreland and McNamara proposed that all assets for the pacification effort should be incorporated in the MACV command structure.¹⁵ Lodge and civilian agency heads in Saigon and Washington resisted, but Komer agreed with Taylor that "defining the civil/military relationship [was] more important than defining civilian agency inter-relationships."¹⁶ Soon Komer moved to Saigon and took over the new Civil Operations and Revolutionary Development Support (CORDS) structure as (civilian) deputy commander of MACV.¹⁷

In strategy, Taylor continued to link pacification and the air war, and he worried that US diplomats might trade in the latter for the chimera of peace talks. He had returned from Saigon with undue optimism: the bombing was working "about as well as we expected," he told the president in early August 1965. It had raised morale in the South and depressed it in the North, made operations harder for PLAF and PAVN forces, and reminded Hanoi of the rising costs of the war.¹⁸ Pointing at Senate majority leader Mike Mansfield, Taylor noted, "Some of our best friends often consider that at some early point in the procedure it would be desirable or even essential to declare a 'cease-fire.'" Doing so would put the South Vietnamese government at a disadvantage, since "the hostile acts of the Viet Cong which must be brought under control—terrorism, sabotage, oppression of the rural population, recruiting and infiltration—do not depend on the use of weapons. The prevention of these acts by the government does." Taylor did not oppose peace feelers, but he warned a cease-fire should only be granted in return for up-front concessions by North Vietnam that allowed South Vietnamese forces to uphold law and order. Taylor conceded that Rolling Thunder could end under such an agreement, and in the coming months he further refined the idea of trading in blue chips for North Vietnamese concessions before talks could advance to a serious stage.[19]

Two days after Christmas 1965, President Johnson called on Taylor for advice. Facing the increasing costs of the war and fearing public dissent in a mid-term election year, Johnson had decided on a bombing pause. The president, who did not expect a positive reaction from Hanoi, thought it might impress the Soviets and score political points at home. Taylor, who generally disapproved of any halt to the air war, allowed that the pause made sense from a domestic and international point of view and added it might put to rest hopes that it could lead to a negotiated settlement. Westmoreland and Admiral Sharp had already registered their protest and wanted to expand the air campaign. This time Taylor supported Johnson's position: the immediate military impact was negligible and was outweighed by the political benefits. Johnson was thinking of announcing a five-day pause; Taylor suggested leaving it open-ended for greater effect.[20]

That did not mean Taylor had softened. In a late January 1966 meeting with the president and the core group of Vietnam policy advisers, Taylor linked Hanoi's resolve to the encouragement North Vietnam's leaders perceived from opposition voices in the United States. Only a resumption of bombing while also strengthening consensus within the United States could get Hanoi to settle.[21] And when State Department officials floated ideas in the summer of 1966 about a cease-fire during the anticipated South Vietnamese elections in September, Taylor made sure Johnson and Rusk knew of his opposition. "I am stoutly on the side of Saigon in this debate," Taylor noted, referring to an ongoing debate between embassy officials and Foggy Bottom. He saw no reason to expect that the NLF would forego attempts to sabotage the election. Proponents of the idea argued that the proposal itself put the communists on the defensive in the court of public opinion. Taylor thought all it would achieve would be to raise doubts about US commitment among government officials in Saigon and leave voters in rural areas exposed to harassment and terrorist attacks. Yet Taylor would not have responded so vigorously if this did not point at a bigger problem: "I have always been afraid of our being maneuvered into a cease-fire without safeguards at the outset of peace negotiations." If the United States proclaimed a unilateral cease-fire, it would be much harder to negotiate a carefully crafted agreement later on.[22]

While he questioned the direction of peace initiatives, Taylor remained concerned about full-blown Americanization of the ground war—even after that had already happened. In November 1965 he opposed a JCS plan for an offensive military strategy in which American forces were to carry the brunt of the attack on PLAF and PAVN units and base camps. Taylor pointed out that this was going to be very heavy fighting and that Americans would take much greater casualties. Moreover, the JCS plan apportioned too many American and South Vietnamese regular forces to "clearing and securing operations" and left anywhere from half to three-quarters of ARVN combat battalions guarding installations in relatively safe areas. This detracted from the ability of the South Vietnamese to engage their enemy in contested regions. Taylor proposed a "joint US/GVN ground force mission, with the US forces concentrating on the destruction of located VC main forces. The clearing mission is preponderantly an ARVN responsibility supplemented when necessary by US forces. The securing mission is the primary function of the Regional and Popular forces," though they might require some support from the ARVN and could later also draw on the national police. Taylor felt that no mission statement should allow South Vietnamese leaders to keep their army out of major campaigns.[23]

Taylor believed it was folly to expect US forces and the Saigon government to extend control over the entire South in short order. Briefing Henry Kissinger for a tour of Vietnam in the fall of 1965, Taylor noted that McNamara "wanted to take over the whole country," and he feared this had led to "an imperial adventure for an indefinite number of years."[24] Taylor agreed with what French counterinsurgency experts had come to call the oil spot approach. Instead of dissipating the military's efforts, the United States should prioritize security of the cities and aim to increase safe areas from 53 percent of the population to 75 or 80 percent by the end of 1966. Taylor observed that American forces had taken over too much of the fighting, a development he had always sought to prevent. He remained convinced that the air campaign against North Vietnam had contributed to slower infiltration of fighters from the North—a dubious claim that did not reflect the increase to over 1,500 men per month in 1965—and greater morale in the South. Whether it had moved Hanoi any closer to negotiations remained to be seen, but in the meantime, the air force and navy should continue their bombing runs.[25]

In February 1966, Taylor and LBJ concluded that Diem's downfall was the war's pivot point. From then on, the United States had been on its descent into inevitable war.[26] Even so, on February 17, Taylor appeared as an upbeat and pugnacious witness before Senator J. William Fulbright's Foreign Relations Committee in a round of public hearings that had already featured critiques from George Kennan and James Gavin.[27] There was, Taylor insisted, a comprehensive strategy, which consisted of four tracks. The most visible ones were the commitment of combat forces and the air campaign against North Vietnam. The former had become necessary because the buildup of South Vietnam's military could not sufficiently outpace the growth of the PLAF and PAVN, and the air campaign boosted morale in the South, slowed infiltration, and demonstrated to Hanoi the cost of the war. But there were also two less visible tracks: nation building and diplomacy. Taylor concluded that the military effort could not lead to victory in the sense of Robert E. Lee's surrender at Appomattox or Japan's aboard the USS *Missouri*. In an exchange with John Sparkman (D, Alabama), who desired a more aggressive strategy, Taylor defined victory as gaining a positive settlement that would allow the South Vietnamese people to live freely.[28] That troubled Fulbright, who wondered whether the United States could stay within limits in the bombing campaign and get Hanoi to concede defeat. Fulbright and Albert Gore (D, Tennessee), who made a similar point about the goal of forcing Hanoi to surrender, exhibited a better sense of the commitment in North Vietnam than Taylor, who thought the means and objective of US strategy were appropriately limited.[29]

Gore, representing the skeptical position shared by the majority, expressed regret for his prior hesitancy to speak out against the war and argued that all it did was help the Soviet Union gain ground in the Cold War in Europe and Latin America. He also worried that the conflict could not be kept limited to Southeast Asia and might lead to nuclear war with China.[30] Wayne Morse (D, Oregon), one of just two dissenters in the vote on the Tonkin Gulf Resolution in August 1964, attacked Taylor as the embodiment of a misguided war effort and of American militarism. The exchange grew sharper as Taylor objected to Morse's conclusion that the American people were sure to tire of the war. This, Taylor shot back, "was good news to Hanoi." In substantive terms, Morse's questions veered from the current situation to whether the United States had violated terms of the 1954 Geneva Accords. He argued there had been false pretense from the outset. Taylor disagreed, reminding the senators that the United States and South Vietnam had not signed that agreement, but he conceded in his opening statement and the subsequent discussion that the goal, a negotiated settlement and an independent South Vietnam, was hard to attain.[31]

Taylor made the case for the Vietnam War as a Cold War battle. He stressed that he did not like the term "domino theory" and did not think neighbors would fall automatically if South Vietnam did. Instead, subversive aggression would spread to a number of vulnerable countries. He also noted that there were no viable alternatives to the present strategy and that he believed the wider importance of the war was to disprove the theory of wars of national liberation.[32] Frank Church (D, Idaho) and Claiborne Pell (D, Rhode Island) shared Gore's fear that a harder hitting air campaign could draw China into the war, a notion Taylor deemed unlikely as long as the targets remained military in nature. Pell contrasted Taylor's statements about the need for American forces to seek out enemy main units—though not guerrilla fighters in general—and the enclave strategy that Gavin had proposed to the committee nine days prior. He found both positions convincing in the moment and wished the two retired generals would debate the issue publicly.[33] Komer, who had considered recruiting other retired generals, like Lauris Norstad, as pro-war witnesses, found Taylor's appearance so persuasive that he ceased his efforts.[34] PFIAB chairman Clark Clifford congratulated Taylor on a magnificent performance: "It had substance, logic and clarity, and these qualities, added to your composure and dignity, made it a memorable occasion." Taylor joked, "At least I can now say that I have lived through two 'Longest Days.'"[35] He hoped it helped educate the public and moved Americans to "roll up our national sleeves and get back to the serious business in South Viet-Nam."[36]

Political infighting in South Vietnam reached a fever pitch in early April 1966. The ARVN's I Corps commander, General Nguyen Chanh Thi, appeared to support mass protests in the Buddhist stronghold of Danang that threatened the fabric of the state. Lyndon Johnson and his Vietnam brain trust expected Ky's government to fall. At their emergency meeting on April 4, Taylor noted that if Buddhist leader Thich Tri Quang became the man behind the throne, "he will tear down everything." Not that Ky had been ideal: when LBJ pointed at his unfortunate statement that the mayor of Danang ought to be shot, Taylor reminded him of "the Hitler statement—but I thought [Ky] had matured." The best one could do, Taylor recommended, was to nudge Ky to step aside so that the military council could retain control.³⁷ But Taylor misread the crisis. Ky reacted with resolve and Thi, whose relationship with Buddhist leaders was tenser than it seemed from Washington, publicly renounced any desire to overthrow the government. In June he left for lifelong exile in the United States.³⁸ The episode illustrated that Taylor had not gained a keener sense of South Vietnam by stepping out of the daily fray of Saigon's politics.

By the spring of 1966, Taylor had come to accept the logic of the body count, noting that enemy capabilities had to degrade once casualties topped infiltration rates, which McNamara now put at 8,000 per month.³⁹ How to count and stop the infiltrators stimulated creative thinking. That summer, McNamara proposed planting sensors by way of airdrops along the Ho Chi Minh trail in Laos and building an electronic fence at the DMZ, an idea that had originated with the Pentagon's Advanced Research Projects Agency and the RAND Corporation. When the JCS rejected the far-fetched scheme, McNamara asked Taylor and William Sullivan to investigate the concept with a group of ARPA scientists in Santa Barbara. McNamara believed sensors would allow military intelligence to provide more accurate estimates of the pace of infiltration. Some areas could be designated denial barriers, because MACV could call for air strikes as soon as sensors showed activity. Sullivan recalled that neither he nor Taylor, who had nurtured the scheme in 1961 when he was impressed by presentations of ARPA operatives in Vietnam and told Lansdale to develop plans for electronic surveillance of South Vietnam's borders, thought much of it. McNamara overruled all doubters, sensors were planted, and an electronic fence was built. The results did not justify the effort and expense.⁴⁰

In the meantime Taylor had sharpened his position on diplomacy. At the end of April he told Lyndon Johnson what the US government should demand in return for a bombing pause. As a precondition for peace talks, Taylor wanted "some degree of reduction or elimination of Viet Cong and . . . North Vietnamese activity in the South, or a cessation of infiltration from the North, or a combination of both." Until such moves occurred, to avoid peace talks that the enemy used for grandstanding, the United States had to keep up the air offensive. Taylor recalled the Korean armistice talks: North Korea and China could stall because they had no incentive to settle. Still, if Johnson wanted to negotiate, he had at least six blue chips: cessation of bombing in North Vietnam, halting military operations against Vietcong units, offering to send no additional US forces to South Vietnam, withdrawal of US forces from South Vietnam, offering amnesty and civic rights for NLF fighters and officers, and promising economic aid to North Vietnam. Of course, Taylor noted, these chips should only be traded for an end to PLAF operations, no more infiltration from the North, withdrawal of all PAVN units, and dissolution of the NLF as a political movement. Taylor thought a comprehensive deal could be built on ending US bombing raids in return for a termination of PLAF and PAVN military operations.[41]

Kissinger, who was then trying to set up back channels to Hanoi, learned about Taylor's plans from Harriman. He thought Taylor was naive, as his scheme left the communists in control of much of South Vietnam. Kissinger preferred the establishment of checkpoints in South Vietnam and Laos to verify the end of North Vietnamese infiltration.[42] Ambassador Lodge, too, questioned the feasibility of Taylor's suggestions. He noted that American negotiators should indeed proceed from an understanding that "initiation and discussions does not mean the advent of peace" and that Hanoi had to be pressured to come to a prompt settlement. Lodge feared that any leaks to the press linking pauses in the bombing and a cease-fire might make it impossible to resume bombing later in the face of pressure from public opinion. While it might be possible to resume offensive operations on the ground, he concluded Taylor's proposal did not "reach terrorism in the Viet Cong areas," and this would open up American and South Vietnamese forces to charges of operating in places deemed off limits in the agreement.[43]

By February 1967, Taylor had worked out a more detailed proposal, building toward a full-blown cease-fire, which would end American bombing in North Vietnam as well as the three kinds of war in the South: the "big war" of PAVN and PLAF main units, the "little war" of local guerrillas, and the "criminal war" waged by saboteurs and terrorists. One would have to expect breaches of the truce because PAVN units depended on resupplies and PLAF units had to steal from the people. One would also have to expect delaying tactics from communist negotiators akin to what had happened in Korea. It was thus best to start with normalization, seeking diplomatic channels that would allow American and North Vietnamese negotiators to meet. Taylor thought this might lead to a slow decline in fighting, especially if talks were conducted in secret and American diplomats could show their Vietnamese counterparts what kind of settlement to expect. Moreover, the United States could punish North Vietnam for missing deadlines, presumably by stepping up the air campaign. For Taylor, a halt to the bombing and a cease-fire were the desired outcomes and could therefore not be preconditions for negotiations.[44]

The close linkage of bombing and talking in Taylor's thinking was further illustrated by the contrast with more extreme hawks, like Rostow and the JCS, who advocated for an unrestrained air war. Taylor reminded the president in May 1967 that industrial targets whose destruction could force North Vietnam to quit simply did not exist. By then Johnson had long approved striking petroleum, oil, and lubricant facilities, a category of targets that had once proved so significant in the air war against Nazi Germany. In Vietnam, it did not shift the balance of resolve. Taylor cautioned against rendering the regime powerless and unable to conduct peace talks, and the nuance in his approach frustrated the president. Taylor's distinction of relative success against infiltration, which the United States had never intended to stop but did curtail, served as a case in point.[45] Yet, uncomfortable as he was with Rostow's lack of restraint, Taylor had not shifted into the peace camp. In October 1967 he was among those advisers who argued Kissinger's back channel diplomacy should be abandoned. In this he was joined by Rusk, Supreme Court Justice Abe Fortas, and Clifford, but not McNamara, who had spent much of 1967 in search of an exit strategy.[46]

In the summer of 1967, Taylor found himself on another mission to South Vietnam, this time accompanied by PFIAB chairman Clark Clifford. Lyndon Johnson told the leaders of allied nations he was sending "my most experienced and trusted advisers" to review the situation in Vietnam and consult with the members of the Manila group (the seven countries with armed forces in Vietnam: the United States, Australia, New Zealand, the Philippines, Thailand, South Vietnam, and South Korea) "on all aspects of the Vietnam problem." The president combined optimism and a plea for more troops: "We must meet and defeat whatever Hanoi may do in the South, while continuing to deal effectively with thrusts across the border by North Vietnamese forces and with the infiltration routes and sources of supply in North Vietnam." LBJ also thought "the Vietnamese themselves fully recognize that they must do more and General Westmoreland feels substantial need for additional external help."[47] It was thus a central part of Taylor and Clifford's mission to persuade US allies to make a greater effort in Vietnam.

Johnson's emissaries found a combination of resolve and bewilderment. Taylor concluded that the leaders of America's allies believed the policy was right, but they recognized they were losing the global public relations battle. Worse, Taylor noted, the American people were turning against the war in greater numbers, especially among elites who shaped public opinion. Clifford thought of Washington as "the miasma of pessimism." To counter these trends and establish a unified narrative of the challenges in Vietnam and the soundness of American policy, Taylor proposed a public relations strategy. For international audiences, he recommended monthly coordinating meetings of State Department officials and representatives of the Manila group, sharing background papers that could be placed in all embassies of the seven nations, and instructions to their ambassadors to defend the Southeast Asia policy vigorously. A year later, Clifford came to identify this trip as the starting point of his concerns about the war, but in 1967 he still seemed to share Taylor's optimism.[48]

Taylor told the press there was no lack of resolve. The allies were prepared to increase the pressure in Vietnam, but "the question is how to accomplish it." The problem, Taylor held, was to do well enough "in the big war against the major units" to allow for improvements to long-term pacification and nation-building efforts. He admitted that South Vietnam's politics remained unsettled, but he expressed optimism about "constitutional procedures which are moving forward" toward national elections in the fall. Taylor conceded that opinions in the Manila group were split on his suggested blockade of Haiphong, which could have been read as a declaration of war: "everyone would like to have the harbor of Haiphong closed, but, of course, there is a price to pay for it." Questions about restraint aside, Taylor made clear that allied support for South Vietnam was stronger than the American public seemed to perceive. He noted that there were 47,000 Korean combat troops in Vietnam, and when a reporter pointed out there also were 56,000 US troops in South Korea, Taylor remarked, implausibly, "It would be very interesting for you if you listed all the large contributions to South Vietnam and compared them with Korea. You will find that the Free World contribution on a percentage basis is higher in South Vietnam than it was in Korea."[49] Yet to most Americans it probably did not mean much that there were 55,000 officers and men from allied countries as well as 800,000 South Vietnamese fighting alongside half a million Americans. What loomed largest was that 6,350 Americans had died in Vietnam in 1966; for 1967 the count would be 11,363.[50]

After Tet

To meet the grave threat of eroding support for the war effort, Taylor thought a group of experts should speak at universities, talk to reporters, and appear on all major political television programs to convey why the United States fought and how the war could be won. Lodge could lead them as a senior statesman with broad expertise on Vietnam. For other members, Taylor proposed General William E. DePuy, the commander of 1st Infantry Division in Vietnam and former MACV operations chief; Philip Habib, former head of the political section of the Saigon embassy; a diplomat or military officer who knew the pacification program (Taylor suggested Richard Holbrook and Komer's White House aide Lieutenant Colonel Robert Montague); Leroy Wehrle, who was due to return to the United States after several years as economist at the Saigon embassy; and a State Department official familiar with attempts to open negotiations with the North Vietnamese. Given several months, Taylor hoped, these men would rebuild public confidence. He remained convinced that US strategy for the war was well defined and that the American people would approve if they were properly informed.[51]

Lyndon Johnson crafted his own public relations approach that fall. He relied heavily on his bully pulpit in speeches and press conferences and leaned on Rusk, McNamara (despite the latter's growing doubts about the war that prompted him to urge Johnson on November 1 to find a way out), and Westmoreland to persuade the American people that victory was near. Taylor reemphasized the need for a comprehensive public education campaign in mid-November. He noted that the White House should target opinion-makers in the media, political and business elites and other influential public figures, such as teachers and ministers, the general public, and selected foreign audiences. He thought this could be achieved through "speeches, news conferences and T.V. appearances of US officials; citizens committees in large cities supported from Washington by speakers and literature." Taylor also proposed "White House briefings of big shots of the political, business and publicity media worlds; trips to Vietnam by senior citizens on the model of the Election Observer trip; visits to the United States by Asian leaders with a stake in the outcome in Vietnam." And he hoped "a government sponsored T.V. program to answer citizens' questions bearing on Vietnam" could reclaim the narrative.[52] Johnson stuck with the familiar routine of high-profile speeches and an optimistic message. In so doing, he inadvertently elevated the 1968 Tet Offensive from military struggle to political calamity.

Like Johnson, and indeed seemingly all key officials, Taylor did not show much awareness of the ramifications of Le Duan's ascent to power in Hanoi by 1964. In his year-end review in 1967, Taylor noted Ho Chi Minh had to comprehend he was not in a position to step up attacks in the South or sustain the same level of casualties as in 1966 and 1967 for much longer. By that calculus, retreat into small war while negotiating seemed the best option. This was a case of mirror imaging, assessing what Taylor would have done in Ho's position, and it showed a troubling lack of empathy. For the new PFIAB chairman to not be aware of the significant shifts in Hanoi, particularly the aggressiveness and intransigence of Le Duan and his inner circle, suggests American intelligence agencies provided little useful insight into the mind-set of North Vietnam's leaders.[53] How then could the United States force the DRV to negotiate? How could one assess whether airpower was having a substantial psychological effect?

At home, too, Taylor was losing his grip on the war. He had been critical of Lyndon Johnson on domestic public opinion since 1965. But there never was an honest public accounting for why the United States was engaged in war in Vietnam, how it was fought, and why the American people needed to remain patient.[54] Under the circumstances, it almost seems surprising that anti-war sentiment (and anti-war effort) did not surge more markedly before mid-1967. In his memoir, Taylor remained quiet about Johnson's public relations campaign in late 1967. He agreed with Johnson's assessment: from the vantage point of late 1967, 1968 looked like the year in which the war could be won. His take on a speech by Senator Edward Kennedy on January 25 in Boston, counseling de-escalation, illustrated Taylor's thinking: "I know of no military men who have been on the ground in Viet-Name who support such proposals. They are familiar with the lessons of military history that an energetic offensive, properly conducted, shortens combat and thereby reduces the loss of life and property." Taking to the defensive could only increase the suffering; it invited "slow but costly attrition, progressive discouragement, mounting loss of morale and eventual defeat."[55] That the enemy might launch massive countrywide attacks did not enter Taylor's mind on the eve of the Tet Offensive.

Instead of victory 1968 brought turmoil. At the end of January, Vietnam's communist forces launched their largest offensive yet. In the United States, politicians and the public initially rallied behind the president, but that soon changed. Signifying the shift, at the end of February, Walter Cronkite's assessment of the situation as a stalemate in his CBS News broadcast from Vietnam convinced Lyndon Johnson he had lost the support of the American people. At that point Taylor was invested in discussions over how many additional troops the Pentagon should deploy. The *New York Times* soon reported that Westmoreland had requested

206,000 men, on top of the over half a million US troops who were already in Vietnam. Taylor pointed at the distinction between a contingency plan for an all-out offensive—for which Westmoreland would have needed over 700,000 men—and the immediate request of 25,000 men to facilitate the counterattacks already under way. This was not a simple misunderstanding between military men and civilians, however. JCS chairman Earle Wheeler, the driving force behind the request for 206,000 men, intended to force the president to call up the reserve and restore American forces in Europe, Korea, and at home that had been depleted.[56]

Taylor attempted to stiffen the president's resolve. In early February, before he knew just how many American soldiers Westmoreland and the JCS hoped to add, at a time when speculations reached only as high as 45,000, Taylor advised LBJ to send fifteen additional battalions. Their main contribution to the war effort, he thought, was "in demonstrating to the world, including Hanoi, that we mean business." Closing with his usual pitch, Taylor implored Johnson to "maintain the bombing of the north at maximum levels of effectiveness," but he also noted it was high time to "review and clarify our military and political objectives for the remainder of this year."[57] Taylor did not recommend holding on to every inch of ground. On February 14, contrary to Westmoreland's plans, Taylor told the president that US forces should withdraw from the besieged outpost at Khe Sanh in northwestern South Vietnam. He applied a logic similar to the 1953 decisions to cede forward posts in Korea: the cost of defending Khe Sanh was greater than the benefit of holding on.[58] In a famous photograph, Johnson and his national security adviser, Walt Rostow, are shown huddling over a relief map of Khe Sanh at the White House. Indeed, when Rostow alerted the president to Taylor's concerns, he also noted that the map was set up in the Situation Room.[59] Taylor may have had a sound operational calculus, but he did not gauge the president's mind-set.

In early March, Taylor summarized the two distinctly different views of the Tet Offensive prevalent in Washington. One group held that despite all initial success, the enemy had exposed himself and the time was right for American and South Vietnamese forces to press on to victory; the other group believed the enemy had hit vital nerve centers, South Vietnamese armed forces had given up on pacification and retrenched in the cities, government leaders were deeply divided, and the United States could only hope to stem the tide by an even greater commitment to uncertain ends. Taylor attributed these divergent interpretations to a common ailment of all Vietnam War assessments: everyone read the data selectively and proceeded to view events with predetermined conclusions in mind. He agreed with the optimistic reading, but conceded the pessimistic assessment had some merit in the short term.

Above all, he warned of drawing premature conclusions before Westmoreland's counteroffensive had ended. Taylor did not dismiss outright the basic fear of the pessimists that "Viet-nam is a sponge with an inexhaustible capacity for absorbing US resources and, hence, at some point we must call a halt." Taylor accurately concluded that the PLAF faced great difficulties in finding new recruits in the South. Lacking hard evidence, he also asserted that North Vietnam could not maintain current rates of infiltration of men and supplies and that the communists' logistics system was strained to the breaking point. This was, he closed hopefully, the fourteenth year of the war for both Vietnamese regimes and "it is hard to believe that Hanoi is enjoying the conflict or can hold out indefinitely as the pessimists believe." Consequently, "these considerations encourage the belief that an end—or at least the start of negotiations—may not be far off" as long as the United States kept up the pressure in South Vietnam and continued bombing the North. He knew the American people were unwilling to endure a protracted stalemate. Now was the time to get more aggressive.[60]

Taylor assumed President Johnson could not stomach withdrawal but was unlikely to escalate further. He proposed three "program packages worth serious consideration." Option A, which amounted to staying the course, provided none of the requested 206,000 additional troops. Option B, staying the course with moderately more manpower, suggested a "partial acceptance of General Westmoreland's recommendation." Both called for new strategic guidance; buildup of the strategic reserve; no negotiation initiative; the withdrawal of the San Antonio formula as the basis for peace talks, which held the United States would cease bombing North Vietnam in return for Hanoi's guarantee not to increase the rate of infiltration; and pressure on Nguyen Van Thieu's government to do better. Taylor's third option called for full approval of Westmoreland's request and a "major effort to rally the homefront." He conceded that there was a fourth possibility: "We can lower our objective to a compromise resulting in something less than an independent Viet-Nam free from attack or we can drop back further and content ourselves with punishing the aggressor to the point that we can withdraw, feeling that the 'War of Liberation' technique has at least been somewhat discredited as a cheap method of Communist expansion." Taylor thought Westmoreland should concentrate forces around the cities, thus temporarily exposing remote areas. Once there were enough reserves, he could conduct limited operations into Laos, Cambodia, or the DMZ. Underwriting it all was continued bombing of North Vietnam and expansion of South Vietnam's armed forces, which should take over in the Mekong delta and replace American forces in the countryside and in strongholds along the DMZ.[61]

Taylor concluded that the Pentagon should deploy 25,000 additional men for now and consider further contingency plans. But when the Wise Men, a group of retired officers and former government officials, met in late March, he found the mood changed. Whereas the November 1967 meeting had shown widespread support for the limited war strategy, now all but three participants objected: Taylor, Robert Murphy, and Abe Fortas. Some of the hawks, most notably Acheson and Bundy, could no longer imagine a successful outcome. Taylor believed his fellow Wise Men had made up their minds from media and newspaper coverage, since the briefings given by Philip Habib, CIA officer George Carver, and General DePuy did not warrant an overly pessimistic assessment. He also suspected civilians in the Pentagon who had turned against the war had privately approached some of his colleagues. Above all, Taylor thought the debate over unattainable military victory was misguided—military victory had never been the American objective in Vietnam.[62]

The Wise Men's advice contributed to Lyndon Johnson's decision not to seek reelection. He made the announcement in a televised address on March 31 that began with the words "Tonight I want to speak to you of peace in Vietnam and Southeast Asia."[63] Talks began in Paris in May, with Harriman and Cyrus Vance as the American chief negotiators, but in 1968 this did not proceed much beyond considering the framework and the question of under what conditions the United States would stop bombing North Vietnam.[64] Taylor stuck to his hardline position: a bombing pause should follow only on significant concessions by Hanoi. Harriman, Vance, and a growing number of State and Defense Department officials held that a bombing pause would signal good faith to Hanoi's leaders. Johnson vacillated and ultimately determined only in late October to end Rolling Thunder entirely, but that was a function of the presidential elections and a last-ditch effort to boost the chances of Vice President Hubert Humphrey.[65]

Taylor had experienced major setbacks in 1968. His influence waned and the cornerstone of his strategy, strategic bombing to force Hanoi to come to terms, had crumbled. He had tried to keep Johnson focused on expanding the air war, but gained an increasing number of opponents, including Clifford, who deemed the war unwinnable, and Paul Nitze, who now ran the Defense Department's foreign policy and strategy shop. In May, Taylor supported recommendations by Ambassador Ellsworth Bunker not to cease bombing in North Vietnam "for an inadequate return" on the diplomatic track. US negotiators should continue talks about a complete cessation of bombing, but in the meantime air strikes should be expanded between the 19th and 20th parallel.[66] This raised the hackles of Clifford's deputies. In their May 25 staff meeting, Nitze complained that Taylor's pleas were based on the assumption that North Vietnam would quit once the pain got too great. He concluded: "How do we *know*? We don't!" Clifford's right-hand man, Paul Warnke, agreed: "We aren't doing anything we haven't already done—What Taylor is saying is to threaten that we'll slug them—but we can't slug them any more than we already have done—& we didn't break their will before why sh[ou]ld we be able to break it now??"[67] Airpower had hit its limits and no one could say with certainty that victory could be won. Nevertheless, Lyndon Johnson still listened to hawks, like Rostow and Taylor, more than to Clifford and Harriman.[68]

Taylor had taken over as PFIAB chairman just as the magnitude of the Tet Offensive sank in. His central questions were whether US intelligence had missed critical clues and what one might do to improve signals intelligence to gauge infiltration rates from North Vietnam to the South. Here, Taylor recommended strengthened aerial surveillance.[69] With respect to Tet, Taylor concluded that the sense of uneasiness felt by commanders in Vietnam, most notably General Fred Weyand in Saigon, which had led to just enough preparedness to defend the capital region, had not reached the proper pitch in Washington. He ascribed this partly to fragmented intelligence data points and the sheer amount of clutter, but stressed that intelligence coordination in Washington and between field offices and higher headquarters needed to be more comprehensive and timely.[70]

In the months after Tet, better intelligence data helped Taylor alert Lyndon Johnson to an imminent enemy offensive. The recent lull in fighting in Vietnam, he concluded, was a result of the enemy's need to integrate a massive influx of new fighters. Despite very heavy losses, North Vietnamese army units, PLAF main forces, and local irregular forces stood some 18,000 men above their pre-Tet manpower level. At the July 30 Tuesday lunch Lyndon Johnson asked Taylor, who was not a regular member of the influential lunch group, to consider whether the lull in fighting indicated any willingness of Hanoi to engage in the Paris talks. Taylor rushed to talk to Clifford, Rusk, CIA director Richard Helms,

Bunker, and new MACV commander General Creighton Abrams. He did not find time to consult with his fellow board members, in part because his assessment indicated great urgency. The enemy was building up strength for another wave of attacks, the third in a sequence initiated by the Tet Offensive. Taylor estimated it would commence in the first half of August and focus on the coastal area in I Corps running from the DMZ to Danang, Ban Me Thuot in the highlands, Loc Ninh near the Cambodian border, and Saigon itself.[71] So it did, and as in the initial Tet Offensive and another wave in the spring, enemy forces were exposed in vulnerable positions and the PLAF was left decimated.

Positive operational developments notwithstanding, Taylor watched the emerging Paris talks and the war itself with growing concern. In a meeting in late May to assess whether Hanoi would capitulate during negotiations if the United States kept bombing, Taylor noted, "We are hurting ourselves by restricting the bombing."[72] Taylor proposed to take aim entirely at the political will of the leadership in Hanoi, without specifying how exactly that could be done. This struck Rusk as overly defined by political goals and fraught with political risks. In a role reversal, the secretary of state argued that airpower should be used primarily for operational purposes, whereas the retired general aimed at political goals. To Rusk, it still made sense to focus on bombing supply depots in the North and destroying men and material on the infiltration routes of the Ho Chi Minh trail. He seemed to think the war could be won in the South.[73] In July, Taylor doubled down: peace talks were at a stalemate and US airpower had done quite well before the talks had started, before political decisions imposed undue limitations.[74] Clifford rejected Taylor's premise. On a recent trip to Vietnam he had come to realize the war could not be won, and worse, he suspected Thieu's government was most interested in keeping the protection of 540,000 American soldiers and marines and the "golden stream" of money from Washington. Moreover, he decided Taylor's other assumption, that the United States had an "*obligation* absolute" to stay in Vietnam, was equally false.[75] When Taylor returned to his idea, first voiced in the aftermath of the Tet Offensive, to link the intensity of bombing in North Vietnam to the level of attacks in the South, Clifford shot back that the United States had to get out of Vietnam, not get drawn deeper into a war with the DRV.[76]

In the midst of the 1968 presidential election campaign, Taylor warned President Johnson that recent positive signals in the Paris talks could be a trap or an indication how much North Vietnam was hurting. Once again his mind returned to Korea: surely, leadership in Hanoi had drawn the conclusion that the United States would shift into a defensive posture on the battlefield if negotiations seemed to progress. Was October 1968 like the fall of 1951 all over again? Taylor speculated that there were "factors in the Hanoi-Peking-Moscow triangular relationship, unknown to us, which push them to this decision." It seemed possible that the losses in the South and the cost of the war in general had finally made Hanoi consider returning to a lower-intensity effort. It greatly helped the American cause that the home front had calmed—Taylor's odd take on the events of summer 1968—and the election campaigns did not suggest Hanoi would find a more pliant administration in office in 1969. Taylor allowed that "these guesses may be far from the mark." He deployed them in an effort to remind Johnson, US negotiators, and the American people that rushing into a cease-fire would not make for peace.[77]

In his memoir, while the war had not yet ended, Taylor concluded that all foreign commitments could come at a steep price in lives, treasure, and social and political upheaval at home. He remained convinced that an independent South Vietnam was a cornerstone of American strategy for Southeast Asia, yet he acknowledged that intelligence on North Vietnam was sparse and that it proved impossible at critical junctures to project how Hanoi would respond to American actions. Even anticipating Saigon's actions proved unreliable. Instead of sound intelligence, American policymakers and strategists had to rely on conjecture from the Korean War; if North Vietnam's leaders behaved like those of China and North Korea, increased military pressure could lead to a favorable negotiated settlement. Of course, they did not, and Taylor's lessons instead served as an indictment of the intelligence services and the national security establishment.[78]

Taylor came to conclude that the war was lost at home, and he consistently lamented the lack of a comprehensive media and information campaign. He felt bitterness toward the press and television reporters, but he knew the fault lay with the White House and inefficiency in the American system of governance. Few experienced operators survived a change in administrations, and every four or eight years lessons had to be learned anew. Leaders were thus "likely to be new and untrained" and "likely to be timid as well."[79] Taylor had advised a strategy of gradual escalation to minimize the risk of war spinning out of control, but he recognized this meant "to apply limited force with limited means to gain limited results. While this carefully controlled violence may have had some justification at the start, it ended by defeating its own purposes . . . [and] ended by assuring a prolonged war which carried with it the dangers of expansion."[80] Pulled in two directions, Taylor regretted the restraint put on the use of airpower, but still found the tight control exercised by the White House on targets wholly appropriate. What may have made a difference was that the Johnson administration ultimately decided not to "flatten everything in and around Hanoi . . . it would have made it extremely difficult to continue [the war] effectively" if North Vietnam kept going after such an assault.[81] More generally, he expressed deep skepticism about the feasibility of limited war against a determined enemy.[82]

Taylor had continued his quest to improve the decision-making apparatus in the late 1960s. In 1968, for example, he invited Gordon Gray to participate in an IDA study of "the evolution and current status of the national security process at the level of the President and his principal advisers."[83] Taylor held on to his belief that the State and Defense Departments worked at cross purposes and that the JCS were structurally hampered and could not provide the measured advice the president and secretary of defense needed to hear.[84] In his retrospective on the PFIAB's activities, Taylor made clear that for reasons of security and efficiency it should remain a neutral and apolitical group of presidential appointees rather than a watchdog for congressional committees that oversee the intelligence community. He was proud of his efforts: the intelligence community operated more smoothly; the CIA had benefited from the establishment of a deputy directorate for science and technology (in 1963); the DIA, founded in 1961, had centralized data gathering and analysis within the Defense Department; the shift from service attachés to a single defense attaché (in 1964) had streamlined performance at US embassies; new technologies and increased funding had strengthened the signals intelligence program; an NSA-operated global communications system reported critical intelligence to key offices in Washington more speedily; protection against electronic eavesdropping had been improved; the introduction of uniform standards allowed for more stringent criteria in the issuance of security clearances; and, in Vietnam, signals intelligence, clandestine agents, more coordinated interrogation of POWs, and more keen analysis of captured documents had led to a much improved intelligence collection effort.[85]

There remained room for improvement. Taylor concluded the president did not receive sufficiently up-to-date intelligence in moments of crisis like the Tet Offensive, early warning capabilities could stand further tweaking, and too many different agencies and departments without proper coordination conducted evaluations of military capabilities. Moreover, as science and technology advanced, signals intelligence had to follow, which required greater resources and better communications. Taylor noted that the NSA had suffered from frequent turnover in leadership and recommended longer tours of duty for its director. He considered US espionage efforts "inadequate," though the explanation remains redacted in the document. The US counterintelligence effort suffered from a lack of authorization to use audio surveillance devices against foreign agents within the United States. Taylor worried, too, that the DIA did not receive the full support of all military departments and offices, and he fell back on an older critique when he noted that NSC policy guidance to the intelligence community was vague and needed more frequent updating. On the whole, Taylor noted "the increasing importance of the national intelligence effort to our security," stressed the importance of attracting the best and brightest Americans to work in this field, and admonished the administration to speak out forcefully against "an unhappy tendency in Congress, the press and elsewhere to denigrate intelligence in the public eye and to undermine public confidence in our intelligence agencies, particularly the CIA."[86] Taylor, who still relished debate and remained tolerant of opposing views, had, with growing age and based on his experiences in the Vietnam War, discovered an enemy in parts of the media.

Taylor as Critic

Observing the national scene after 1968, Taylor feared that domestic fallout from the Vietnam War had destroyed the Cold War consensus. He opposed the termination of the draft because he believed the American people had to be invested in national service if mobilization for the Cold War was to be seen as an all-out effort. But as long as the limited war option was retained, Americans could take solace in their relative strength even in times of declining military and economic power.[87] Wars of national liberation, guerrilla tactics, and determined foes were here to stay, and politicians, soldiers, and the public had to recognize that power projection was difficult and costly. The Vietnam War had shown "our ineffective use of available power arising from the bias or inexperience of officials, from self-imposed restrictions on the use of military power, and from the ineptitude of our diplomacy in exploiting military success." In the coming years Americans were likely to turn against the military, view war as unheroic, and lack the will to conduct it successfully. Cold War strategy required a new conception of national security and a renewed commitment to national unity.[88]

Taylor proposed a test of the national interest before pursuing a war. Presidents and their advisers needed to address four measures: "the gain to be anticipated from its success, the probable cost of achieving this success, the probability of failure, and the additive cost which failure would entail." How to interpret these in any given crisis was in the eye of the beholder. As late as 1972, Taylor still thought an independent South Vietnam could be sustained and that probable gains of victory outweighed the costs of the war effort; most others, even within the Nixon administration, had come to a different conclusion.[89] For future limited wars, Taylor recommended that the president needed to be certain of sustained popular support and rely on a military prepared to win quickly and decisively. In Vietnam, a declaration of war would have been better than Johnson's reliance on the Tonkin Gulf Resolution. Taylor did not know that President Johnson had floated the idea of asking for additional authorization to deploy ground forces in June 1965 and that Senate majority leader Mike Mansfield had advised against it because he could not guarantee smooth passage and did not think the Senate should dictate military actions.[90]

Oddly, Taylor's assessment in 1972 was no more pessimistic than what he had presented in his spring 1966 lectures at Lehigh University. There, too, he had pointed at the need to weigh carefully the cost of intervention and anticipated consequences of inaction. While Vietnam had required intervention and offered an opportunity to confront war of national liberation, the United States had to be careful not to deplete the strategic reserve and become embroiled in unnecessary wars that could only attrite American power. Local allies had to be willing and able to fight their own wars; foreigners could provide assistance, but they could not impose a legitimate government or establish viable social order. In crises, careful selectivity was key, and in Taylor's view the Eisenhower administration had crossed a critical line in Vietnam in 1954. He concluded that this step was taken consciously, in hopes that Diem would assert his rule, and based on the recognition that inaction was worse. At that point it would have been better to treat clandestine support for an insurgency like open aggression and attack North Vietnam and the infiltration and resupply routes through Laos. And in South Vietnam the United States had never fully integrated war fighting and pacification.[91]

Until the Paris agreement was signed, Taylor held out hope for a positive end of the war. When former CIA and NSC officer Chester Cooper, whom Taylor had hired as an assistant director at the IDA, published *The Lost Crusade,* one of the earliest critical reflections on how the Kennedy and Johnson administration had made political and strategic decisions, Taylor responded that any conclusions depended on the as yet uncertain outcome. "If it ends in the 'free choice' by the South Vietnamese people which you advocate in your book," Taylor noted hopefully, "I would say that the crusade has achieved its prime objective."[92] Cooper had foresworn the logic that the ends justified the means when he resigned from the White House staff in March 1966. He thought the tepid response characteristic of Taylor's defensiveness and detachment: "perhaps it was too much to ask Taylor to peel off the six layers of armor." Later on, in a 1999 interview, Cooper noted that no one other than Taylor's wife and son (Cooper seemed unaware there were two sons) broke through Taylor's armor.[93] Cooper's editor was less forgiving and reminded Taylor that his own *Uncertain Trumpet* had once equally attempted to raise questions that the public should debate.[94]

In a 1979 interview Taylor noted the lessons he had drawn from Vietnam since the Paris Accords. He reiterated that Lyndon Johnson should not have sent ground forces without a declaration of war. Taylor admitted that this was his conclusion in hindsight, albeit one he had already stressed in the later years of the war. This reflected his concern that the Kennedy and Johnson administrations failed to craft a consistent message to convey the importance of the conflict to the American people. The main failing, however, was in intelligence. Taylor conceded the US government never understood its ally—quite unlike in Korea— and knew next to nothing about North Vietnam and its leaders. One issue Taylor and others had taken into account, on the other hand, was the British experience in Malaya, a case of successful counterinsurgency, albeit against a very different enemy in an incomparable political and geographic environment.[95] Here, Taylor's recollection matches recent historical research on William Westmoreland, who visited Malaysia in early 1964 and who had studied the conflict closely as superintendent at West Point.[96]

Taylor, who remained the PFIAB chair until the spring of 1970, did not have much influence on the Nixon administration. The only occasions when he was invited to the White House were affairs with dozens, sometimes hundreds of guests: an April 18, 1969, reception for the American Society of Newspaper Editors; a May 15, 1969, armed forces breakfast, which put him in the same room as Arthur Radford; a dinner honoring Ambassadors Charles Bohlen, David Bruce, Robert Murphy, and Llewellyn Thompson that same evening; and the April 10, 1970, state dinner for West German chancellor Willy Brandt. Nixon met with

Taylor's PFIAB only once, on April 14, 1969. By the time of the next meeting, on June 5, 1970, retired admiral George Anderson had taken over as chairman.[97]

Taylor maintained his ties to Henry Kissinger, the national security adviser and chief negotiator of the Paris Accords. As part of the transition from the Johnson to the Nixon administration, Taylor and Kissinger had talked about the linkage of troop withdrawals and cease-fire talks. Taylor favored seeking an agreement on bilateral withdrawals, but he doubted that the North Vietnamese were prepared to accept it. Unilateral troop withdrawals were fraught with risk, though perhaps a limited action after an agreement with Saigon might yield positive results. Bringing back some American troops would buy goodwill from a restive public at home, and if the ARVN could step up, it might also send a strong message to Hanoi that the communists could not win the war. The fundamental trap to avoid, Taylor told Kissinger in March 1969, was creating an unstoppable dynamic in which limited unilateral withdrawals made any future bilateral agreement less likely while at the same time raising expectations of the American people that the war was winding down and their boys were coming home.[98]

Once Kissinger had attained an initial agreement with his North Vietnamese counterpart Le Duc Tho in the fall of 1972, he sought Taylor's advice in a Sunday evening phone conversation. Taylor, pointing at his experience with intransigent communists in Korea, expressed concern over several issues. Kissinger assured him that the first, the obviously unworkable National Reconciliation Council, comprised of representatives of Thieu's government and the NLF, was merely a smokescreen designed to allow all parties to sign the agreement. Taylor's bigger concern was with the fragments of the text Hanoi had released to American news media. He wondered why Kissinger did not counter with a fuller version, but he was most concerned with the absence of any mention that ammunition could be replaced after a cease-fire. Kissinger noted he still wanted to negotiate and could not make the text public before it was completed. He assured Taylor that ammunition restocking was part of the agreement and that the Nixon administration retained the right to supply the ARVN in the postwar period. Indeed, this was significant enough to warrant another call from Kissinger the next morning once he had had a chance to review the full text.[99]

Taylor kept coming back to the difficulty of judging the agreement from Hanoi's text. In so doing, he inadvertently put his finger on a critical flaw in the cease-fire agreement: Hanoi's text was different from the English-language agreement, and the differences were not adjudicated in the January 1973 accords. Critically, where the English-language text spoke of a war between two countries, the Vietnamese-language text referred to a civil war and two regions.[100] Even though Kissinger admitted to duplicity only on the National Reconciliation Council, one might read the entire conversation as one in which he implied this was not an agreement meant to last. Instead, it was supposed to allow the ARVN to win the war after the cease-fire.[101] Yet neither Taylor nor Kissinger believed Saigon could capitalize on its advantages, which, Kissinger promised, included unlimited military and economic aid. Taylor identified the basic problem: the regime in Saigon had never lost its inferiority complex relative to the United States and South Vietnam feared the homogeneity of the North. Hanoi's dictators held the advantage in mobilizing all resources for a total war effort.[102]

Unlike McNamara and Rostow, who sparred bitterly in the mid-1990s, Taylor did not produce a postwar piece about the Vietnam War.[103] When he addressed questions in interviews, he was closer to the unrepentant Rostow than the tormented McNamara: the United States had lost a winnable war and fought a necessary one. In 1981 Taylor reflected on the muddled conception of victory. Initially, he thought, there had been a clear and attainable objective: to prevent South Vietnam from falling to communism and permit the people to choose their own government. But this became "garbled and confused to the point where no one seemed to understand it." Once American ground forces arrived in 1965, political and military objectives were never again brought into alignment. This was the ultimate failure of American strategy and of the national security system. Taylor noted that the president was the sole authority to "harmonize national resources." The general remained bitter about biased reporting from journalists who were often new to the job and always under pressure to report something fit to print, but he understood the deeper structural flaws. As he put it, he was still a Clausewitzian, but the dictum of war as the ultimate extension of policy needed to be amended. Taylor held that "military power is one of many forms of national power which are used to achieve national and international goals. When war comes, it needs to be preeminent, but all the rest must be coordinated and focused on the national goal."[104]

Looking beyond the Vietnam War, Taylor concluded that Washington had to adjust to a multipolar order. As early as 1966 he had argued that Washington needed to prepared for a world in which wars of national liberation and the rise of China added complexity to the Cold

War. To meet these threats, military means and social and economic programs had to be integrated in policy-making at home and in implementation abroad. The critical issues were finding talented and well-trained officials for overseas missions and weighing carefully the projected costs and benefits of investments and interventions.[105] Taylor had hoped that the senior interdepartmental group offered the right structure, and in his later commentary he expressed deep disappointment in the State Department's lack of leadership. His fear that American credibility and global power were at stake persisted: "If we leave Vietnam with our tail between our legs, the consequences of this defeat in the rest of Asia, Africa, and Latin America would be disastrous."[106] Since that had now happened, the question was how the United States could bounce back from defeat.

Taylor made the case for rearmament, following a maxim of Frederick the Great: "diplomacy without arms is music without instruments." He feared that since the 1950s "the gap between the hopes, aspirations, and expectations of American policy and the realities of military power has constantly widened." American diplomats and soldiers now faced an environment in which enemies and adversaries had grown much stronger.[107] He also worried that the new all-volunteer military, which had been one of the results of the Vietnam War, was unsuited to modern war and heavy casualties.[108] Taylor remained wedded to a conception of warfare that had been shaped by the industrial age: it was defined by mass, mobility, and firepower and was measured in men and machines. He feared "our national policy has become too lightly armed for security or success in the turbulent world which awaits us."[109] Yet as the 1980s dawned, information technology, smart bombs, and a host of new weapons and communications systems were about to offer the false allure of silver bullets.

Taylor's concern went beyond arms and budgets. He lamented the lack of an integrated policy statement resembling the Basic National Security Policy documents of the Eisenhower years. Since then, Pentagon planners had gathered presidential statements and those of foreign policy actors at the White House, in the cabinet, or in Congress to keep abreast of America's commitments and objectives. Yet the United States was committed to defend, protect, or build states almost anywhere in the world, and military tasks ranged from preparedness for major wars, protecting foreign markets and suppliers of raw materials, providing military assistance, and intervening in crises from Latin America to the Middle East, sub-Saharan Africa, and Asia and the Pacific. Political instability in supplier countries, perhaps supported by the Soviet Union, "could produce serious fluctuations in the output of the American economy that would injure the national prosperity and impair our ability to conduct and sustain military operations." In case of war, the navy appeared hard pressed to maintain control of shipping lanes from North America to Europe, to operate in the eastern Mediterranean, and to protect American interests in Southeast Asia and the southwest Pacific. The army could meet peacetime needs, but the reserves were depleted and mobilization required a return of conscription.[110]

Civil-military relations and the relationship between the executive branch and Congress also troubled Taylor, who worried about the lack of public support for any one of his hypothetical conflict scenarios. In particular, he noted that the fallout from the Vietnam War and the War Powers Act of 1973 made it likely the American people and their representatives in Washington would be caught in a lengthy debate rather than be prepared to intervene decisively in future crises. Since neither the relative weakness of the armed forces nor tense civil-military relations and congressional retrenchment were closely guarded secrets, an enterprising adversary could deem the moment right for political subversion or lower-scale military actions in an attempt to spread communism or deny the United States access to critical resources and strategic bases.[111]

In Taylor's assessment, the US nuclear deterrent remained strong, but the ability to defend Western Europe was now "extremely doubtful." Warsaw Pact forces that were "readily available for an attack are superior in numbers, better equipped with modern weapons, and backed by a deep communication zone," whereas American forces in southern Germany relied on a tenuous supply network from the North Sea port of Bremerhaven. Nevertheless, Taylor assumed that Soviet leaders understood the high risk of an attack and he concluded that while the American position in Western Europe seemed indefensible, it was not untenable. He advised American policymakers to avoid making commitments in the Middle East and Africa, where the United States lacked suitable bases and the Soviet Union, China, and Cuba had been particularly active in recent years.[112]

The United States did not have to bear the burden by itself. NATO and other allies contributed to defense and Washington should seek new "economic allies able and willing to enter into long-term contracts to provide us with essential imports." Above all, Americans needed to come to terms with the limits of power and with the declining standing of the United States in the world that restricted the freedom of action.[113] Taylor was sufficiently alarmed by the direction of detente and the finer points of strategic arms limitation talks to join the Committee on the Present Danger in 1976 as one of its founding members. He did not take an active part, but his presence added to the organization's cachet in military affairs. Taylor was joined by former CNO Elmo Zumwalt, Goodpaster, Ridgway, Lemnitzer, Rusk, Nitze, Gray, former CIA director William Colby, and leading neoconservatives who would play important roles in the Ronald Reagan administration.[114]

Taylor advocated for the expansion of conventional forces that could protect vital maritime lines of communication from "new bases in the South Atlantic, Southwest Pacific, southern Africa, and the approaches to the Persian Gulf." He calculated that an annual defense budget at 8 percent of the gross national product, instead of the current 5.7 percent, would meet the needs of the armed forces.[115] Yet unlike his former assistant and long-time friend Goodpaster, Taylor also believed the United States did not need to maintain a lead in the numerical count of nuclear missiles. Goodpaster recounted in 1976 that they had "a current disagreement on the subject of strategic nuclear weapons." Whereas Goodpaster held to the notion that the United States had to maintain "rough equivalence" with the Soviets, Taylor thought it was sufficient to maintain the capability to destroy the necessary targets in Russia, independent of whether the United States had more or fewer warheads than the Soviet Union.[116]

Taylor brought together several strands of his thinking on international security, the Cold War, and the national security establishment in *Precarious Security*, his final book. He decried "the progressive decline in power of the United States and its principal allies, the economic ills of the industrialized world, the continued malevolence of the Soviet Union backed by a growing military strength, the disruption of the power balance in the Mediterranean-Middle East, and growing unrest in the underdeveloped world." At home, Taylor worried that too many people had lost faith in government, the nation appeared divided, and society seemed decadent.[117] He feared, too, that "national security" had been "used as an excuse for illegal encroachments on civil liberties or as a cloak to conceal official blunders, misdoings, and even crimes" and that the War Powers Act hobbled the president's ability to make timely decisions.[118] The traits Taylor saw in contemporary society "in history have often preceded the decadence of civilization and the appearance of predatory barbarians at its gates."[119]

Taylor was troubled because he regarded public support of foreign and domestic policies as a foundation of efficient governance. To counter the decline, he proposed replacing the NSC with a national policy council, wherein foreign and defense policy could be weighed alongside economics, welfare, and social policies. Taylor reasoned that this could rebuild trust, but he also assumed that the complex problems of the Cold War era required a holistic approach with careful coordination rather than piecemeal arrival of frequently contrary policy proposals on the president's desk. Americans needed to understand that national security went far beyond military affairs.[120] Moreover, a reorganization of the national security establishment could perhaps restore the balance of power between the White House and Congress. The latter, Taylor complained, had inserted itself too heavily in foreign policy, broken Nixon's promises to South Vietnam, "botched the 1975 trade bill by interjecting the extraneous issue of Jewish emigration from the USSR," and left foreign governments wondering who was in charge in Washington.[121]

Taylor feared that population growth and limited resources would destabilize China, Indonesia, Africa, the Middle East, and Latin America. Signs of starvation in South Asia and migrant streams from Mexico to the United States were just the beginning. Against this stood the five power centers that Nixon and Kissinger had identified: the United States, the USSR, Western Europe, Japan, and China, where the unsettled succession of Mao and Zhou Enlai complicated the picture. Taylor expected the gravest threats to global order from fuel and food shortages, and he projected that the 1980s would be defined by armed conflicts, social turbulence, political turmoil, and natural disasters as well as increasing tensions between Muslims and Jews, Hindus and Muslims, North and South Korea, and China and the Soviet Union. Geopolitics and the superpowers still mattered, but demographic change, environmental factors, and economics all threatened to disrupt peace, and the world had to be viewed along a north-south fault line as well as the familiar east-west divide.[122] Taylor detected the most immediate conflict potential in the troubled Turkish-Greek relationship in the eastern Mediterranean and that of Israel and its neighbors in the Middle East.[123] The security of the United States rested on properly balanced strategic and conventional armed forces, a recalibrated relationship between the executive and legislative branches, strong alliances, and the most efficient deployment of military and civilian means at the president's disposal.[124]

With his focus on areas outside of Europe and on the proper organization of national security decision-making, Taylor was hardly in the mainstream of the Committee on the Present Danger, which was primarily concerned with Soviet gains in the arms race. Taylor pleaded his case in the inaugural issue of *International Security*. He did not see much merit in a line item comparison of armed forces because the number of army divisions, planes, ships, ICBMs, IRBMs, and nuclear warheads did not reflect quality. Soviet numerical superiority could be accepted as long as American arms were better. Neither side, Taylor noted, really knew what it had in its strategic nuclear arsenal. Nobody had ever conducted anything beyond partial tests and one could only speculate how well an ICBM might perform from launch to detonation. The new technology of multiple, independently targetable warheads (MIRVs) made it even more difficult to draw firm comparisons of capabilities. Taylor concluded that "inadequacy of weapons data and the inherent incomparability of such factors as missile numbers, accuracy, reliability, megatonnage, and indestructibility" made a direct comparison of American and Soviet assets inutile. The better assumption for force structure planning was the certain capacity to destroy the enemy's arsenal.[125]

The picture was less reassuring in conventional arms. Here, too, Taylor did not advocate that the United States needed to match the Soviets one for one. After all, Taylor mused, they needed some seventy divisions at the Sino-Soviet border and in Eastern Europe just to keep other communist regimes in check. But the United States still lacked ample conventional forces in Western Europe, Korea, and Japan, and in the strategic reserve so as to deter the Soviet Union and retain the ability to react to crises in far-flung places. Western Europe seemed in particular danger, when measured in forces-in-being, a fact worsened by "alarming political and economic debility" of European NATO members, and the situation in the Mediterranean and Middle East as well as Northeast Asia seemed only marginally better. But, Taylor concluded, while it was important to build up conventional forces, the better measure of the nation's overall strength was unity of purpose, a leader respected by all sides, and "effectual integrated power."[126]

Two years later, with the mood in the country caught between a desire to reduce the federal government and frustration with America's weakness in crises in Iran and at the Horn of Africa, Taylor proposed a review of priorities in the national interest. He suggested a study of three major threats to provide for more rational reallocation of resources: a surprise attack on the American nuclear arsenal, a massive conventional attack on NATO, and hostile efforts to cut America's vital supplies. Taylor deemed the first scenario highly unlikely, but the consequences of letting down one's guard on nuclear deterrence were too dire to contemplate. An attack on NATO was slightly more realistic, particularly since the Soviets could expect to win the early battles, but the effects of nuclear deterrence still made it seem far-fetched. The greatest vulnerability rested in the ease with which global shipping of oil could be attacked. Taylor's list of potential threats included hostile forces sinking tankers near the Persian Gulf, renewed fighting between Israel and its neighbors coupled with another oil embargo, overthrow of governments in the Middle East, larger scale fighting in southern Africa, and sabotage at sea or in ports. Meeting these threats required "liberal allocation of resources to all branches of government, civil and military, capable to making a significant contribution to its prevention or the moderation of its consequences." War and preparedness had become so complex that they required a full-blown national effort at all times.[127]

Taylor, though instinctively a hawk, did not think national security should take precedence over domestic policies. Instead, he advocated for more carefully calibrated defense spending and efficient bureaucracy and decision-making. To strengthen the nuclear deterrent, Taylor proposed a shift away from the triad of land-based ICBMs, bombers, and submarine-launched ballistic missiles. Hardening silos could not protect ICBMs. Taylor argued that SLBMs and cruise missiles could be just as destructive and did not require fixed sites. Implementing the shift would free force planners from having to consider expected losses in an enemy's first strike, which in turn further reduced the required number of missiles and warheads to destroy the enemy's arsenal. To enhance NATO, Taylor recommended quality over quantity. The United States should deploy the most modern weapon systems, ranging from precision-guided munitions and tactical nuclear missiles to cruise missiles that could hit targets deep inside the Soviet Union, improved nuclear artillery shells, and neutron bombs. Concurrently, the European allies had to raise their readiness and NATO needed to overhaul its logistics system. The mission to protect trade routes and oil producing areas was not entirely a military one, but here, too, constant readiness was required.[128]

Taylor wanted a versatile force that could meet the whole array of threats at an acceptable price. The fiction of a two-war or even just a one-and-a-half-war policy had to be abandoned. Taylor thought it would not be a loss since the United States had not maintained sufficient capabilities in the first place. Instead, the armed forces had to maintain military superiority in the western hemisphere, control sea lanes, provide a ready reserve of at least four divisions that could "sustain combat of moderate intensity" for two months, and build "a specialized antiterrorist force drawn from all elements of the military establishment ready to prevent, frustrate, or retaliate for acts of international terrorism." Presuming the Carter administration would raise the defense budget by 3 percent, Taylor estimated there would not be enough money for the current sixteen army divisions and three marine divisions as well as a 600,000-man reserve. Global reach through new weapons, enhanced air and sea lift, and a stronger navy could allow for less manpower. The great advantage, Taylor noted, was a functions-based budget that funded the highest priorities. Giving up on chasing numerical equivalency in the nuclear or conventional fields would make such forces more affordable. In all facets, but nowhere more so than in the trade-protection mission, military and political and economic means had to be fully integrated. Taylor feared that the economic threat could easily be overshadowed by the nuclear or conventional arms calculus, and he warned politicians to stay alert.[129]

Reflecting on his career in the national security establishment, Taylor noted that the primary deficiencies involved the joint chiefs, the secretary of defense, and their relationship to the White House. In a 1977 talk, with Arleigh Burke and other contemporaries in the audience, Taylor reiterated that the JCS system had never worked to its fullest potential. The chiefs were simply too divided by service interests to provide visionary advice. The process was slow and indecisive. Taylor recalled that when he served as John F. Kennedy's adviser, he could get a paper on the president's desk quickly and that often a decision was made before the JCS position paper had even arrived. So what, if it was more deeply considered? By the time it appeared, the chiefs' advice was no longer useful.[130] Taylor remained frustrated by his inability to overhaul the system in the 1960s, when he had tried to strengthen the position of the chairman. The position of the JCS remained contested and some military officers and civilian policymakers still thought in terms of a sharp divide between military and political issues. Taylor, who had worked in both realms, held that "there's no such thing as a pure military component of a Presidential problem on which the Chiefs can render pure military advice."[131]

Taylor revisited the issue in one of his last public appearances. Already battling with the disease that would kill him three years later—amyotrophic lateral sclerosis—he nevertheless gave biting testimony for Senate and House committees in 1984, in hearings that eventually led to the Goldwater-Nichols Act of 1986, which empowered the JCS chairman as well as regional commanders and reduced the influence of the service chiefs. Taylor had asked for more, returning to his 1950s notion that the JCS ought to be replaced by a general-in-chief or at least a committee whose members did not represent individual armed services. The JCS, he remarked, had "rarely, if ever, performed an advisory role of any importance at the top level of national policy." Taylor was particularly concerned that the armed forces of the United States still grew haphazardly and that "there is in our organization no place where a decision is made as to what the strategic capabilities of our armed forces should be."[132]

Taylor was in prominent company. In January 1982, Air Force general and JCS chairman David Jones had advanced his reform proposal, fully aware that previous efforts launched by President Eisenhower (formally) and Taylor and McNamara (informally) had failed to affect major change.[133] When the time came to testify before the House Armed Services Investigations Subcommittee later that spring, Taylor joined an illustrious list of witnesses, including Lemnitzer, LeMay, and Admiral Thomas Moorer, JCS chairman from 1970 to 1974, as well as three former defense secretaries and Robert Komer. LeMay and Taylor agreed on the need for reform, Moorer offered the minority view that the system was working and that trying to fix it amounted to "spend[ing] millions rearranging furniture, changing letterheads, changing phone numbers."[134] In a study of the national security apparatus throughout the Cold War, "Brute" Krulak concluded that the JCS should be streamlined and that the Defense Department had become a bloated bureaucracy that stood in the way of timely decision-making. Krulak recommended that the secretary of defense be removed from the military chain of command and that the JCS be tasked with providing unfiltered counsel to the president and Congress. Where Taylor desired a general-in-chief, Krulak wanted to return to the World War II practice of a body of equals.[135]

At that point, Taylor had determined that overspending on defense, too, had negative consequences. Once Ronald Reagan was in office and the seemingly unlimited defense buildup had accelerated, Taylor stated his concerns in a November 1981 *Washington Post* editorial. Sounding like Eisenhower, Taylor warned that the apparent economic crisis was certain to complicate Reagan's military policy. The administration, Taylor noted, was trying to do too many things at once and there was a dire need to define strategic priorities. It made no sense to engage in every arms race once baseline conditions of defense and deterrence were met. Taylor surmised that "the overall military goal of the Reagan policy, as set forth by its exponents is to match or surpass Soviet military strength with forces able to fight, presumably successfully, anywhere at any time for an indefinite duration." This was misguided. Taylor asked, "Does that mean, one wonders, that we should increase our Army from its present 16 divisions to match the Soviets' 170 and then expect our forces to fight the latter anywhere, say in Siberia?" Surely not, but without presidential guidelines no scenario seemed too far-fetched.

Taylor concluded that the main power bases that had to be defended were the homeland and US allies, the Western Hemisphere, and critical overseas markets and sea lanes. To do so, "first priority will be given to the readiness of existing forces to perform their assigned tasks." To spend defense dollars more efficiently, "every major [new] unit and weapons system must be justified by its contribution to an approved task, the latter arising from a policy goal that in turns derives from the need to counter a recognized threat." Once again parting ways with some of his colleagues on the Committee on the Present Danger, Taylor held that "numerical parity with the Soviets would cease to be a matter of concern and an arms race would be irrelevant." He believed such a state of affairs served the strategic needs of the United States, but it also had great political appeal since it demonstrated to citizens what their tax dollars were spent on and how they benefited from trade and markets protected by the armed forces. It offered "a reasonable chance to remain safe without going broke in the process." Taylor's program read like a militarized version of George Kennan's containment proposals in 1946 and 1947: economic strength, properly safeguarded, would ultimately trump the Soviet system.[136] Two months earlier Taylor had summed up his own views: "How Much for Defense? Only What's Essential."[137]

Taylor did not live to see the end of the Cold War. By early 1985 his illness had progressed to the point where he had almost entirely lost his voice and could barely get around his apartment. Hospitalizations at Walter Reed grew more frequent, and eventually Taylor had to accept being confined to a wheelchair. That he did not do. In January 1987 he broke his collarbone in a fall when he tried to get on his walker. Worse, Taylor had lost consciousness and, though he awoke from his coma after a few days, ensuing complications included pneumonia. Taylor did not leave the hospital again. He died on Easter Sunday, April 19, 1987. Among the outpouring of tributes were those of President Reagan, Belgium's King Baudouin, Jacqueline Kennedy Onassis, and veterans of the 101st Airborne Division who had fought with Taylor in World War II and who now delivered a final salute at his gravesite in Arlington National Cemetery.[138]

Epilogue

Maxwell Taylor's experience in the Cold War highlights four interrelated themes that have defined the US national security state and also shed light on the nature of strategy. First, the warfare state will guide decision-makers to seek military solutions to political problems. Sometimes that is appropriate, but at other times, as in Vietnam, it can drown out other approaches. Second, strategy and bureaucracy often work at cross-purposes. Again, decisions leading to the Vietnam War offer an illustration: instead of aligning means, ends, and political objectives, US strategy suffered from the collision of politics and policy with operational art and military planning. The various bureaucracies, though linked in the National Security Council, sought separate solutions. Third, strategy in general has increasingly become the fault line between operational art and politics and policy. It should be the connective tissue. Fourth, powerful and influential individuals served as contingent actors in the historical drama, but their options were limited by Cold War structures, ranging from bureaucracies that channeled possible actions to mind-sets that made it difficult not to view the problem at hand through the lens of the wider conflict and recent experiences. As they say in military and policy circles, if all you have is a hammer, everything looks like a nail. But what if you had several different hammers all trying to strike the nail at once?

Taylor himself made a consistent argument for the likelihood of limited war, one he first stated—remarkably early—in his 1948 lecture in London. Consequently, he remained throughout the 1950s, 1960s, and 1970s a champion of preparedness for both conventional and limited nuclear warfare, and by 1961 he had also come to recognize the threat posed to American interests overseas by insurgencies and revolutionary war. His response evolved, from heavy emphasis on firepower and land forces—befitting Taylor's roles at West Point, in Berlin, in Korea, and at the Pentagon in the 1940s and 1950s—to better balance of air, sea, and land forces in the 1960s and in his commentaries, books, and articles in the 1970s. To some degree this was a direct lesson of the Korean War, where, Taylor concluded, artillery and airpower had forced the enemy to make political concessions and accept a diplomatic settlement. When he tried to apply this lesson in Vietnam, it proved ill suited, but there is no indication that Taylor changed his thinking on how to combat revolutionary armies. Yet when he addressed global strategy for the 1970s and 1980s, he proposed moderation in the nuclear arms race and, sounding more like Dwight Eisenhower and less like the Maxwell Taylor of the 1950s, warned of economic and financial limits to American power. All throughout, he remained a consistent critic of the national security bureaucracy, especially the NSC and JCS, even though he had briefly lapsed into toleration when he got to run the joint chiefs for a president and defense secretary whose thinking on strategy was fairly close to his own.

Toward the end of his life, Taylor took one more parting shot at the JCS. His testimony contributed to the 1986 legislation put forward by Senator Barry Goldwater (R, Arizona) and Representative William Nichols (D, Alabama). The Goldwater-Nichols Act was the most profound reorganization of the defense establishment since the National Security Act in 1947. It was also a response to long-term concerns over flawed processes in strategy and operations that dated back to the Vietnam War. Goldwater and Nichols aimed to end interservice rivalry and clarify the chain of command. Most significantly, the law enhanced the position of the JCS chairman, who no longer had to report dissenting opinions, and elevated regional combatant commanders, who no longer received orders from their service chiefs. Yet for all the seeming simplicity this legislation introduced, the US military has not grown more adept at meeting challenges since the end of the Cold War.[1] The evidence suggests that civilian leaders since the early 1990s have selected JCS chairmen based as much on their malleability as on their strategic acumen, and the civil-military divide has deepened.[2]

At the end of the Cold War it seemed the United States—and liberal democracy—had triumphed.[3] The quick victory against Iraq in 1991 further underscored America's standing as the world's sole superpower and emboldened defense intellectuals, policymakers, and the military establishment to assume that a combination of precision-guided munitions, computing and satellite technology, more realistic training, and proper doctrine for the application of military force had triggered a revolution in military affairs (RMA) that offered a clean break with the past. The future of warfare appeared to be defined by precision air and missile strikes, power projection by the air force and navy, and a lighter touch on the ground by fast-moving army and marine brigades.[4] This failed to take into account enduring lessons of military history: the enemy always gets to have a say in shaping the nature of war, enemies need not be states, and weaker enemies will find ways to exploit the superpower's vulnerabilities instead of seeking a main force battle. Soon, the United States found itself in a world in which "new wars," waged as much by criminal actors and warlords as by state governments and their armed forces erupted in the Balkans, in sub-Saharan Africa, and elsewhere.[5]

The September 11, 2001, attack on the United States and the subsequent War on Terror exposed two fundamental problems: the RMA could not protect the country against threats from non-state actors and asymmetrical warfare bogged down US armed forces in Afghanistan and Iraq. Both problems had antecedents in the Cold War, and Taylor had grappled with them since the 1950s. For one, preparedness for a full spectrum of operations from peacekeeping to limited and perhaps even general war taxed the armed forces and made it difficult to design proper doctrine, force structure, and operational and strategic plans. Here, the emphasis placed by Defense Secretary Donald Rumsfeld on transformation to Special Forces and lightning strikes that could exploit openings created by shock-and-awe application of airpower proved ill suited to the realities of warfare and politics in the Middle East and Central Asia, which required patience and a larger number of ground forces than the Pentagon had been willing to concede.[6] The adjustment from conventional thinking to counterinsurgency doctrine after 2006 did not fundamentally change the equation, not even in Iraq, where operational success did not yield long-term political stability.[7] While the wars in Afghanistan and Iraq have ended, in the sense of US declarations of the end of missions, both also remained unresolved in 2018.

But for all the strife and struggle in America's wars in the twenty-first century, the main unresolved issues that bedeviled Maxwell Taylor are still on display in Washington. Civil-military relations remain tense, even though for the moment there is an usual concentration of power in the hands of military men. The ways in which policy guidance is translated into strategy and from there into operational plans remain tenuous, and despite the confluence of generals in key offices at the White House and Pentagon, there still appears to be only a bare thread linking operational excellence and policy objectives.[8] Throughout 2017, defense intellectuals and commentators on the political scene often took refuge from the chaos swirling around Donald Trump's administration by pointing at "the adults in the room," usually referring to the army and marine generals who had settled in their roles as defense secretary (James Mattis), national security adviser (H. R. McMaster), and White House chief of staff (John Kelly, initially the homeland security secretary). When President Trump delivered one of his most measured and carefully crafted speeches, in late August 2017, about the war in Afghanistan, commentators and scholars almost instantly noted this sounded less like Trump, who as a candidate had thundered against continuing the losing effort in Afghanistan that to him seemed to offer little but a waste of energy and resources, and more like his generals, who wanted to extend the American presence in that country.[9]

The adults-in-the-room narrative seemed to take a hit when John Kelly rushed to the president's defense in an October 2017 controversy over whether Trump had mishandled a condolence call to the widow of an American soldier who had been killed alongside three of his comrades in an ambush in Niger. And those invested in the public discourse over race and commemoration took notice of Kelly's statement that Confederate general Robert E. Lee was "a good man" and that the Civil War could have been avoided if only both sides had been willing to compromise. It is unnecessarily alarmist to state the nation was in the midst of a slow-moving military coup, but the rise of the generals did have a negative effect on strategy.[10]

There is an imbalance in civil-military relations when generals not only advise on strategy, but also define policy. Mattis and McMaster are deep thinkers, but they could not detach themselves from the loss of lives and treasure that had already occurred, and their instinct seemed to be to double down. Mattis and his coeditor Kori Schake pointed out as much in 2016 when they concluded there was a problem with generals taking too strong a lead in defining strategy.[11] Generals are prone to becoming skilled managers of violence, but they still approach strategy more from the perspective of means and military ends than from that of the wider political objective.[12] Through the Vietnam War, Taylor had displayed the same tendencies. Finally, if indeed the military has become the sole remaining vestige of national identity, or at least the last institution left standing that the far left and the far right and almost everyone in between can trust, albeit often more in an idealized image, then having its top commanders (current or former) at the heart of "our bitter and divisive politics" could be crippling to the nation.[13] The short-term salve against the volatility of a president may lead to a deeper loss of identity and worse rifts in political culture. It has done little to fix the problems that have bedeviled American strategy in most wars dating back to 1945, and in that larger sense many of the challenges Maxwell Taylor faced while serving in Berlin and Korea, on the JCS, at the White House, and in Vietnam remain.

Acknowledgments

No scholar truly works alone. I have built this study of Maxwell Taylor and US Cold War strategy and civil-military relations on the foundation laid by many students of the Cold War, American military history, international and diplomatic history, policy history, and strategic studies. Their contributions are referenced in the notes and bibliography, but I would like to thank Pierre Asselin, Beth Bailey, Robert Citino, William Donnelly, Kate Epstein, George Herring, Mark Lawrence, Brian Linn, Fredrik Logevall, Peter Mansoor, John McNay, Lien-Hang T. Nguyen, Carol Reardon, Brian Holden Reid, Adam Seipp, Mark Stoler, Jeremi Suri, David Ulbrich, Bruce Vandervort, Andrew Wiest, Jim Willbanks, and Jonathan Winkler for insightful comments, critical questions, strategic advice, and support when it was most needed.

More archivists and librarians than I could possibly thank in a short space made it possible to conduct efficient and productive research at the institutions noted in the bibliography. Jeff Kozak at the Marshall Library, Suzanne Christoff at West Point, Michael Lynch, Shannon Schwaller and Rich Baker at the Army Heritage and Education Center, Valoise Armstrong at the Eisenhower Library, and Carol Leadenham at the Hoover Institution in particular went beyond their usual tasks and duties to track down materials and enrich this book. Tim Nenninger took time out of his working retirement to explore partially declassified materials kept in the "top secret vault" at the National Archives. And without grants, fellowships, and other support from the Ohio University History Department, the College of Arts and Sciences, and the Vice President for Research as well as the Army Heritage and Education Center, the Center of Military History, and the Eisenhower Foundation, I could not have visited over a dozen archives and research libraries in the past couple of years.

Some debts go back a long time. At the University of Maryland, Jon Sumida, Shu Guang Zhang, Keith Olson, Jeffrey Herf, John Lampe,

Randy Papadopoulos, Sandy Cochran, and George Quester were critical in forming my scholarship at an early stage, and fellow Ph.D. alumni Stephen Johnson, Sheldon Goldberg, and Nicholas Schlosser continued to provide sound advice as well as great company whenever I returned to Washington, D.C. At my early teaching stops, Norwich University and New Mexico Tech, Reina Pennington, Jim Ehrman, Tom Taylor, Lewis Greenstein, Mary Dezember, the late Alexander Prusin, and Scott Zeman helped me become a better teacher, which in turn has greatly improved my writing and scholarship. At Ohio University, I owe many debts. Special thanks, in no particular order, go to Katherine Jellison, John Brobst, Steve Miner, Lon Hamby, Patrick Barr-Melej, Ziad Abu-Rish, Assan Sarr, Alec Holcombe, Paul Milazzo, Brian Schoen, Chester Pach, Joshua Hill, Marvin Fletcher, and Robert Ingram for their comments and questions as well as for making the department and the Contemporary History Institute places of vibrant scholarship. If my colleagues commented by choice, students did so by (implied) coercion—and they added much to this study by their willingness to engage questions and readings in seminars and colloquia as well as by their own research contributions. In particular, I am grateful to Adam Givens, Seth Givens, Lindsay Kittle, Caitlin Bentley, Fred Coventry, Matt Johnson, Caleb Greene, Heather Salazar, Alexander Lovelace, Robert Venosa, Mitchell Smith, Mike Rattanasengchanh, Tyler Esno, Luke Griffith, Matt Jacobs, Jasper Verschoor, Guy Aldridge, Samuel Miner, and Precious Oluwasanya (the latter two also for critical research assistance). Soldier-scholars Steve Wills (a sailor), Jeff Mills, and Eric Burke forced me to think in different ways about civil-military relations and the linkage of operations and strategy. Over the years, it has become impossible for me to think about scholarship and teaching as separate pursuits. I am also grateful to our community of scholars and teachers who are interested in War and Peace, one of our strongest curricular themes and a fast rising undergraduate major, and who hail from departments as close as political science and as far as physics or information and telecommunications systems. Thanks especially to Nukhet Sandal, Robin Muhammad, Haley Duschinski, Mike Sweeney, Gillian Berchowitz, and the late Patricia Weitsman. They have all forced me to think about broader audiences and relevancy. At the University Press of Kentucky, Melissa Hammer and her team of editors—and the readers they chose—have helped me make this a much better book.

On a personal note, and most essentially, I would like to thank those whose support has allowed me to pursue a career in the academy and stay relatively sane: my parents and my partner, Susan Longfield Karr.

Notes

Introduction

1. Brian McAllister Linn, *Elvis's Army: Cold War GIs and the Atomic Battlefield* (Cambridge, Mass.: Harvard Univ. Press, 2016).
2. Robert S. McNamara with Brian VanDeMark, *In Retrospect: The Tragedy and Lessons of Vietnam* (New York: Crown, 1995), 54.
3. John M. Taylor, *General Maxwell Taylor: The Sword and the Pen* (New York: Doubleday, 1989), 22.
4. Robert Buzzanco, *Masters of War: Military Dissent and Politics in the Vietnam Era* (Cambridge, UK: Cambridge Univ. Press, 1996), Thomas E. Ricks, *The Generals: American Military Command from World War II to Today* (New York: Penguin, 2012).
5. H. R. McMaster, *Dereliction of Duty: Johnson, McNamara, the Joint Chiefs of Staff, and the Lies that Led to Vietnam* (New York: Harper, 1997).
6. Douglas C. Kinnard, *The Certain Trumpet: Maxwell Taylor and the American Experience in Vietnam*. Washington, D.C.: Brassey's, 1991.
7. Maxwell D. Taylor, *Swords and Plowshares* (New York: Norton, 1972); John Taylor, *General Maxwell Taylor*.
8. Taylor, *Swords and Plowshares;* John Taylor, *General Maxwell Taylor*.
9. Taylor, *Swords and Plowshares*, 16–17.

1. West Point

1. Eisenhower to Marshall, 24 September 1945, Eisenhower Pre-Presidential Papers, principal file, box 80, folder: Marshall, George C. (5), Dwight D. Eisenhower Presidential Library, Abilene, Kansas (DDEL).
2. Richard F. Haynes, "The Defense Unification Battle, 1947–1950: The Army," *Prologue: The Journal of the National Archives* 7, no. 1 (1975): 27–31; Steven L. Rearden, *Council of War: A History of the Joint Chiefs of Staff, 1942–1991* (Washington, D.C.: Joint History Office, Joint Chiefs of Staff, 2012), 64–69; William A. Taylor, *Every Citizen a Soldier: The Campaign for Universal Military Training after World War II* (College Station: Texas A&M Univ. Press, 2014).
3. Taylor, *Swords and Plowshares*, 112–122; Theodore J. Crackel, *West Point: A Bicentennial History* (Lawrence: Univ. Press of Kansas, 2002), 211–215.

4. Taylor to Eisenhower, 19 August 1945, Eisenhower Pre-Presidential Papers, principal file, box 117, folder: U.S. Military Academy (4), DDEL.

5. P.D.H., Memorandum to the Army Commander, United States Third Army, 12 September 1945, Paul D. Harkins Papers, box 1, folder 7, US Army Heritage and Education Center, Carlisle, Pennsylvania (AHEC).

6. Patton to Taylor, 13 September 1945, George S. Patton Papers, box 4, folder 20, US Military Academy Library, Special Collections, West Point (USMA).

7. Eisenhower to Taylor, 21 August 1945, Eisenhower Pre-Presidential Papers, principal file, box 117, folder: United States Military Academy (4), DDEL.

8. Eisenhower to Marshall, 27 July 1945, in *The Papers of Dwight D. Eisenhower*, vol. 6, *Occupation, 1945*, ed. Alfred D. Chandler Jr. and Louis Galambos (Baltimore, Md.: Johns Hopkins Univ. Press, 1978), 203; John Taylor, *General Maxwell Taylor*, 22.

9. Eisenhower to Forrestal, 7 February 1948, in *The Papers of Dwight D. Eisenhower*, vol. 9, *The Chief of Staff*, ed. Alfred D. Chandler Jr. and Louis Galambos (Baltimore, Md.: Johns Hopkins Univ. Press, 1978), 2242–2256. The list is on pages 2252–2253.

10. Eisenhower to Houghton, 8 February 1947, in *The Papers of Dwight D. Eisenhower*, vol. 8, *The Chief of Staff*, ed. Alfred D. Chandler Jr. and Louis Galambos (Baltimore, Md.: Johns Hopkins Univ. Press, 1978), 1502–1503; Taylor to Eisenhower, 1 July 1947, Eisenhower Pre-Presidential Papers, principal file, box 117, folder: United States Military Academy (2), DDEL.

11. Taylor, diary, 7 July 1947, Taylor Papers, box 1, National Defense University (NDU).

12. Eisenhower to Taylor, 26 June 1947, in *Eisenhower Papers*, vol. 8, 1781–1783.

13. Eisenhower to Taylor, 2 January 1946, in *The Papers of Dwight D. Eisenhower*, vol. 7, *The Chief of Staff*, ed. Alfred D. Chandler Jr. and Louis Galambos (Baltimore, Md.: Johns Hopkins Univ. Press, 1978), 710–712.

14. Taylor to Eisenhower, 8 January 1946, Eisenhower Pre-Presidential Papers, principal file, box 117, folder: U.S. Military Academy (3), DDEL.

15. Marshall to MacArthur, 2 August 1945, in *The Papers of George Catlett Marshall*, vol. 5, *"The Finest Soldier," January 1, 1945–January 7, 1947*, ed. Larry I. Bland (Baltimore, Md.: Johns Hopkins Univ. Press, 2003), 256–257. For Marshall's visit to Berchtesgaden, recorded as a fishing trip, see page xxvi.

16. Taylor to Marshall, 4 September 1947, Marshall Papers, box 138, folder 5, George C. Marshall Library, Virginia Military Institute, Lexington, Virginia (GCML).

17. Taylor, *Swords and Plowshares*, 21–26; John Taylor, *General Maxwell Taylor*, 11–18.

18. Taylor, *Swords and Plowshares*, 22–28.

19. Taylor, "Leading the American Soldier," address to the First Class, US Military Academy, 27 May 1946, quoted in Captain Mark H. Smith, "The Superintendency of Maxwell Taylor: Planting the Seeds of Leader Development" (West Point, N.Y.: US Military Academy, December 1988), 10, Digital Collections, USMA, http://digital-library.usma.edu/cdm/singleitem/collection/p16919c0111/id/49/rec/1 (accessed 5 August 2016).

20. Maxwell D. Taylor interviewed by Colonel Richard Manion, first interview (1972, no specific date), 5–6, Taylor Papers, box 1, AHEC.

21. Crackel, *West Point*, 204.

22. *Annual Report of the Superintendent, United States Military Academy, 1946*, 7, Digital Collections, USMA, http://digital-library.usma.edu/cdm/singleitem/collection/superep/id/52/rec/56 (accessed 1 December 2015).

23. *Annual Report of the Superintendent of the U.S. Military Academy, 1947*, 12, Digital Collections, USMA, http://digital-library.usma.edu/cdm/singleitem/collection/superep/id/53/rec/58 (accessed 2 August 2016).

24. *Annual Report of the Superintendent, United States Military Academy, 1948*, 16, Digital Collections, USMA, http://digital-library.usma.edu/cdm/singleitem/collection/superep/id/54/rec/60 (accessed 3 August 2016); *Annual Report of the Superintendent, United States Military Academy, 1949*, 9, Digital Collections, USMA, http://digital-library.usma.edu/cdm/singleitem/collection/superep/id/56/rec/1 (accessed 23 December 2016).

25. Edward M. Coffman, *The Regulars: The American Army, 1898–1941* (Cambridge, Mass.: Harvard Univ. Press, 2004), 375.

26. Taylor to Eiler, 28 February 1986, Keith E. Eiler Papers, box 27, folder 19, Hoover Institution Archives, Stanford University, Palo Alto, California (HIA).

27. Taylor, *Swords and Plowshares*, 56–62; John Taylor, *General Maxwell Taylor*, 56–66.

28. Samuel Eliot Morrison, *History of U.S. Naval Operations in World War II*, vol. 9, *Sicily—Salerno—Anzio, January 1943–June 1944* (Boston: Little, Brown, 1954), 241–242; Robert Murphy, *Diplomat among Warriors* (Garden City, N.Y.: Doubleday, 1964), 195.

29. Taylor, *Swords and Plowshares*, 62–64.

30. Ibid., 64–69.

31. Williamson Murray and Allan R. Millett, *A War to Be Won: Fighting the Second World War* (Cambridge, Mass.: Harvard Univ. Press, 2001), 468.

32. Taylor, *Swords and Plowshares*, 97–102; Rick Atkinson, *The Guns at Last Light: The War in Western Europe, 1944–1945* (New York: Henry Holt, 2013), 450–468.

33. Taylor, "Our Army," 6 April 1946, Taylor Papers, box 2, folder: Speeches 1945–1947, NDU.

34. Attachment to Ewell to Goodpaster, 5 December 1957, Goodpaster Papers, White House (1954–1961), box 15, folder 24, GCML.

35. Maxwell Taylor, "West Point Looks Ahead" (pamphlet) (West Point, N.Y.: US Military Academy, 1946), 1; Compton to Colonel Robert Sink, 23 April 1946, MIT, Office of the President, 1930–1959 (Compton-Killian), AC 4, box 226, folder 3, Institute Archives and Special Collections, MIT Libraries, Cambridge, Massachusetts.

36. Taylor, "The West Point Curriculum," 16 May 1946, Taylor Papers, box 2, folder: West Point 1945–1949, NDU.

37. Taylor, "West Point Looks Ahead," 2.

38. Ibid., 5.

39. Ibid., 3.

40. Colonels Alexander, Jones, and Reeder to Taylor, 31 January 1946, Divi-

sion of the Third Class into three-year and four-year components, Records of the United States Military Academy, S. 161, file 351.051, Curriculum, Return to the Four Year Course, 1946, RG 404, USMA.

41. Taylor interviewed by Manion, Section 1, 14, and Section 3 (8 December 1972), 7–9.

42. Report of the Board of Consultants, 7 November 1945, enclosure to Academic Board Meeting, 11 April 1946, 64–75, Records of the United States Military Academy, Proceedings of the Academic Board, 1946, RG 404, USMA.

43. Taylor, diary, 5 and 6 November 1945, Taylor Papers, box 1, NDU.

44. Report of the Board of Consultants, 65–66.

45. Taylor's Remarks to the Board of Consultants, 5 November 1945, in Proceedings of the Academic Board, 1946, 76–77, Records of the United States Military Academy, RG 404, USMA.

46. Frank James Price, *Troy H. Middleton: A Biography* (Baton Rouge: Louisiana State Univ. Press, 1974), 33–36.

47. Report of the Board of Consultants, 67–69.

48. Middleton to Taylor, 16 November 1945, Special Collections, item 241: Maxwell Taylor Letters, USMA.

49. *Annual Report of the Superintendent, United States Military Academy, 1946*, 14–16.

50. *Annual Report of the Superintendent, United States Military Academy, 1948*, 12–13.

51. Ibid., 23.

52. Eisenhower to Taylor, 2 January 1946, in *Eisenhower Papers*, 7:710–712; Taylor, *Swords and Plowshares*, 112–115.

53. *Annual Report of the Superintendent, United States Military Academy, 1947*, 20, 23.

54. Ibid., 23.

55. Taylor to Eisenhower, 11 May 1946, in Proceedings of the Academic Board, 1946, 100–101.

56. Lance Betros, *Raised from Granite: West Point since 1902* (College Station: Texas A&M Univ. Press, 2012), 131, 247–249.

57. This information comes from Higgins's account in John Taylor, *General Maxwell Taylor*, 148–149.

58. The discussion of the 11 May meeting and Taylor to Chief of Staff, War Department, 10 May 1946, are in Proceedings of the Academic Board, 1946, 99–101.

59. Taylor, "The West Point Curriculum," 16 May 1946.

60. *Annual Report of the Superintendent, United States Military Academy, 1947*, 1.

61. Roger H. Nye, "George A. Lincoln: Architect in National Security," in *Issues of National Security in the 1970s: Essays Presented to Colonel George A. Lincoln on His Sixtieth Birthday*, ed. Amos A. Jordan Jr. (New York: Praeger, 1967), 3–20, Taylor quoted on 6–7.

62. Fred Kaplan, *The Insurgents: David Petraeus and the Plot to Change the American Way of War* (New York: Simon and Schuster, 2013), 4–10.

63. Lincoln to Colonel Paul Caraway, National War College, 11 March 1948,

George A. Lincoln Papers, box 8, folder: Correspondence Files Jan–Oct 1947, USMA.

64. Crackel, *West Point*, 214. The source for this assertion is a conversation with Sumner Willard that took place more than four decades after the events. Willard had joined the faculty as a language professor in 1963. Beukema's papers at West Point do not suggest deep antagonism.

65. *Annual Report of the Superintendent, United States Military Academy, 1947*, 15.

66. Thomas J. Fleming, *West Point: The Men and Times of the U.S. Military Academy* (New York: Morrow, 1969), 344; Betros, *Carved from Granite*, 134–135.

67. Enclosure to Beukema to Lieutenant General Charles D. Herron, 21 February 1951, Beukema Papers, box 2, folder: Col B—H to 1 Jan 1952, USMA.

68. Beukema to Dr. Charles Fairman, 30 August 1948, Beukema Papers, box 3, folder: Col B—F to 1 Jan 1952; "Chronology of Department of Social Sciences," undated, Beukema Papers, box 4, folder: Beukema on academic matters, USMA.

69. Beukema to Hans Heymann Jr., Assistant Editor, *Columbia Journal of International Affairs*, 8 April 1947 (quoted), Beukema Papers, box 2, folder: Col B—H to 1 Jan 1952, USMA.

70. Taylor, "West Point Looks Ahead," 3–4.

71. Ibid., 6.

72. Ibid., 7.

73. Lincoln to Lieutenant William W. Whitson, Ground General School, Fort Riley, Kansas, 8 September 1948, Lincoln Papers, box 8, folder: Correspondence Files Sep–Dec 1948, USMA.

74. *Annual Report of the Superintendent, United States Military Academy, 1948*, 5.

75. Comparison of Class Hours Devoted to Soc Sci-Humanities and Science-Engineering, undated, Lincoln Papers, box 96, folder: Curriculum Study Misc. Undated Materials, USMA.

76. Taylor, *Swords and Plowshares*, 26–28; Coffman, *The Regulars*, 260.

77. *Annual Report of the Superintendent, United States Military Academy, 1947*, 37.

78. Taylor to Eisenhower, 21 October 1946, Eisenhower Pre-Presidential Papers, principal file, box 117, folder: U.S. Military Academy (3), DDEL; Eisenhower to Taylor, 23 October and 22 November 1946, in *Eisenhower Papers*, 8:1331–1332, 1390–1391. As late as 1967, Taylor congratulated Secretary of the Army Stanley Resor for maintaining the postseason ban. Taylor to Resor, 22 November 1967, Harold K. Johnson Papers, Series I: Correspondence, Personal, Army Chief of Staff, box 111, folder 1, AHEC.

79. Linn, *Elvis's Army*, 27.

80. John E. Bodnar, *The "Good War" in American Memory* (Baltimore, Md.: Johns Hopkins Univ. Press, 2010); Michael R. Dolski, *D-Day Remembered: The Normandy Landings in American Collective Memory* (Knoxville: Univ. of Tennessee Press, 2016), 37–58.

81. *Annual Report of the Superintendent, United States Military Academy, 1948*, 1–2.

82. *Annual Report of the Superintendent, United States Military Academy, 1949*, 2–3.

83. *Annual Report of the Superintendent, United States Military Academy, 1952*, 6, Digital Collections, USMA, http://digital-library.usma.edu/cdm/singleitem/collection/superep/id/59/rec/1 (accessed 23 December 2016).

84. Taylor, *Sword and Plowshares*, 45; John Taylor, *General Maxwell Taylor*, 43.

85. John Taylor, *General Maxwell Taylor*, 92–93.

86. *Annual Report of the Superintendent, United States Military Academy, 1947*, 39.

87. Taylor, diary, 9 and 10 July 1947, Taylor Papers, box 1, NDU.

88. Linn, *Elvis's Army*, 25–26.

89. Taylor, *Every Citizen a Soldier*, 93–99.

90. Taylor to Governor Kelly (Michigan), 14 October 1946, Records of the United States Military Academy, S. 161, file 351: Criticisms, USMA, 1946–1948, RG 404, USMA.

91. Emmett G. Lenihan, Chairman Subcommittee, National Defense Committee, American Legion to Taylor, 11 June 1947, Records of the United States Military Academy, S. 161, file 351: Military Academy 1946–1948, RG 404, USMA.

92. Major General Moore to Rear Admiral Holloway, Superintendent, US Naval Academy, 8 November 1949, Records of the United States Military Academy, S. 161, file 351: Military Academy 1946–1948, RG 404, USMA.

93. Persons to Taylor, 3 May 1946; Taylor to Persons, 4 May 1946; Persons to Taylor, 10 May 1946; Taylor to Persons, 12 May 1946, all in Records of the United States Military Academy, S. 161, file 351: Military Academy 1946–1948, RG 404, USMA.

94. Taylor quoted in John W. Masland and Laurence I. Radway, *Soldiers and Scholars: Military Education and National Policy* (Princeton, N.J.: Princeton Univ. Press, 1957), 108.

95. Taylor to Thomason, 18 June 1946; Taylor to Governor Kelly, 14 October 1946, all in Records of the United States Military Academy, S. 161, file 351: Criticisms, USMA, 1946–1948, RG 404, USMA. Taylor's conversations with Representative R. Ewing Thomason (D, TX), a member of the House Military Affairs Committee, continued into 1947.

96. Maxwell D. Taylor, *West Point: Its Objectives and Methods* (West Point, N.Y.: US Military Academy, 1947), 1.

97. Ibid., 3–5, quotation on 3.

98. Ibid., 6–13.

99. Betros, *Carved from Granite*, 89.

100. Taylor, *West Point: Its Objectives and Methods*, 13–15.

101. Eisenhower to Taylor, 13 June 1947, in *Eisenhower Papers*, 8:1751–1752.

102. Taylor, *West Point: Its Objectives and Methods*, 19.

103. Report of Trip to Europe, 26 March to 20 May 1948, by Colonel Gatchell, Professor and Head of Department of Mechanics, and Colonel Bartlett, Professor and Head of Department of Electricity, 12, Lincoln Papers, box 8, folder: Correspondence Files March–April 1948, Special Collections, USMA.

104. Robert Gates Speech, United States Military Academy, 25 February 2011, http://archive.defense.gov/Speeches/Speech.aspx?SpeechID=1539 (accessed May 19, 2016).

105. Eisenhower to Taylor, 21 August 1947, in *Eisenhower Papers,* 9:1886–1888; Taylor to Eisenhower, 30 September 1947, Eisenhower Pre-Presidential Papers, principal file, box 117, folder: United States Military Academy (2), DDEL.

106. *Annual Report of the Superintendent, United States Military Academy, 1947,* 21–22.

107. *Annual Report of the Superintendent, United States Military Academy, 1948,* 25.

108. Eisenhower to Taylor, 24 April 1947, in *Eisenhower Papers,* 8:1663. There is no record of a discussion of the appointment in the Proceedings of the Academic Board, 1947.

109. *Annual Report of the Superintendent, United States Military Academy, 1946,* 2.

110. *Annual Report of the Superintendent, United States Military Academy, 1947,* 25.

111. Lincoln to Taylor, 27 July 1948, Lincoln Papers, box 8, folder: Correspondence Files Jul–Aug 1948, USMA.

112. Taylor, "West Point Looks Ahead," 6.

113. Linn, *Elvis's Army,* 26–27.

114. Crackel, *West Point,* 220–223.

115. Maxwell D. Taylor, n.d., "Personal, World War II," 90–92, Taylor Papers, box 1, folder: World War II Operations: Lessons of World War II, NDU, quotation on page 90.

116. Taylor, "Postwar Trends in American Strategy," 27 May 1948, talk at Imperial Defence College, 3–4, Taylor Papers, box 2, folder: Speeches 1947–49, NDU.

117. Ibid., 4–6.

118. Ibid., 7–10.

119. Ibid.,10–13, quotation on 11.

120. Ibid.,13–16.

121. Ibid., 17–21.

122. Notes for Use by General Omar Bradley in Testimony before the Senate Armed Services Committee, 25 March 1948, Lincoln Papers, box 37, folder: Gen Omar Bradley Lecture 1948, USMA.

123. Taylor to Westmoreland, 7 August 1961, Westmoreland Papers, box 2, folder: WCW—Military—Gen.—1961 Aug., South Caroliniana Library, University of South Carolina (SCL).

124. Taylor to Westmoreland, 17 May 1960, Westmoreland Papers, box 13, folder: WCW—Military—Topical—Letters of Congratulations (Feb.–18 May 1960), SCL.

125. Robert Griffith, ed., *Ike's Letters to a Friend, 1941–1958* (Lawrence: Univ. Press of Kansas, 1984), 58 (12 August 1949).

126. Beukema to R. Parker Kuhn, 14 December 1949, Beukema Papers, box 1, folder: Col B—K to 1 Jan 1952, USMA.

127. Proceedings of the Academic Board, 1949, 1–29, Records of the United States Military Academy, RG 404, USMA.

128. Taylor, diary, 28 January 1949, Taylor Papers, box 1, NDU.

129. Lincoln to Taylor, 6 December 1948, Lincoln Papers, box 8, folder: Correspondence Files Sep–Dec 1948, USMA.

130. "Some Reflections on Leadership," address by General Maxwell D. Taylor at The Citadel, Charleston, South Carolina, 21 January 1956, James A. Van Fleet Papers, box 19, folder 34, GCML.

131. Maxwell D. Taylor, "Military Leadership: What Is It? Can It Be Taught?" *Distinguished Lecture Series* (Washington, D.C.: National Defense University, spring 1977), 84–93.

2. Cold War Frontiers

1. Taylor to Baruch, 19 January 1949, Baruch Papers, box 136, folder: Taylor, Maxwell D., Public Policy Papers, Department of Rare Manuscripts and Special Collections, Princeton University Library (PUL).

2. Taylor interviewed by Manion, Section 3, 16 (quoted); Taylor to Eisenhower, 26 August 1949, Eisenhower Pre-Presidential Papers, principal file, box 115, folder: Taylor, Maxwell D., DDEL; Lucius D. Clay, *Decision in Germany* (Garden City, N.Y.: Doubleday, 1950), 227–244.

3. Theodor Scharnholz, "German-American Relations at the Local Level: Heidelberg, 1948–1955," in *GIs in Germany: The Social, Economic, Cultural, and Political History of the American Military Presence*, ed. Thomas W. Maulucci and Detlef Junker (Cambridge, UK: Cambridge Univ. Press, 2013), 142–160.

4. Phillip A. Karber and Jerald A. Combs, "The United States, NATO, and the Soviet Threat to Western Europe: Military Estimates and Policy Opinions, 1945–1963," *Diplomatic History* 22, no. 3 (1998), 399–429; Dewery A. Browder, "Appendix: Population Statistics for U.S. Military in Germany, 1945–2000," in Maulucci and Junker, eds., *GIs in Germany*, 347–352.

5. Lawrence S. Kaplan, *The United States and NATO: The Formative Years* (Lexington: Univ. Press of Kentucky, 1984).

6. Hans-Jürgen Schraut, "U.S. Forces in Germany, 1945–1955," in *U.S. Military Forces in Europe: The Early Years, 1945–1950*, ed. Simon W. Duke and Wolfgang Krieger (Boulder, Colo.: Westview Press, 1993), 153–180 (esp. 169–172).

7. McCloy to Handy, 20 June 1950, Thomas T. Handy Papers, box 3, folder F-33, GCML.

8. Frank L. Howley, *Berlin Command* (New York: Putnam, 1950).

9. David G. Coleman, "The Berlin-Korea Parallel: Berlin and American National Security in Light of the Korean War," *Australasian Journal of American Studies* 18, no. 1 (1999), 19–41.

10. Daniel F. Harrington, *Berlin on the Brink: The Blockade, the Airlift, and the Early Cold War* (Lexington: Univ. Press of Kentucky, 2012).

11. Paul Steege, *Black Market, Cold War: Everyday Life in Berlin, 1946–1949* (Cambridge, UK: Cambridge Univ. Press, 2007), 192–271.

12. Robert P. Grathwol and Donita M. Moorhus, *Cold War Outpost: American Forces in Berlin, 1945–1994* (Washington, D.C.: Department of Defense, Legacy Resource Management Program, 1994), 60–62.

13. Taylor, *Swords and Plowshares*, 123–125.
14. Taylor, "Berlin Situation," 14 November 1949, Taylor Papers, box 3, folder: Maxwell Taylor Speeches, Public Pronouncements, Briefings, NDU.
15. Briefing for Admiral Sherman, 27 March 1950, Taylor Papers, box 3, folder: Maxwell Taylor Speeches, Public Pronouncements, Briefings, NDU.
16. Taylor to Handy, 15 December 1949, Handy Papers, box 5, folder F-5, GCML.
17. Thomas Alan Schwartz, *America's Germany: John J. McCloy and the Federal Republic of Germany* (Cambridge, Mass.: Harvard Univ. Press, 1991), 114.
18. Hubert G. Schmidt and Elisabeth Erdmann, "Economic Assistance to West Berlin, 1949–1951," 2, Historical Division, Office of the US High Commissioner for Germany, Records of the U.S. High Commissioner for Germany, Office of the Executive Secretary, General Records, 1947–1952, box 5, folder: 249, RG 466, NARA.
19. Ann Tusa and John Tusa, *The Berlin Blockade* (London: Hodder and Stoughton, 1988), 375; Hermann-Josef Rupieper, *Der besetzte Verbündete: Die amerikanische Deutschlandpolitik 1949–1955* (Opladen: Westdeutscher Verlag, 1991), 180–181.
20. Briefing talk given by MDT to VIPs visiting Berlin (undated), 5–6, Taylor Papers, box 3, folder: Maxwell Taylor Speeches, Public Pronouncements, Briefings, NDU. Emphasis in original.
21. Taylor, "Comments to the ECA Advisory Committee" (undated) and talk to be given at luncheon, 8 February 1950, at Kaiserstr. Club, Taylor Papers, box 3, folder: Maxwell Taylor Speeches, Public Pronouncements, Briefings, NDU.
22. Taylor, statement for *Berliner Wirtschaftsblatt*, 31 July 1950, Taylor Papers, box 3, folder: Maxwell Taylor Speeches, Public Pronouncements, Briefings—2 Sep 49–19 Jan 51, NDU.
23. Taylor interviewed by Manion, Section 3, 18.
24. Excerpt from the Journal of Colonel H. P. Jones, Chief of the Division of Economic Affairs of the Office of the United States High Commissioner for Germany, in Department of State, *Foreign Relations of the United States, 1949*, vol. 3, *Council of Foreign Ministers; Germany and Austria* (Washington, D.C.: Government Printing Office, 1975), 430–431; Taylor, "Berlin Situation."
25. Schmidt and Erdmann, *Economic Assistance*, 13–19, Taylor quoted on 17.
26. Tusa, *Berlin Blockade*, 376.
27. Schmidt and Erdmann, *Economic Assistance*, 33.
28. Rupieper, *Der besetzte Verbündete*, 183–184; Henrik Bering, *Outpost Berlin: The History of the American Military Forces in Berlin, 1945–1994* (Chicago: edition q, 1995), 140–141; Ann Tusa, *The Last Division: Berlin and the Wall* (London: Hodder and Stoughton, 1996), 36.
29. Briefing talk given by MDT to VIPs visiting Berlin (undated), 4–5, Taylor Papers, box 3, folder: Maxwell Taylor Speeches, Public Pronouncements, Briefings, NDU.
30. Taylor, speech before the German World Economic Society, 2 October 1950, 3, Taylor Papers, box 3, folder: Maxwell Taylor Speeches, Public Pronouncements, Briefings—2 Sep 49–19 Jan 51, NDU.
31. Tusa, *Last Division*, 36; Grathwol and Moorhus, *Cold War Outpost*, 68.

32. Tusa, *Berlin Blockade*, 373.
33. Howley, *Berlin Command*, 14–15.
34. Riddleberger to Acheson, 13 September 1949, in Department of State, *Foreign Relations of the United States, 1949*, 3:378–380.
35. Taylor to Acting Secretary of State, 25 September 1949, in Department of State, *Foreign Relations of the United States, 1949*, 3:392–393; Taylor to McCloy, 28 September 1949 and 1 October 1949, in Department of State, *Foreign Relations of the United States, 1949*, 3:393–399.
36. Kotikov's 10 October 1949 letter in Taylor to Acheson, 11 October 1949, in Department of State, *Foreign Relations of the United States, 1949*, 3:411–412; the western commandants' 21 November response is in McCloy to Acting Secretary of State, 22 November 1949, in Department of State, *Foreign Relations of the United States, 1949*, 3:431–432; Kotikov's December 19 letter is in Babcock to Acheson, 31 December 1949, in Department of State, *Foreign Relations of the United States, 1949*, 3:434–436.
37. Quoted in Tusa, *Last Division*, 46.
38. Acheson to McCloy, 31 January 1950, in Department of State, *Foreign Relations of the United States, 1950*, vol. 4, *Central and Eastern Europe; the Soviet Union* (Washington, D.C.: United States Government Printing Office, 1980), 819–820.
39. Taylor, Briefing—National Defense College, 17 April 1950, Taylor Papers, box 3, folder: Maxwell Taylor Speeches, Public Pronouncements, Briefings—2 Sep 49–19 Jan 51, NDU.
40. For a celebratory East German perspective, see Gerhard Keiderling, *Berlin 1945–1986: Geschichte der Hauptstadt der DDR* (Berlin: Dietz Verlag, 1987), 391–393.
41. Byroade to McCloy and Taylor, 9 February 1950, in Department of State, *Foreign Relations of the United States, 1950*, 4:824–825.
42. Memorandum by the Secretary of the Army (Pace), Referred to the National Security Council by the Secretary of Defense (Johnson), 28 April 1950, in Department of State, *Foreign Relations of the United States, 1950*, 4:844–847.
43. Briefing for Admiral Sherman, 27 March 1950; Taylor for *Welt im Film*, 13 April 1950; Taylor to Hasker, NBC, 14 April 1950, all in Taylor Papers, box 3, folder: Maxwell Taylor Speeches, Public Pronouncements, Briefings—2 Sep 49–19 Jan 51, NDU.
44. Speech by General Taylor to officers of tactical units, 22 May 1950, 7, Taylor Papers, box 3, folder: Maxwell Taylor Speeches, Public Pronouncements, Briefings—2 Sep 49–19 Jan 51, NDU.
45. Pace memorandum, 28 April 1950.
46. Wendelin to Taylor, 3 August 1950, Historical Report on Security Aspects of Deutschlandtreffen, Records of the U.S. High Commissioner to Germany, Miscellaneous Files Relating Primarily to Berlin, box 3, folder: Deutschlandtreffen, RG 466, NARA.
47. Handy to Taylor, 12 June 1950, Handy Papers, box 5, folder F-5, GCML.
48. Taylor, statement to the press, 29 May 1950, Taylor Papers, box 3, folder: Maxwell Taylor Speeches, Public Pronouncements, Briefings—2 Sep 49–19 Jan 51, NDU.

49. Acheson to McCloy, 28 October 1949, in Department of State, *Foreign Relations of the United States, 1949*, 3:429–430.
50. Rupieper, *Der besetzte Verbündete*, 193–199.
51. Taylor to McCloy, 3, 5, and 17 April 1950, in Department of State, *Foreign Relations of the United States, 1950*, 4:836–838, 839–840, 842–843.
52. Taylor to McCloy, 11 May 1950, in *Foreign Relations of the United States, 1950*, 4:855–856; editorial note, in Department of State, *Foreign Relations of the United States, 1950*, 4:860–861.
53. Tusa, *Last Division*, 31.
54. Schwartz, *America's Germany*, 67.
55. Taylor to McCloy, 12 April 1950, in Department of State, *Foreign Relations of the United States, 1950*, 4:841–842.
56. Taylor, speech to the ECA Committee including Vice Chancellor Blücher and Economics Minister Erhard, 24 July 1950, Taylor Papers, box 3, folder: Maxwell Taylor Speeches, Public Pronouncements, Briefings—2 Sep 49–19 Jan 51, NDU.
57. Taylor to Gruenther, 10 September 1949, Gruenther Papers, General Correspondence Series, box 18, folder: Taylor, Maxwell D., DDEL.
58. Taylor to Acting Secretary of State, 7 October 1949; McCloy to Acting Secretary of State, 7 October 1949; and Editorial Note, all in Department of State, *Foreign Relations of the United States, 1949*, 3:526–531.
59. Briefing speech given by MDT to VIPs visiting Berlin (undated), 8, Taylor Papers, box 3, folder: Maxwell Taylor Speeches, Public Pronouncements, Briefings, NDU; Nicholas J. Schlosser, *Cold War on the Airwaves: The Radio Propaganda War against East Germany* (Champaign: Univ. of Illinois Press, 2015), 47–74.
60. Acheson to McCloy and Taylor, 1 April 1950, in Department of State, *Foreign Relations of the United States, 1950*, 4:835–836.
61. Taylor, *Swords and Plowshares*, 125–126; McCloy in Schwartz, *America's Germany*, 115.
62. Coleman, "Berlin-Korea Parallel," 24–33.
63. Byroade to McCloy, 28 July 1950, and paper prepared by McCloy, Handy, and Taylor, 29 August 1950, in Department of State, *Foreign Relations of the United States, 1950*, 4:867–887.
64. M.D.T., "A Review of the Berlin Situation," 10 August 1950, Records of the U.S. High Commissioner for Germany, Office of the Executive Secretary, Miscellaneous Files Relating to Berlin, M to P, box 5, folder: Hold Page, RG 466, NARA.
65. Paper by McCloy, Handy, and Taylor, 869–870.
66. Ibid., 871–873; MDT, "A Review of the Berlin Situation."
67. Paper by McCloy, Handy, and Taylor, 875–877.
68. Ibid., 884–887.
69. M.C. 30, 18 November 1950, Report by the Standing Group to the Military Committee on Military Aspects of German Participation in the Defense of Western Europe, NATO Archive, International Military Staff, http://archives.nato.int/military-aspects-of-german-participation-in-defence-of-western-europe-3;isad (accessed 21 December 2016); Schwartz, *America's Germany*, 113–155;

Sheldon A. Goldberg, *From Disarmament to Rearmament: The Reversal of U.S. Policy toward West Germany, 1946–1955* (Athens: Ohio Univ. Press, 2017).

70. Taylor to McCloy, 7 October 1950, in Department of State, *Foreign Relations of the United States, 1950*, 4:891–893.

71. Ewan Butler, *Berlin 1955* (New York: Praeger, 1955), 161.

72. Taylor to Handy and McCloy, 16 November 1950, Records of the U.S. High Commissioner for Germany, U.S. High Commissioner John J. McCloy, Top Secret General Records, 1949–1952, box 3: 1950, folder: November 1950, Top Secret Documents, McCloy Project (II), RG 466, NARA.

73. Taylor to McCloy, 27 September 1950, in Department of State, *Foreign Relations of the United States, 1950*, 4:888–889.

74. Marshall to Lay, 18 October 1950, in Department of State, *Foreign Relations of the United States, 1950*, 4:893–894.

75. Memorandum for the Joint Chiefs of Staff Representative on the National Security Council Staff (Wooldridge), 30 October 1950, in Department of State, *Foreign Relations of the United States, 1950*, 4:897–898.

76. Jones to Taylor, 27 November 1950, "One Year's Stockpile for Berlin," Records of the U.S. High Commissioner for Germany, Miscellaneous Files Relating Primarily to Berlin, box 3, folder: Economics, RG 466, NARA.

77. Rupieper, *Der besetzte Verbündete*, 147–148.

78. Taylor interview by Mannion, Section III, 19.

79. Rupieper, *Der besetzte Verbündete*, 148–149.

80. McCloy to Taylor, 24 January 1951, Handy Papers, box 5, folder F-5, GCML.

81. Handy to McCloy, 23 June 1950, Handy Papers, box 3, folder F-33, GCML.

82. Quoted in Jean Edward Smith, *Lucius D. Clay: An American Life* (New York: Henry Holt, 1990), 647.

83. Department of State, Confidential Memorandum of Conversation, "Berlin," 12 February 1958. National Security Archive, Berlin Crisis Collection, http://nsarchive.chadwyck.com/nsa/documents/BC/00092/all.pdf (accessed 28 March 2015).

84. Taylor, *Swords and Plowshares*, 127.

85. Ibid., 123–130.

86. Paul D. Harkins interviewed by Ted Gittinger, 10 November 1981, 2, The Association for Diplomatic Studies and Training Foreign Affairs Oral History Project, LBJ Library (LBJL).

87. Taylor interviewed by Manion, Section 3, 20–21.

88. Taylor interviewed by Manion, Section 2, 10 November 1972, 16.

89. Brian McAllister Linn, *The Echo of Battle: The Army's Way of War* (Cambridge, Mass.: Harvard Univ. Press, 2007), 151–160.

90. David Jablonsky, *War by Land, Sea, and Air: Dwight Eisenhower and the Concept of Unified Command* (New Haven, Conn.: Yale Univ. Press, 2010), 141–183.

91. John Sager, "Universal Military Training and the Struggle to Define American Identity during the Cold War," *Federal History* 5, no. 1 (2013), 57–74; Taylor, *Every Citizen a Soldier*.

92. Collins to Eisenhower, 5 June 1951, Eisenhower to Collins, 20 December 1951, and Collins to Eisenhower, 11 February 1952, all in Eisenhower Pre-Presidential Papers, principal file, box 25, folder: Collins, J. Lawton (1), DDEL.

93. T. R. Fehrenbach, *This Kind of War: A Study in Unpreparedness* (New York: Macmillan, 1963); Thomas E. Hanson, *Combat Ready? The Eighth U.S. Army on the Eve of the Korean War* (College Station: Texas A&M Univ. Press, 2010); Linn, *Elvis's Army*, 9–47.

94. Steven T. Ross, *American War Plans 1945–1950: Strategies for Defeating the Soviet Union* (London: Frank Cass, 1996); Edward N. Kaplan, *To Kill Nations: American Strategy in the Air-Atomic Age and the Rise of Mutually Assured Destruction* (Ithaca, N.Y.: Cornell Univ. Press, 2015), 19–46.

95. Department of State, *Foreign Relations of the United States, 1950*, vol. 1, *National Security Affairs; Foreign Economic Policy* (Washington, D.C.: Government Printing Office, 1977), 234–92; David T. Fautua, "The 'Long Pull' Army: NSC 68, the Korean War, and the Creation of the Cold War Army," *Journal of Military History* 61, no. 1 (1997): 93–120.

96. Quoted in Forrest Pogue, *George C. Marshall*, vol. 4, *Statesman, 1945–1959* (New York: Viking, 1987), 427.

97. Steven Casey, *Selling the Korean War: Propaganda, Politics, and Public Opinion in the United States, 1950–1953* (Oxford, UK: Oxford Univ. Press, 2008), 205–263.

98. Richard Squires, *Auf dem Kriegspfad: Aufzeichnungen eines englischen Offiziers* (Berlin: Rutten and Loening, 1951).

99. George F. Hoffmann, *Cold War Casualty: The Court-Martial of Major General Robert W. Grow* (Kent, Ohio: Kent State Univ. Press, 1993), 1.

100. Address by Lieutenant General Maxwell D. Taylor at the Army War College, Carlisle Barracks, 27 October 1952, 3–4, Taylor Papers, box 3, folder: Miscellaneous Messages and Speeches, 1951–1954, NDU.

101. Taylor to Secretary of the Army, 24 August 1951, Directives to CINCFE Respecting the ROK Force to Be Developed, *Declassified Documents Online* (DDO), http://tinyurl.galegroup.com/tinyurl/3g88i2 (accessed 10 September 2016).

102. Taylor to Gray, 31 October 1951, DDO, http://tinyurl.galegroup.com/tinyurl/3g8BN3 (accessed September 10, 2016).

103. Maxwell D. Taylor, "Notes from Far East Trip," 10 May 1951, Henry S. Aurand Papers, box 45, "General Correspondence: [1951] T-Z (1)," DDEL; Matthew B. Ridgway, *The Korean War* (Garden City, N.Y.: Doubleday, 1967), 192–193.

104. Morris J. MacGregor Jr., *Integration of the Armed Forces, 1940–1965* (Washington, D.C.: US Army Center of Military History, 1981), 432–433.

105. Enclosure to Taylor to Ridgway, 4 February 1954, "The Preponderant Role of the Infantry," 2, Taylor Papers, box 2, folder: Korea, (D), NDU.

106. Rupieper, *Der besetzte Verbündete*, 121–122.

107. Hays to Taylor, 24 March 1951, and Taylor to Hays, 4 April 1951, Records of the U.S. High Commissioner for Germany, Office of the Executive Director, General Hays's Files, 1949–1951, box 1, folder: Miscellaneous Military, RG 466, NARA.

108. Robert W. Coakley, Karl E. Cocke, and Daniel P. Griffin, *Demobilization Following the Korean War* (Washington, D.C.: Histories Division, Office of the Chief of Military History, 1968), 1–2.

109. Steven L. Rearden, *History of the Office of the Secretary of Defense: The Formative Years, 1947–1950* (Washington, D.C.: Historical Office, Office of the Secretary of Defense, 1984), 309–384; Doris M. Condit, *History of the Office of the Secretary of Defense*, vol. 2, *The Test of War, 1950–1953* (Washington, D.C.: Historical Office, Office of the Secretary of Defense, 1988), 223–306.

110. Taylor interviewed by Manion, Section 3, 22–24.

111. Pace to Lovett, 26 December 1951, Submission of Materiel for Use in Briefing the Armed Services Committee of the House of Representatives, Enclosure: "Attainment of Preparedness Objectives," Records of the Army Staff, Security Classified Correspondence, 1948–1954, box 246, folder: 032.2, RG 319, NARA.

112. Major General Reuben Jenkins, discussion memorandum, 16 July 1952, "Army Strength and Structure for FY 1953," Records of the Army Staff, Security Classified Correspondence, 1948–1954, box 307, folder: 320 Programs 34 thru 39, RG 319, NARA. Taylor noted his approval on 21 July 1952.

113. Pace to Lovett, 26 December 1951.

114. Statement of the Secretary of the Army before the Subcommittee on Armed Services, Committee on Appropriations, House of Representatives, 5th Draft, 29 January 1952, 2 (Off the Record section), Records of the Army Staff, Security Classified Correspondence, 1948–1954, box 246, folder: 032.2, RG 319, NARA.

115. Enclosure to Pace to Lovett, 26 December 1951, "Support of ROK Forces."

116. Republican minority leader Joseph Martin read MacArthur's letter in the House. H. W. Brands, *The General vs. the President: MacArthur and Truman at the Brink of Nuclear War* (New York, Doubleday, 2016), 280–286.

117. Stephen Taaffe, *MacArthur's Korean War Generals* (Lawrence: Univ. Press of Kansas, 2016), 2.

118. J. Lawton Collins, *War in Peacetime: The History and Lessons of Korea* (Boston: Houghton Mifflin, 1969), 326.

119. Taylor interviewed by Manion, Section 3, 25.

120. Brigadier General George E. Martin, Staff Section Report for the Period 1–28 February 1953, Records of Eighth U.S. Army, 1946–56, Assistant Chief of Staff, G-3, Command Reports 1952–1953, box 96, folder: Book I G3 Section for February 1953, RG 338, NARA.

121. Eighth Army, Command Report No. 29, 1–12, 50.

122. Enclosure to Taylor to Ridgway, 4 February 1954, 2, Taylor Papers, box 2, folder: Korea (D), NDU.

123. Taylor to Ridgway, 4 February 1954.

124. Enclosure to Taylor to Ridgway, 4 February 1954, "The Preponderant Role of the Infantry."

125. Headquarters, United States Eighth Army, G-3 Section, Periodic Operations Report, 13 February 1953, Annex B, Records of Eighth U.S. Army, 1946–1956, box 96, folder: Book IV, G3 Section for February 1953, RG 338, NARA.

126. Period Intelligence Report No. 947, 13 February 1953, Records of

Eighth U.S. Army, 1946–1956, Assistant Chief of Staff, G-2, Periodic Intelligence Reports, box 74, folder: Feb. 1, 1953 to Feb. 28, 1953, RG 338, NARA.

127. Collins, *War in Peacetime*, 318–322; Taylor, *Swords and Plowshares*, 136–137.

128. Taylor interviewed by Manion, Section 3, 25–26.

129. Ibid., 26.

130. James Van Fleet, "The Truth about Korea, Part I: From a Man Now Free to Speak," *Life*, May 11, 1953, 126–142; James Van Fleet, "The Truth about Korea, Part II: How We Can Win with What We Have," *Life*, May 18, 1953, 156–172.

131. Enclosure to Clark to Eisenhower, 19 January 1953, "Statement on Ammunition Situation in Far East Command," Eisenhower Papers as President (Ann Whitman File), Administration Series, box 10, folder: Clark, Gen. Mark, DDEL.

132. Taylor to Williams, 27 May 1953, Samuel T. Williams Papers, box 4, folder 18, HIA.

133. Major General Porter to the Adjutant General, 23 March 1953, "Report on Visit to Far East," and Major General C. D. Eddleman, discussion memorandum, 20 April 1953, "Visit to Korea by Senior Commander," Records of the Army Staff, Security Classified Correspondence, 1948–1954, 1953, box 411, folder: 091 Korea—10—1953, RG 319, NARA.

134. Colonel Hugh P. Harris, Assistant Chief of Staff, G-3, Staff Section Report for the Period 1–31 March 1953, Records of Eighth U.S. Army, 1946–56, Assistant Chief of Staff, G-3, Command Reports 1952–1953, March 1953, box 98, folder: Book I G3 Section for March 1953, RG 338, NARA.

135. Colonel Hugh P. Harris, Assistant Chief of Staff, G-3, Annex B: Headquarters, United States Eighth Army, Period Operations Reports, 26, 27, and 28 March 1953, Records of Eighth U.S. Army, 1946–1956, box 98, folder: Book VII G3 Section for March 1953, RG 338, NARA.

136. Periodic Intelligence Reports No. 985 (23 March 1953), No. 986 (24 March 1953), No. 987 (25 March 1953), No. 988 (26 March 1953), 989 (27 March 1953), 990 (28 March 1953), 991 (29 March 1953), 992 (30 March 1953), and 993 (31 March 1953), all in Records of Eighth U.S. Army, 1946–1956, G-2 Period Intelligence Reports, box 75, RG 338, NARA.

137. Enclosure 1 to G-2 Periodic Intelligence Report No. 993.

138. Periodic Intelligence Reports 987, 990, and 991.

139. Eighth Army Command Report 29, April 1953, 53; Eighth Army Command Report 29, Section II: Supporting Documents, Book 1: Office of the Chief of Staff, *Monthly Narrative Summary for April 1953*.

140. Eighth Army, *Narrative Summary for April 1953*, 1–2; Xiaobing Li, *China's Battle for Korea: The 1951 Spring Offensive* (Bloomington: Indiana Univ. Press, 2014), 235.

141. Shu Guang Zhang, *Mao's Military Romanticism: China and the Korean War, 1950–1953* (Lawrence: Univ. Press of Kansas, 1995), 232–250; Peng Dehuai, "My Story of the Korean War," and Chai Chengwen, "The Korean Truce Negotiations," in *Mao's Generals Remember Korea*, ed. Xiaobing Li, Allan R. Millett, and Bin Yu (Lawrence: Univ. Press of Kansas, 2001), 30–37.

142. Eighth Army, *Narrative Summary for April 1953*, 2.

143. Briggs to Secretary of State, 26 April 1953, Records of the Army Staff, Security Classified Correspondence, 1948–1954, 1953, box 411, folder: 091 Korea—10—1953, RG 319, NARA.

144. Zhang, *Mao's Military Romanticism*, 242; Li, *China's Battle for Korea*, 236.

145. Clark to JCS, 30 May 1953, *DDO*, http://tinyurl.galegroup.com/tinyurl/3g8FD2 (accessed 10 September 2016).

146. William I. Stueck, *The Korean War: An International History* (Princeton, N.J.: Princeton Univ. Press, 1995); Masuda Hajimu, *Cold War Crucible: The Korean Conflict and the Postwar World* (Cambridge, Mass.: Harvard Univ. Press, 2015).

147. Headquarters, United States Eighth Army, Command Report, May 1953, 2, 51, Records of the Army Adjutant General, box 1476, folder: May 1953, RG 407, NARA.

148. Eighth Army Command Report, May 1953, 3.

149. Taylor interviewed by Manion, first interview, 27–28. The best military history, albeit thus far ending in mid-1951, is Allan R. Millett, *The War for Korea: They Came from the North, 1950–1951* (Lawrence: Univ. Press of Kansas, 2010).

150. Fehrenbach, *This Kind of War*, 620; Anthony Farrar-Hockley, *The British Part in the Korean War*, vol. 2, *An Honourable Discharge* (London: HMSO, 1995), 377.

151. Clarke to Walter Hermes, 20 March 1968, Bruce Clarke Papers, box 1, folder: Undated + 1962–69, Special Collections and Manuscripts, USMA.

152. Periodic Intelligence Report No. 1095, 11 July 1953, Records of Eighth U.S. Army, 1946–1956, G-2, Periodic Intelligence Reports, box 79, July 1, 1953 to July 31, 1953, RG 338, NARA.

153. S.L.A. Marshall, *Pork Chop Hill: The American Fighting Man in Action, Korea, Spring 1953* (New York: Morrow, 1956), 15. For enemy casualties: Period Intelligence Report No. 1095.

154. Walter Hermes, *The United States Army in the Korean War: Truce Tent and Fighting Front* (Washington, D.C.: US Army Center for Military History, 1966), 465–478.

155. Clark to JCS, 17 July 1953, Eisenhower Papers as President (Ann Whitman File), International Series, box 35, folder: Korea 1953 (2), DDEL.

156. Headquarters, United States Eighth Army, Command Report, June 1953, 1–3, Records of the Army Adjutant General, box 1477, folder: June 1953, RG 407, NARA.

157. Hermes, *Truce Tent and Fighting Front*, 477; Clay Blair, *The Forgotten War: America in Korea, 1950–1953* (New York: Times Books, 1987), 974–975.

158. Conrad Crane, *American Airpower Strategy in Korea, 1950–1953* (Lawrence: Univ. Press of Kansas, 2000), 160.

159. Collins, n.d., memorandum for the Secretary of the Army, "Report of Chief of Staff's Visit to Far East Command," 22–30 June 1953, Collins Papers, box 22, folder: Trip to Far East Command, June 22–July 2, 1953, DDEL.

160. Blair, *Forgotten War*, 973; Crane, *Airpower in Korea*, 158–162.

161. Taylor interview by Stanley Karnow, 1979, http://openvault.wgbh.org/catalog/vietnam-f7ff45-interview-with-maxwell-d-maxwell-davenport-taylor-1979-part-1-of-4 (accessed 9 February 2016).

162. Headquarters, United States Eighth Army, Command Report, July 1953, 1, Records of the Army Adjutant General, box 1478, July 1953, RG 407, NARA.

163. Colonel R. T. Finn, Assistant Chief of Staff, G-1, 31 July 1953, G-1 Staff Section Feeder Report to Eighth U.S. Army Command Report July 1953, Records of Eighth U.S. Army, 1946–56, Assistant Chief of Staff, G-1, Command Reports, 1951–53, 1955, box 8, folder: G-1 Command Report for July, RG 338, NARA.

164. Periodic Intelligence Reports Nos. 1099 (15 July 1953) and 1111 (27 July 1953) and Enclosure No. 1 to Periodic Intelligence Report 1111, Records of Eighth U.S. Army, 1946–1956, G-2, Periodic Intelligence Reports, box 79, folder: July 1, 1953 to July 31, 1953, RG 338, NARA.

165. Headquarters, United States Eighth Army, Command Report, July 1953, 2, Records of the Army Adjutant General, box 1478, folder: July 1953, RG 407, NARA.

166. Lieutenant Colonel Kenneth C. Jones, Asst Adjutant General to Commanding Generals, All Corps; Commanding Generals, All Divisions; Chief, Korean Military Advisory Group; Commanding Officers, All Area Commands and Groups, 11 July 1953, Records of the Army Adjutant General, box 1477, folder: June 1953, RG 407, NARA.

167. Captain Helgeson, Military History Section, 20 August 1953, G1 Command Report for July, Records of Eighth U.S. Army, 1946–56, Assistant Chief of Staff, G-1, Command Reports, 1951–53, 1955, box 8, folder: G-1 Command Report for July, RG 338, NARA.

168. Headquarters, United States Eighth Army, Command Report, September 1953, 2, Records of the Army Adjutant General, box 1480, folder: Sept 1953, RG 407, NARA.

169. [John E. Hull], *The Autobiography of General John E. Hull, 1895–1975* (N.p.: Miriam Anderson, Mary Von Bargen, Mildred Head, and Dorothy A. Lynch, 1978), 180–183; Headquarters, United States Army Pacific, *The Handling of Prisoners of War during the Korean War*, Fort Shafter, Hawaii: Military History Office, US Army Pacific, June 1960, 96.

170. Headquarters, United States Eighth Army, Command Report, August 1953, 1–3, Records of the Army Adjutant General, box 1479, folder: Aug 1953, RG 407, NARA.

171. Headquarters, United States Eighth Army, Command Report, September 1953, 1, 3, Records of the Army Adjutant General, box 1480, folder: Sept 1953, RG 407, NARA.

172. Jack Raymond, *Power at the Pentagon* (New York: Harper and Row, 1964), 115.

173. Headquarters, United States Eighth Army, Quarterly Historical Report, 1 Jan 54—31 Mar 54, 1–3, Records of the Army Adjutant General, box 1482, folder: Jan–Mar 1954, RG 407, NARA.

174. Eisenhower, memorandum for the Secretary of State, the Secretary

of Defense, the Mutual Security Administrator, 31 July 1953, "Assistance to Korea," Eisenhower Papers as President (Ann Whitman File), box 36, folder: Dulles/Korea/Security Policy, DDEL.

175. Colonel John C. Lackas, Assistant Comptroller of International Affairs, to Under Secretary of the Army, 31 August 1953, "U.S. Expenditures for, and Contributions to, ROK Other Than the Direct Cost of the U.S. War Effort in Korea," Records of the Army Staff, Security Classified Correspondence, 1948–1954, 1953, box 411, folder: 091 Korea—10—1953, RG 319, NARA.

176. Eighth Army Historical Report, 1 Jan 54—31 Mar 54, 173–174.

177. Taylor to Williams, 17 July 1954, Samuel T. Williams Papers, box 7, folder 12, HIA.

178. Headquarters, United States Eighth Army, Quarterly Historical Report, 1 Oct 53–31 Dec 53, 1–3, Records of the Adjutant General, box 1481, folder: Oct–Dec 1953, RG 407, NARA.

179. Jenkins to Taylor, 6 October 1953, Records of the Army Staff, Security Classified Correspondence, 1948–1954, 1953, box 411, folder: 091 Korea—10—1953, RG 319, NARA.

180. Ibid.

181. Taylor, *Swords and Plowshares,* 153; Glen R. Hawkins, *United States Army Force Structure and Force Design Initiatives, 1939–1989* (Washington, D.C.: US Army Center of Military History, 1991), 27–28; John B. Wilson, *Maneuver and Firepower: The Evolution of Divisions and Separate Brigades* (Washington, D.C.: US Army Center of Military History, 1998), 271.

182. T. Michael Booth and Duncan Spencer, *Paratrooper: The Life of Gen. James Gavin* (New York: Simon and Schuster, 1994).

183. James M. Gavin, *War and Peace in the Space Age* (New York: Harper, 1958), 132–37.

184. Ibid., 137–139; James M. Gavin, "New Divisional Organization," *Army-Navy-Air Force Register* 76, no. 3923 (12 February 1955): 1–2; James M. Gavin, "Cavalry, and I Don't Mean Horses," *Harper's Magazine* 208, no. 1247 (April 1954), 54–60.

185. Personal note for the Supreme Commander by Field Marshal Montgomery, 4 January 1954, Norstad Papers, Personal Name Series, box 74, folder: Montgomery, Field Marshal (2), DDEL.

186. SGM-1-55, North Atlantic Military Committee, Standing Group, 10 January 1955, *Memorandum for the Supreme Allied Commander Europe, the Supreme Allied Commander Atlantic, the Channel Committee, the Canada–United States Regional Planning Group,* Annex A to Appendix B to Enclosure J, 38–41, NATO Archive, International Military Staff, Brussels.

187. General John E. Hull interviewed by Lieutenant Colonel James W. Wurman, Section 8, 22 April 1974, 14, Hull Papers, box 1, AHEC.

188. Taylor to Ridgway, 2 May 1954, Matthew B. Ridgway Papers, Series 2, box 18, folder: Correspondence (Army Chief of Staff), T, AHEC.

189. Eighth Army Report, 1 July 54—30 Sept. 54, 5.

190. Headquarters, United States Eighth Army, Quarterly Historical Report, 1 Oct 54—31 Dec 54, 5, Records of the Adjutant General, box 1484, folder: July 1–Dec 31, 1954, RG 407, NARA.

191. Dulles to Hoover, 14 February 1955, John Foster Dulles Papers, Personnel Series, box 10, folder: T (1), DDEL.
192. Affidavit of General Maxwell Taylor, US District Court for the Southern District of New York, General William C. Westmoreland against CBS, Inc., et al., 13 December 1983, ProQuest History Vault (PQV), http://congressional.proquest.com/histvault?q=000591-004-0112 (accessed January 8, 2017).

3. Reformer and Strategist?

1. Maxwell D. Taylor, *The Uncertain Trumpet* (New York: Harper and Brothers, 1960), 28–29; Taylor, *Swords and Plowshares,* 156.
2. "And Now—The Atomic Army: Exclusive Interview with Gen. Maxwell D. Taylor, Chief of Staff, U.S. Army," *U.S. News and World Report* (3 February 1956), 64–73, quotation on 64.
3. John Taylor, *General Maxwell Taylor,* 191–192.
4. Stevens to Gruenther, 16 March 1955, Gruenther Papers, NATO Series, box 4, folder: Stevens, Honorable Robert T., DDEL.
5. Dwight D. Eisenhower, "Special Message to the Congress on Reorganization of the Defense Establishment," 3 April 1958, available online by Gerhard Peters and John T. Woolley, *The American Presidency Project,* http://www.presidency.ucsb.edu/ws/?pid=11340 (accessed 23 December 2016).
6. Saki Dockrill, *Eisenhower's New Look National Security Policy, 1953–1961* (Houndmills, UK: Macmillan Press, 1996); Richard M. Leighton, *History of the Office of the Secretary of Defense: Strategy, Money, and the New Look, 1953–1956* (Washington, D.C.: Office of the Secretary of Defense, Historical Office, 2001).
7. Williams to Taylor, 22 September 1955, Williams Papers, box 11, folder 18, HIA.
8. Taylor, *Uncertain Trumpet,* 5–6, quotation on 5.
9. Ibid., 4.
10. NSC 162/2, 30 October 1953, in Department of State, *Foreign Relations of the United States, 1952–1954,* vol. 2, *National Security Affairs,* part 1 (Washington, D.C.: Government Printing Office, 1984), 577–97; Gerard Clarfield, *Security with Solvency: Dwight D. Eisenhower and the Shaping of the American Military Establishment* (Westport, Conn.: Praeger, 1999); William McClenahan Jr. and William H. Becker, *Eisenhower and the Cold War Economy* (Baltimore, Md.: Johns Hopkins Univ. Press, 2011).
11. Staff of the Senate Republican Policy Committee, "National Defense Under the Republican Administration," 10 March 1955, 3, Charles E. Wilson Papers, box 51, folder: Senate Republican Memo, March 10, 1955, Anderson University, Indiana (AU).
12. Leighton, *New Look,* 65–113, 231–276, 307–333, 359–378, 471–488, 605–630.
13. "National Defense Under the Republican Administration," 6.
14. Semiannual Report of the Secretary of Defense and the Semiannual Reports of the Secretary of the Army, Secretary of the Navy, Secretary of the Air Force, January 1 to June 30, 1957, I-8, Wilson Papers, box 25, folder: Federal government (2), AU.

15. Helmut Hammerich, *Das Heer 1950 bis 1970: Konzeption, Organisation, Aufstellung* (Munich: R. Oldenbourg Verlag, 2006); Bruno Thoß, *NATO-Strategie und nationale Vertedigungsplanung: Planung und Aufbau der Bundeswehr unter den Bedingungen einer massiven atomaren Vergeltungsstrategie 1952–1960* (Munich: R. Oldenbourg Verlag, 2006).

16. Robert J. Watson, *History of the Joint Chiefs of Staff*, vol. 5, *The Joint Chiefs of Staff and National Policy, 1953–1954* (Washington, D.C.: Historical Division, Joint Chiefs of Staff, 1986), 32–34.

17. Eisenhower to Gruenther, 26 September 1951, Eisenhower Pre-Presidential Papers, principal file, box 48, folder: Gruenther, Alfred M. (1), DDEL.

18. Goodpaster, 6 July 1955, memorandum of conference with the president on 29 June 1955, Eisenhower Papers as President (Ann Whitman File), Ann Whitman Diary Series, box 6, folder: ACW Diary July 1955 (5), DDEL.

19. Taylor, remarks at Armed Forces Staff College, November 1956, "Mission of the United States Army," Taylor Papers, Digital Collection, NDU, https://digitalndulibrary.ndu.edu/cdm/compoundobject/collection/taylor/id/1084/rec/6 (accessed 23 December 2016), quotation on 15.

20. "And Now—the Atomic Army," 64–65, 68–69, quotation on 69.

21. Taylor, "Mission of the United States Army," 13–14.

22. "And Now—the Atomic Army," 66–67.

23. Taylor, *The Uncertain Trumpet*, 29–30, 36–46.

24. Armstrong to Taylor, 17 June 1957 and 14 September 1965, Armstrong Papers, box 61, folder 28, PUL.

25. Taylor, *The Uncertain Trumpet*, 30–32.

26. Ibid., 32–34.

27. Linn, *Elvis's Army*, 87–90.

28. Quoted in Leighton, *New Look*, 614; Statement of General Maxwell D. Taylor before the Subcommittee on Department of Defense Appropriations, House of Representatives, Relative to the Department of the Army Budget for Fiscal Year 1957, 1 February 1956, Taylor Papers, Digital Collection, NDU, https://digitalndulibrary.ndu.edu/cdm/compoundobject/collection/taylor/id/484/rec/37 (accessed 26 December 2016); Byron R. Fairchild and Walter S. Poole, *The History of the Joint Chiefs of Staff*, vol. 7, *The Joint Chiefs of Staff and National Policy, 1957–1960* (Washington, D.C.: Office of Joint History, Office of the Chairman of the Joint Chiefs of Staff, 2000), 31–42.

29. Statement by General Maxwell D. Taylor before the Senate Armed Services Committee, 20 February 1956, 8, Records of the U.S. Joint Chiefs of Staff, Chairman's File, Admiral Radford, 1953–1957, box 22, folder: 111 (1956), RG 218, NARA.

30. Army Staff, 9 May 1956, "Discussion of Major Issues," Section I, 1–2, Records of the Army Staff, Records of the Office of the Chief of Information, box 1, folder: Current Army Thinking on Major Issues 1956, RG 319, NARA.

31. Griffith, ed., *Ike's Letters to a Friend*, 168–169 (20 August 1956).

32. Fairchild and Poole, *The History of the Joint Chiefs of Staff*, 7:31–42; Linn, *Elvis's Army*, 68.

33. Drew Pearson, *Diaries, 1949–1959*, ed. Tyler Abell (New York: Holt, Rinehart and Winston, 1974), 509; Donald A. Carter, *Forging the Shield: The*

U.S. Army in Europe, 1951–1962 (Washington, D.C.: US Army Center of Military History, 2014), 358–368.

34. Robert J. Watson, *History of the Office of the Secretary of Defense*, vol. 4, *Into the Missile Age, 1956–1960* (Washington, D.C.: Historical Office, Office of the Secretary of Defense, 1997), 127–155.

35. Taylor, "The Mission of the Army," 6–8, quotation on 8.

36. Washington Center of Foreign Policy Research, Johns Hopkins University, *Developments in Military Technology and Their Impact on United States Strategy and Foreign Policy* (Washington, D.C.: Government Printing Office, 1959).

37. Eisenhower to Dulles, 8 September 1953, Eisenhower Papers as President (Ann Whitman File), International Series, box 36, folder: Dulles/Korea/Security Policy, DDEL, emphasis in original.

38. Dwight D. Eisenhower, "The Central Role of the President in the Conduct of Security Affairs," in Jordan, ed., *Issues of National Security*, 206–219; E. Bruce Geelhoed, *Charles E. Wilson and Controversy at the Pentagon, 1953 to 1957* (Detroit, Mich.: Wayne State Univ. Press, 1979).

39. Nicholas Michael Sambaluk, *The Other Space Race: Eisenhower and the Quest for Aerospace Security* (Annapolis, Md.: Naval Institute Press, 2015).

40. Maxwell D. Taylor, "Reflections on the American Military Establishment," in *Evolution of the American Military Establishment since World War II*, ed. Paul R. Schratz (Lexington, Va.: George C. Marshall Research Foundation, 1978), 7–22.

41. Oral History Interview with Andrew J. Goodpaster, 1 of 3, on 25 April 1967 by Ed Edwin, 35–42, DDEL; Oral History Interview with John S. D. Eisenhower, 2 of 2, on 10 March 1972 by Dr. Maclyn Burg, 3, 29–31, DDEL.

42. Dulles to Eisenhower, 23 July 1958, Eisenhower Papers as President (Ann C. Whitman File), Dulles-Herter Series, box 10, folder: Dulles, July 1958, DDEL.

43. Matthew B. Ridgway, *Soldier: The Memoirs of Matthew B. Ridgway* (New York: Harper, 1956), 274–275.

44. Wilson, *Maneuver and Firepower*, 264–268.

45. Oral History Interview with Matthew Ridgway by Maurice Matloff, part 2, on 18 April 1984, 1, Ridgway Papers, box 34: Oral Histories, AHEC.

46. Gavin, *War and Peace in the Space Age*, 155.

47. Andrew J. Bacevich, *The Pentomic Era: The U.S. Army between Korea and Vietnam* (Washington, D.C.: National Defense Univ. Press, 1986), 14–16.

48. Ridgway, *Soldier*, 264–273, quotation on page 271.

49. Andrew J. Bacevich, "The Paradox of Professionalism: Eisenhower, Ridgway, and the Challenge to Civilian Control, 1953–1955," *Journal of Military History* 61, no. 2 (1997), 303–333.

50. Ridgway, *Soldier*, 317–321, 323–332.

51. Taylor, "Reflections on the American Military Establishment," 14–15.

52. Ridgway, *Soldier*, 320.

53. Ridgway to Taylor, 17 May 1955, Ridgway Papers, Series 2, box 18, folder: Correspondence (Army Chief of Staff), T, AHEC.

54. Ridgway, *Soldier*, 74–75, 107–145.

55. Ingo Trauschweizer, *The Cold War U.S. Army: Building Deterrence for Limited War* (Lawrence: Univ. Press of Kansas, 2008), 48–80.

56. Taylor, *Swords and Plowshares*, 166.

57. Donald A. Carter, "Eisenhower Versus the Generals," *Journal of Military History* 71, no. 4 (2007): 1169–1199; Linn, *Echo of Battle*, 151–192.

58. Quoted in Andreas Wenger, "The Politics of Military Planning: Evolution of NATO's Strategy," 175, in *War Plans and Alliances in the Cold War: Threat Perceptions in East and West*, ed. Vojtech Mastny, Sven G. Holtsmark, and Andreas Wenger (London: Routledge, 2006), 165–192.

59. Address by General Maxwell Taylor to the National Strategy Seminar at the Army War College, Carlisle Barracks, Pennsylvania, 6 June 1956, "The Role of the Army in National Strategy," Taylor Papers, Digital Collection, NDU, https://digitalndulibrary.ndu.edu/cdm/compoundobject/collection/taylor/id/1223/rec/84 (accessed 23 December 2016).

60. Douglas Kinnard, "Civil-Military Relations: The President and the General," *Parameters* 15, no. 2 (1985): 19–29; Jay M. Parker, "The Colonels' Revolt: Eisenhower, the Army, and the Politics of National Security" (Newport, R.I.: Naval War College, 1994); John Taylor, *General Maxwell Taylor*, 207–212.

61. Quoted in John Taylor, *General Maxwell Taylor*, 209.

62. Palmer to Brigadier General Phillips, 19 July 1961, Williston Palmer Papers, box 5, folder: Taylor, Maxwell D, USMA.

63. Westmoreland interview by Lieutenant Colonel Martin L. Ganderson, 1982, 69–72, Westmoreland Papers, box 13, SCL.

64. Watson, *Into the Missile Age*, 76–84.

65. Taylor, *Uncertain Trumpet*, 38–39; Kenneth W. Condit, *History of the Joint Chiefs of Staff*, vol. 6, *The Joint Chiefs of Staff and National Policy, 1955–1956* (Washington, D.C.: Historical Office, Joint Staff, 1992), 25–32.

66. Taylor, *Uncertain Trumpet*, xiii–xiv.

67. Maxwell Taylor, "Missions of the U.S. Army," Armed Forces Staff College, November 1956, 12–13, Taylor Papers, Digital Collection, NDU, https://digitalndulibrary.ndu.edu/cdm/compoundobject/collection/taylor/id/1084/rec/70 (accessed 23 December 2016); Maxwell Taylor, "Security through Balanced Deterrence," Calvin Bullock Forum, 10 December 1956, Taylor Papers, Digital Collection, NDU, https://digitalndulibrary.ndu.edu/cdm/compoundobject/collection/taylor/id/1028/rec/67 (accessed 23 December 2016).

68. Jonathan M. Soffer, *General Matthew B. Ridgway: From Progressivism to Reaganism, 1895–1993* (Westport, Conn.: Praeger, 1998), 184–88.

69. Template of Taylor's letter, 28 November 1955, Goodpaster Papers, box 18, folder 12, GCML.

70. Brigadier General Twiggs to Delafield, 19 December 1955, Delafied Family Papers, box 18, folder 54, Department of Rare Books and Special Collections, PUL.

71. Arthur W. Radford interview, 1965, 4, John Foster Dulles Oral History Collection, PUL.

72. Goodpaster, memorandum of conference with the president, 26 May 1956, Nuclear History Collection, Digital National Security Archive (DNSA), http://nsarchive.chadwyck.com.proxy.library.ohiou.edu/nsa/documents/NH/00088/all.pdf (accessed 28 March 2015), quotations on 2 and 3.

73. Quoted in Taylor, *Uncertain Trumpet*, 51.

74. "Building the National Defense Program," 14 May 1956, Council on Foreign Relations Records, box 447, folder 3, Public Policy Papers, Department of Rare Books and Special Collections, PUL and audio recording, http://diglib.princeton.edu/audio/findingaids/MC104-56B.mp3 (accessed 22 March 2017).
75. Trauschweizer, *Cold War U.S. Army*, 58–70.
76. Linn, *Echo of Battle*, 167–181; Linn, *Elvis's Army*, 86–88.
77. Office of the Deputy Chief of Staff for Military Operations, Memorandum for Record, 15 May 1956, Briefing for Chief of Staff on Army Organization 1960–1970 (PENTANA), 3–4, AHEC Library.
78. Eddleman interviewed by Colonel L. G. Smith and Lieutenant Colonel M. G. Swindler, session 4, 15 April 1975, 28–29, Eddleman Papers, box 2, AHEC.
79. Westmoreland interview by Ganderson, 31.
80. Carter, *Forging the Shield*, 256–259.
81. Kalev I. Sepp, "The Pentomic Puzzle: The Influence of Personality and Nuclear Weapons on U.S. Army Organization, 1952–1958," *Army History* 51 (2001): 1–13; John J. McGrath, *The Brigade: A History* (Fort Leavenworth, Kans.: Combat Studies Institute Press, 2004), 59.
82. Bacevich, *Pentomic Era*, 103–106, 115–119.
83. Quoted in Hawkins, *United States Army Force Structure and Force Design Initiatives*, 35.
84. "Summary of Remarks by General Maxwell D. Taylor at Quantico Conference, 23 June 1956," Taylor Papers, Digital Collection, NDU, https://digitalndulibrary.ndu.edu/cdm/compoundobject/collection/taylor/id/1203/rec/82 (accessed 23 December 2016).
85. Quoted in Bacevich, *Pentomic Era*, 68.
86. Remarks by General Maxwell D. Taylor before the House Armed Services Committee, 29 January 1957, 3, Records of the U.S. Joint Chiefs of Staff, Chairman's File, Admiral Radford, 1953–1957, box 22, "111 (1958 Budget)," RG 218, NARA.
87. Headquarters, Continental Army Command, TOE 57T ROTAD, 10 August 1956, AHEC Library; Headquarters, Department of the Army, TOE 57D, 31 July 1958, AHEC Library.
88. John K. Mahon and Romana Danysh, *Infantry, Part I: Regular Army* (Washington, D.C.: Office of the Chief of Military History, US Army, 1972), 92; McGrath, *The Brigade*, 62.
89. Office of the Deputy Chief of Staff for Personnel, 15 August 1956, Combat Arms Regimental System: Outline Plan (Draft), Records of the Army Staff, Records of the Office of the Chief of Information, entry 45, box 1, folder: Combat Arms 1956, RG 319, NARA; John Taylor, *General Maxwell Taylor*, 198–199.
90. Taylor, *Swords and Plowshares*, 171.
91. Eisenhower to Wilson, 5 January 1955, Wilson Papers, box 24, folder: Eisenhower, Dwight David 1954–1955, AU.
92. R. P. Hunnicutt, *Patton: A History of the American Main Battle Tank* (Novato, Calif.: Presidio Press, 1984), 149–150; Wilson, *Maneuver and Firepower*, 286.
93. Headquarters, United States Army, Europe, Office of the Commander in Chief, 13 September 1961, Priorities Governing the Issue of New Equipment

to Troops in USAREUR, Norstad Papers, box 61, folder: Clarke, Bruce C. (4), DDEL.

94. Marc Trachtenberg, *A Constructed Peace: The Making of the European Settlement, 1945–1963* (Princeton, N.J.: Princeton Univ. Press, 1999), 191.

95. Taylor to Norstad, 21 April 1958, Norstad Papers, box 98, folder: Chief of Staff Army (2), DDEL.

96. General Bennett interviewed by Lieutenant Colonel Smith and Lieutenant Colonel Hatcher, vol. 1, tape 5, 21 April 1976, 10–12, Bennett Papers, Oral History, box 1, AHEC.

97. Brigadier General J. K. Wilson, Artillery Commander, to Assistant Commandant, The Artillery and Missile School, Fort Sill, 1 May 1958, Records of the United States Continental Army Command, U.S. Army Schools, Artillery and Guided Missile School, Fort Sill, box 9, folder: Organization and Planning Files: Reorganization of the Inf Div Arty, RG 546, NARA.

98. Memorandum for Record, 5 November 1958, General Palmer's Discussion with SACEUR, on the Subject Review of USAREUR's Strength, Norstad Papers, box 104, folder: Memorandum for Record 1957–1958–1959 (4), DDEL; Carter, *Forging the Shield*, 299–334.

99. Linn, *Elvis's Army*, 90–93.

100. Address by Lieutenant General Harold K. Johnson, Deputy Chief of Staff for Military Operations, to Canadian National Defense College, 10 January 1964, Modern Land Weaponry and Methods of Warfare, 4, Johnson Papers, box 56, folder: Speech Reference File-Personal (4 of 4), thru 1968, AHEC.

101. Anthony B. Herbert, *Soldier* (New York: Holt, Rinehart and Winston, 1973), 77–79.

102. Eddleman interviewed by Smith and Swindler, section 4, 29–30.

103. Ingo Trauschweizer, "Learning with an Ally: The U.S. Army and the *Bundeswehr* in the Cold War," *Journal of Military History* 72, no. 2 (2008): 477–508.

104. Wilson, *Maneuver and Firepower*, 296–310; McGrath, *The Brigade*, 61–65.

105. Trauschweizer, *Cold War U.S. Army*, 48–113.

106. Maxwell D. Taylor, "The World-Wide Role and Capability of the Army," *Army Combat Forces Journal* 6, no. 2 (1955): 24–26, quotations on 25.

107. Minutes of press conference held by General Taylor, 10 January 1956, 5.

108. Chairman's Staff Group to Radford, 11 October 1956, Statements by General Taylor, *DDO*, http://tinyurl.galegroup.com/tinyurl/3g62D0 (accessed 10 September 2016).

109. Address by General Maxwell D. Taylor before the National Press Club, 19 December 1957; Question and Answer Period Following General Taylor's Address before the National Press Club, transcript, both in Taylor Papers, box 7, folder: C/S Speeches, file no. 3, 1957, NDU, quotations on 4 and 5.

110. Address by General Maxwell D. Taylor at the Third Annual Meeting, Association of the United States Army, 28 October 1957, Taylor Papers, box 7, folder: C/S/ Speeches, file no. 3, 1957, NDU.

111. Statement by General Maxwell D. Taylor before the Subcommittee on

Department of Defense Appropriations of the Committee on Appropriations, U.S. Senate, 9 June 1958, Taylor Papers, box 7, folder: C/S Speeches, file no. 4, 1958, NDU.

112. J.C.S. 2285/2, memorandum by the Chief of Staff, U.S. Army, 18 June 1958, Strategic Mobility for U.S. Forces, Records of the Joint Chiefs of Staff, Central Decimal File 1958, CCS381 (11–22–57), section 2, RG 218, NARA.

113. Roger J. Spiller, *"Not War But Like War": The American Intervention in Lebanon,* Leavenworth Paper No. 3 (Fort Leavenworth, Kans.: US Army Command and General Staff College, 1981); Carter, *Forging the Shield,* 341–358; Linn, *Elvis's Army,* 213–214.

114. Stump to Wilson, 24 June 1957, Wilson Papers, box 25, folder: Federal government (2), AU.

115. John Foster Dulles, "Challenge and Response in United States Policy," *Foreign Affairs* 36, no. 1 (1957): 25–43.

116. Kaplan, *To Kill Nations,* 133–139.

117. John P. McConnell to White, 30 September 1957, "Report of the Board of Officers," Thomas D. White Papers, box 6, folder: General White: McConnell Report, LOC.

118. Nathan F. Twining, *Neither Liberty nor Safety: A Hard Look at U.S. Military Policy and Strategy* (New York: Holt, Rinehart and Winston, 1966), 102–120, quotation on 115.

119. SM-109-57, 8 February 1957, Appendix to Enclosure "A" to JCS 2073/1353, "Over-all Strategic Concept for the Defense of the NATO Area," Records of the Joint Chiefs of Staff, Geographic File 1957, CCS092 Western Europe (3-12-48) (2), section 73, RG 218, NARA.

120. Fairchild and Poole, *The History of the Joint Chiefs of Staff,* 7:11–29; Robert S. Jordan, *An Unsung Soldier: The Life of General Andrew J. Goodpaster* (Annapolis, Md.: Naval Institute Press, 2013), 85–86.

121. Taylor, "Building the National Defense Program."

122. Kai Bird, *The Chairman: John J. McCloy and the Making of the American Establishment* (New York: Simon and Schuster, 1992), 464, claims Kissinger "borrowed heavily" from Taylor's talk. See Niall Ferguson, *Kissinger,* vol. 1, *1923–1968: The Idealist* (New York, Penguin Press, 2015), 332–353, on Kissinger's role at the council.

123. Henry A. Kissinger, *Nuclear Weapons and Foreign Policy* (Garden City, N.Y.: Doubleday, 1957).

124. *The Mike Wallace Interview,* 13 July 1958, Harry Ransom Center, Univ. of Texas, http://www.hrc.utexas.edu/multimedia/video/2008/wallace/kissinger_henry.html (accessed 10 October 2016).

125. Goodpaster Papers, series 5, White House, box 18, folder 13, GCML.

126. Griffith, *Ike's Letters,* 199 (26 February 1958).

127. Gordon Gray, "Memorandum of Meeting with the President (Wednesday, August 24, 9 a.m.), August 25, 1960," Report of Panel of President's Science Advisory Committee on Weapons Technology for Limited Warfare, White House Office: Office of the Staff Secretary, 1952–1961, Subject Series: Alphabetical Subseries, box 23, folder: Science Advisory Committee (6), DDEL.

128. Bacevich, *Pentomic Era*, 20–21, 49–51.
129. Russell to Taylor, 28 October 1955, Russell Collection, Congressional, Legislative, box 136, folder 3, RRL; Linn, *Elvis's Army*, 132–190.
130. Taylor to Russell, 7 December 1955, Russell Collection, Congressional, Legislative, box 136, folder 3, RRL.
131. General Maxwell D. Taylor, "The Army's Era of Management," article for publication in *Armed Forces Management* (October 1956), Taylor Papers, Digital Collection, NDU, https://digitalndulibrary.ndu.edu/cdm/compoundobject/collection/taylor/id/1152/rec/74 (accessed 26 December 2016).
132. William H. Donnelly, "Bilko's Army: A Crisis in Command?" *Journal of Military History* 75, no. 4 (2011), 1183–1215; Linn, *Elvis's Army*, 68–71.
133. Carter, "Eisenhower versus the Generals," 1191.
134. Taylor to Williams, 15 September 1955, Williams Papers, box 11, folder 18, HIA.
135. Eisenhower to Wilson, 21 December 1955, Eisenhower Papers as President (Ann Whitman File), Administration Series, box 40, folder: Wilson, Chas. E. (Sec Def)—1955 (1), DDEL.
136. Department of Defense, Office of Public Information, Minutes of Press Conference Held by General Maxwell D. Taylor, Tuesday, 10 January 1956, The Pentagon, 3, Eisenhower Papers as President (Ann Whitman File), Administration Series, box 37, folder: Taylor, Gen. Maxwell D., DDEL.
137. Taylor to Williams, 15 September 1955, Williams Papers, box 11, folder 18, HIA.
138. Goodpaster, memorandum for record, 3 April 1956, Eisenhower Papers as President (Ann Whitman File), DDE Diary Series, box 15, folder: Apr. '56 Goodpaster, DDEL.
139. John Eisenhower, 20 August 1957, "Memorandum of Conference with the President on August 16, 1957," White House Office, Office of the Staff Secretary, Subject Series, Department of Defense Subseries box 1, folder: Department of Defense, Vol. II (1), DDEL.
140. Taylor to Norstad, 29 May 1958, Norstad Papers, box 81, folder: Taft thru Thierry (2), DDEL.
141. J. R. Killian Jr., July 15, 1959, "Notes of Matters Discussed with the President at Meeting on July 14, 1959," White House Office: Office of the Staff Secretary, 1952–1961, Subject Series: Alphabetical Subseries box 23, folder: Science Advisory Committee (6), DDEL.
142. "Statement by the President on the Proposed Transfer of the Army Ballistic Missiles Agency to the National Aeronautics and Space Administration," 21 October 1959, *American Presidency Project*, http://www.presidency.ucsb.edu/ws/?pid=11563 (accessed 26 December 2016).
143. Taylor to Wilber Brucker, 22 October 1959, quoted in John Taylor, *General Maxwell Taylor*, 224.
144. Gavin interview by Lieutenant Colonel Donald G. Andrews and Lieutenant Colonel Charles H. Ferguson, 1975, 41 and 44, Gavin Papers, box 1, AHEC.
145. Gavin, notes, 23 June 1981, Gavin Papers, box 27, folder: Gavin's Opinion of General Eisenhower, Correspondence, AHEC.
146. Entry for 29 October, Chronology in file: Other People's Statements on

Satellite and Missile Programs, Senate Papers of Lyndon Baines Johnson, box 356, LBJL.

147. Gavin to Taylor and Brucker, 23 December 1957 (with handwritten note: approved, Wilber Brucker, 8 January 1958), and Gavin to Lemnitzer, 16 June 1975, both in Gavin Papers, box 20, folder: Correspondence, 1957, 1975, AHEC.

148. Westmoreland to Bradley Biggs, 12 August 1975, Gavin Papers, box 27, folder: Westmoreland, AHEC; Westmoreland, notes for *A Soldier Reports*, 7, Westmoreland Papers, Personal Papers—Topical—Writings—*Soldier Reports* (1976)—Notes (ca. 1974), folder 3, SCL.

149. Gavin, *War and Peace in the Space Age*.

150. Gavin to James F. Hollingsworth, undated, Gavin Papers, box 20, folder: Correspondence on Nuclear Issues in 1950s, Newsletters on Nuclear Tests, Retirement, AHEC.

151. Transcript of press conference, General James M. Gavin, Boston, Massachusetts, 6 pm, 3 February 1966, Gavin Papers, box 19, folder: Vietnam: Transcript on Gavin's Press Conference, February, AHEC.

152. Security Resources Panel of the Science Advisory Committee, Deterrence and Survival in the Nuclear Age, 7 November 1957, White House Office Files, Office of the Special Assistant for National Security Affairs, NSC Series, Policy Papers Subseries, box 22, folder: NSC 5724 (2), DDEL.

153. Quoted in David L. Snead, *The Gaither Committee, Eisenhower, and the Cold War* (Columbus: Ohio State Univ. Press, 1999), 101.

154. Ibid., 157–181; Linda McFarland, *Cold War Strategist: Stuart Symington and the Search for National Security* (Westport, Conn.: Praeger, 2001), 77–101; Christopher A. Preble, *John F. Kennedy and the Missile Gap* (DeKalb: Northern Illinois Univ. Press, 2004), 52–101.

155. Snead, *Gaither Committee*.

156. Taylor, "Unified Command Post Concept for the Organization of the Department of Defense (Personal Views of the Chief of Staff, U.S. Army)," undated, Taylor Papers, box 7, folder: C/S Speeches, file no. 4, 1958, NDU; Taylor to Gruenther, 18 February 1958, Gruenther Papers, Red Cross Series, box 14, folder: Defense Reorganization Advisory Group (4), DDEL.

157. Statement by the president on the Defense Reorganization Bill, 28 May 1958, *American Presidency Project*, http://www.presidency.ucsb.edu/ws/?pid=11076 (accessed 26 December 2016).

158. Statement by General Maxwell D. Taylor to the Senate Armed Services Committee on Reorganization of the Department of Defense, 3 July 1958, Taylor Papers, box 7, folder: C/S Speeches, file no. 4, 1958, NDU.

159. Briefing by General Maxwell D. Taylor for new members of the 86th Congress, 29 January 1959, "The Army Today," 5, Taylor Papers, box 8, folder: C/S Speeches, file no. 5, 1959, NDU.

160. Statement by General Maxwell Taylor (ret.) before the Aeronautical and Space Sciences Committee and the Preparedness Investigation Subcommittee of the Senate Armed Services Committee, 4 February 1960, Taylor Papers, box 11, folder: General Taylor Testimony, 1960, NDU.

161. Chester J. Pach Jr. and Elmo Richardson, *The Presidency of Dwight D. Eisenhower*, rev. ed. (Lawrence: Univ. Press of Kansas, 1991), 213.

162. Taylor's statement, 4 February 1960.

163. Address of General Maxwell D. Taylor before the U.S. Army War College, Carlisle Barracks, Pennsylvania, 5 February 1960, "The Uncertain Trumpet," Taylor Papers, Digital Collection, NDU, https://digitalndulibrary.ndu.edu/cdm/compoundobject/collection/taylor/id/1734/rec/95 (accessed 23 December 2016), quotations on 5 and 8.

164. For example, in a speech at the New York City University Club on 12 March, his Armed Forces Day address in Houston on 19 May, a lecture at the Air War College the following day, a speech at the University of Missouri on 22 September, and one at the California Institute of Technology on 12 October, Taylor Papers, Digital Collection, NDU, https://digitalndulibrary.ndu.edu/cdm/search/collection/taylor (accessed 23 December 2016).

165. Statement of General Maxwell D. Taylor before the Subcommittee on National Policy Machinery, 14 June 1960, Central Intelligence Agency, Electronic Reading Room (CIA), https://www.cia.gov/library/readingroom/document/cia-rdp91-00965r000300100028-7 (accessed 14 February 2017).

166. This was also the argument and chapter title of the opening salvo of Taylor's *Uncertain Trumpet*, 1–10.

167. Maxwell Taylor, "Limited War," National War College, 18 November 1960, Taylor Papers, Digital Collection, NDU, https://digitalndulibrary.ndu.edu/cdm/compoundobject/collection/taylor/id/1867/rec/106 (accessed 23 December 2016).

168. Oral History Interview with Lyman L. Lemnitzer, 1 of 2, by David C. Berliner, 21 November 1972, 10, Columbia University Oral History Project, DDEL; Ricks, *The Generals*, 219.

169. Taylor, *Swords and Plowshares*, 169; Trachtenberg, *Constructed Peace*, 147–56.

170. Goodpaster, 10 March 1959, "Memorandum of Conference with the President March 6, 1959," White House Office, Office of the Staff Secretary. Subject Series, Department of Defense Subseries, box 1, folder: Department of Defense, Vol. III (5), DDEL.

171. Phone conversation, Herter and Taylor, 1 July 1959, Christian Herter Papers, box 12, folder: CAH Telephone Calls 5/4/59 to 12/31/59 (3), DDEL.

172. Eisenhower, Remarks at Fort Benning, Georgia, after Watching a Demonstration of New Army Equipment, 3 May 1960, *American Presidency Project*, http://www.presidency.ucsb.edu/ws/?pid=11769 (accessed 26 December 2016).

173. Taylor, *Uncertain Trumpet*, 121, 123.

174. Maxwell Taylor, "Our Great Military Fallacy," *Look*, 24 November 1959, 27–31; Maxwell Taylor, "Our Critical Military Need: One Defense Chief," *Look*, 22 December 1959, 111–121; Maxwell Taylor, "How We Can Survive," *Look*, 19 January 1960, 56–63.

175. Taylor, *Uncertain Trumpet*, 17.

176. Ibid., 47–79.

177. Ibid., 112–129.

178. Ibid., 175–177.

179. Morris Janowitz, *The Professional Soldier: A Social and Political Portrait* (New York: Free Press, 1960), 359.

180. Question and Answer Period, National Press Club Address, 19 December 1957, 1, Taylor Papers, box 7, folder: C/S Speeches, file no. 3, 1957, NDU.
181. Oral History Interview with General Lucius D. Clay, 2 of 2, by Ed Edwin, 16 March 1967 98, DDEL. It is unclear how Clay rationalized Gavin's service as ambassador to France.
182. Oral History Interview with Arleigh A. Burke, 4 of 4, by John T. Mason Jr., 12 January 1973, 233, DDEL.
183. Oral History Interview with Nathan F. Twining, 4 of 4, by John T. Mason Jr., 12 September 1967, 209, 249–250, DDEL.
184. Taylor, *Uncertain Trumpet*, 71.
185. The President's News Conference, 13 January 1960, *American Presidency Project*, http://www.presidency.ucsb.edu/ws/?pid=12131 (accessed 5 May 2015).
186. Gray, memorandum of meeting with the president, 17 February 1960, Nuclear History Collection, DNSA, http://nsarchive.chadwyck.com.proxy.library.ohiou.edu/nsa/documents/NH/00225/all.pdf (accessed 28 March 2015).
187. David Alan Rosenberg, "The Origins of Overkill: Nuclear Weapons and American Strategy, 1945–1960," *International Security* 7, no. 4 (1983): 3–71.

4. Camelot's Strategist

1. Maxwell Taylor, "Security Will Not Wait," *Foreign Affairs* 39, no. 2 (1961): 174–184; Armstrong to Phil [Quigg], 15 October 1960, Armstrong Papers, box 61, folder 28, Public Policy Papers, PUL.
2. Kennedy to Taylor, 4 May 1961, Taylor Papers, box 46, folder C, NDU; Kenneth O'Donnell to McNamara, 27 June 1961, Papers of President Kennedy, National Security Files, Meetings and Memoranda, box 327: Staff Memoranda, Taylor, Maxwell, 1961: January–August, JFKL.
3. Taylor to Kennedy, 26 June 1961, Taylor Papers, box 17, folder B, NDU.
4. McMaster, *Dereliction of Duty*, 13–17.
5. Jordan, *An Unsung Soldier*, 55–114.
6. Jablonsky, *War by Air, Land, and Sea*, 171–181.
7. David Halberstam, *The Best and the Brightest* (New York: Random House, 1972).
8. Bundy, memorandum for the president, 16 May 1961, White House Organization, Papers of President Kennedy, National Security Files, box 405, folder: Memos to the President, 5/6/61–5/28/61, JFKL.
9. President Kennedy's Appointment Books, Jan. 1, 1961–Dec. 31, 1961, and Jan. 1, 1962–Dec. 31, 1962, JFKL.
10. Andrew Preston, *The War Council: McGeorge Bundy, the NSC, and Vietnam* (Cambridge, Mass.: Harvard Univ. Press, 2006).
11. McMaster, *Dereliction of Duty*, 8–23; Earle Wheeler interview by Chester Clifton, 1964, 23–26; Taylor interview by Elspeth Rostow, 26 April 1964, 11–13, John F. Kennedy Oral History Collection, JFKL.
12. Willy Brandt, *People and Politics: The Years 1960–1975*, trans. J. Maxwell Brownjohn (Boston: Little, Brown, 1976), 19; "USA/Taylor: Durchbruch nach Berlin," *Der Spiegel*, 16 August 1961.

13. Andrew J. Goodpaster, "The Role of the Joint Chiefs of Staff in the National Security Structure," in Jordan, *Issues of National Security*, 220–247, quotation and Taylor's interpretation on 234–235.

14. Philip Nash, "Bear *Any* Burden? John F. Kennedy and Nuclear Weapons," in *Cold War Statesmen Confront the Bomb: Nuclear Diplomacy since 1945*, ed. John Lewis Gaddis et al. (Oxford, UK: Oxford Univ. Press, 1999), 120–40; Lawrence S. Kaplan et al., *History of the Office of the Secretary of Defense*, vol. 5, *The McNamara Ascendancy, 1961–1965* (Washington, D.C.: Historical Office, Office of the Secretary of Defense, 2006), 293–322.

15. Taylor, *Uncertain Trumpet*, 146.

16. Taylor interview by Rostow, 12 April 1964, 4, JFKL.

17. Kaplan, *To Kill Nations*, 174.

18. Taylor interview by Rostow, 12 April 1964, 1–2.

19. McNamara to Kennedy, 20 February 1961, Tab II, 10–11, Records of Robert S. McNamara, Defense Programs and Operations, "Report to the President, FY 1962 Budget," box 10, RG 200, NARA.

20. Ibid., Annex A, Attachment 2: Limited War Proposals.

21. Taylor, "American Commitments and Military Capabilities," 18 January 1960 talk at Council on Foreign Relations, Records of the Council on Foreign Relations, box 453, folder 1, Public Policy Papers, PUL.

22. Kaplan, *McNamara Ascendancy*, 72–95.

23. Maxwell D. Taylor, *Responsibility and Response* (New York: Harper and Row, 1967), 6.

24. Ibid., 12.

25. Ibid., 12–15, quotation on 15.

26. Taylor, remarks at the Printing Week Dinner, New York, 15 January 1962, Norstad Papers, box 81, "Taft thru Thierry (2)," DDEL.

27. Taylor to Rostow, 14 May 1962, Papers of President Kennedy, National Security Files, Subject Series, box 294, folder: Basic National Security Policy 6/22/62 and undated [1 of 2], JFKL.

28. Taylor to Bundy and Julian Ewell, 25 March 1962; Taylor to Kennedy, 3 April 1962; Rusk to Kennedy, 13 April 1962, all in Papers of President Kennedy, National Security Files, Trips and Conferences, box 251A, folder: Maxwell D. Taylor's Trip, Europe, 3/62, JFKL.

29. Kennedy to Taylor, 22 April 1961, Papers of President Kennedy, National Security Files, Meetings and Memoranda, box 327: Staff Memoranda, Taylor, Maxwell, 1961: January–August, JFKL.

30. U.S. Senate, Hearing Held before the Select Committee to Study Governmental Operations with Respect to Intelligence Activities, 9 July 1975, Evening Session, 5, https://www.maryferrell.org/showDoc.html?docId=1368#relPageId=1&tab=page (accessed 18 April 2017).

31. Appointment Books of President Kennedy, 21 January–31 December 1961, JFKL.

32. Taylor interview by Rostow, 12 April 1964, 9, 14–15.

33. Taylor, *Swords and Plowshares*, 184–194.

34. Seymour M. Hersh, *The Dark Side of Camelot* (New York: Little, Brown, 1997), 273–277.

35. Luis Aguilar, ed., *Operation Zapata: The "Ultrasensitive" Report and Testimony of the Board of Inquiry on the Bay of Pigs* (Frederick, Md.: University Publications of America, 1981), 344, 350–351.

36. Walter S. Poole, *The Joint Chiefs of Staff and National Policy*, vol. 8, *1961–1964* (Washington, D.C.: Office of Joint History, Office of the Chairman of the Joint Chiefs of Staff, 2011), 107–120.

37. Jack B. Pfeiffer to John H. Wright, Chief, Information and Privacy Division, OIS, 6 December 1984, Attachment 3: "The Taylor Committee Investigation of the Bay of Pigs," 9 November 1984, 6–8, National Security Archive, http://nsarchive.gwu.edu/NSAEBB/NSAEBB355/bop-v014.pdf (accessed 31 January 2018).

38. Aguilar, *Operation Zapata*, 44–53.

39. Program review by Lansdale, 18 January 1962, in Department of State, *Foreign Relations of the United States, 1961–1963*, vol. 10, *Cuba, January 1961–September 1962* (Washington, D.C.: Government Printing Office, 1997), 710–718; Lansdale to Special Group (Augmented), 25 July 1962, National Security Archive, http://nsarchive2.gwu.edu/nsa/cuba_mis_cri/620725%20Review%20°f%200p.%20Mongoose.pdf (accessed 31 January 2018).

40. Poole, *JCS 1961–1964*, 159–161; US Senate, *Select Committee to Study Governmental Operations, Alleged Assassination Plots Involving Foreign Leaders: An Interim Report*, November 20, 1975 (Washington, D.C.: Government Printing Office, 1975), 154–156.

41. Taylor interview by Rostow, 12 April 1964, 16.

42. Ibid., 17.

43. Jeffrey H. Michaels, "Managing Counterinsurgency: The Special Group (CI), 1962–1966," *Journal of Strategic Studies* 35, no. 1 (2012): 33–61.

44. Taylor to Bundy, 11 June 1962, PQV, http://congressional.proquest.com/histvault?q=002948-007-0035 (accessed 8 January 2017).

45. Bundy, draft of National Security Action Memorandum 131, 13 March 1962, PQV, http://congressional.proquest.com/histvault?q=100469-001-0216 (accessed 8 January 2017).

46. Thomas A. Parrott, memorandum for the President, 22 March 1962, Taylor Papers, box 45, folder D, NDU.

47. Taylor to Kennedy, 2 June 1962, Progress in the Counterinsurgency Program, Papers of President Kennedy, National Security Files, Meetings and Memoranda, box 319, folder: Special Group (CI), General, 6 April 1961–7 June 1962, JFKL; Taylor to Kennedy, 4 June 1962, Progress in the Counterinsurgency Program, Taylor Papers, box 45, folder D, NDU.

48. National Security Action Memorandum 182, 24 August 1962, Counterinsurgency Doctrine, Records of the National Security Council, National Security Action Memorandum, box 2, RG 273, NARA.

49. General Maxwell Taylor, "A National Program to Combat Subversive Insurgency," 18 May 1962, Taylor Papers, box 20, folder A, NDU, quotation on page 6; Maxwell Taylor, "Our Evolving Strategy of National Security," 11 June 1962 address at University of Pittsburgh, Attorney General Papers of Robert F. Kennedy, box 75, folder: Taylor, Leslie-Taylor, William, JFKL.

50. Taylor, "National Program to Combat Subversive Insurgency," 6–9, quotation on 6 and 7.

51. Ibid., 10–23, quotation on 17.

52. Ibid., 23–25, quotations on 24.

53. Kennedy, Remarks at West Point to the Graduating Class of the U.S. Military Academy, 6 June 1962, *American Presidency Project*, http://www.presidency.ucsb.edu/ws/?pid=8695 (accessed 19 February 2017); Taylor, speech notes, 18 June 1962, "Development of the National Program to Combat Subversive Insurgencies," Taylor Papers, box 20, folder A, NDU.

54. Taylor, address at University of Pittsburgh, 10–12.

55. Hope M. Harrison, *Driving the Soviets up the Wall: Soviet-East German Relations, 1953–1961* (Princeton, N.J.: Princeton Univ. Press, 2003).

56. Michael Beschloss, *The Crisis Years: Kennedy and Khrushchev, 1960–1963* (New York: HarperCollins, 1991), 224–227; Frederick Kempe, *Berlin 1961: Kennedy, Khrushchev, and the Most Dangerous Place on Earth* (New York: Putnam, 2011), 210–268.

57. John F. Kennedy, Radio and Television Report to the American People on Berlin, 25 July 1961, JFKL, https://www.jfklibrary.org/Research/Research-Aids/JFK-Speeches/Berlin-Crisis_19610725.aspx (accessed 29 April 2017); Kempe, *Berlin 1961*, 307–318.

58. Ingo Trauschweizer, "Tanks at Checkpoint Charlie: Lucius Clay and the Berlin Crisis, 1961–1962," *Cold War History* 6, no. 2 (2006): 205–228; W. R. Smyser, *Kennedy and the Berlin Wall: "A Hell of a Lot Better than a War"* (Lanham, Md.: Rowman and Littlefield, 2009).

59. Taylor to Rusk, 31 July 1961, PQV, http://congressional.proquest.com/histvault?q=002869-005-0601 (accessed 15 January 2017).

60. Taylor to Kennedy, 21 July 1961, Berlin Airlift, Papers of President Kennedy, National Security Files, box 81A, folder: Germany—Berlin, General, 7/19/61–7/22/61, JFKL.

61. Taylor, 27 July 1961, "Considerations for the Desirability of a New Berlin Airlift," Appendix to Taylor to Kennedy, 28 July 1961, PQV, http://congressional.proquest.com/histvault?q=002869-005-0557 (accessed 3 February 2017).

62. Bundy to Taylor, 31 August 1961, Papers of President Kennedy, National Security Files, box 82A, folder: Germany—Berlin, General, 8/29/61–8/31/61, JFKL; Taylor to Kennedy, 1 September 1961, Suggested Language of Rules for Engagement in the Berlin Corridor, Papers of President Kennedy, National Security Files, box 82A, folder: Germany—Berlin, General, 9/1/61–9/5/61, JFKL; Seth A. Givens, "Cold War Capital: The United States, the European Allies, and the Fight for Berlin, 1945–94" (Ph.D. diss., Ohio University, 2018).

63. Lemnitzer to Norstad, 31 August 1961; Taylor to Kennedy, 1 September 1961, both in Records of Robert S. McNamara, Defense Programs and Operations, box 82, folder: Air Access (to Berlin 1961), RG 200, NARA.

64. Taylor interview by Rostow, 26 April 1964, 16.

65. Ibid., 16.

66. Taylor to Kennedy, 18 August 1961, Further Information on Troop Movement to Berlin, Papers of President Kennedy, National Security Files, box 82, folder: Germany—Berlin, General, 8/18/61–8/20/61, JFKL; Carter, *Forging the Shield*, 417–420.

67. Legere to Taylor, 28 August 1961, Papers of President Kennedy, National

Security Files, Henry Kissinger Series, box 463, folder: 32 Secret Sealed Package, JFKL.

68. Trauschweizer, "Tanks at Checkpoint Charlie."

69. Kennedy to Norstad, 20 October 1961, Norstad Papers, Policy Files Series, box 86, folder: Berlin-LIVE OAK 1961, 1 Sep–31 Dec (2), DDEL; National Security Action Memorandum 109, 23 October 1961, Records of the National Security Council, National Security Action Memorandum (NSAM), RG 273, NARA.

70. Minutes of National Security Council Meeting, 19 July 1961, in Department of State, *Foreign Relations of the United States, 1961–1963*, vol. 14, *Berlin Crisis, 1961–1962* (Washington, D.C.: Government Printing Office, 1993), 219–22; Sean Maloney, "Berlin Contingency Planning: Prelude to Flexible Response," *Journal of Strategic Studies* 25, no. 1 (2002): 99–134.

71. Gregory Pedlow, "Flexible Response Before MC 14/3: General Lauris Norstad and the Second Berlin Crisis," *Storia delle Relazione Internazionali* 13, no. 1 (1998): 235–268.

72. Norstad to JCS, 21 September 1961, Norstad Papers, Subject Series, box 103, "Joint Chiefs of Staff 1957 thru Oct 1961, Vol. I (3)," DDEL.

73. Draft, HWF, 6 October 1961, General Norstad's Discussions with the JCS on Monday, 2 October, Norstad Papers, Subject Series, box 105, folder: Memorandum for Record II 1960–1961 (2), DDEL.

74. Taylor to Kennedy, 3 October 1961, General Norstad's Proposal for U.S. Reinforcements to NATO, Papers of President Kennedy, President's Office Files, Subjects, box 103, folder: NATO-Norstad Meetings, JFKL.

75. Taylor to Kennedy, 22 November 1961, Support of Conventional Forces in the 1963 Budget, National Security Files, Departments and Agencies, box 175, folder: Defense Budget FY63 11/61–12/61, JFKL.

76. "Notes on the 481st National Security Council Meeting, May 1, 1961," in Department of State, *Foreign Relations of the United States, 1961–1963*, vol. 24, *Laos Crisis* (Washington, D.C.: Government Publishing Office, 1994), 162–164.

77. Rostow to Kennedy, Next Steps in Viet-Nam, 21 June 1961, DNSA, http://nsarchive.chadwyck.com.proxy.library.ohiou.edu/nsa/documents/VI/00831/all.pdf (accessed 28 March 2015).

78. Taylor to Kennedy, "Reply to Diem's Request for a 100,000 Man Increase in the Army of Viet-nam," 29 June 1961, DNSA, http://nsarchive.chadwyck.com.proxy.library.ohiou.edu/nsa/documents/VI/00833/all.pdf (accessed 28 March 2015).

79. Bromley Smith, memorandum of conversation with General Clifton, 3 July 1961, DNSA, http://nsarchive.chadwyck.com.proxy.library.ohiou.edu/nsa/documents/VI/00836/all.pdf (accessed 28 March 2015).

80. Edward Miller, *Misalliance: Ngo Dinh Diem, the United States, and the Fate of South Vietnam* (Cambridge, Mass.: Harvard Univ. Press, 2013), 214–227.

81. Taylor, memorandum for the president, 26 July 1961, Southeast Asian Planning, Attorney General Papers of Robert F. Kennedy, box 205, folder: Vietnam, Section 1: 4/27/61–11/15/61 (folder 1 of 2), JFKL.

82. Kennedy to Taylor, 7 August 1961, PQV, http://congressional.proquest.com/histvault?q=002246-001-0109 (accessed 8 January 2017).

83. Taylor and Rostow to Kennedy, 27 July 1961, Issues for Decision—South-

east Asia Meeting, Friday, July 28, Papers of President Kennedy, National Security Files, box 405, folder: Memos to the President, 7/61, JFKL.

84. David Milne, *America's Rasputin: Walt Rostow and the Vietnam War* (New York: Hill and Wang, 2008), 31–34, 89–95.

85. Edmund F. Wehrle Jr., "'A Good Bad Deal': John F. Kennedy, W. Averell Harriman, and the Neutralization of Laos, 1961–1962," *Pacific Historical Review* 67, no. 3 (1998): 349–377; William J. Rust, *So Much to Lose: John F. Kennedy and American Policy in Laos* (Lexington: Univ. Press of Kentucky, 2014).

86. Draft instructions from the president to General Taylor, 12 October 1961, Papers of President Kennedy, National Security Files, box 251A, folder: Taylor Trip (A), Vietnam, 10/12/61–10/19/61, JFKL.

87. "Paper Prepared by the Taylor Mission," October 18, 1961, in Department of State, *Foreign Relations of the United States, 1961–1963*, vol. 1, *Vietnam, 1961* (Washington, D.C.: Government Printing Office, 1988), 388–390.

88. Rostow to Taylor, 16 October 1961, in Department of State, *Foreign Relations of the United States, 1961–1963*, 1:381–382.

89. *The Pentagon Papers*, part 4, B. 1, 111–114, NARA, https://www.archives.gov/research/pentagon-papers (accessed 23 April 2017); J. P. Harris, *Vietnam's High Ground: Armed Struggle for the Central Highlands, 1954–1965* (Lawrence: Univ. Press of Kansas, 2016).

90. Felt to Rostow, 2 November 1961, in Department of State, *Foreign Relations of the United States, 1961–1963*, 1:465–466.

91. McConaughy to Nolting, 20 October 1961, in Department of State, *Foreign Relations of the United States, 1961–1963*, 1:407–411.

92. Nolting to Rusk, 18 October 1961, Papers of President Kennedy, National Security Files, box 251A, folder: Taylor Trip (A), Vietnam, 10/12/61–10/19/61, JFKL.

93. Taylor, memorandum for the record, 19 October 1961, "Meeting Held at Field Command Headquarters, ARVN," in Department of State, *Foreign Relations of the United States, 1961–1963*, 1:395–398.

94. Nolting to Rusk, 20 October 1961, in Department of State, *Foreign Relations of the United States, 1961–1963*, 1:399–400.

95. Nolting to Rusk (from Taylor for Under Secretary Johnson, McNamara, Bundy, Lemnitzer, Dulles), 25 October 1961; Nolting to Rusk (Eyes Only from Taylor for the President, Rusk and Johnson, McNamara, Lemnitzer), 25 October 1961, both in Papers of President Kennedy, National Security Files, box 251A, folder: Taylor Trip (B), Vietnam, 10/20/61–10/25/61, JFKL.

96. Young to Rusk (from Taylor for Johnson, Bundy, and Ewell), 27 October 1961, Papers of President Kennedy, National Security Files, box 251A, folder: Taylor Trip (C), Vietnam, 10/26/61–10/31/61, JFKL.

97. Bundy to Taylor, 28 October 1961, in Department of State, *Foreign Relations of the United States, 1961–1963*, 1:443.

98. Lansdale to Taylor, 21 and 23 October 1961, in Department of State, *Foreign Relations of the United States, 1961–1963*, 1:411–416, 418–423.

99. Nolting to Rusk, 28 October 1961; Lemnitzer to McNamara, 31 October 1961, both in Department of State, *Foreign Relations of the United States, 1961–1963*, 1:444–446, 463–464.

100. McGarr to Felt, 23 October 1961; Nolting to Rusk, 25 October 1961; McGarr to Lemnitzer, 2 November 1961, all in Department of State, *Foreign Relations of the United States, 1961–63*, 1:424–427, 431–433, 470–474; McNamara, *In Retrospect*, 47; Graham A. Cosmas, *MACV: The Joint Command in the Years of Escalation, 1962–1967* (Washington, D.C.: US Army Center of Military History, 2006), 21–29.

101. Nolting to Rusk (Eyes Only for the President from General Taylor), 1 November 1961, Papers of President Kennedy, National Security Files, box 251A, folder: Taylor Trip (D), Vietnam, 11/1/61–11/13/61, JFKL.

102. Wood to U. Alexis Johnson, 25 October 1961, in Department of State, *Foreign Relations of the United States, 1961–1963*, 1:436–440.

103. Harriman to Kennedy, 12 November 1961, in Department of State, *Foreign Relations of the United States, 1961–1963*, 1:580–582.

104. Paper prepared by Galbraith, 3 November 1961, in Department of State, *Foreign Relations of the United States, 1961–1963*, 1:474–476.

105. Mansfield to Kennedy, 2 November 1961, in Department of State, *Foreign Relations of the United States, 1961–1963*, 1:467–470.

106. Yuen Foong Khong, *Analogies at War: Korea, Munich, Dien Bien Phu, and the Vietnam Decisions of 1965* (Princeton, N.J.: Princeton Univ. Press, 1992), 83–85.

107. WHB, memorandum for the record, 6 November 1961, "Meeting to Discuss the Recommendations of the Taylor Mission to South Viet-Nam," in Department of State, *Foreign Relations of the United States, 1961–1963*, 1:532–534.

108. McNamara to Kennedy, 5 November 1961, in Department of State, *Foreign Relations of the United States, 1961–1963*, 1:538–540.

109. George W. Ball, *The Past Has Another Pattern: Memoirs* (New York: Norton, 1982), 366–367.

110. WHB, memorandum for the record, 6 November 1961.

111. "Notes of a Meeting," The White House, 11 November 1961, in Department of State, *Foreign Relations of the United States, 1961–1963*, 1:577–578.

112. Bundy to Rusk, National Security Action Memorandum 111, 22 November 1961, Records of the National Security Council, National Security Action Memorandum, box 1, RG 273, NARA.

113. Bundy, memorandum for the president, 15 November 1961, Papers of President Kennedy, National Security Files, box 405, folder: Memos to the President, 11/161–11/20/61, JFKL; "Notes on the National Security Council Meeting," 15 November 1961, in Department of State, *Foreign Relations of the United States, 1961–1963*, 1:607–610.

114. Taylor to Lemnitzer, 27 February 1962, Taylor Papers, box 17, folder H, NDU.

115. Robert H. Johnson to Rostow, 16 November 1961; Neilson to Murrow, 17 November 1961, both in Department of State, *Foreign Relations of the United States, 1961–1963*, 1:639–642.

116. Rusk to Kennedy, 24 November 1961, "Defoliant Operations in Viet-Nam," Rusk Papers, series 4, box 9, folder 4, RRL.

117. William A. Buckingham Jr., *Operation Ranch Hand: The Air Force and Herbicides in Southeast Asia, 1961–1971* (Washington, D.C.: Office of Air Force History, 1982).

118. *Hearing before the Committee on Armed Services, United States Senate on General Maxwell Taylor for Appointment as Chairman of the Joint Chiefs of Staff, August 9, 1962* (Washington, D.C.: Government Printing Office, 1962), 3.
119. Ibid., 7–9.
120. Taylor interview by Rostow, 21 June 1964, 1.
121. Clifton to Robert F. Kennedy, 14 September 1962, Papers of Attorney General Robert Kennedy, box 75, folder: Taylor, Leslie-Taylor, William, JFKL.
122. Poole, *JCS 1961–1964*, 165.
123. Taylor interview by Rostow, 12 April 1964, 17.
124. Ernest R. May and Philip D. Zelikow, eds., *The Kennedy Tapes: Inside the White House during the Cuban Missile Crisis*, vol. 3 (Cambridge, Mass.: Harvard Univ. Press, 1997), 58–63, 194–195, 206–211.
125. McMaster, *Dereliction of Duty*, 24–31.
126. Taylor interview by Rostow, 21 June 1964, 4–5.
127. Kaplan, *To Kill Nations*, 179.
128. McMaster, *Dereliction of Duty*, 27–31; Poole, *JCS 1961–1964*, 184–185.
129. Taylor interview by Rostow, 21 June 1964, 7–8.
130. Ibid., 5–6.
131. Thomas Blanton, William Burr, and Svetlana Savranskaya, eds., *The Underwater Cuban Missile Crisis: Soviet Submarines and the Risk of Nuclear War*, National Security Archive Electronic Briefing Book No. 399, http://nsarchive2.gwu.edu/NSAEBB/NSAEBB399/ (accessed 11 October 2017).
132. Alexander Fursenko and Timothy Naftali, *"One Hell of a Gamble": The Secret History of the Cuban Missile Crisis, 1958–1964* (New York: Norton, 1997).
133. Taylor to Kennedy, 16 November 1962, PQV, http://congressional.proquest.com/histvault?q=002243-012-0001 (accessed 20 January 2017).
134. Taylor interview by Rostow, 21 June 1964, 9.
135. William H. Sullivan, *Obbligato 1939–1979: Notes on a Foreign Service Career* (New York: Norton, 1984), 179.
136. Ibid.,178–181.
137. McMaster, *Dereliction of Duty*, 155–158.
138. Neil Sheehan, *A Bright Shining Lie: John Paul Vann and America in Vietnam* (New York: Random House, 1988), 203–265, 340–343; David M. Toczek, *The Battle of Ap Bac: They Did Everything but Learn from It* (Westport, Conn.: Greenwood, 2001); Mark Moyar, *Triumph Forsaken: The Vietnam War, 1954–1965* (Cambridge, UK: Cambridge Univ. Press, 2006), 187–188.
139. Jane E. Stromseth, *The Origins of Flexible Response: NATO's Debate over Strategy in the 1960s* (New York: St. Martin's Press, 1988); Trauschweizer, *Cold War U.S. Army*, 120–146.
140. Taylor to McNamara, 12 November 1963, McNamara Records, Defense Programs and Organizations, box 31, RG 200, NARA.
141. Taylor interview by Rostow, 21 June 1964, 13.
142. Poole, *JCS 1961–1964*, 12–15, quotations on 13.
143. Ibid., 70–74.
144. Ibid., 56–60.
145. Ibid., 75–77.
146. Kaplan, *McNamara Ascendancy*, 5–6; Preston, *War Council*.

147. Mark Perry, *Four Stars: The Inside Story of the Forty-Year Battle between the Joint Chiefs of Staff and America's Civilian Leaders* (Boston: Houghton Mifflin, 1989), 111–131; McMaster, *Dereliction of Duty*, 22–23.

148. Office of the White House Press Secretary, 1 October 1962, Remarks at Swearing-In Ceremony of General Maxwell Taylor as Chairman of the Joint Chiefs of Staff, PQV, http://congressional.proquest.com/histvault?q=002245-009-0909 (accessed 8 January 2017).

149. McMaster, *Dereliction of Duty*, 54–55.

150. C. Richard Nelson, *The Life and Work of General Andrew J. Goodpaster: Best Practices in National Security Affairs* (Lanham, Md.: Rowman and Littlefield, 2016).

151. Poole, *JCS 1961–1964*, 99–106, quotation on 104.

152. Taylor interview by Rostow, 21 June 1964, 9–11.

153. McCone, "Memorandum for the Record, February 29, 1964, Discussion at the NSC Meeting," in Department of State, *Foreign Relations of the United States, 1964–1968*, vol. 10, *National Security Policy* (Washington, D.C.: US Government Printing Office, 2001), 45–46; Thomas P. McIninch, "The Oxcart Story," Central Intelligence Agency, Studies Archives Indexes, 15, no. 1 (1996), https://www.cia.gov/library/center-for-the-study-of-intelligence/kent-csi/vol15no1/html/v15i1a01p_0001.htm (accessed 7 July 2018).

154. Quoted in Raymond, *Power at the Pentagon*, 329–331.

155. Preston, *War Council*, 122–125.

156. Hilsman, Review of *The Certain Trumpet* by Douglas Kinnard, *Parameters* 22, no. 3 (1992): 115–116.

157. James G. Blight, Janet M. Lang, and David A. Welch, *Virtual JFK: Vietnam if Kennedy Had Lived* (Lanham, Md.: Rowman Littlefield, 2009).

158. Taylor interview by Karnow, part 1 of 4.

159. Ibid., part 3 of 4.

160. National Security Action Memorandum 288, 17 March 1964, in Department of State, *Foreign Relations of the United States, 1964–1968*, vol. 1, *Vietnam, 1964* (Washington, D.C.: Government Printing Office, 1992), 172–173.

161. Mark Clodfelter, *The Limits of Air Power: The American Bombing of North Vietnam* (New York: Free Press, 1989), 44–47, quotations on 47.

162. Colby and McCone, "Memorandum for the Record, 21 February 1964, Presidential Meeting on Vietnam, 20 February 1964," Papers of President Johnson, John McCone Memoranda, box 1, folder: Meetings with the President, 6 January 1964—2 April 1964, LBJL.

163. McCone, "Memorandum for the Record, 13 March 1964, Meeting with the President, attended by Secretaries Rusk and McNamara, Mr. Bundy, and Mr. McCone—To discuss South Vietnam Report," Papers of President Johnson, John McCone Memoranda, box 1, folder: Meetings with the President, 6 January 1964—2 April 1964, LBJL.

164. McCone, "Memorandum for the Record, 16 May 1964, National Security Council meeting—16 May 1964"; McCone, "Memorandum for the Record, 16 May 1964, NSC Meeting on Friday, 15 May at Noon," both in Papers of President Johnson, John McCone Memoranda, box 1, folder: Meetings with the President, 3 April 1964—20 May 1964, LBJL.

165. McCone, "Memorandum for the Record, 26 June 1964, Discussion on Southeast Asia—6:00 p.m.—25 June 1964," Papers of President Johnson, John McCone Memoranda, box 1, folder: Meetings with the President, 4 January 1964—28 April 1965, LBJL.

166. McMaster, *Dereliction of Duty;* Nicholas J. Schlosser, ed., *The Greene Papers: General Wallace M. Greene Jr. and the Escalation of the Vietnam War* (Quantico, Va.: History Division, US Marine Corps, 2015), 1–17

5. Architect of the Vietnam War

1. Taylor interview by Rostow, 12 April 1964, 3.
2. Taylor, *Swords and Plowshares,* 226–228.
3. Kinnard, *Certain Trumpet,* 134–162.
4. Johnson to Taylor, 2 July 1964, in Department of State, *Foreign Relations of the United States, 1964–1968,* 1:538; Kinnard, *Certain Trumpet,* 135.
5. Robert R. Tomes, *Apocalypse Then: American Intellectuals and the Vietnam War, 1954–1975* (New York: New York Univ. Press, 1998), 103–111.
6. U. Alexis Johnson interviewed by Richard Rusk, March 1985, part 2, 10, Dean Rusk Oral History Collection, RRL.
7. William H. Sullivan interviewed by Paige E. Mulhollan, Interview 1, 21 July 1972, 16–17, PQV, http://congressional.proquest.com/histvault?q=002276-016-0691 (accessed 11 January 2017); Fredrik Logevall, *Choosing War: The Lost Chance for Peace and the Escalation of War in Vietnam* (Berkeley: Univ. of California Press, 1999), 164–165.
8. McCone, "Memorandum for the Record, 26 June 1964, Discussion on Southeast Asia—6:00 p.m.—25 June 1964," Papers of President Johnson, John McCone Memoranda, box 1, folder: Meetings with the President, 4 January 1964—28 April 1965, LBJL.
9. Rostow to Taylor, 23 September 1964, Papers of Walt W. Rostow, box 13, folder: Southeast Asia, LBJL.
10. Sullivan interview by Mulhollan, 19.
11. Taylor interview by Rostow, 26 April 1964, 18.
12. Taylor and James Killen to AID, 8 October 1964, Charles T. R. Bohannan Papers, box 34, folder 8, HIA.
13. Lien Hang T. Nguyen, *Hanoi's War: An Interntional History of the War for Peace in Vietnam* (Chapel Hill: Univ. of North Carolina Press, 2012); Pierre Asselin, *Hanoi's Road to the Vietnam War, 1954–1965* (Berkeley: Univ. of California Press, 2013).
14. Remarks of the President and General Maxwell Taylor at Swearing-In Ceremony of General Taylor as Ambassador to Viet Nam, 2 July 1964, PQV, http://congressional.proquest.com/histvault?q=002795-019-0574 (accessed 8 January 2017).
15. Taylor to Rusk, 8 July 1964, in Department of State, *Foreign Relations of the United States, 1964–68,* 1:539–542, quotation on 542.
16. Logevall, *Choosing War,* 183–185.
17. Thomas L. Ahern Jr., *The CIA and the Generals: Covert Support to Military Government in South Vietnam* (Washington, D.C.: Central Intelligence

Agency, Center for the Study of Intelligence, 2009), 25–27, https://www.cia.gov/library/readingroom/document/5076e89c993247d4d82b62ed (accessed 10 July 2018).

18. Rowan to Johnson, 11 July 1964, in Department of State, *Foreign Relations of the United States, 1964–68,* 1:544–545, quotation on 545.

19. Brigadier General C. A. Youngdale, J2 Portion of U.S. Mission Council Weekly Summary, 20 July 1964, Records of United States Forces in Southeast Asia, HQ MACV, Historians Background Material Files, box 5, folder: U.S. Mission Council (Working File, Part 1 of 2), RG 472, NARA.

20. William Bundy, Courses of Action for South Vietnam, 8 September 1964, PQV, http://congressional.proquest.com/histvault?q=002789-001-0222 (accessed 8 January 2017).

21. Taylor to Rusk, 15 July 1964, in Department of State, *Foreign Relations of the United States, 1964–1968,* 1:547–548.

22. Taylor to Rusk, 15 July 1964, in Department of State, *Foreign Relations of the United States, 1964–1968,* 1:548–552.

23. Taylor to Rusk, 17 July 1964, in Department of State, *Foreign Relations of the United States, 1964–1968,* 1:553–554.

24. Forrestal to Bundy, 22 July 1964, in Department of State, *Foreign Relations of the United States, 1964–1968,* 1:558–561.

25. JCS to McNamara, 27 July 1964; Forrestal to Rusk, 31 July 1964, both in Department of State, *Foreign Relations of the United States, 1964–1968,* 1:583–585, 587–588.

26. McCone to Johnson, 28 July 1964, in Department of State, *Foreign Relations of the United States, 1964–1968,* 1:585–587.

27. Unger to Rusk, 27 July 1964; Taylor to Rusk, 27 July 1964, both in Department of State, *Foreign Relations of the United States, 1964–1968,* 1:579–583.

28. Taylor to Rusk, 3 August 1964, in Department of State, *Foreign Relations of the United States, 1964–1968,* 1:593–594.

29. Taylor, *Swords and Plowshares,* 319.

30. Taylor to Rusk, 7 August 1964, in Department of State, *Foreign Relations of the United States, 1964–1968,* 1:646–647.

31. "Taylor's View: 'A Pyrrhic Victory,'" *Washington Sunday Star,* 18 July 1971.

32. Taylor to McNamara, 3 February 1964, PQV, http://congressional.proquest.com/histvault?q=002243-013-0232 (accessed 19 January 2017).

33. Taylor to Rusk, 9 August 1964, PQV, http://congressional.proquest.com/histvault?q=003221-001-0188 (accessed 14 January 2017); Clodfelter, *Limits of Air Power,* 49–51.

34. Taylor to Rusk, 9 August 1964, in Department of State, *Foreign Relations of the United States, 1964–1968,* 1:654–656.

35. Taylor to Rusk for the president, 10 August 1964, in Department of State, *Foreign Relations of the United States, 1964–1968,* 1:656–662.

36. Ibid., quotation on 662.

37. Taylor to Rusk, 18 August 1964, in Department of State, *Foreign Relations of the United States, 1964–1968,* 1:689–693, quotations on 690.

38. Sibley, memorandum for the record, 14 August 1964, in Department of

State, *Foreign Relations of the United States, 1964–1968*, 1:665–668, quotations on 666.

39. Wheeler to McNamara, 14 August 1964, in Department of State, *Foreign Relations of the United States, 1964–1968*, 1:681–682.

40. Sharp to Westmoreland, 14 August 14, 1964, in Department of State, *Foreign Relations of the United States, 1964–1968*, 1:680–681.

41. Bundy to Johnson, 14 August 1964, in Department of State, *Foreign Relations of the United States, 1964–1968*, 1:679–680.

42. Taylor to Rusk, McNamara, Wheeler, 30 October 1964, Westmoreland Collection, box 1, folder 3, AHEC.

43. Taylor to Rusk for the president, 17 August 1964, in Department of State, *Foreign Relations of the United States, 1964–1968*, 1:684–688.

44. JCS to McNamara, 27 August 1964, in Department of State, *Foreign Relations of the United States, 1964–1968*, 1:713–717, quotations on 714 and 715.

45. Ibid., 717.

46. Bundy to Johnson, 31 August 1964, in Department of State, *Foreign Relations of the United States, 1964–1968*, 1:723–724.

47. Taylor to Rusk, 6 September 1964, in Department of State, *Foreign Relations of the United States, 1964–1968*, 1:733–736; Taylor, "Chronology of Events while Ambassador to the Republic of Viet-Nam, July 1964–July 1965," 3, Taylor Papers, box 52, folder E, NDU.

48. Westmoreland to Taylor, 6 September 1964, in Department of State, *Foreign Relations of the United States, 1964–1968*, 1:736–742.

49. Bundy to Johnson, 8 September 1964, in Department of State, *Foreign Relations of the United States, 1964–1968*, 1:746–749, quotations on 746, 749.

50. "Memorandum of a Meeting," White House, 9 September 1964, in Department of State, *Foreign Relations of the United States, 1964–1968*, 1:749–755.

51. National Security Action Memorandum 314, 10 September 1964, in Department of State, *Foreign Relations of the United States, 1964–1968*, 1:758–760.

52. Taylor to Rusk, 19 September 1964, in Department of State, *Foreign Relations of the United States, 1964–68*, 1:761–763.

53. Taylor, Chronology July 1964–July 1965, 5–7, quotation on 6.

54. Komer to U. Alexis Johnson, 3 March 1967, Papers of Robert W. Komer, box 7, folder: RWK CHRON FILE January–March 1967, LBJL.

55. Greene, "Attended Joint Chiefs White House Conference with the President," 4 March 1964, 7, Wallace M. Greene, Jr. Papers, box 1, file 1—Notes and Papers on Situation in S. Vietnam, vol. 1 (2 Jan—16 Aug 1964), item 7, Marine Corps University Archive, Quantico, Virginia.

56. Taylor interview by Karnow, part 3 of 4; William Westmoreland interview for *Vietnam: A Television History,* 1981, http://openvault.wgbh.org/catalog/vietnam-b463a4-interview-with-william-c-william-childs-westmoreland-1981 (accessed 13 February 2016).

57. Conversation with Taylor, 25 November 1964, Lyndon B. Johnson Presidential Recordings, Miller Center, University of Virginia, https://millercenter.org/

the-presidency/secret-white-house-tapes/conversation-maxwell-taylor-november-25-1964 (accessed 4 February 2018).

58. Paper prepared by Taylor, 26 November 1964, *American Presidency Project*, http://www.presidency.ucsb.edu/vietnam/showdoc.php?docid=150 (accessed 13 May 2015).

59. Taylor to Rusk, 10 November 1965, in Department of State, *Foreign Relations of the United States, 1964–1968*, 1:899–900.

60. Taylor to McNamara, 3 November 1965, in Department of State, *Foreign Relations of the United States, 1964–1968*, 1:882–884.

61. Taylor to State, Defense, White House, CIA, 2 November 1964, in Department of State, *Foreign Relations of the United States, 1964–1968*, 1:879–880.

62. Westmoreland to Wheeler, 27 November 1964, Westmoreland Papers, box 33, folder: Eyes Only Message file 1 Jan—31 Dec 64 [2 of 2], LBJL; William Bundy, memorandum of meeting on Southeast Asia, 27 November 1964, McNamara Records, Defense Programs and Operations, box 63, folder: SVN—Memo to Pres, Dec. 64, RG 200, NARA.

63. Taylor to Johnson, 17 November 1964, in Department of State, *Foreign Relations of the United States, 1964–1968*, 1:908–909.

64. J2 Portion of U.S Mission Council Weekly Summaries for 18–25 Oct and for 22–29 Nov, Records of United States Forces in Southeast Asia, HQ MACV, Historians Background Material Files, box 16, folders: Mission Council Meeting—26 Oct 1964 and Mission Council Meeting—30 Nov 1964, RG 472, NARA.

65. Paper prepared by Taylor, 26 November 1964; Taylor, *Swords and Plowshares*, 382.

66. Killen to Taylor, 17 October 1964, Subject: National Police, Records of United States Forces in Southeast Asia, HQ MACV, Historians Background Material Files, box 16, folder: Mission Council Meeting—26 Oct 1964, RG 472, NARA.

67. Taylor, The Current Situation in South Viet-Nam, November 1964, PQV, http://congressional.proquest.com/histvault?q=002795-001-0625 (accessed 18 January 2017).

68. "Position paper on Southeast Asia," paper prepared by the Executive Committee, Washington, D.C., 2 December 1964; Johnson to Taylor, 3 December 1964, both in Department of State, *Foreign Relations of the United States, 1964–1968*, 1:969–974 and 974–978.

69. Johnson to Taylor, 3 December 1964.

70. McGeorge to William Bundy, 7 December 1964, *DDO*, tinyurl.galegroup.com/tinyurl/4AWRy7 (accessed 27 December 2016); Preston, *War Council*, 150–151.

71. Diddy and Maxwell Taylor to Williston Palmer, 16 November 1964, Williston Palmer Papers, box 5, Taylor, Maxwell D., USMA.

72. Paper prepared by Taylor, 26 November 1964.

73. Taylor interview by Karnow, part 1 of 4.

74. Taylor to Johnson, 24 November 1964, in Department of State, *Foreign Relations of the United States, 1964–1968*, 1:935–936.

75. Notes on a meeting, White House, 1 December 1964, *American Presidency Project*, http://www.presidency.ucsb.edu/vietnam/showdoc.php?docid=29 (accessed 13 May 2015).

76. McGeorge Bundy's notes, 1 December 1964, Papers of McGeorge Bundy, box 1, folder: December 1, 1964, LBJL.
77. Notes on a meeting, 1 December 1964.
78. Taylor, *Swords and Plowshares*, 327.
79. Taylor to Rusk for the president, 6 January 1965, section 4 of 5, PQV, http://congressional.proquest.com/histvault?q=003221-002-0001 (accessed 19 January 2017).
80. Taylor, Chronology July 1964–July 1965, 8.
81. Preston, *War Council*, 174–175.
82. Taylor to Rusk for the president, 6 January 1965, section 5 of 5.
83. George C. Herring, *LBJ and Vietnam: A Different Kind of War* (Austin: Univ. of Texas Press, 1994).
84. Bundy, meeting notes, 6 January 1965, Bundy Papers, box 1, folder: January 6, 1965, LBJL.
85. John Taylor quotes from RFK letter in family papers: John Taylor to McNamara, 4 January 1988, McNamara Papers, box 1:16, folder: Taylor, Maxwell D. and family, LOC.
86. Bundy to Johnson, 6 March 1965.
87. Bundy to Johnson (Personal and Sensitive), 24 March 1965, PQV, http://congressional.proquest.com/histvault?q=002795-020-0351 (accessed 16 January 2017).
88. Benjamin T. Harrison and Christopher L. Mosher, "John T. McNaughton and Vietnam: The Early Years as Assistant Secretary of Defense, 1964–195," *History* 92, no. 308 (2007): 496–514.
89. Bundy to Johnson, 24 March 1965.
90. Westmoreland to Sharp, 8 February 1965, Westmoreland Papers, box 33, folder: Eyes Only Message File 1 Jan—31 Mar 65: TO [1 of 2], LBJL.
91. Taylor, Chronology July 1964–July 1965, 8, 10.
92. Taylor to Rusk, 7 February 1965, General Records of the Department of State, Central Foreign Policy Files, 1964–1966, box 2950, folder: POL 27 Viet S., 2/5/65, RG 59, NARA; Statement by the President upon Ordering Withdrawal of American Dependents from South Viet-Nam, 7 February 1965, *American Presidency Project*, http://www.presidency.ucsb.edu/ws/?pid=27252 (accessed 3 February 2017).
93. Johnson to Taylor, 8 February 1965, General Records of the Department of State, Central Foreign Policy Files, 1964–1966, box 2950, folder: POL 27 Military Operations, Viet S., 2/8/65, RG 59, NARA; Bundy, meeting notes, 10 February 1965, Bundy Papers, box 1, folder: February 10, 1965, LBJL.
94. Taylor to Rusk, 12 February 1965, PQV, http://congressional.proquest.com/histvault?q=002795-018-0031 (accessed 14 January 2017).
95. Ibid.
96. Clodfelter, *Limits of Airpower*, 59–61.
97. Westmoreland interview for *Television History*; Taylor, *Swords and Plowshares*, 337–338.
98. Bromley Smith to Johnson, 23 February 1965, PQV, http://congressional.proquest.com/histvault?q=002789-017-1153 (accessed 8 January 2017).
99. Taylor to Johnson, 23 February 1965, in Department of State, *Foreign*

Relations of the United States, 1964–1968, vol. 2, *Vietnam, January–June, 1965* (Washington, D.C.: Government Printing Office, 1996), 349–350.

100. Embassy Saigon (Miller) to State, 24 December 1964, Summary of Conversation of December 20, PQV, http://congressional.proquest.com/histvault?q=002791-010-0264 (accessed 19 January 2017); Nguyen Cao Ky, *Twenty Years and Twenty Days* (New York: Stein and Day, 1976), 53–55.

101. Taylor to Rusk, 25 December 1964, PQV, http://congressional.proquest.com/histvault?q=002791-009-0535 (accessed 25 January 2017).

102. Embassy Saigon (Zorthian) to Rusk, 24 December 1964, PQV, http://congressional.proquest.com/histvault?q=002791-009-0535 (accessed 25 January 2017).

103. Taylor to Johnson, 23 February 1965.

104. Taylor to Johnson, 31 March 1965, Joint US-GVN Programs in the Non-Military Field in South Viet-Nam, PQV, http://congressional.proquest.com/histvault?q=002795-019-0569 (accessed 8 January 2017).

105. Taylor's Weekly Report for the President, 24 March 1965, *DDO:* tinyurl.galegroup.com/tinyurl/4RGWG1 (accessed 24 February 2017).

106. Taylor to Johnson, 6 January 1965, section 3 of 5, in Department of State, *Foreign Relations of the United States, 1964–1968*, 2:21–22.

107. Paper by Taylor, [1 April 1965], PQV, http://congressional.proquest.com/histvault?q=002795-023-0140 (accessed 11 January 2017).

108. Taylor Paper, 1 April 1965.

109. Taylor to Bundy, 17 April 1965, PQV, http://congressional.proquest.com/histvault?q=003221-002-0533 (accessed 18 January 2017).

110. Taylor, *Swords and Plowshares*, 339–340.

111. Taylor to Bundy, 17 April 1965.

112. Taylor's Assessment of the Overall Situation in Vietnam, 7 March 1965, PQV, http://congressional.proquest.com/histvault?q=002793-020-0909 (accessed 14 January 2017).

113. Taylor to Diem, 1 October 1963, copied in Harkins to Rusk, 1 October 1963, PQV, http://congressional.proquest.com/histvault?q=002783-005-0718 (accessed 14 January 2017).

114. Taylor's assessment, 7 March 1965.

115. Preston, *War Council*, 171.

116. Taylor to Rusk, 4 March 1965, PQV, http://congressional.proquest.com/histvault?q=002793-005-0417 (accessed 8 January 2017).

117. Taylor to Johnson, 2 March 1965, PQV, http://congressional.proquest.com/histvault?q=002791-012-0739 (accessed 19 January 2017).

118. Taylor to Rusk, 12 March 1965 (Saigon 2941), General Records of the Department of State, Central Foreign Policy Files, 1964–1966, box 2954, folder: POL 27 Viet S., 3/11/65, RG 59, NARA.

119. Taylor to Rusk, 12 April 1965 (Saigon 3332), Goodpaster Papers, box 80, folder 5, GCML.

120. Taylor to Rusk, 14 April 1965, in Department of State, *Foreign Relations of the United States, 1964–1968*, 2:554–555.

121. Taylor to Rusk, 14 April 1965 (Dept. 3384), PQV, http://congressional.proquest.com/histvault?q=003221-002-0533 (accessed 18 January 2017).

122. Bundy to Johnson, 14 April 1965, in Department of State, *Foreign Relations of the United States, 1964–1968*, 2:556.

123. Taylor to Rusk, 14 April 1965 (Dept. 3373), Goodpaster Papers, box 80, folder 5, GCML.

124. McNamara, "Remarks Regarding Situation in Vietnam as Departing for Meeting in Hawaii," 19 April 1965; "Remarks by McNamara on Departure from Honolulu," 20 April 1965, both in McNamara Records, Records Relating to Vietnam and Southeast Asia, box 180, Book 3, Tab 110 and 111, NARA.

125. Bundy to Taylor, 15 April 1965, PQV, http://congressional.proquest.com/histvault?q=002795-002-0135 (accessed 11 January 2017).

126. Bundy, notes of a meeting, 9 March 1965, Bundy Papers, box 1, folder: March 9, 1965, LBJL.

127. U.S. Grant Sharp, *Strategy for Defeat: Vietnam in Retrospect* (San Rafael, Calif.: Presidio Press, 1978), 77–80, differs from McNamara to Johnson, 21 April 1965, which paints a picture of agreement on airpower and ground forces. Papers of President Johnson, National Security File, Country File—Vietnam, box 74, folder: 1965 Troop Decision, LBJL.

128. Taylor interview by Karnow, part 3 of 4; Westmoreland interview for *Television History*.

129. Taylor to Rusk (Eyes Only for McNamara), 23 April 1965, Papers of President Johnson, National Security File, National Security Council History, box 41, folder: Deployment of Major U.S. Forces to Vietnam, July, 1965, vol. 3, LBJL.

130. McNamara to Johnson, 21 April 1965.

131. Rusk to Taylor, 22 April 1965, in Department of State, *Foreign Relations of the United States, 1964–1968*, 2:602–603.

132. Taylor to Rusk, 26 April 1965, General Records of the Department of State, Central Foreign Policy Files, 1964–1966, box 2958, folder: POL 27 Military Operation, Viet S, 4/26/65, RG 59, NARA.

133. Taylor, Chronology July 1964–July 1965, 11.

134. Ball to Taylor and Johnson, 1 June 1965, in Department of State, *Foreign Relations of the United States, 1964–1968*, 2:704–706; Qiang Zhai, *China and the Vietnam Wars, 1950–1975* (Chapel Hill: Univ. of North Carolina Press, 2000).

135. McNamara to Johnson, 21 April 1965.

136. Quoted in Clodfelter, *Limits of Air Power*, 68.

137. Taylor to Rusk, 17 April 1965 and 17 May 1965, PQV, http://congressional.proquest.com/histvault?q=002789-011-0712 (accessed 25 January 2017).

138. Taylor to Rusk, 5 July 1965, PQV, http://congressional.proquest.com/histvault?q=002789-011-0712 (accessed 25 January 2017).

139. Taylor, Chronology July 1964–July 1965, 13.

140. Taylor to Rusk, 5 June 1965, in Department of State, *Foreign Relations of the United States, 1964–1968*, 2:719–724.

141. Westmoreland to Taylor, 30 May 1965, Comparison of the Rural Reconstruction Situation, 25 January and 25 April, Records of United States Forces in Southeast Asia, HQ MACV, Historians Background Material Files, box 9, folder: COMUSMACV's Files 1965 (I), RG 472, NARA.

142. Taylor to Rusk for the president, 30 June 1965, General Records of the Department of State, Central Foreign Policy Files, 1964–1966, box 2962, folder: POL 27, Viet S., 6/28/65, RG 59, NARA.

143. Westmoreland to Wheeler, 30 June 1965, Records of United States Forces in Southeast Asia, HQ MACV, Historians Background Material Files, box 9, folder: COMUSMACV's Files 1965 (II), RG 472, NARA.

144. Quoted in Khong, *Analogies at War*, 159.

145. Johnson, Tape 11, 2–3 [July 25, 1965], U. Alexis Johnson Papers, box 1, folder: Diaries, LBJL.

146. Johnson, Tape 14, 4–5 [August 1967], U. Alexis Johnson Papers, box 1, folder: Diaries, LBJL.

147. Bundy to the president, 24 July 1965, The History of Recommendations for Increased US Forces in Vietnam, Papers of President Johnson, National Security File, Country File—Vietnam, box 74, folder: 1965 Troop Decision, LBJL.

148. Bundy to Johnson, 30 June 1965, PQV, http://congressional.proquest.com/histvault?q=002962-003-0001, accessed January 10, 2017.

149. Johnson, Tape 11, 3 [August 1965], U. Alexis Johnson Papers, box 1, folder: Diaries, LBJL.

150. Memorandum of conversation, 16 July 1965, Meeting with GVN, attached to American Embassy Saigon (Manfull) to State, 27 July 1965, PQV, http://congressional.proquest.com/histvault?q=002793-004-0602 (accessed 19 January 2017); Cooper and Unger for Bundies, 18 July 1965, General Records of the Department of State, Central Foreign Policy Files, 1964–1966, box 2963, folder: POL 27 Military Operations, Viet S, 7/17/65, RG 59, NARA.

151. Taylor to Rusk for the president, 17 June 1965, General Records of the Department of State, Central Foreign Policy Files, 1964–1966, box 2961, folder: POL 27 Military Operations, Viet S, 6/16/65, RG 59, NARA.

152. *Sunday Mirror*, 4 July 1965.

153. Taylor, *Swords and Plowshares*, 348–357; *The Big Picture* ("The Screaming Eagles in Vietnam," Episode TV-714, 1967), https://www.youtube.com/watch?v=fZCiOthZKFc (accessed 18 May 2016).

154. McNamara, *In Retrospect*, 118–119; Secretary Rusk's News Conference of 2 August 1965, 27, Rusk Papers, Series II. Secretary of State, box 3, folder 58, RRL.

155. Taylor to Rusk, 11 July 1965, Papers of President Johnson, National Security File, National Security Council History, box 43, folder: Deployment of Major US Forces to Vietnam, July, 1965, vol. 6, LBJL.

156. Taylor, *Responsibility and Response*, 26–31; Taylor, *Swords and Plowshares*, 366.

157. Taylor, *Responsibility and Response*, 31–32.

158. Ibid., 23–24.

159. Gregory A. Daddis, *No Sure Victory: Measuring U.S. Army Effectiveness and Progress in the Vietnam War* (Oxford, UK: Oxford Univ. Press, 2011).

160. Taylor, *Responsibility and Response*, 27.

161. Taylor's notes, "Vietnam Report," 9, Papers of W. Averell Harriman, box 514, folder: Taylor, Maxwell D., LOC.

162. Taylor, *Responsibility and Response*, 21.

163. Logevall, *Choosing War*, 273–278
164. Taylor to Rusk, 24 July 1965, PQV, http://congressional.proquest.com/histvault?q=002793-004-0452 (accessed 17 January 2017).
165. Taylor, "Vietnam Report," 13–14.
166. Enclosure to Taylor to Ridgway, 4 February 1954, "The Significance of Oriental Military Manpower," Taylor Papers, box 2, folder: Korea (D), NDU.

6. Wise Man?

1. Taylor, *Swords and Plowshares*, 365.
2. Memorandum for the record (name redacted), 7 October 1965, Discussion with General Maxwell D. Taylor on the President's Foreign Intelligence Advisory Board, CIA, https://www.cia.gov/library/readingroom/document/cia-rdp80b01676r000500010044-0 (accessed 14 February 2017).
3. Taylor to Rusk, 3 May 1968, Papers of President Johnson, National Security File, Subject File, box 41, folder: President's Foreign Intelligence Advisory Board, LBJL.
4. Johnson, Tape 14, 8 [August 1967], U. Alexis Johnson Papers, box 1, folder: Diaries, LBJL.
5. Kaplan, *McNamara Ascendancy*, 36–37.
6. Harriman to Taylor, 28 October 1965, Harriman Papers, box 514, folder: Taylor, Maxwell D., LOC.
7. Taylor to Harriman, 30 October 1965, Harriman Papers, box 514, folder: Taylor, Maxwell D., LOC.
8. Taylor to Johnson, 17 January 1966, *DDO*, tinyurl.galegroup.com/tinyurl/4R4DU8 (accessed 4 February 2018).
9. Major General Fairbourn, memorandum for record, 8 March 1966, Subject: First Meeting of the Senior Interdepartmental Group (SIG), in Department of State, *Foreign Relations of the United States, 1964–68*, 33:148–151.
10. Taylor to Johnson, 17 January 1966.
11. Schwartz, Record of Agreement and Decisions of the Senior Interdepartmental Group Meeting, 26 July 1966, in Department of State, *Foreign Relations of the United States, 1964–68*, 33:82–83.
12. National Security Action Memorandum 341, 2 March 1966, Direction, Coordination, and Supervision of Interdepartmental Activities Overseas, Records of the National Security Council, National Security Action Memorandum, box 4, RG 273, NARA; memorandum for Director of Central Intelligence (author's name redacted), 10 October 1966, CIA Reaction to General Maxwell Taylor's Report on the U.S. Counterinsurgency Program, CIA, https://www.cia.gov/library/readingroom/document/cia-rdp78-06202a000100090002-1 (accessed 4 February 2018).
13. Komer to Johnson, 2 March 1966, in Department of State, *Foreign Relations of the United States, 1964–68*, 33:130–131.
14. Komer to Taylor, 11 August, 1966, Komer Papers, box 7, folder: CHRON FILE July–September 1966 [1 of 2], LBJL.
15. Komer to McNamara, 29 September 1966, Komer Papers, box 7, folder: CHRON FILE July–September 1966 [1 of 2], LBJL.

16. Komer to Taylor, 26 November 1966, Komer Papers, box 7, folder: CHRON FILE October–December 1966 [2 of 3], LBJL.

17. Frank Leith Jones, *Blowtorch Bob: Robert Komer, Vietnam, and American Cold War Strategy* (Annapolis, Md.: Naval Institute Press, 2013), 93–151.

18. Bundy, notes of a meeting, 2 August 1965, Bundy Papers, box 1, folder: August 2, 1965, LBJL.

19. Taylor to Johnson, 7 September 1965, A Cease-Fire in South Viet Nam, *DDO*, tinyurl.galegroup.com/tinyurl/4RGpR5 (accessed 24 February 2017).

20. Conversation with Taylor and McNamara, 28 December 1965, Johnson Recordings, Miller Center, https://millercenter.org/the-presidency/secret-white-house-tapes/conversation-maxwell-taylor-and-robert-mcnamara-december-28 (accessed 3 February 2018).

21. Meeting in the Cabinet Room, 28 January 1966, Resumption of Bombing, Papers of President Johnson, Meeting Notes File, box 1, folder: January 28, 1966—1:20 p.m., LBJL.

22. Taylor to Johnson and Rusk, 9 August 1966, Cease-Fire during Viet-Nam Elections, *DDO*, tinyurl.galegroup.com/tinyurl/4AXQY1 (accessed 27 December 2016).

23. Taylor, 19 November 1965, Concept of Employment of US/GVN Forces (no recipient noted), *DDO*, tinyurl.galegroup.com/tinyurl/4QzxT5 (accessed 23 February 2017).

24. From Kissinger's notes in Ferguson, *Kissinger*, 1:636.

25. Taylor, *Swords and Plowshares*, 363–364.

26. Conversation with Taylor, 1 February 1966, Johnson Recordings, Miller Center, https://millercenter.org/the-presidency/secret-white-house-tapes/conversation-maxwell-taylor-and-telephone-operator-february (accessed 4 February 2018).

27. *The Vietnam Hearings*, with an Introduction by J. William Fulbright (New York: Vintage Books, 1966), 167–226.

28. Ibid., 182.

29. Ibid., 204–207, 211.

30. Joseph A. Fry, *The American South and the Vietnam War: Belligerence, Protest, and Agony in Dixie* (Lexington: Univ. Press of Kentucky, 2015), 128–134.

31. *Vietnam Hearings*, 186–191.

32. Ibid., 168–170.

33. Ibid., 213–220.

34. Komer to Moyers, 18 February 1966, Komer Papers, box 6, folder: CHRON FILE February 1966 [1 of 2], LBJL.

35. Clifford to Taylor, 21 February 1966; Taylor to Clifford, 22 February 1966, both in Papers of Clark Clifford, box 41, folder: Taylor, Maxwell D., LOC.

36. Taylor to Williams, 22 February 1966, Samuel T. Williams Papers, box 22, folder 10, HIA.

37. Valenti, meeting in the Cabinet Room, 5 April 1966, Papers of President Johnson, Meeting Notes File, box 1 folder: April—1:00 p.m., LBJL.

38. Douglas Martin, "Gen. Nguyen Chanh Thi, 84, Seen as Hero in Vietnam, Dies," *New York Times*, 26 June 2007.

39. Valenti, meeting in Cabinet Room, 11 March 1966, Papers of President Johnson, Meeting Notes File, box 1, folder: March 11, 1966—12:35 p.m., LBJL.

40. Rufus Phillips, *Why Vietnam Matters: An Eyewitness Account of Lessons Not Learned* (Annapolis, Md.: Naval Institute Press, 2008), 104; Annie Jacobsen, *The Pentagon's Brain: An Uncensored History of DARPA, America's Top Secret Military Research Agency* (New York: Little, Brown, 2015), 202–210; Sharon Weinberger, *The Imagineers of War: The Untold History of DARPA, the Pentagon Agency that Changed the World* (New York: Knopf, 2017), 79–80.

41. Taylor to Johnson, 27 April 1966, Assessment and Use of Negotiations Blue Chips, DDO, tinyurl.galegroup.com/tinyurl/4AW5K3 (accessed 27 December 2016).

42. Ferguson, *Kissinger*, 1:678–679; James G. Hershberg, *Marigold: The Lost Chance for Peace in Vietnam* (Stanford, Calif.: Stanford Univ. Press, 2012), 630–683.

43. Lodge to Rostow, 17 June 1966, PQV, http://congressional.proquest.com/histvault?q=002789-005-0564 (accessed 17 January 2017).

44. Taylor to Johnson, 20 February 1967, Possible Forms of Negotiations with Hanoi, DDO, tinyurl.galegroup.com/tinyurl/4AXjx0 (accessed 31 January 2018).

45. Taylor to Johnson, 11 May 1967, in Department of State, *Foreign Relations of the United States, 1964–68*, vol. 5, *Vietnam, 1967* (Washington, D.C.: Government Printing Office, 2002), 410–411.

46. Ferguson, *Kissinger*, 1:770–771.

47. State to US embassies, President Johnson's personal message to Thanom, Holt, Marcos, Thieu, Park and Holyoake requesting their concurrence for sending Clark Clifford and Gen. Maxwell Taylor to Saigon, 18 July 1967, DDO, tinyurl.galegroup.com/tinyurl/4AVpu7 (accessed 27 December 2016.)

48. Clifford, Talk with LBJ, 4 August 1968, hand-written notes, Clifford Papers, box 1, folder 1, LBJL.

49. Press Conference of General Maxwell D. Taylor and Clark Clifford upon Returning from Southeast Asia, 5 August 1967, Papers of President Johnson, National Security File, Country File—Vietnam, box 211, folder 5, LBJL.

50. Statistics on casualties, NARA, https://www.archives.gov/research/military/vietnam-war/casualty-statistics.html#category (accessed 20 April 2017).

51. Taylor to Johnson, 25 August 1967, Clifford Papers, box 41, folder: Taylor, Maxwell D., LOC.

52. Taylor to Johnson, 17 November 1967, DDO, tinyurl.galegroup.com/tinyurl/4QvME0 (accessed 23 February 2017).

53. Taylor, *Swords and Plowshares*, 379–382.

54. Ibid., 376–378.

55. Taylor to Johnson, 30 January 1968, Papers of President Johnson, National Security File, Files of Walt W. Rostow, box 6, folder 7, LBJL.

56. Taylor, *Swords and Plowshares*, 383–388.

57. Taylor to Johnson, 10 February 1968, Further Reinforcements for VietNam, Clifford Papers, box 2, folder 3, LBJL.

58. Taylor to Johnson, 14 February 1968, Khe Sanh, Clifford Papers, box 2, folder 5, LBJL

59. Rostow to Johnson (Eyes Only), 13 February 1968, Papers of President Johnson, National Security File, Files of Walt W. Rostow, box 6, folder 8, LBJL.

60. Taylor memorandum, 9 March 1965, attached to Rostow to Johnson, 9 March 1968, PQV, http://congressional.proquest.com/histvault?q=002795-010-0001 (accessed 17 January 2017).

61. Taylor, Viet-Nam Alternatives [elsewhere identified as 2 March 1968], Clifford Papers, box 1, folder 10, LBJL.

62. Taylor, *Swords and Plowshares*, 388–392.

63. Johnson, The President's Address to the Nation Announcing Steps to Limit the War in Vietnam and Reporting His Decision Not to Seek Reelection, 31 March 1968, *American Presidency Project*, http://www.presidency.ucsb.edu/ws/?pid=28772 (accessed 3 October 2017).

64. Pierre Asselin, *A Bitter Peace: Washington, Hanoi, and the Making of the Paris Agreement* (Chapel Hill: Univ. of North Carolina Press, 2002), 5–13.

65. Taylor, *Swords and Plowshares*, 393–398.

66. Taylor to Johnson, 13 May 1968, Papers of President Johnson, National Security File, Files of Walt W. Rostow, box 6, folder 7, LBJL.

67. Elsey, notes of Secretary of Defense Clifford's 0930 Saturday [25 May 1968] Staff Meeting, Papers of George Elsey, box 1, folder: CMC/GME May 1—June 30, 1968 [3 of 3], LBJL.

68. Milne, *America's Rasputin*, 231–235.

69. Taylor to Johnson, 23 February 1968; Taylor to Rostow, 19 April 1968; Taylor to Rostow, 10 June 1968, all in Papers of President Johnson, National Security File, Subject File, box 41, folder: President's Foreign Intelligence Advisory Board, LBJL.

70. Taylor to Johnson, 7 June 1968, Evaluation of the Quality of U.S. Intelligence Bearing on the TET Offensive, January 1968, Papers of President Johnson, National Security File, Intelligence File, box 6, folder: Foreign Intelligence Advisory Board, vol. 2 (1 of 4), LBJL.

71. Taylor to Johnson, 2 August 1968, Evaluation of the Lull in Enemy Activities in South Viet-Nam, Papers of President Johnson, National Security File, Subject File, box 41, folder: President's Foreign Intelligence Advisory Board, LBJL.

72. Clifford, notes for meeting, 25 May 1968, Clifford Papers, box 1, folder 3, LBJL.

73. Rusk to Johnson, 31 July 1968, *DDO*, tinyurl.galegroup.com/tinyurl/4AVs46 (accessed 4 February 2018).

74. Taylor to Johnson, 17 July 1968, The Stalemate in Paris, Elsey Papers, box 2, folder: CMC/GME July 1—August 31, 1968 [2 of 3], LBJL.

75. Elsey, notes on Secretary of Defense Clifford's 22 and 24 July 1968 meetings, Elsey Papers, box 2, folder: CMC/GME July 1—August 31, 1968 [3 of 3], LBJL, emphasis in the original.

76. Taylor to Johnson, 30 July 1968; Elsey, notes of Clifford's staff meeting on 31 July 1968, both in Elsey Papers, box 2, folder: CMC/GME July 1—August 31, 1968 [2 of 3], LBJL.

77. Taylor to Johnson, 24 October 1968, *DDO*, tinyurl.galegroup.com/tinyurl/4AXpu7 (accessed 27 December 2016).

78. Taylor, *Swords and Plowshares*, 399–401; Taylor to Helms, 23 February

1968, PQV, http://congressional.proquest.com/histvault?q=000591-005-1274 (accessed 8 January 2017).

79. Taylor, *Swords and Plowshares*, 400–402, quotations on 402.

80. Ibid., 403.

81. Quoted in Clodfelter, *Limits of Air Power*, 143.

82. Taylor, *Swords and Plowshares*, 404–408.

83. Taylor to Gray, 12 June 1968, Gordon Gray Papers, box 1, folder: Miscellaneous Correspondence, 1967–68, DDEL.

84. Taylor to Gruenther, 9 January 1969, Gruenther Papers, U.S. Army Series, box 7, folder: T—Miscellaneous (1), DDEL.

85. Taylor to Johnson, 25 November 1968, Papers of President Johnson, National Security File, Intelligence File, box 6, folder: Foreign Intelligence Advisory Board, vol. 2 (1 of 4), LBJL.

86. Ibid.

87. Taylor, *Swords and Plowshares*, 417–421.

88. Ibid., 409–413, quotation on 410.

89. Ibid., 413–416, quotation on 413.

90. Mansfield to Johnson, 9 June 1965, PQV, http://congressional.proquest.com/histvault?q=002962-003-0001 (accessed 10 January 2017).

91. Taylor, *Responsibility and Response*, 42–64.

92. Chester L. Cooper, *The Lost Crusade: America in Vietnam* (New York: Dodd, 1970); Taylor to Cooper, 9 May 1970, Papers of Chester Cooper, box 10, folder: Correspondence, LBJL.

93. Cooper to Thomas Lipscomb, 12 May 1970, Cooper Papers, box 10, folder: Correspondence, LBJL; Chester Cooper interview, no. 2, by Jonathan Persoff, 10 August 1999, 20, Cooper Papers, box 3, folder: Vietnam General, LBJL.

94. Thomas Lipscomb to Taylor, 11 May 1970, Cooper Papers, box 10, folder: Correspondence, LBJL.

95. Taylor interview by Karnow, part 3 of 4.

96. Gregory A. Daddis, *Westmoreland's War: Reassessing American Strategy in Vietnam* (Oxford, UK: Oxford Univ. Press, 2014), 2, 57.

97. Presidential daily diaries, Richard M. Nixon Virtual Presidential Library, https://www.nixonlibrary.gov/virtuallibrary/documents/dailydiary.php (accessed 18 April 2017).

98. Taylor to Kissinger, 13 January 1969 and 19 March 1969, PQV, http://congressional.proquest.com/histvault?q=102564-001-0899 (accessed 8 January 2017).

99. Transcripts of conversations, Kissinger and Taylor, 29 October 1972 and 30 October 1972, PQV, http://congressional.proquest.com/histvault?q=101096-014-0170 (accessed 8 January 2017).

100. Asselin, *Bitter Peace*, 185.

101. Larry Berman, *No Peace, No Honor: Nixon, Kissinger, and Betrayal in Vietnam* (New York: Free Press, 2001), argues Nixon intended to reignite the air war, too, once North Vietnam had broken the agreement.

102. Conversation, Kissinger and Taylor, 29 October 1972.

103. McNamara, *In Retrospect*; Walt W. Rostow, "The Case for the War," *Times Literary Supplement*, 9 June 1995; Walt W. Rostow, "Vietnam and Asia,"

Diplomatic History 20, no. 3 (1996): 467–471; Milne, *America's Rasputin*, 241–258.

104. Robert S. Gallagher, "Memories of Peace and War: An Exclusive Interview with General Maxwell D. Taylor," *American Heritage Magazine* 32, no. 3 (1981), https://www.americanheritage.com/index.php/content/memories-peace-and-war (accessed 7 July 2018).

105. Taylor, *Responsibility and Response*, 65–80.

106. Quoted in Gabriel Kolko, *Anatomy of a War: Vietnam, the United States, and the Modern Historical Experience* (New York: Pantheon, 1985), 113.

107. Maxwell D. Taylor, "National Policy Too Lightly Armed," in *Grand Strategy for the 1980s*, ed. Bruce Palmer Jr. (Washington, D.C.: American Enterprise Institute for Public Policy Research, 1978), 3–17, quotations on 3.

108. Gallagher, "Memories of Peace and War."

109. Taylor, "Too Lightly Armed," 3.

110. Ibid., 4–9, quotation on 6.

111. Ibid., 9.

112. Ibid., 10–14.

113. Ibid., 15–17.

114. Charles Tyroler II, ed., *Alerting America: The Papers of the Committee on the Present Danger* (Washington, D.C.: Pergamon-Brassey's, 1984), 3–9.

115. Taylor, "Too Lightly Armed," 14–15.

116. General Andrew J. Goodpaster interview by Colonel William D. Johnson and Lieutenant Colonel James C. Ferguson, section 3, 25 February 1976, 68, Goodpaster Papers, box 43, folder 8, GCML.

117. Maxwell D. Taylor, *Precarious Security* (New York: Norton, 1976), ix.

118. Ibid., 2 (quotation) and 29–36.

119. Ibid., xi.

120. Ibid., 1–4.

121. Ibid., 43–50, quotation on 47.

122. Ibid., 4–13.

123. Ibid., 17–28.

124. Ibid., 124–136.

125. Maxwell D. Taylor, "The United States—A Military Power Second to None?" *International Security* 1, no. 1 (1976): 49–55, quotation on 51.

126. Ibid., 53–55.

127. Maxwell D. Taylor, "Changing Military Priorities," *AEI Foreign Policy and Defense Review* 1, no. 3 (1979): 2–13, quotation on 5.

128. Ibid., 5–7.

129. Ibid., 7–13, quotation on 7–8.

130. Taylor, "Reflections on the American Military Establishment," 7–22.

131. Ibid., 19.

132. Deborah M. Kyle, "Congress Serious about Defense Reform; 33 Senate Witnesses Endorse Change," *Armed Forces Journal International* 121, no. 7 (February 1984): 10–24, Taylor quoted on 20.

133. James Kitfield, *Prodigal Soldiers: How the Generation of Officers Born of Vietnam Revolutionized the American Style of War* (New York: Simon and Schuster, 1995), 246.

134. Ibid., 251–253, Moorer quoted on 253.
135. Victor S. Krulak, *Organization for National Security: A Study* (Cambridge, Mass.: US Strategic Institute Publishing Office, 1983), 113–128.
136. Maxwell D. Taylor, "Reagan's Military Policy Is in Trouble," *Washington Post*, 2 November 1981.
137. Maxwell D. Taylor, "How Much for Defense? Only What's Essential," *Washington Post*, September 1, 1981.
138. John Taylor, *General Maxwell Taylor*, 383–386.

Epilogue

1. Gordon Nathaniel Lederman, *Reorganizing the Joint Chiefs of Staff: The Goldwater-Nichols Act of 1968* (Westport, Conn.: Greenwood Press, 1999; James R. Locher III, *Victory on the Potomac: The Goldwater-Nichols Act Unifies the Pentagon* (College Station: Texas A&M Univ. Press, 2002); Steven T. Wills, "Replacing the Maritime Strategy: The Change in Naval Strategy from 1989 to 1994" (Ph.D. diss., Ohio University, 2017).
2. Mark Perry, *The Pentagon's Wars: The Military's Undeclared War against America's Presidents* (New York: Basic Books, 2017).
3. Francis Fukuyama, *The End of History and the Last Man* (New York: Free Press, 1992).
4. Douglas A. Macgregor, *Transformation under Fire: Reevaluating How America Fights* (Westport, Conn.: Praeger, 2003); Robert R. Tomes, *US Defense Strategy from Vietnam to Operation Iraqi Freedom: Military Innovation and the New American Way of War, 1973–2003* (London: Routledge, 2007); John Sloan Brown, *Kevlar Legions: The Transformation of the U.S. Army, 1989–2005* (Washington, D.C.: US Army Center of Military History, 2011); Brian D. Laslie, *The Air Force Way of War: Tactics and Training after Vietnam* (Lexington: Univ. Press of Kentucky, 2015).
5. Mary Kaldor, *New and Old Wars: Organised Violence in a Global Era*, 3rd ed. (Cambridge, UK: Polity Press, 2012).
6. Michael R. Gordon and Bernard E. Trainor, *Cobra II: The Inside Story of the Invasion and Occupation of Iraq* (New York: Pantheon, 2006).
7. Peter R. Mansoor, *Surge: My Journey with General David Petraeus and the Remaking of the Iraq War* (New Haven: Yale Univ. Press, 2013); David Fitzgerald, *Learning to Forget: US Army Counterinsurgency Doctrine and Practice from Vietnam to Iraq* (Stanford, Calif.: Stanford Univ. Press, 2013); Aaron B. O'Connell, ed., *Our Latest Longest War: Losing Hearts and Minds in Afghanistan* (Chicago: Univ. of Chicago Press, 2017).
8. Ingo Trauschweizer, "Should Military Men Draft Our Nation's Security Strategy?" *The Conversation*, 3 January 2018, https://theconversation.com/should-military-men-draft-our-nations-security-strategy-89415 (accessed 28 January 2018).
9. Aaron O'Connell on NPR's *Studio 1A*, 22 August 2017; Bryan Bender and Wesley Morgan, "Generals Win Key Fight over Afghanistan They Lost with Obama," *Politico*, 22 August 2017, https://www.politico.com/story/2017/08/22/trump-generals-afghanistan-241922 (accessed 7 July 2018).

10. Stephen Kinzer, "America's Slow-Motion Military Coup," *Boston Globe*, 16 September 2017, http://www.bostonglobe.com/opinion/2017/09/16/america-slow-motion-military-coup/WgzYW9MPBIbsegCwd4IpJN/story.html; Masha Gessen, "John Kelly and the Language of the Military Coup," *New Yorker*, 20 October 2017, https://www.newyorker.com/news/news-desk/john-kelly-and-the-language-of-the-military-coup.

11. Kori Schake and Jim Mattis, "A Great Divergence?" and "Ensuring a Civil-Military Connection," in *Warriors and Citizens: Americans Views of Our Military* (Stanford, Calif.: Hoover Institution Press, 2016), 1–20, 287–326 (especially 6 and 301–306).

12. See also Michael Geyer, "German Strategy in the Age of Machine Warfare, 1914–1945," in *Makers of Modern Strategy from Machiavelli to the Nuclear Age*, ed. Peter Paret (Princeton, N.J.: Princeton, Univ. Press, 1986), 527–597.

13. Retired General David Barno and Nora Bensahel make that point specifically about John Kelly and the position of the White House Chief of Staff: "Why No General Should Serve as White House Chief of Staff," *War on the Rocks*, 12 September 2017, https://warontherocks.com/2017/09/why-no-general-should-serve-as-white-house-chief-of-staff/.

Bibliography

Archives and Research Libraries

Caroliniana Library, University of South Carolina, Columbia, South Carolina

William C. Westmoreland Papers

Central Intelligence Agency

Electronic Reading Room

Dwight D. Eisenhower Presidential Library, Abilene, Kansas

Henry M. Aurand Papers
J. Lawton Collins Papers
Dwight D. Eisenhower Pre-Presidential Papers
Dwight D. Eisenhower Papers as President (Anne Whitman File)
Gordon Gray Papers
Alfred M. Gruenther Papers
Christian Herter Papers
Lauris Norstad Papers
Oral History Collection
White House Central Files
White House Office Files

George C. Marshall Library, Lexington, Virginia

Lucius D. Clay Papers
Andrew Goodpaster Papers
Thomas T. Handy Papers
George C. Marshall Papers
James Van Fleet Papers

Hoover Institution Archives, Stanford University, Stanford, California

Charles T. R. Bohannan Papers
Keith E. Eiler Papers

270   Bibliography

Edward Lansdale Papers
Samuel T. Williams Papers

Institute Archives and Special Collections, MIT Libraries, Cambridge, Massachusetts

MIT, Office of the President, 1930–1959 (Compton-Killian).

John F. Kennedy Presidential Library, Boston, Massachusetts

Appointment Books of President Kennedy
Digital Collections
Papers of John F. Kennedy, Presidential Papers, National Security Files
Papers of John F. Kennedy, President's Office Files
Papers of Robert F. Kennedy, Attorney General Files

Library of Congress, Washington, D.C.

Papers of Clark M. Clifford
Papers of W. Averell Harriman
Papers of Frank Kowalski Jr.
Papers of Curtis E. LeMay
Papers of Robert S. McNamara
Papers of Nathan F. Twining
Papers of Thomas D. White

Lyndon B. Johnson Presidential Library, Austin, Texas

Oral History Collection
Papers of McGeorge Bundy
Papers of Chester L. Cooper
Papers of George M. Elsey
Papers of Lyndon B. Johnson, US Senate
Papers of Lyndon B. Johnson, Presidential Papers
Papers of U. Alexis Johnson
Papers of Robert W. Komer
Papers of Walt W. Rostow
Papers of William C. Westmoreland

Miller Center, University of Virginia

Lyndon B. Johnson Presidential Recordings

National Archives and Records Administration, College Park, Maryland

Digital Collection: *The Pentagon Papers*
RG 59: Records of the Department of State
RG 200: Records of Robert S. McNamara [RG now decommissioned, but number remains in the finding aid]
RG 218: Records of the Joint Chiefs of Staff

RG 273: Records of the National Security Council
RG 319: Records of the U.S. Army Staff
RG 338: Records of U.S. Army Commands
RG 407: Records of the Army Adjutant General
RG 466: Records of the U.S. High Commissioner for Germany
RG 472: Records of United States Forces in Southeast Asia
RG 546: Records of the United States Continental Army Command

National Defense University, Fort McNair, Washington, D.C.

Digital Collections
Maxwell D. Taylor Papers

National Security Archive, George Washington University, Washington, D.C.

Berlin Crisis Collection
Digital Collections

NATO Archive, Casteau, Belgium

Digital Collections
International Military Staff

Nicholson Library, Anderson University, Anderson, Indiana

Charles E. Wilson Papers

Princeton University Library, Rare Books and Special Collections, Princeton, New Jersey

Hamilton Fish Armstrong Papers
Bernard M. Baruch Papers
Council on Foreign Relations Records
Delafield Family Papers
John Foster Dulles Papers
Oral History Collection

Richard M. Nixon Virtual Presidential Library, Yorba Linda, California

Presidential Daily Diaries

Richard Russell Library for Political and Research Studies, Athens, Georgia

Oral History Collection
Dean Rusk Papers
Richard Russell Collection

US Army Heritage and Education Center, Carlisle, Pennsylvania

Donald V. Bennett Papers
Charles L. Bolte Papers

Bruce C. Clarke Papers
J. Lawton Collins Papers
Garrison H. Davidson Papers
William E. DePuy Papers
Clyde Eddleman Papers
Julian J. Ewell Papers
James M. Gavin Papers
Andrew Goodpaster Papers
Paul D. Harkins Papers
John E. Hull Papers
Harold K. Johnson Papers
Matthew B. Ridgway Papers
Maxwell D. Taylor Papers
John L. Throckmorton Papers
William C. Westmoreland Collection
Earle G. Wheeler Papers

US Marine Corps University, Library and Archive, Quantico, Virginia

Wallace M. Greene Jr. Papers
Victor S. Krulak Papers

US Military Academy Library, Special Collections and Archives, West Point, New York

Herman Beukema Papers
Bruce Cooper Clarke Papers
Digital Collections
George A. Lincoln Papers
Williston Palmer Papers
RG 404: Records of the U.S. Military Academy
Special Collections, Item 241: Maxwell Taylor Letters

Published Primary Sources

Aguilar, Luis, ed. *Operation Zapata: The "Ultrasensitive" Report and Testimony of the Board of Inquiry on the Bay of Pigs.* Frederick, Md.: University Publications of America, 1981.

"And Now—The Atomic Army: Exclusive Interview with Gen. Maxwell D. Taylor, Chief of Staff, U.S. Army." *U.S. News and World Report* (3 February 1956), 64–73.

Bland, Larry I., ed. *The Papers of George Catlett Marshall.* Vol. 5, *"The Finest Soldier," January 1, 1945–January 7, 1947.* Baltimore, Md.: Johns Hopkins Univ. Press, 2003.

Chandler, Alfred D., Jr., and Louis Galambos, eds. *The Papers of Dwight D. Eisenhower.* Vol. 6, *Occupation, 1945.* Baltimore, Md.: Johns Hopkins Univ. Press, 1978.

———, eds. *The Papers of Dwight D. Eisenhower.* Vol. 7, *The Chief of Staff.* Baltimore, Md.: Johns Hopkins Univ. Press, 1978.

———, eds. *The Papers of Dwight D. Eisenhower.* Vol. 8, *The Chief of Staff.* Baltimore, Md.: Johns Hopkins Univ. Press, 1978.

———, eds. *The Papers of Dwight D. Eisenhower.* Vol. 9, *The Chief of Staff.* Baltimore, Md.: Johns Hopkins Univ. Press, 1978.

Department of Defense. *Report of the Office the Secretary of Defense Vietnam Task Force.* Washington, D.C.: Office of the Secretary of Defense, 1969. Released in their entirety by the National Archives in 2011, http://www.archives.gov/research/pentagon-papers.

Department of State. *Foreign Relations of the United States.* Multiple volumes for 1949–1968. Washington, D.C.: Government Printing Office, 1975–2003.

Griffith, Robert, ed. *Ike's Letters to a Friend, 1941–1958.* Lawrence: Univ. Press of Kansas, 1984.

Headquarters, United States Army Pacific. *The Handling of Prisoners of War during the Korean War.* Fort Shafter, Hawaii: Military History Office, US Army Pacific, June 1960.

May, Ernest R., and Philip D. Zelikow, eds. *The Kennedy Tapes: Inside the White House during the Cuban Missile Crisis.* 3 vols. Cambridge, Mass.: Harvard Univ. Press, 1997.

Peters, Gerhard, and John T. Woolley. *The American Presidency Project.* ProQuest History Vault (PQV).

Schlosser, Nicholas J., ed. *The Greene Papers: General Wallace M. Greene Jr. and the Escalation of the Vietnam War.* Quantico, Va.: History Division, US Marine Corps, 2015.

Taylor, Maxwell D. "Military Leadership: What Is It? Can It Be Taught?" *Distinguished Lecture Series,* 84–93. Washington, D.C.: National Defense University, spring 1977.

———. *West Point: Its Objectives and Methods.* West Point, N.Y.: US Military Academy, 1947.

———. "West Point Looks Ahead." Pamphlet. West Point, N.Y.: US Military Academy, 1946.

Twining, Nathan F. *Neither Liberty nor Safety: A Hard Look at U.S. Military Policy and Strategy.* New York: Holt, Rinehart and Winston, 1966.

US Declassified Documents Online (DDO). https://www.gale.com/c/us-declassified-documents-online.

The Vietnam Hearings, with an Introduction by J. William Fulbright. New York: Vintage Books, 1966.

Washington Center of Foreign Policy Research, Johns Hopkins University. *Developments in Military Technology and Their Impact on United States Strategy and Foreign Policy.* Washington, D.C.: Government Printing Office, 1959.

Memoirs and Articles by Participants

Ball, George W. *The Past Has Another Pattern: Memoirs.* New York: Norton, 1982.

Brandt, Willy. *People and Politics: The Years 1960–1975*. Translated by J. Maxwell Brownjohn. Boston: Little, Brown, 1976.
Butler, Ewan. *Berlin 1955*. New York: Praeger, 1955.
Clay, Lucius D. *Decision in Germany*. Garden City, N.Y.: Doubleday, 1950.
Collins, J. Lawton. *War in Peacetime: The History and Lessons of Korea*. Boston: Houghton Mifflin, 1969.
Dulles, John Foster. "Challenge and Response in United States Policy." *Foreign Affairs* 36, no. 1 (1957): 25–43.
Gallagher, Robert S. "Memories of Peace and War: An Exclusive Interview with General Maxwell D. Taylor." *American Heritage Magazine* 32, no. 3 (1981). https://www.americanheritage.com/index.php/content/memories-peace-and-war.
Gavin, James M. "Cavalry, and I Don't Mean Horses." *Harper's Magazine* 208, no. 1247 (April 1954), 54–60.
———. "New Divisional Organization." *Army-Navy-Air Force Register* 76, no. 3923 (12 February 1955): 1–2.
———. *War and Peace in the Space Age*. New York: Harper, 1958.
Herbert, Anthony B. *Soldier*. New York: Holt, Rinehart and Winston, 1973.
Howley, Frank L. *Berlin Command*. New York: Putnam, 1950.
[Hull, John E.] *The Autobiography of General John E. Hull, 1895–1975*. N.p.: Miriam Anderson, Mary Von Bargen, Mildred Head, and Dorothy A. Lynch, 1978.
Johnson, U. Alexis, with Jef Olivarius McAllister. *The Right Hand of Power*. Englewood Cliffs, N.J.: Prentice-Hall, 1984.
Krulak, Victor S. *Organization for National Security: A Study*. Cambridge, Mass.: US Strategic Institute Publishing Office, 1983.
Ky, Nguyen Cao. *Twenty Years and Twenty Days*. New York: Stein and Day, 1976.
LeMay, Curtis E., with MacKinlay Kantor. *Mission with LeMay: My Story*. New York: Doubleday, 1965.
McNamara, Robert S., with Brian VanDeMark. *In Retrospect: The Tragedy and Lessons of Vietnam*. New York: Crown, 1995.
Pearson, Drew. *Diaries, 1949–1959*. Edited by Tyler Abell. New York: Holt, Rinehart and Winston, 1974.
Phillips, Rufus. *Why Vietnam Matters: An Eyewitness Account of Lessons Not Learned*. Annapolis, Md.: Naval Institute Press, 2008.
Ridgway, Matthew B. *Soldier: The Memoirs of Matthew B. Ridgway*. New York: Harper, 1956.
———. *The Korean War*. Garden City, N.Y.: Doubleday, 1967.
Rostow, Walt W. "Vietnam and Asia." *Diplomatic History* 20, no. 3 (1996): 467–471.
Sharp, U. S. Grant. *Strategy for Defeat: Vietnam in Retrospect*. San Rafael, Calif.: Presidio Press, 1978.
Squires, Richard. *Auf dem Kriegspfad: Aufzeichnungen eines englischen Offiziers*. Berlin: Rutten Loening, 1951.
Sullivan, William H. *Obbligato 1939–1979: Notes on a Foreign Service Career*. New York: Norton, 1984.

Taylor, Maxwell D. "Changing Military Priorities." *AEI Foreign Policy and Defense Review* 1, no. 3 (1979): 2–13.
———. "How We Can Survive." *Look,* 19 January 1960, 56–63.
———. "Our Critical Military Need: One Defense Chief." *Look,* 22 December 1959, 111–121.
———. "Our Great Military Fallacy." *Look,* 24 November 1959, 27–31.
———. *Precarious Security.* New York: Norton, 1976.
———. "Reagan's Military Policy Is in Trouble." *Washington Post,* 2 November 1981.
———. *Responsibility and Response.* New York: Harper and Row, 1967.
———. "Security Will Not Wait." *Foreign Affairs* 39, no. 2 (1961): 174–184.
———. *Swords and Plowshares.* New York: Norton, 1972.
———. *The Uncertain Trumpet.* New York: Harper and Brothers, 1960.
———. "The United States—A Military Power Second to None?" *International Security* 1, no. 1 (1976): 49–55.
——— "The World-Wide Role and Capability of the Army." *Army Combat Forces Journal* 6, no. 2 (1955): 24–26.
Van Fleet, James. "The Truth about Korea, Part I: From a Man Now Free to Speak." *Life,* May 11, 1953, 126–142.
———. "The Truth about Korea, Part II: How We Can Win with What We Have." *Life,* May 18, 1953, 156–172.
Westmoreland, William C. *A Soldier Reports.* New York: Doubleday, 1976.

Secondary Literature

Ahern, Thomas L., Jr. *The CIA and the Generals: Covert Support to Military Government in South Vietnam.* Washington, D.C.: Central Intelligence Agency, Center for the Study of Intelligence, 2009.
Asselin, Pierre. *A Bitter Peace: Washington, Hanoi, and the Making of the Paris Agreement.* Chapel Hill: Univ. of North Carolina Press, 2002.
———. *Hanoi's Road to the Vietnam War, 1954–1965.* Berkeley: Univ. of California Press, 2013.
Atkinson, Rick. *The Guns at Last Light: The War in Western Europe, 1944–1945.* New York: Henry Holt, 2013.
Bacevich, Andrew J. *The New American Militarism: How Americans Are Seduced by War.* Oxford, UK: Oxford Univ. Press, 2005.
———. "The Paradox of Professionalism: Eisenhower, Ridgway, and the Challenge to Civilian Control, 1953–1955." *Journal of Military History* 61, no. 2 (1997): 303–333.
———. *The Pentomic Era: The U.S. Army between Korea and Vietnam.* Washington, D.C.: National Defense Univ. Press, 1986.
Barrett, David M. *Uncertain Warriors: Lyndon Johnson and His Vietnam Advisers.* Lawrence: Univ. Press of Kansas, 1993.
Bender, Bryan, and Wesley Morgan. "Generals Win Key Fight over Afghanistan They Lost with Obama." *Politico,* 22 August 2017. https://www.politico.com/story/2017/08/22/trump-generals-afghanistan-241922.

Bering, Henrik. *Outpost Berlin: The History of the American Military Forces in Berlin, 1945–1994*. Chicago: edition q, 1995.
Berman, Larry. *No Peace, No Honor: Nixon, Kissinger, and Betrayal in Vietnam*. New York: Free Press, 2001.
Beschloss, Michael. *The Crisis Years: Kennedy and Khrushchev, 1960–1963* (New York: HarperCollins, 1991.
Betros, Lance. *Raised from Granite: West Point since 1902*. College Station: Texas A&M Univ. Press, 2012.
Bird, Kai. *The Chairman: John J. McCloy and the Making of the American Establishment*. New York: Simon and Schuster, 1992.
Blair, Clay. *The Forgotten War: America in Korea, 1950–1953*. New York: Times Books, 1987.
Blight, James G., Janet M. Lang, and David A. Welch. *Virtual JFK: Vietnam if Kennedy Had Lived*. Lanham, Md.: Rowman and Littlefield, 2009.
Bodnar, John E. *The "Good War" in American Memory*. Baltimore, Md.: Johns Hopkins Univ. Press, 2010.
Booth, T. Michael, and Duncan Spencer. *Paratrooper: The Life of Gen. James Gavin*. New York: Simon and Schuster, 1994.
Brands, H. W. *The General vs. the President: MacArthur and Truman at the Brink of Nuclear War*. New York, Doubleday, 2016.
Brown, John Sloan. *Kevlar Legions: The Transformation of the U.S. Army, 1989–2005*. Washington, D.C.: US Army Center of Military History, 2011.
Buckingham, William A., Jr. *Operation Ranch Hand: The Air Force and Herbicides in Southeast Asia, 1961–1971*. Washington, D.C.: Office of Air Force History, 1982.
Buzzanco, Robert. *Masters of War: Military Dissent and Politics in the Vietnam Era*. Cambridge, UK: Cambridge Univ. Press, 1996.
Carter, Donald A. "Eisenhower Versus the Generals." *Journal of Military History* 71, no. 4 (2007): 1169–1199.
———. *Forging the Shield: The U.S. Army in Europe, 1951–1962*. Washington, D.C.: US Army Center of Military History, 2014.
Casey, Steven. *Selling the Korean War: Propaganda, Politics, and Public Opinion in the United States, 1950–1953*. Oxford, UK: Oxford Univ. Press, 2008.
Clarfield, Gerard. *Security with Solvency: Dwight D. Eisenhower and the Shaping of the American Military Establishment*. Westport, Conn.: Praeger, 1999.
Clodfelter, Mark. *The Limits of Air Power: The American Bombing of North Vietnam*. New York: Free Press, 1989.
Coakley, Robert W., Karl E. Cocke, and Daniel P. Griffin. *Demobilization Following the Korean War*. Washington, D.C.: Histories Division, Office of the Chief of Military History, 1968.
Coffman, Edward M. *The Regulars: The American Army, 1898–1941*. Cambridge, Mass.: Harvard Univ. Press, 2004.
Coleman, David G. "The Berlin-Korea Parallel: Berlin and American National Security in Light of the Korean War." *Australasian Journal of American Studies* 18, no. 1 (1999): 19–41.
Condit, Doris M. *History of the Office of the Secretary of Defense*. Vol. 2, *The*

Test of War, 1950–1953. Washington, D.C.: Historical Office, Office of the Secretary of Defense, 1988.
Condit, Kenneth W. *History of the Joint Chiefs of Staff.* Vol. 6, *The Joint Chiefs of Staff and National Policy, 1955–1956.* Washington, D.C.: Historical Office, Joint Staff, 1992.
Cooper, Chester L. *The Lost Crusade: America in Vietnam.* New York: Dodd, 1970.
Cosmas, Graham A. *MACV: The Joint Command in the Years of Escalation, 1962–1967.* Washington, D.C.: US Army Center of Military History, 2006.
Crackel, Theodore J. *West Point: A Bicentennial History.* Lawrence: Univ. Press of Kansas, 2002.
Crane, Conrad. *American Airpower Strategy in Korea, 1950–1953.* Lawrence: Univ. Press of Kansas, 2000.
Daddis, Gregory A. *No Sure Victory: Measuring U.S. Army Effectiveness and Progress in the Vietnam War.* Oxford, UK: Oxford Univ. Press, 2011.
———. *Westmoreland's War: Reassessing American Strategy in Vietnam.* Oxford, UK: Oxford Univ. Press, 2014.
Dockrill, Saki. *Eisenhower's New Look National Security Policy, 1953–1961.* Houndmills, UK: Macmillan Press, 1996.
Dolski, Michael R. *D-Day Remembered: The Normandy Landings in American Collective Memory.* Knoxville: Univ. of Tennessee Press, 2016.
Donnelly, William H. "Bilko's Army: A Crisis in Command?" *Journal of Military History* 75, no. 4 (2011): 1183–1215.
Duke, Simon W., and Wolfgang Krieger, eds. *U.S. Military Forces in Europe: The Early Years, 1945–1950.* Boulder, Colo.: Westview Press, 1993.
Fairchild, Byron R., and Walter S. Poole. *The History of the Joint Chiefs of Staff.* Vol. 7, *The Joint Chiefs of Staff and National Policy, 1957–1960.* Washington, D.C.: Office of Joint History, Office of the Chairman of the Joint Chiefs of Staff, 2000.
Farrar-Hockley, Anthony. *The British Part in the Korean War.* Vol. 2, *An Honourable Discharge.* London: HMSO, 1995.
Fautua, David T. "The 'Long Pull' Army: NSC 68, the Korean War, and the Creation of the Cold War Army." *Journal of Military History* 61, no. 1 (1997): 93–120.
Fehrenbach, T. R. *This Kind of War: A Study in Unpreparedness.* New York: Macmillan, 1963.
Fergsuon, Niall. *Kissinger.* Vol. 1, *1923–1968: The Idealist.* New York, Penguin Press, 2015.
Fitzgerald, David. *Learning to Forget: US Army Counterinsurgency Doctrine and Practice from Vietnam to Iraq.* Stanford, Calif.: Stanford Univ. Press, 2013.
Fleming, Thomas J. *West Point: The Men and Times of the U.S. Military Academy.* New York: Morrow, 1969.
Fry, Joseph A. *The American South and the Vietnam War: Belligerence, Protest, and Agony in Dixie.* Lexington: Univ. Press of Kentucky, 2015.
Fukuyama, Francis. *The End of History and the Last Man.* New York: Free Press, 1992.

Fursenko, Alexander, and Timothy Naftali. *"One Hell of a Gamble": The Secret History of the Cuban Missile Crisis, 1958–1964.* New York: Norton, 1997.
Gaddis, John Lewis. *Strategies of Containment: A Critical Appraisal of American National Security Policy during the Cold War,* rev. ed. Oxford, UK: Oxford Univ. Press, 2005.
Gaddis, John Lewis, Philip H. Gordon, Ernest R. May, and Jonathan Rosenberg, eds. *Cold War Statesmen Confront the Bomb: Nuclear Diplomacy since 1945.* Oxford, UK: Oxford Univ. Press, 1999.
Geelhoed, E. Bruce. *Charles E. Wilson and Controversy at the Pentagon, 1953 to 1957.* Detroit, Mich.: Wayne State Univ. Press, 1979.
Givens, Seth A. "Cold War Capital: The United States, the European Allies, and the Fight for Berlin, 1945–94." Ph.D. diss., Ohio University, 2018.
Goldberg, Sheldon A. *From Disarmament to Rearmament: The Reversal of U.S. Policy toward West Germany, 1946–1955.* Athens: Ohio Univ. Press, 2017.
Goldstein, Gordon M. *Lessons in Disaster: McGeorge Bundy and the Path to War in Vietnam.* New York: Times Books, 2008.
Gole, Henry G. *General William E. DePuy: Preparing the Army for Modern War.* Lexington: Univ. Press of Kentucky, 2008.
Gordon, Michael R., and Bernard E. Trainor. *Cobra II: The Inside Story of the Invasion and Occupation of Iraq.* New York: Pantheon, 2006.
Grathwol, Robert P., and Donita M. Moorhus. *Cold War Outpost: American Forces in Berlin, 1945–1994.* Washington, D.C.: Department of Defense, Legacy Resource Management Program, 1994.
Halberstam, David. *The Best and the Brightest.* New York: Random House, 1972.
Hammerich, Helmut. *Das Heer 1950 bis 1970: Konzeption, Organisation, Aufstellung.* Munich: R. Oldenbourg Verlag, 2006.
Hanson, Thomas E. *Combat Ready? The Eighth U.S. Army on the Eve of the Korean War.* College Station: Texas A&M Univ. Press, 2010.
Harrington, Daniel F. *Berlin on the Brink: The Blockade, the Airlift, and the Early Cold War.* Lexington: Univ. Press of Kentucky, 2012.
Harris, J. P. *Vietnam's High Ground: Armed Struggle for the Central Highlands, 1954–1965.* Lawrence: Univ. Press of Kansas, 2016.
Harrison, Benjamin T., and Christopher L. Mosher, "John T. McNaughton and Vietnam: The Early Years as Assistant Secretary of Defense, 1964–195." *History* 92, no. 308 (2007): 496–514.
Harrison, Hope M. *Driving the Soviets up the Wall: Soviet-East German Relations, 1953–1961.* Princeton, N.J.: Princeton Univ. Press, 2003.
Hawkins, Glen R. *United States Army Force Structure and Force Design Initiatives, 1939–1989.* Washington, D.C.: US Army Center of Military History, 1991.
Haynes, Richard F. "The Defense Unification Battle, 1947–1950: The Army." *Prologue: The Journal of the National Archives* 7, no. 1 (1975): 27–31.
Hermes, Walter. *The United States Army in the Korean War: Truce Tent and Fighting Front.* Washington, D.C.: US Army Center for Military History, 1966.
Herring, George C. *LBJ and Vietnam: A Different Kind of War.* Austin: Univ. of Texas Press, 1994.
Hersh, Seymour M. *The Dark Side of Camelot.* New York: Little, Brown, 1997.

Hershberg, James G. *Marigold: The Lost Chance for Peace in Vietnam*. Stanford, Calif.: Stanford Univ. Press, 2012.

Hoffmann, George F. *Cold War Casualty: The Court-Martial of Major General Robert W. Grow*. Kent, Ohio: Kent State Univ. Press, 1993.

Hunnicutt, R. P. *Patton: A History of the American Main Battle Tank*. Novato, Calif.: Presidio Press, 1984.

Jablonsky, David. *War by Land, Sea, and Air: Dwight Eisenhower and the Concept of Unified Command*. New Haven, Conn.: Yale Univ. Press, 2010.

Jacobsen, Annie. *The Pentagon's Brain: An Uncensored History of DARPA, America's Top Secret Military Research Agency* (New York: Little, Brown, 2015.

Janowitz, Morris. *The Professional Soldier: A Social and Political Portrait*. New York: Free Press, 1960.

Jones, Frank Leith. *Blowtorch Bob: Robert Komer, Vietnam, and American Cold War Strategy*. Annapolis, Md.: Naval Institute Press, 2013.

Jordan, Amos A., Jr., ed. *Issues of National Security in the 1970s: Essays Presented to Colonel George A. Lincoln on His Sixtieth Birthday*. New York: Praeger, 1967.

Jordan, Robert S. *An Unsung Soldier: The Life of General Andrew J. Goodpaster*. Annapolis, Md.: Naval Institute Press, 2013.

Kaldor, Mary. *New and Old Wars: Organised Violence in a Global Era*, 3rd ed. Cambridge, UK: Polity Press, 2012.

Kaplan, Edward N. *To Kill Nations: American Strategy in the Air-Atomic Age and the Rise of Mutually Assured Destruction*. Ithaca, N.Y.: Cornell Univ. Press, 2015.

Kaplan, Fred. *The Insurgents: David Petraeus and the Plot to Change the American Way of War*. New York: Simon and Schuster, 2013.

Kaplan, Lawrence S. *The United States and NATO: The Formative Years*. Lexington: Univ. Press of Kentucky, 1984.

Kaplan, Lawrence S., Ronald D. Landa, and Edward J. Drea. *History of the Office of the Secretary of Defense*. Vol. 5, *The McNamara Ascendancy, 1961–1965*. Washington, D.C.: Historical Office, Office of the Secretary of Defense, 2006.

Karber, Phillip A., and Jerald A. Combs. "The United States, NATO, and the Soviet Threat to Western Europe: Military Estimates and Policy Opinions, 1945–1963." *Diplomatic History* 22, no. 3 (1998): 399–429.

Keiderling, Gerhard. *Berlin 1945–1986: Geschichte der Hauptstadt der DDR*. Berlin: Dietz Verlag, 1987.

Kempe, Frederick. *Berlin 1961: Kennedy, Khrushchev, and the Most Dangerous Place on Earth*. New York: Putnam, 2011.

Khong, Yuen Foong. *Analogies at War: Korea, Munich, Dien Bien Phu, and the Vietnam Decisions of 1965*. Princeton, N.J.: Princeton Univ. Press, 1992.

Kinnard, Douglas. *The Certain Trumpet: Maxwell Taylor and the American Experience in Vietnam*. Washington, D.C.: Brassey's, 1991.

———. "Civil-Military Relations: The President and the General." *Parameters* 15, no. 2 (1985): 19–29.

Kissinger, Henry A. *Nuclear Weapons and Foreign Policy*. Garden City, N.Y.: Doubleday, 1957.

Kitfield, James. *Prodigal Soldiers: How the Generation of Officers Born of Vietnam Revolutionized the American Style of War.* New York: Simon and Schuster, 1995.

Kohn, Richard H. "The Danger of Militarization in an Endless War on Terrorism." *Journal of Military History* 73, no. 1 (2009): 177–208.

Kolko, Gabriel. *Anatomy of a War: Vietnam, the United States, and the Modern Historical Experience.* New York: Pantheon, 1985.

Kyle, Deborah M. "Congress Serious about Defense Reform; 33 Senate Witnesses Endorse Change." *Armed Forces Journal International* 121, no. 7 (February 1984): 10–24.

Laslie, Brian D. *The Air Force Way of War: Tactics and Training after Vietnam.* Lexington: Univ. Press of Kentucky, 2015.

Lederman, Gordon Nathaniel. *Reorganizing the Joint Chiefs of Staff: The Goldwater-Nichols Act of 1968.* Westport, Conn.: Greenwood Press, 1999.

Leighton, Richard M. *History of the Office of the Secretary of Defense: Strategy, Money, and the New Look, 1953–1956.* Washington, D.C.: Office of the Secretary of Defense, Historical Office, 2001.

Li, Xiaobing. *China's Battle for Korea: The 1951 Spring Offensive.* Bloomington: Indiana Univ. Press, 2014.

Li, Xiaobing, Allan R. Millett, and Bin Yu, eds. *Mao's Generals Remember Korea.* Lawrence: Univ. Press of Kansas, 2001.

Linn, Brian McAllister. *The Echo of Battle: The Army's Way of War.* Cambridge, Mass.: Harvard Univ. Press, 2007.

———. *Elvis's Army: Cold War GIs and the Atomic Battlefield.* Cambridge, Mass.: Harvard Univ. Press, 2016.

Locher, James R., III. *Victory on the Potomac: The Goldwater-Nichols Act Unifies the Pentagon.* College Station: Texas A&M Univ. Press, 2002.

Logevall, Fredrik. *Choosing War: The Lost Chance for Peace and the Escalation of War in Vietnam.* Berkeley: Univ. of California Press, 1999.

Macgregor, Douglas A. *Transformation under Fire: Reevaluating How America Fights.* Westport, Conn.: Praeger, 2003.

MacGregor, Morris J., Jr. *Integration of the Armed Forces, 1940–1965.* Washington, D.C.: US Army Center of Military History, 1981.

Mahon, John K., and Romana Danysh. *Infantry, Part I: Regular Army.* Washington, D.C.: Office of the Chief of Military History, US Army, 1972.

Maloney, Sean. "Berlin Contingency Planning: Prelude to Flexible Response." *Journal of Strategic Studies* 25, no. 1 (2002): 99–134.

Mansoor, Peter R. *Surge: My Journey with General David Petraeus and the Remaking of the Iraq War.* New Haven: Yale Univ. Press, 2013.

Marshall, S.L.A. *Pork Chop Hill: The American Fighting Man in Action, Korea, Spring 1953.* New York: Morrow, 1956.

Masland, John W., and Laurence I. Radway. *Soldiers and Scholars: Military Education and National Policy.* Princeton, N.J.: Princeton Univ. Press, 1957.

Mastny, Vojtech, Sven G. Holtsmark, and Andreas Wenger, eds. *War Plans and Alliances in the Cold War: Threat Perceptions in East and West.* London: Routledge, 2006.

Masuda, Hajimu. *Cold War Crucible: The Korean Conflict and the Postwar World.* Cambridge, Mass.: Harvard Univ. Press, 2015.
Maulucci, Thomas W., and Detlef Junker, eds. *GIs in Germany: The Social, Economic, Cultural, and Political History of the American Military Presence.* Cambridge, UK: Cambridge Univ. Press, 2013.
McClenahan, William, Jr., and William H. Becker. *Eisenhower and the Cold War Economy.* Baltimore, Md.: Johns Hopkins Univ. Press, 2011.
McFarland, Linda. *Cold War Strategist: Stuart Symington and the Search for National Security.* Westport, Conn.: Praeger, 2001.
McGrath, John J. *The Brigade: A History.* Fort Leavenworth, Kans.: Combat Studies Institute Press, 2004.
McMaster, H. R. *Dereliction of Duty: Johnson, McNamara, the Joint Chiefs of Staff, and the Lies that Led to Vietnam.* New York: Harper, 1997.
Michaels, Jeffrey H. "Managing Counterinsurgency: The Special Group (CI), 1962–1966." *Journal of Strategic Studies* 35, no. 1 (2012): 33–61.
Miller, Edward. *Misalliance: Ngo Dinh Diem, the United States, and the Fate of South Vietnam.* Cambridge, Mass.: Harvard Univ. Press, 2013.
Millett, Allan R. *The War for Korea: They Came from the North, 1950–1951.* Lawrence: Univ. Press of Kansas, 2010.
Milne, David. *America's Rasputin: Walt Rostow and the Vietnam War.* New York: Hill and Wang, 2008.
Morrison, Samuel Eliot. *History of U.S. Naval Operations in World War II.* Vol. 9, *Sicily—Salerno—Anzio, January 1943–June 1944.* Boston: Little, Brown, 1954.
Moyar, Mark. *Triumph Forsaken: The Vietnam War, 1954–1965.* Cambridge, UK: Cambridge Univ. Press, 2006.
Murphy, Robert. *Diplomat among Warriors.* Garden City, N.Y.: Doubleday, 1964.
Murray, Williamson, and Allan R. Millett. *A War to Be Won: Fighting the Second World War.* Cambridge, Mass.: Harvard Univ. Press, 2001.
Nelson, C. Richard. *The Life and Work of General Andrew J. Goodpaster: Best Practices in National Security Affairs.* Lanham, Md.: Rowman and Littlefield, 2016.
Nguyen, Lien Hang T. *Hanoi's War: An International History of the War for Peace in Vietnam.* Chapel Hill: Univ. of North Carolina Press, 2012.
O'Connell, Aaron B., ed. *Our Latest Longest War: Losing Hearts and Minds in Afghanistan.* Chicago: Univ. of Chicago Press, 2017.
Pach. Chester J., Jr., and Elmo Richardson. *The Presidency of Dwight D. Eisenhower,* rev. ed. Lawrence: Univ. Press of Kansas, 1991.
Palmer, Bruce Palmer, Jr., ed. *Grand Strategy for the 1980s.* Washington, D.C.: American Enterprise Institute for Public Policy Research, 1978.
Paret, Peter, ed. *Makers of Modern Strategy from Machiavelli to the Nuclear Age.* Princeton, N.J.: Princeton Univ. Press, 1986.
Parker, Jay M. "The Colonels' Revolt: Eisenhower, the Army, and the Politics of National Security." Newport, R.I.: Naval War College, 1994.
Parrish, Thomas. *Berlin in the Balance: The Blockade, the Airlift, the First Major Battle of the Cold War.* Reading, Mass.: Addison-Wesley, 1998.

Pedlow, Gregory. "Flexible Response Before MC 14/3: General Lauris Norstad and the Second Berlin Crisis." *Storia delle Relazione Internazionali* 13, no. 1 (1998): 235–268.

Perry, Mark. *Four Stars: The Inside Story of the Forty-Year Battle between the Joint Chiefs of Staff and America's Civilian Leaders.* Boston: Houghton Mifflin, 1989.

———. *The Pentagon's Wars: The Military's Undeclared War against America's Presidents.* New York: Basic Books, 2017.

Pogue, Forrest. *George C. Marshall.* Vol. 4, *Statesman, 1945–1959.* New York: Viking, 1987.

Poole, Walter S. *The Joint Chiefs of Staff and National Policy.* Vol. 8, *1961–1964.* Washington, D.C.: Office of Joint History, Office of the Chairman of the Joint Chiefs of Staff, 2011.

Preble, Christopher A. *John F. Kennedy and the Missile Gap* (DeKalb: Northern Illinois Univ. Press, 2004.

Preston, Andrew. *The War Council: McGeorge Bundy, the NSC, and Vietnam.* Cambridge, Mass.: Harvard Univ. Press, 2006.

Price, Frank James. *Troy H. Middleton: A Biography.* Baton Rouge: Louisiana State Univ. Press, 1974.

Raymond, Jack. *Power at the Pentagon.* New York: Harper and Row, 1964.

Rearden, Steven L. *Council of War: A History of the Joint Chiefs of Staff, 1942–1991.* Washington, D.C.: Joint History Office, Joint Chiefs of Staff, 2012.

———. *History of the Office of the Secretary of Defense: The Formative Years, 1947–1950.* Washington, D.C.: Historical Office, Office of the Secretary of Defense, 1984.

Ricks, Thomas E. *The Generals: American Military Command from World War II to Today.* New York: Penguin, 2012.

Rosenberg, David Alan. "The Origins of Overkill: Nuclear Weapons and American Strategy, 1945–1960." *International Security* 7, no. 4 (1983): 3–71.

Ross, Steven T. *American War Plans 1945–1950: Strategies for Defeating the Soviet Union.* London: Frank Cass, 1996.

Rostow, Walt W. "The Case for the War." *Times Literary Supplement,* 9 June 1995.

Rupieper, Hermann-Josef. *Der besetzte Verbündete: Die amerikanische Deutschlandpolitik 1949–1955.* Opladen: Westdeutscher Verlag, 1991.

Rust, William J. *So Much to Lose: John F. Kennedy and American Policy in Laos.* Lexington: Univ. Press of Kentucky, 2014.

Sager, John. "Universal Military Training and the Struggle to Define American Identity during the Cold War." *Federal History* 5, no. 1 (2013): 57–74.

Sambaluk, Nicholas Michael. *The Other Space Race: Eisenhower and the Quest for Aerospace Security.* Annapolis, Md.: Naval Institute Press, 2015.

Schake, Kori, and Jim Mattis, eds. *Warriors and Citizens: American Views of Our Military.* Stanford, Calif.: Hoover Institution Press, 2016.

Schlosser, Nicholas J. *Cold War on the Airwaves: The Radio Propaganda War against East Germany.* Champaign: Univ. of Illinois Press, 2015.

Schratz, Paul R., ed. *Evolution of the American Military Establishment since World War II.* Lexington, Va.: George C. Marshall Research Foundation, 1978.

Schwartz, Thomas Alan. *America's Germany: John J. McCloy and the Federal Republic of Germany.* Cambridge, Mass.: Harvard Univ. Press, 1991.

Sepp, Kalev I. "The Pentomic Puzzle: The Influence of Personality and Nuclear Weapons on U.S. Army Organization, 1952–1958." *Army History* 51 (2001): 1–13.

Sheehan, Neil. *A Bright Shining Lie: John Paul Vann and America in Vietnam.* New York: Random House, 1988.

Shulimson, Jack, and Graham A. Cosmas. *The Joint Chiefs of Staff and the War in Vietnam, 1960–1968.* 3 vols. Washington, D.C.: Office of Joint History, Joint Chiefs of Staff, 2009–2012.

Smith, Jean Edward. *Lucius D. Clay: An American Life.* New York: Henry Holt, 1990.

Smyser, W. R. *Kennedy and the Berlin Wall: "A Hell of a Lot Better than a War."* Lanham, Md.: Rowman and Littlefield, 2009.

Snead, David L. *The Gaither Committee, Eisenhower, and the Cold War.* Columbus: Ohio State Univ. Press, 1999.

Soffer, Jonathan M. *General Matthew B. Ridgway: From Progressivism to Reaganism, 1895–1993.* Westport, Conn.: Praeger, 1998.

Sorley, Lewis. *Honorable Warrior: General Harold K. Johnson and the Ethics of Command.* Lawrence: Univ. Press of Kansas, 1998.

Spiller, Roger J. *"Not War But Like War": The American Intervention in Lebanon.* Leavenworth Paper No. 3. Fort Leavenworth, Kans.: US Army Command and General Staff College, 1981.

Steege, Paul. *Black Market, Cold War: Everyday Life in Berlin, 1946–1949.* Cambridge, UK: Cambridge Univ. Press, 2007.

Stewart, Richard, ed., *American Military History.* Vol. 2, *The United States Army in a Global Era, 1917–2008.* Washington, D.C.: US Army Center of Military History, 2010.

Stromseth, Jane E. *The Origins of Flexible Response: NATO's Debate over Strategy in the 1960s.* New York: St. Martin's Press, 1988.

Stueck, William I. *The Korean War: An International History.* Princeton, N.J.: Princeton Univ. Press, 1995.

Taaffe, Stephen. *MacArthur's Korean War Generals.* Lawrence: Univ. Press of Kansas, 2016.

Taylor, John M. *General Maxwell Taylor: The Sword and the Pen.* New York: Doubleday, 1989.

Taylor, William A. *Every Citizen a Soldier: The Campaign for Universal Military Training after World War II.* College Station: Texas A&M Univ. Press, 2014.

Thomas, Evan. *Ike's Bluff: President Eisenhower's Secret Battle to Save the World.* New York: Little, Brown, 2012.

Thoß, Bruno. *NATO-Strategie und nationale Verteidigungsplanung: Planung und Aufbau der Bundeswehr unter den Bedingungen einer massiven atomaren Vergeltungsstrategie 1952–1960.* Munich: R. Oldenbourg Verlag, 2006.

Toczek, David M. *The Battle of Ap Bac: They Did Everything but Learn from It.* Westport, Conn.: Greenwood, 2001.

Tomes, Robert R. *Apocalypse Then: American Intellectuals and the Vietnam War, 1954–1975.* New York: New York Univ. Press, 1998.

———. *US Defense Strategy from Vietnam to Operation Iraqi Freedom: Military Innovation and the New American Way of War, 1973–2003*. London: Routledge, 2007.
Trachtenberg, Marc. *A Constructed Peace: The Making of the European Settlement, 1945–1963*. Princeton, N.J.: Princeton Univ. Press, 1999.
Trauschweizer, Ingo. *The Cold War U.S. Army: Building Deterrence for Limited War*. Lawrence: Univ. Press of Kansas, 2008.
———. "Learning with an Ally: The U.S. Army and the *Bundeswehr* in the Cold War." *Journal of Military History* 72, no. 2 (2008): 477–508.
———. "Tanks at Checkpoint Charlie: Lucius Clay and the Berlin Crisis, 1961–1962." *Cold War History* 6, no. 2 (2006): 205–228.
Tusa, Ann. *The Last Division: Berlin and the Wall*. London: Hodder and Stoughton, 1996.
Tusa, Ann, and John Tusa. *The Berlin Blockade*. London: Hodder and Stoughton, 1988.
Tyroler, Charles, II, ed. *Alerting America: The Papers of the Committee on the Present Danger*. Washington, D.C.: Pergamon-Brassey's, 1984.
Watson, Robert J. *History of the Joint Chiefs of Staff*. Vol. 5, *The Joint Chiefs of Staff and National Policy, 1953–1954*. Washington, D.C.: Historical Division, Joint Chiefs of Staff, 1986.
———. *History of the Office of the Secretary of Defense*. Vol. 4, *Into the Missile Age, 1956–1960*. Washington, D.C.: Historical Office, Office of the Secretary of Defense, 1997.
Wehrle, Edmund F., Jr. "'A Good Bad Deal': John F. Kennedy, W. Averell Harriman, and the Neutralization of Laos, 1961–1962." *Pacific Historical Review* 67, no. 3 (1998): 349–377.
Weinberger, Sharon. *The Imagineers of War: The Untold History of DARPA, the Pentagon Agency that Changed the World*. New York: Knopf, 2017.
West, Bing. *The Wrong War: Grit, Strategy, and the Way Out of Afghanistan*. New York: Random House, 2011.
Wills, Steven T. "Replacing the Maritime Strategy: The Change in Naval Strategy from 1989 to 1994." Ph.D. diss., Ohio University, 2017.
Wilson, John B. *Maneuver and Firepower: The Evolution of Divisions and Separate Brigades*. Washington, D.C.: US Army Center of Military History, 1998.
Woods, Randall B. *Shadow Warrior: William Egan Colby and the CIA*. New York: Basic Books, 2013.
Zhai, Qiang. *China and the Vietnam Wars, 1950–1975*. Chapel Hill: Univ. of North Carolina Press, 2000.
Zhang, Shu Guang. *Mao's Military Romanticism: China and the Korean War, 1950–1953*. Lawrence: Univ. Press of Kansas, 1995.

Index

Abrams, General Creighton, 152, 190
Absolute Weapon, The (Brodie), 19
Acheson, Dean, 19, 40, 43, 46, 54–55, 188
Adenauer, Konrad, 43
AFAK (Armed Forces Assistance to Korea), 63, 64, 67
Afghanistan war, 209, 210
Africa, 104, 137, 198, 199, 202
African American soldiers, 52
airborne divisions, 22–23
Air Force, 25, 31, 68, 78, 89, 91
airpower, 31, 119, 126; dominant role in modern warfare, 30; "Douhet theory" on, 155; enemy, 52; excessive reliance on, 74; in Korean War, 62, 88, 153; strategic bombing, 156, 159, 173, 188; in Vietnam War, 120, 135; in World War II, 119. *See also* Rolling Thunder, Operation
Alexander, Brigadier General, 26
Alexander, Colonel Roger, 20
Alexander, Field Marshal Sir Harold, 12
alliance politics, 72
Alsop, Joseph, 94
American Legion, 23
Anderson, Admiral George, 127, 130, 196
Anderson, Robert B., 99
Annapolis (Naval Academy), 19, 26, 32, 33
arms race, 69, 77, 80, 84, 201, 205, 206, 208

Armstrong, Hamilton Fish, 72, 101
Army Department, 22, 24, 28
Army Hour, The (radio program), 90
Army Intelligence, 51
Army War College, 51, 79, 96
ARVN (Army of the Republic of Vietnam), 120–21, 138, 150, 196; counterinsurgency and, 175; coup against Diem and, 134; I Corps, 140, 143, 144, 167, 179, 190; in Laos, 147; MACV and, 162; Ranger units, 122; shortcomings of, 128–29; Special Forces, 140; US troops in supporting role, 163. *See also* Vietnam, South (Republic of Vietnam)
Asia, 104, 137, 198
ATFA (Atomic Field Army), 77
atomic battlefield, 66, 82; effect of radiation, 85; money/manpower limits and, 73; number of troops and, 77
atomic weapons. *See* nuclear (atomic) weapons

Badoglio, Marshal Pietro, 11, 12
Ball, George, 124, 163–64
Barrel Roll, Operation, 156
Baruch, Bernard, 37
Basic National Security Policy papers, 98, 198
battle group concept, 65–66
Baudouin, king of Belgium, 206
Baxter, James Phinney, 15

285

286 Index

Bennett, Donald, 84
Berlin crises, 3, 32, 36–49, 72, 74, 76, 207; airlift to West Berlin (1948), 38, 115; Allied military strength and, 45, 46; building of Wall (1961), 102, 114; Kennedy and, 101, 113–17; West Berlin and refugees from East Germany, 113; West Berlin economic situation, 39–40
Beukema, Herman, 19, 20, 26, 33
Big Picture, The (army television program), 90, 168
Bissell, Richard, 107, 124
Blücher, Franz, 43
Bohlen, Charles, 195
Bolling, General Alexander R., 51
Bolté, General Charles, 49
Bonin Islands, 32
Bourne, Commandant Geoffrey (British Army), 41, 44
Bowie, Robert, 46
Bowles, Chester, 117, 123
Boy Scouts of America, 8
Bracken, John, 24
Bradley, General Omar, 7, 8, 11, 13, 32, 94
Brandt, Willy, 49, 102, 195
Braun, Wernher von, 91
Briggs, Ellis, 58, 61, 63, 67
Britain, 29, 30; Berlin Crisis and, 42, 45, 47, 49; economic performance in World War II, 17; Korean War and, 62; war in Malaya, 37, 195; West Berlin economy and, 39
Brodie, Bernard, 19
Bruce, David, 195
Brucker, Wilber, 72, 93
building block principle, 85
Bundy, McGeorge, 102, 115, 152, 188; escalation of land war in Vietnam and, 144–45, 162, 166; Taylor criticized by, 155
Bundy, William, 162
Bunker, Ellsworth, 189, 190
bureaucracy, 3, 90, 97, 98, 101, 109; counterinsurgency policy and, 174; dogma in strategy and, 98; linked in NSC, 207; Taylor as master manipulator within, 4; unified, 6, 112
Burke, Arleigh, 1, 74, 99, 102, 106, 204
Buzzanco, Robert, 2
Byroade, Henry, 42

Cambodia, 119, 144, 159, 188
Cao Dai sect, in Vietnam, 165
Carboni, General Giacomo, 11, 12
Carroll, Joseph, 126
Carter, Jimmy, 204
Carver, George, 188
Castro, Fidel, 100, 104, 107, 108, 109
China, 30, 41, 51, 117, 128, 191; artillery attacks on Taiwan Strait islands, 67; atomic weapons capability of, 144; insurgencies and, 137; in Korean War, 53, 54, 55, 59, 62, 153, 154, 180; political role in Africa, 199; as power center, 201; rift with Soviet Union, 104; rise of, 197; Vietnam War and, 164, 178, 179
Church, Senator Frank, 179
CIA (Central Intelligence Agency), 51, 110, 133, 173; Bay of Pigs invasion and, 106, 107–8; directorate for science and technology, 192; public confidence in, 193; Vietnam War and, 123, 124, 139, 141, 159
CINCPAC, 61, 87
Citadel, The, 34
civil-military relations, 2, 3, 99, 209, 210; Taylor's impact on, 101; unresolved issues in, 4
Clark, General Mark, 52, 55, 56–57; performance of ROK troops and, 60; prisoner exchange in Korea and, 58; retirement of, 66
Clarke, General Bruce C., 15, 60, 116
Clausewitz, Carl von, 28, 97
Clay, General Lucius, 37, 39, 48, 99
Clifford, Clark, 172, 179, 180, 182–83, 188, 190

Clifton, General Chester, 102
Co, General Nguyen Huu, 167
Colby, William, 200
Cold War, 1, 3, 6, 11, 104, 205; Army's role in, 82; Berlin blockade and, 37, 49; complexities of, 197–98, 201; end of, 206, 208; expansion of, 38, 46; perpetual military mobilization and, 69; strategy and, 28, 71, 76–77; US domestic political climate and, 50–51; Vietnam War and, 166, 178, 179, 193
Collins, General J. Lawton, 11, 49, 50, 51, 55, 58, 67
colonialism, 111, 123
combat readiness, 54, 64, 78, 80
Command and General Staff College, 11, 28, 85
Committee on the Present Danger, 200, 206
communications systems, 12, 38, 67, 83, 84, 92, 198; air strikes against, 152; in atomic battlefield, 77; command levels and, 85; Communist network in Vietnam, 158; increasing importance of, 66; NSA-operated, 192; rebuilding after Korean War and, 64; signals intelligence and, 192–93; West Point curriculum and, 15
communism, 30, 95; in China, 41, 51; insurgencies and, 111; lack of incentive for workers under, 39; in South Vietnam, 121; threat of spread to emerging nations, 104
Compton, Karl, 14, 15, 16, 20
Congo, 101
Congress, US, 1, 6, 20, 27, 74, 95, 198; defense budgets and, 70, 94; unified war planning and, 69
containment policy, 58
conventional war, 3, 35, 68, 111
Cooper, Chester, 194, 195
CORDS (Civil Operations and Revolutionary Development Support), 175

Council on Foreign Relations, 5, 81, 88, 104
counterinsurgency, 1, 3, 105, 109, 137, 209; changes in US armed forces required by, 112–13; numerical superiority required for, 170; oil spot approach to, 177; South Vietnam as laboratory for, 110, 112; South Vietnamese army and paramilitary, 154
"criminal war," 169, 181
Cronkite, Walter, 134, 185
Cuba, 104, 111, 126; Bay of Pigs invasion, 100, 101, 102, 106–8, 109, 131; political role in Africa, 199
Cuban Missile Crisis, 109, 126–28, 142
Cushman, John, 97

Davidson, General Garrison, 13–14, 85
Dean, Major General William, 63
Decker, General George, 117, 131
defense budgets, 73, 89, 105, 113, 204; function-based model, 103; Korean War and, 50, 51, 53, 70; missile technology and, 94; as percentage of gross national product, 200
Defense Department, 6, 68, 93, 96, 189; budgets called for, 53, 70; centralized data gathering and analysis at, 192; Cold War strategy and, 76–77; focus on general war, 97; paramilitary operations and, 108; study group on unification of armed forces, 32; Vietnam War and, 123. *See also* War Department
Defense Reorganization Act, 95
de Gaulle, Charles, 106
Delafield, Brigadier General John Ross, 81
demobilization, postwar, 5, 49
Democratic Party, 76, 80
Democratic Republic of Vietnam (DRV). *See* Vietnam, North (DRV)

288   Index

DePuy, General William E., 97, 184, 188
desegregation, in US military, 51, 52
DIA (Defense Intelligence Agency), 126, 173, 192, 193
Diem, Ngo Dinh, 118, 119, 122, 125, 153, 160; autocratic methods of, 121; coup against, 120–21, 133–35, 139, 169; downfall as pivot point of Vietnam War, 178
diplomacy, 168–69
domino theory, 169, 179
Dulles, Allen, 19, 106
Dulles, John Foster, 63, 67, 75, 76

ECA (Economic Cooperation Administration), 39, 40
economics: Eisenhower administration and, 69, 70, 99; political instability in supplier countries, 198–99; West Berlin economic situation, 39–40, 42, 43–44; World War II and, 17
Eddleman, General Clyde, 82, 85
Egypt, 104
Eighth Army, US, 3, 47, 57, 59, 60, 62; atomic weapons and, 61; casualties in Korea, 56; defensive mission in Korean War, 55; ethnic composition of, 52; preparedness of, 50; tasks in Korea after armistice, 63–65
Eisenhower, Dwight D., 1, 6, 8, 15, 18, 101, 198; as Army Chief of Staff, 17; on containment of limited war, 89; defense policy, 79; Defense Reorganization Act and, 95; elected US president, 53; Korean War and, 58, 60; on limits of American power, 208; missile technology and, 91, 94–95; multilateral nuclear force proposal and, 129; as NATO commander, 48; nuclear deterrence strategy, 2; as president of Columbia University, 8, 32; reform of JCS and, 205; rehabilitation program for Korea and, 64; retirement of, 109; study group on disarmament and, 98; on tactical atomic weapons, 81; Taylor's relationship with, 68–78; on *The Uncertain Trumpet*, 100; universal military training (UMT) and, 50; on value of West Point, 7; West Point curriculum and, 25, 26, 34; West Point sports and, 22; in World War II, 12, 13, 28, 36; on worldwide presence of US forces, 75
Eisenhower, Major John S. D., 76
engineering, in West Point curriculum, 15, 16, 21, 25; balanced curriculum at West Point and, 5, 6, 35; "general engineering education," 10; specialized training, 14
Erhard, Ludwig, 43
Europe, Eastern, 100
Europe, Western, 31, 70, 71, 84, 91, 133, 199; defense of, as main task for US armed forces, 37; Korean War and, 44, 48; possibility of tactical nuclear war in, 88; as power center, 201; scenario of Soviet overrun, 71; US troops in, 113, 202
European Command, US, 38

Far East Command, US, 3, 67
FEAF (Far Eastern Air Forces), 61
Felt, Admiral Harry, 120
firepower, 4, 65, 71, 85; battle group concept and, 66; geography and, 55; German war planning and, 52; in Korean War, 55, 57, 71; pentomic division and, 82; tactical atomic weapons and, 70
flexible response strategy, 73, 78, 80, 97; Eisenhower and, 81; fears about possible Soviet actions, 76; Kennedy and, 105; NATO and, 129; practical application of, 101–2; as vague concept, 101, 103
Foreign Affairs (journal), 72, 101
Foreign Intelligence Advisory Board, 101

Forrestal, James, 7–8
Forrestal, Michael, 141
Forsythe, George, 79
Fortas, Justice Abe, 182
France, 5, 9, 15, 129; Berlin Crisis and, 42, 45, 49; nuclear weapons of, 106; war in Indochina, 37, 59, 166, 170; West Berlin economy and, 39
Free German Youth (FDJ), 42
Fulbright, Senator J. William, 178

Gaither, H. Rowan, 94
Gaither Committee, 93–94
Gaither Report, 96
Galbraith, John Kenneth, 123
Ganeval, General Jean (French Army), 41, 44
Gardiner, Colonel William, 11
Gatchell, Colonel O. J., 15
Gates, Robert, 25
Gates, Thomas, 70
Gavin, General James, 1, 8, 12, 77, 91, 178; on adaptability of armored forces, 65–66; career derailment of, 93; defensive enclave strategy of, 163; proposal to replace JCS, 99
Geneva Accords (1954), 159, 178
German War Academy, 11
Germany, East (GDR), 38, 51, 113, 114; control of access to West Berlin and, 115; paramilitary forces of, 44–46; supply routes through, 41
Germany, in World War II, 17
Germany, West, 40, 42, 45; NATO forces in, 115; rearmament of, 46, 48, 52, 68, 70; US ground forces in, 37, 80, 85; West Berlin's ties to, 43
Giap, General Vo Nguyen, 170
Gilpatric, Roswell, 103, 104, 134
Goldwater, Senator Barry, 208
Goldwater-Nichols Act (1986), 1, 204, 208
Goodpaster, Colonel Andrew, 76, 89, 91–92, 100, 132, 200; escalation of land war in Vietnam and, 167;
Kennedy administration and, 101
Gore, Senator Albert, Sr., 178, 179
Gray, Gordon, 51, 100, 173, 192, 200
Greek Civil War, 104
Greene, Marine Commandant Wallace, 1–2, 131, 136, 148
Grow, General Robert, 51
Gruenther, General Arthur, 7, 8, 38, 66, 68, 94
guerrilla warfare, 86–87, 97, 104, 111
Gulf War, first (1991), 208

Habib, Philip, 184, 188
Hagood, General Johnson, 100
Handy, General Thomas T., 7, 8, 39, 47, 50; German rearmament supported by, 46; on Taylor's leadership in Berlin, 43, 48
Hannah, John, 64
Harkins, Brigadier General Paul, 6–7, 49, 59, 122
Harriman, Averell, 19, 119, 123, 173–74, 188
Harris, Captain Theodore R., 63
Hasker, Ed, 42
Hays, Major General George, 52–53
Hazlett, Everett "Swede," 32, 74, 89
helicopters, 121, 122, 124, 128, 155, 167; mobility of cavalry units and, 66; shot down by communist guerrillas, 129
Helms, Richard, 134, 189
Herbert, Anthony, 85
Heusinger, General Adolf (German Army), 52, 66
Higgins, General Gerald "Jerry," 7, 12, 18–19, 90
Hilsman, Roger, 119, 133, 134
Hitler, Adolf, 28, 69, 91
Hmong fighters, 118
Hoa Hao sect, in Vietnam, 140, 165
Ho Chi Minh, 104, 119, 135, 143, 184–85
Ho Chi Minh trail, 119, 139, 141; plan to plant airdropped sensors along, 180; US air campaigns against, 156, 190

Index

Holbrook, Richard, 184
Hop Tac Plan, 143
Houghton, Amory, 8
Howley, Brigadier General Frank, 38, 39, 41
Huebner, General Clarence, 37, 39
Huk Rebellion, in the Philippines, 104
Hull, General John E., 66–67
Humphrey, Hubert, 188
Hungary, crisis in, 87
Huong, Tran Van, 150, 154

ICBMs (intercontinental ballistic missiles), 93–94, 96, 100, 130, 202, 203. *See also* nuclear (atomic) weapons
IDA (Institute for Defense Analysis), 172, 192, 194
Imperial Defence College (London), 29
Indonesia, 87, 104
In Retrospect (McNamara), 168
intelligence community, 111, 135, 172, 173, 192, 193
International Security (journal), 202
interservice rivalries, 95, 208
Iran, 202
Iraq war, 209
IRBMs (intermediate-range ballistic missiles), 94, 202
Israel, 201, 203
Janowitz, Morris, 99

Japan, 30, 50, 201; postwar constitution and defense, 70; Taylor in, 9, 10; US forces in during Cold War, 32, 52, 202; in World War II, 13, 17
JCS (Joint Chiefs of Staff), 1, 6, 46, 72, 192; Army size/structure and, 74; Bay of Pigs invasion and, 107; Berlin crises and, 47, 115; chain of command and, 95; empowered chairman of, 94; escalation of land war in Vietnam and, 161; Gavin's proposal to replace, 99; as general staff for the defense secretary, 2; German rearmament and, 52; Korean War and, 49; limited war and, 75; near dysfunctionality in mid-1950s, 68; size/composition of US forces and, 53; Special Group (CI) and, 112; strategic reserve and, 87; Taylor as chairman of, 3, 35, 125–36; Taylor's criticism of, 204–5; Vietnam War and, 123, 149
Jenkins, Major General Reuben, 65
Jenner, Senator William, 50–51
Johnson, General Harold K., 85, 159, 160
Johnson, Lyndon B. (LBJ), 2, 3, 93, 135, 170; air war in Vietnam and, 160, 176; American public opinion and, 185; counterinsurgency policy and, 173, 174; decision not to seek reelection, 188; escalation of land war in Vietnam and, 145, 148, 160–61, 166, 194; Great Society project, 138; negotiations in Vietnam War and, 180–81; on pacification in Vietnam, 147; political instability in South Vietnam and, 153; proposed increase in Vietnam troop deployments and, 186; Taylor as ambassador to South Vietnam and, 137; Tet Offensive and, 184
Johnson, U. Alexis, 124, 138, 147, 150, 155; on air and ground war in Vietnam, 164; on deployment of US ground forces in Vietnam, 166
Jones, Air Force General David, 205
Jones, Colonel Harris, 26
Jones, Howard, 39, 40
JSOPs (Joint Strategic Objective Plans), 130, 131
Jupiter ballistic missile, 92, 96

Karnow, Stanley, 134
Kelly, John, 210
Kennan, George, 178, 206
Kennedy, Senator Edward, 185

Kennedy, John F. (JFK), 1, 75, 76, 97, 101; Berlin Wall crisis and, 113–17; counterinsurgency and, 111, 112–13; Cuban Missile Crisis and, 127–28; Indochina insurgencies and, 117–25; integrated war plan and, 100; JCS and, 102–3; as senator, 94, 103; Taylor as adviser to, 3, 204; Taylor as JCS chairman and, 125–36
Kennedy, Matthew Maxwell Taylor, 2
Kennedy, Robert, 2, 106, 108, 124, 155
Khanh, General Nguyen, 135, 138, 142, 143, 146; expansion of war supported by, 143; forced out of power, 145; loyalty to Tran Van Huong, 150; "March North" propaganda campaign, 141; political instability in South Vietnam and, 148; tenuous hold on power, 147–48, 154
Khrushchev, NIkita, 93, 111, 113, 127, 142
Killian, James, 92
Kim Il-Sung, 58
Kinnard, General Douglas, 2
Kissinger, Henry, 88–89, 177, 181, 182, 196, 201
Komer, Robert, 175, 179, 184, 205
Korea, North, 44, 53, 180, 191, 201; casualties in Korean War, 62; military strength of, 55; plan to use atomic bombs against, 61
Korea, South (ROK), 3, 30, 32, 64, 201; armed forces in Vietnam/Indochina, 59, 163, 182, 183; military strength of, 51, 54, 58; poor performance of ROK troops, 60; structure of armed forces, 65; US troops in, 202
Korean War, 28, 46, 49, 81, 104, 207; atomic weapons as deterrent and, 69; balance of forces, 56; battles for outposts, 58, 60; casualties, 56, 57–58, 59, 60, 61, 62; defense budgets and, 50, 51, 53,

70; geography and, 55; impact on Berlin situation, 44, 45, 47–48, 49; lessons from, 71, 170; as limited war, 72, 88; potential atomic escalation, 54, 58, 61–62; POW issue, 58, 63; race relations in US military and, 52; reconstruction after, 63–64; reserve officers and, 90; size/composition of US forces and, 52–53; stalemate and armistice talks, 54, 58, 61–63. *See also* Eighth Army, US
Kosygin, Alexai, 156
Kotikov, General Alexander (Soviet Army), 40–41
Krulak, Marine General Victor "Brute," 113, 134, 205
Ky, Nguyen Cao, 157, 165, 166, 167, 179–80

languages, in West Point curriculum, 7, 9, 17, 26, 34, 35
Lansdale, Air Force Brigadier General Edward, 108, 120, 122, 180
Laos, 101, 110, 112, 144; air strikes in, 138, 141, 149; American military operations in, 188; Ho Chi Minh trail in, 180; neutralization of, 119, 123; North Vietnamese infiltration through, 118, 119, 145, 146, 194; Pathet Lao communist insurgency in, 117, 118, 142; proposal for ground intervention in, 120; Royal Lao forces, 146, 147; South Vietnamese forces in, 159
Latin America, 104, 110, 174, 198, 201
Lebanon, 87
Le Duan, 184, 185
Lee, General William, 12
Legere, Laurence, 116
LeMay, General Curtis E., 1–2, 61, 69, 102, 130; Berlin airlift and, 115; JSOPs and, 130, 131; reform of JCS and, 205; Taylor as JCS chairman and, 136; on West Point curriculum, 25

Lemnitzer, General Lyman, 8, 74, 97, 115, 129, 200; Bay of Pigs invasion and, 107–8; as NATO commander, 117, 125; reform of JCS and, 205; Vietnam War and, 122, 124, 125

limited war, 3, 35, 68, 78–89, 97; defense budgets and, 89; in Europe, 87; force structure adapted to, 75; in Korea, 72; nuclear (atomic) weapons, 14, 78–79, 129; pentomic division and, 81–82; as "philosophy of weakness," 88; public debate about, 89; in Third World countries, 100

Lincoln, Colonel George A., 19, 21, 27, 33–34

local war, 72, 73, 81, 169, 170

Lodge, Senator Henry Cabot, Jr., 89, 133, 134, 167, 181

logistics, 46, 67, 85, 120, 121, 143; budgets for, 64; flexible response strategy and, 73; insurgencies and, 111; of NATO, 203; protection of, 122; Vietnam War and, 163, 166, 167, 187

Lost Crusade, The (Cooper), 194–95

Lovett, Robert, 53–54

Lynch, Grayston, 107

MAAG (Military Assistance and Advisory Group), 118, 120, 122, 124, 143, 144

MacArthur, General Douglas, 6, 8, 154; relieved of command by Truman, 51, 53; West Point curriculum and, 21

Macmillan, Harold, 113

MACV (Military Assistance Command, Vietnam), 49, 122, 129, 137; airpower and, 148; Hop Tac Plan and, 143; land war escalation and, 158; operations in Laos and, 144; pacification effort and, 175; Taylor's authority over, 138

Maddox, USS, 141

Malayan Emergency, 104, 125, 195

Manchuria, 31

Manchurian Incident, 29

maneuver, 38, 52, 66, 77. *See also* mobility

Manila group, 182, 183

Mansfield, Senator Mike, 123, 175, 194

Maoism, 111

Mao Zedong, 58, 201

Market Garden, Operation, 12

Marshall, General George, 5, 6, 8–9, 19; atomic weapons and, 69; as defense secretary, 47, 51; Taylor on staff of, 11

Marshall Islands, 32

Marshall Plan, 30, 39, 40, 43

"massive retaliation" strategy, 69, 70, 76, 81; abandonment of, 96, 100; Kennedy's opposition to, 97; "measured" retaliation compared with, 91; Taylor's criticism of, 97, 98

mathematics, in West Point curriculum, 6, 7, 16, 24

Mattis, James, 210

McAuliffe, Brigadier General Anthony, 8, 12, 13, 52

McCarthy, Senator Joseph, 50

McCloy, John J., 19, 37, 39, 40, 47, 88; German rearmament supported by, 46; on menace to Berlin from the East, 44

McCone, John, 128, 141, 146, 153

McConnell, John P., 135

McDonald, David, 131

McElroy, Neil, 70, 76–77, 89, 94, 97

McGarr, Lieutenant General Lionel, 85, 122

McMaster, H. R., 2, 210

McNamara, Robert, 2, 75, 96, 132, 172; Bay of Pigs invasion and, 101, 102, 107; coup against Diem and, 134; doubts about Vietnam War, 184; escalation of land war in Vietnam and, 145; flexible response strategy and, 105–6;

land war escalation in Vietnam and, 162; mutual assured destruction notion, 131; on non-nuclear warfare as primary mission, 103; plan to drop sensors along Ho Chi Minh trail, 180; reform of JCS and, 205; Taylor as JCS chairman and, 136; Vietnam War and, 122, 123–24, 197

McNaughton, John, 155, 162

Mendenhall, Joseph, 134

Middle East, 20, 31, 87, 199, 201, 209; destabilization of, 201; nuclear weapons in defense of, 80; power balance in, 200

Middleton, Troy, 15, 16, 17

Military Academy, US. *See* West Point

Military Assistance Command, 110

military units, US: 1st Armored Division, 50; 1st Infantry Division, 184; 1st Marine Division, 57, 58; 6th Armored Division, 51; 7th Infantry Division, 57, 58, 60; 24th Infantry Division, 87; 25th Infantry Division, 57, 59; 82nd Airborne Division, 78, 163; 101st Airborne Division, 12, 23, 51, 57, 83, 85, 168, 206; 173rd Airborne Brigade, 162, 164; I Corps, 60; IX Corps, 64; Seventh Army, 37–38, 83, 84–85; VII Corps, 50, 65–66; X Corps, 53. *See also* Eighth Army, US

Minh, General Duong Van "Big," 120, 121, 135, 139, 145

MIRVs (multiple, independently targetable warheads), 202

"missile gap," 97

missiles, guided, 82, 89–93

mobility, 38, 84, 86, 198; of ARVN, 160; atomic battlefield and, 82–83; West Point education and, 7. *See also* maneuver

Mongoose, Operation, 108–9

Monroe Doctrine, 29

Montague, Lieutenant Colonel Robert, 184

Montgomery, Field Marshal Bernard Law (British Army), 66

Moore, General Bryant E., 22, 33

Moorer, Admiral Thomas, 205

Morrison, Charles E., 26

Morrison, Samuel Eliot, 12

Morse, Senator Wayne, 178–79

Murphy, Robert, 12, 172, 188, 195

Mussolini, Benito, 69

NASA, 92

Nasser, Gamal Abdel, 104

National Defense University, 34

National Guard Association, 23, 27, 81

national liberation, wars of, 104, 179, 193, 197

"National Military Program" (Taylor), 72–73

National Reconciliation Council, 196, 197

National Security Act (1947), 29–30, 132

national security state, 3, 30, 207

National War College, 19, 97, 111

nation-building, 113, 157, 183

NATO (North Atlantic Treaty Organization), 46, 52, 66, 79, 86; Berlin Crisis and, 48; contribution to defense burden, 199; first-strike nuclear war and, 88; forces in West Germany, 115; French nuclear forces and, 106; headquarters of, 84; importance to American security, 68; logistics system, 203; nuclear strategy and, 129; retreat of massive retaliation strategy and, 100; scenarios of attack on, 202; small ground forces of, 105; US army structure as model, 71; Vietnam War and, 169

Naval Academy, US. *See* Annapolis

Navy, US, 30, 78, 91, 160, 199

neoconservatives, 200

neutron bombs, 203

New Deal, 100

New Look, 98
Nhu, Ngo Dinh, 122, 134
Nichols, Representative William, 208
Nitze, Paul, 50, 188–89, 200
Nixon, Richard, 195–96, 201
NLF (National Liberation Front), 119, 129, 196; fighting strength of, 170; North Vietnamese support for, 159; peace talks and, 181; rural population and, 140; US air strikes against, 161. *See also* PLAF; Viet Cong
Nolting, Frederick, 120
Norstad, General Lauris, 84, 115, 116, 129
North Atlantic Treaty (1949), 38
NSA (National Security Agency), 193
NSAM-111 policy paper, 125
NSAM-273 policy paper, 135
NSAM-288 policy paper, 134
NSAM-314 policy paper, 147
NSC (National Security Council), 47, 48, 61, 81, 96, 173; committee structure of, 76; Executive Committee, 126; JCS and, 98; Kennedy administration and, 102; limited war strategy and, 97; linked bureaucracies of, 207; proposed intervention in Laos and, 117; Special Group (CI) and, 112; *Sputnik* launches and, 75; Taylor's proposal for replacement of, 201; Vietnam War and, 125; war scenarios envisioned by, 73–74
NSC 68 policy paper, 41, 50, 53, 103
nuclear (atomic) weapons, 2, 14, 66, 70, 73, 75, 78; of China, 144; delivery systems, 73, 76; as deterrent, 68, 69, 199, 203; first strike with, 78; French *force de frappe*, 106; Kennedy and, 103; Korean War and, 54, 58, 61–62; military operations after nuclear exchange, 77, 80; nuclear test ban agreement, 132; Soviet, 95; tactical, 70, 78, 81, 83–84, 87, 203; US monopoly on, 31. *See also* ICBMs

nuclear war, 1, 3, 81, 114, 127; defense of Europe and, 129; escalation to, 72, 76, 115; ground forces as trip wire to trigger, 80; limited, 14, 79; modernization of army and, 87; mutual assured destruction, 131; tactical, 86; Vietnam War escalation and, 178; worst-and best-case scenarios, 131
Nuclear Weapons and Foreign Policy (Kissinger), 89

Oanh, Nguyen Xuan, 157
Office of Strategic Services, 119
Officer Candidate Schools, 27
Onassis, Jacqueline Kennedy, 206
Oxcart reconnaissance plane, 133

Pace, Frank, 51
pacification, in Vietnam, 135, 138, 139, 147, 183; around Saigon, 142, 143; in coastal areas south of DMZ, 140; counterinsurgency and, 175; effects of Tet Offensive and, 186; foreign troops and, 162; lack of coordination in policies, 146; layered structure of war and, 170; US diplomacy and, 157–58; weakness of South Vietnam regime and, 150
Palmer, Williston B., 68, 79, 85
Parrish, Brigadier General Noel, 103
Pate, Commandant Randolph, 88
Patton, General George, 6–7, 13, 49
PAVN (People's Army of Vietnam), 144, 159; Americanization of ground war and, 176; body counts and, 169; growth of, 178; peace talks and, 181; in South Vietnam, 163, 167; Taylor's underestimation of, 171
Pearson, Drew, 74
Pell, Senator Claiborne, 179
Peng Dehuai, Marshal (Chinese Army), 58
Pentagon, 3, 48, 77, 97, 126, 207; ARPA (Advanced Research Proj-

Index   295

ects Agency), 180; remaking culture of, 130; Taylor as planner at, 49–54
pentomic division, 81–82, 83, 84
Persian Gulf, 200, 203
Persons, Major General Wilton B., 24
PFIAB (President's Foreign Intelligence Advisory Board), 172, 173, 179, 182, 185, 189, 195–96
Philippines, 104, 182
PLAF (People's Liberation Armed Forces), 128, 140, 141, 151, 158, 159; American facilities attacked by, 154, 155; Americanization of ground war and, 176; body counts and, 169; growth of, 178; increased activities of, 165; peace talks and, 181; pursued into Cambodia, 144, 149; Taylor's underestimation of, 171; territorial gains in South Vietnam, 150. *See also* NLF; Viet Cong
Polaris missile, 91
Porter, Major General Ray, 57
Potsdam conference, 19
Power, Thomas, 96
Precarious Security (Taylor), 200
Psychological Strategy Board, 51
psychological warfare, 51
psychology, mass, 35
psychology, military, 17–18, 35
Pye, Lucian, 118

Quang, Thich Tri, 139, 179
Quat, Phan Huy, 157, 159, 165

race relations, in US military, 52
Radford, Admiral Arthur, 2, 68, 69, 81, 91, 94, 195; atomic war plans and, 61; flexible response strategy and, 86; Gavin's retirement and, 93; proposal for troop withdrawal from Europe, 79; Taylor's criticism of, 98; Taylor's statement on "National Military Program" and, 73
Ranch Hand, Operation, 125

RAND Corporation, 128, 180
Reagan, Ronald, 200, 205
Redstone missile system, 92
Republican Party, 70
Republic of Korea (ROK). *See* Korea, South (ROK)
Reserve Officers Association, 24
Reston, James, 113
Reuter, Ernst, 43, 44, 46, 48, 49
Rhee, Syngman, 58, 59, 61, 62, 67, 138
RIAS [*Rundfunk im amerikanischen Sektor*] (US radio in Berlin), 44
Ricks, Thomas, 2
Ridgway, General Matthew, 8, 11, 12, 13, 200; battle group concept and, 66; desegregation in US military advocated by, 52; Korean War and, 55; memoirs of, 80; nuclear strategy and, 77, 78; retirement of, 67, 68; on tactical atomic weapons, 70; in World War II, 78
RMA (revolution in military affairs), 208–9
ROAD (Reorganization Objectives Army Division), 85, 86
Rockefeller, Nelson, 19
Rolling Thunder, Operation, 156, 158, 163–64, 168, 176, 188
Roosevelt, Franklin D., 100
Rostow, Walt, 106, 117–18, 182, 186, 189, 197; in Office of Strategic Services, 119; on Taylor's task in Vietnam, 138
ROTC (Reserve Officer Training Corps), 16, 25, 27, 34
Rusk, Dean, 19, 63, 106, 146, 176, 184, 189; Berlin situation and, 115; in Committee on the Present Danger, 200; Operation Mongoose and, 108; Vietnam War and, 122, 123, 182
Russell, Senator Richard, 90, 109
Russia. *See* Soviet Union [USSR] (Russia)
Ryukyu Islands (Okinawa), 32
SAC (Strategic Air Command), 94, 96, 100, 127

296 Index

Saltonstall, Representative Leverett, 126
Schake, Kori, 210
sea/shipping lanes, control of, 199, 203, 206
SEATO (Southeast Asia Treaty Organization), 118, 120, 122, 124, 125
Senate, US: Armed Services Committee, 32, 73, 90, 94; Church Committee, 106, 108; Foreign Relations Committee, 75, 178; Preparedness Investigation Subcommittee, 96
Sharp, Admiral U. S. Grant, 143–44, 162, 176
Sherman, Admiral Forrest, 42
Shoup, Marine Corps General David, 117, 131
Sibley, General Alden, 143
SIG (Senior Interdepartmental Group), 172, 173, 174–75
Sino-Soviet rift, 104, 146
SLBMs (submarine-launched ballistic missiles), 203
small wars, 81, 86, 87
Smith, Representative Margaret Chase, 126
Smith, General William "Beetle," 12
social sciences, 10, 14, 15, 24; balanced curriculum at West Point and, 5, 35; growing importance of, 17
sociology, 35
Soviet Union [USSR] (Russia), 31, 58, 100, 128, 178, 198; blockade activities against West Berlin, 46–47; containment of, 30; division of Berlin and, 40–41, 43; economic performance in World War II, 17; intention to seize West Berlin, 41–42, 45–46; Jewish emigration from, 201; military strength of, 37, 205–6; nuclear arms race and, 203; nuclear testing sites in, 132; piecemeal conquest of Asia, 88; political role in Africa and the Middle East, 199; as power center, 201; rift with China, 104; Soviet Bloc, 72; superiority in numbers, 78, 80; US technological lead over, 73; Vietnam War and, 156, 164
space race, 87, 90
Spanish Civil War, 31
Sparkman, Representative John, 178
Special Group, 108, 142
Special Group (Augmented), 109, 110
Special Group (CI), 109, 110–11, 112, 173
Speidel, General Hans (German Army), 52, 66, 79
Sputnik satellites, 74–75, 87, 93
Stalin, Joseph, 58
State Department, US, 41, 42, 51, 110; Cold War strategy and, 76–77; coup in Saigon and, 120; Korean War and, 50; Vietnam War and, 170, 172, 183
Stevens, Robert, 63, 68
Stilwell, General Joseph, 9, 11
strategic reserve, 73, 87, 117
Student Conference on United States Affairs, 19
Stump, Admiral Felix, 87–88
Suez Canal crisis, 87
Sukarno, 104
Sullivan, William H., 128, 138, 180
Symingtom, Senator Stuart, 94, 96

Taiwan, 63, 135
Taylor, John Maxwell (older son), 5
Taylor, Lydia "Diddy" Happer (wife), 3, 67, 156
Taylor, Maxwell: as Army Chief of Staff, 8, 34; atomic age strategy and, 28–36; biographies and autobiography of, 2; as cadet at West Point, 6–7, 9; as commander during Berlin Crisis, 3, 36–49; counterinsurgency in Vietnam and, 172–83; as critic of military and strategic policies, 193–206; death of, 206; early life of, 9; Eisenhower's relationship with, 68–78; in the field artillery, 2, 10; histo-

rians' judgments of, 2; in Japan before World War II, 124; as JCS chairman, 125–36; at Kennedy White House, 102–13; Korean War and, 53, 54–67, 104; languages studied by, 5, 10; limited war strategy and, 78–89; memoirs of, 6; as micromanager, 4, 19, 27; "National Military Program," 72–73; as Pentagon planner, 49–54; *Precarious Security*, 200; public relations strategy, 90; as reformer, 13, 35, 94; retirement from the military, 97; as West Point superintendent, 2–3, 13–28, 35; in World War II, 5, 9, 11–13, 206. See also *Uncertain Trumpet, The*

Taylor, Maxwell, Vietnam War and: "controlled escalation" strategy, 152; as hawk for airpower in Vietnam, 148–58; Kennedy administration involvement, 117–25; land war escalation, 158–71; policies after Tet Offensive and, 183–93; Taylor as ambassador to South Vietnam, 109–10, 137–48

Taylor, Thomas Happer (younger son), 5

Taylor, Captain Thomas (son of M. T.), 168

technology, 21, 71, 74–75

terrorism, international, 204

Thailand, 110, 118, 147; armed forces in Vietnam, 182; possible destabilization of, 119; US diplomatic efforts to gain support from, 151

Thang, General Nguyen Duc, 167

Thayer, Sylvanus, 26

Thi, General Nguyen Chanh, 179

Thieu, General Nguyen Van, 157, 167, 187, 190, 196

Third World, 4

Tho, Le Duc, 196

Tho, Nguyen Ngoc, 120

Thompson, Llewellyn, 195

Thomson, James, 170

Throckmorton, General John, 157

Ton, Truong Tai, 167

Tonkin Gulf Resolution (1964), 178, 194

Trudeau, General Arthur, 60

Truman, Harry S., 5, 23, 101, 105; Berlin Crisis and, 37, 44; defense budget and, 70; limits on war in Korea and, 54, 88; MacArthur relieved of command by, 51, 53; universal military training (UMT) and, 50

Trump, Donald, 210

Turkey: aid to, 30; Turkish Brigade in Korean War, 59, 62

Twining, General Nathan, 2, 68, 88, 94, 99

Ulbricht, Walter, 114

Uncertain Trumpet, The (Taylor), 98, 100, 126, 195; Kennedy influenced by, 101, 103; "massive retaliation" strategy critiqued in, 97

Unger, Leonard, 141

United Nations (UN), 30, 47, 116; casualties in Korean War, 60, 61; Korean War and, 53, 55, 56; Vietnam War and, 118

United States: defense of homeland, 206; hearts-and-minds idea and, 104; monopoly on atomic weapons, 31; national security state, 207; "new wars" and, 209; as power center, 201

universal military training (UMT), 6, 50

USAID, 110, 123, 173

USCOB (US Commander, Berlin), 38, 45

USIA (US Information Agency), 110, 123, 140, 173

Vance, Cyrus, 188

Van Fleet, General James, 55, 56–57, 63

Vann, Lieutenant Colonel John Paul, 129

Victor Emmanel II (king of Italy), 12
Viet Cong (VC), 121, 138, 145; aided by North Vietnam, 149, 150, 158; counterinsurgency against, 170. See also NLF
Viet Minh, 59
Vietnam, North (DRV), 104, 142; aid to Viet Cong, 149, 150; air defense capabilities, 135; air war against, 2, 119, 135, 138, 149, 177, 182; Haiphong harbor, 120, 135; inadequate intelligence about, 195; negotiations with, 153, 173, 185; preparations for war against, 143. See also PAVN
Vietnam, South (Republic of Vietnam), 67, 104, 136, 197; Buddhist-Catholic tensions, 142, 145, 153, 179; Buddhist protesters in, 139; communist-controlled areas in, 181; as "counterinsurgency laboratory," 110, 112; coup against Diem (1963), 120–21, 133–35; deployment of US ground forces to, 2; domino theory and, 179; military strength of, 118, 120; political instability in, 147–48, 179–80; provinces under communist assault, 150, 151; sustainability of, 194; Taylor as ambassador to, 3, 109–10, 137–48; US forces in, 120. See also ARVN
Vietnam War, 1, 4, 81, 132, 210; all-volunteer army as result of, 198; American casualties, 157; American public opinion and, 141, 157, 168, 181, 182, 185; Ap Bac battle (1963), 128–29; body counts, 169; Cold War and, 193; comparison with Korea, 190–91, 196; counterinsurgency and, 172–83; defoliants and herbicides used in, 125; dynamic of escalation, 171; Kennedy administration and, 101, 117–25; land war escalation, 158–71; layers to, 169; origins of, 2;

Paris peace talks, 189, 190, 194, 196; proposal to deploy nationalist Chinese forces, 135; Tet Offensive (1968), 184, 185, 186, 189, 190, 192; Tonkin Gulf incident, 141. See also NLF; pacification; Taylor, Maxwell, Vietnam War and
Vinson, Representative Carl, 109
Voice of America, 51

War Department, 10, 13, 14, 16, 38. See also Defense Department
war games, 128
Warnke, Paul, 189
War on Terror, 209
War Powers Act (1973), 199, 200
Wedemeyer, General Albert, 11, 38
Wehrle, Leroy, 184
Welt im Film (German TV program), 42
West Berlin Club, 39
Westmoreland, General William, 32, 79, 82, 93, 158–71; air war in Vietnam and, 156, 162, 165, 176; American strategy in Vietnam and, 187–88; counterinsurgency and, 175; fears about South Vietnamese military, 145–46; increase in troop deployments sought by, 185–86; land war escalation and, 158, 165–66; as MACV leader, 137; pentomic division and, 85; public opinion about Vietnam War and, 184; as West Point superintendent, 112
West Point (US Military Academy), 5, 33, 49, 82, 207; curricular reform at, 6–7, 9, 15; faculty, 27; Graduate Record Examination, 21; honor system, 26; Military Topography and Graphics Department, 20; Social Sciences Department, 19; Tactics Department, 18; Taylor as cadet at, 6–7, 9; Taylor as superintendent of, 2–3, 13–28
"West Point Looks Ahead" (Compton), 14

Weyand, General Fred, 189
Weyland, General Otto, 61
Wheeler, General Earle, 129, 130, 136, 150, 186; air war in Vietnam and, 162; escalation of land war in Vietnam and, 167
White, Thomas, 88, 131
White Sands Missile Range, 92
Wilby, Major General Francis, 14, 15, 33
Williams, General Samuel T. "Hanging Sam," 57, 64, 69
Wilson, Charles "Engine Charlie," 68, 70, 77–78, 81; army missile program and, 91, 92; on military science and technology, 84; Taylor's criticism of, 98
Wise Men, 188

Woods, C. Tyler, 63
World War I, 9, 15, 17, 66
World War II, 5, 6, 11–13, 19, 30, 66; air war against Nazi Germany, 182; Cold War strategy and, 31; JCS structure during, 205; Office of Strategic Services in, 119; remembered as "the good war," 22; reserve officers and, 90; size of armed forces and, 27; studied at West Point, 15, 17; veterans of, 23
Yalta conference, 19
Yelisarov, Colonel A. I. (Soviet Army), 41
Zapata, Operation, 106
Zhou Enlai, 201
Zumwalt, Admiral Elmo, 200